⇛ SLAVE NO MORE ⇚

Slave
NO MORE

*Self-Liberation before
Abolitionism in the Americas*

Aline Helg

*Translated from the French
by Lara Vergnaud*

The University of North Carolina Press
CHAPEL HILL

© 2019 The University of North Carolina Press
All rights reserved

Originally published in French by Editions La Découverte, 2016.

Designed and set in Adobe Text Pro with Bodoni Poster and Type No. 8 WF display types by Rebecca Evans
Manufactured in the United States of America

The University of North Carolina Press has been a member of the Green Press Initiative since 2003.

Cover illustration: Aaron Douglas, *Rise, Shine for Thy Light Has Come*, 1930 (detail); © 2018, ProLitteris, Zurich. Collection of the Howard University Gallery of Art, Washington, D.C. Photograph by Gregory R. Staley.

Library of Congress Cataloging-in-Publication Data
Names: Helg, Aline, 1953– author. | Vergnaud, Lara, translator.
Title: Slave no more : self-liberation before abolitionism in the Americas / Aline Helg ; translated from the French by Lara Vergnaud.
Other titles: Plus jamais esclaves! English
Description: Chapel Hill : University of North Carolina Press, [2019] | Originally published in French by Éditions La Découverte, 2016. | Includes bibliographical references and index.
Identifiers: LCCN 2018036570| ISBN 9781469649627 (cloth : alk. paper) | ISBN 9781469649634 (pbk : alk. paper) | ISBN 9781469649641 (ebook)
Subjects: LCSH: Slavery—America—History. | Slave insurrections—America—History. | Slaves—Emancipation—America. | Slavery—United States—History. | Slave insurrections—United States—History. | Slaves—Emancipation—United States. | Slavery—West Indies—History. | Slave insurrections—West Indies—History. | Slaves—Emancipation—West Indies.
Classification: LCC E446 .H3913 2019 | DDC 306.3/620973—dc23 LC record available at https://lccn.loc.gov/2018036570

For Malika

Contents

Introduction
1

PART I
Settings and Eras

≋ 1 ≋
The Slave Trade and Slavery in the Americas
Transcontinental Trends
17

PART II
*From Conquest to the
End of the Seven Years' War
(1501–1763)*

≋ 2 ≋
Marronage
A Risky but Possible Path to Freedom
43

≋ 3 ≋
Self-Purchase and Military Service
Legal but Limited Paths to Emancipation
64

≋ 4 ≋
Conspiracy and Revolt
The Most Perilous Paths to Freedom
82

PART III
The Age of Revolution and Independence
(1763–1825)

5
Slaves as Actors on the Path to U.S. Independence
113

6
From the Slave Revolt in Saint Domingue to the Founding of the Black Nation of Haiti
140

7
The Shock Waves of the Haitian Revolution
164

8
The Wars of Independence in Continental Iberian America
New Opportunities for Liberation
197

PART IV
Defending Slavery versus Abolitionism
(1800–1838)

9
Marronage and the Purchase of Freedom
Old Strategies in New Times
221

10
Revolts and Abolitionism
245

Epilogue
274

Notes 287

Bibliography 313

Index 337

Figures and Graphs

Figures

Certificate commending James Armistead Lafayette
for his revolutionary war service, 1784   132

Burning of Le Cap, 1793   151

Protector of Slaves Office, Trinidad, 1838   235

Black women selling angu, Brazil, ca. 1820   243

Sketch of a flag taken from the insurgent
slaves at Barbados, 1816   259

To the Friends of Negro Emancipation, 1834   272

Graphs

1. Destinations of Enslaved Africans
Disembarked in the Americas, 1501–1866   19

2. Numbers of Enslaved Africans Disembarked
Each Year in the Americas, 1501–1864   20

SLAVE NO MORE

Introduction

During the mid-eighteenth century, between fifty-three thousand and seventy thousand African captives were brought to the Americas each year to be sold at slave markets. These men, women, and children soon realized that after surviving the long Atlantic crossing in slave ship steerage compartments, they would have to set out on foot, often chained to other slaves, toward the plantation, mine, or home of the master who had purchased them, somewhere on a Caribbean island, in the colony of Georgia, on the Pacific coast of South America, or in Brazil. Whippings, hunger, thirst, disease, and death were omnipresent, but these captives also discovered an unknown world filled with new landscapes, vegetation, food, animals, and inhabitants speaking incomprehensible languages. They saw whites as well as countless other black and lighter-skinned slaves, Amerindians regrouped into rural communities, and an entire, largely mixed, free population active in towns and along roads and rivers. Many among this population free from the tyranny of the whip were emancipated slaves; more still were born of free parents, who were either Africans or descended from deported Africans. In many regions, these "free people of color," as they were called, greatly outnumbered slaves, and in fact represented the large majority of the population. Farther inland, fugitive slaves had established alternative communities outside colonized plantation or mining zones that would eventually become self-sustaining. Even though the slave trade had been growing since the early sixteenth century, and slavery appeared indestructible, some slaves nonetheless succeeded in obtaining freedom for themselves and their family members. Moreover, in places where the slave trade had ended, the number of slaves was declining rapidly. Yet in the years preceding the Seven Years' War (1756–63), nobody in the Americas was questioning the institution of slavery except for some British Quakers and Methodists on the northeastern coast of the continent.

How were these enslaved men and women able to obtain their freedom before movements to abolish slavery in the Americas and Europe were formed? Which strategies did they favor? Did those strategies correspond to specific contexts? How did slaves express themselves as human beings and social actors in their own right, when the laws of the time primarily considered them to be personal property? Did the rise of abolitionism in the second half of the eighteenth century change the means through which slaves freed themselves? Were slaves and abolitionists able to join forces to bring an end to the slave trade and slavery?

This book aims to answer these questions, all while striving to illuminate the perspective of the enslaved. My goal is not to establish a hierarchy of the different ways of fighting for freedom, for example by glorifying runaway or rebelling slaves over those who endured slavery until their deaths: for any slave, survival itself was a victory. Instead, I focus on those who, alone or collectively, were able to obtain their freedom, at times through force, self-sacrifice, ruse, or patience, and at others by chance. I examine how individuals and groups of slaves became free at the same time that slavery was expanding, thereby undermining the very foundations of racial bondage.

My work situates slaves' quest for freedom within the more general framework of a fight for survival under the particularly alienating and oppressive circumstances of slavery. All slaves thought up strategies to make their enslavement less unbearable. Like other exploited classes, they simultaneously resorted to compromise and to more or less active and obvious resistance, and only exceptionally opted for armed rebellion, whose risks were well known. Unlike other subaltern classes, slaves' exceptional status as "personal property" meant that asserting their humanity—by starting a family, for example, or cultivating a social life or personal project—was already, for them, a patent rejection of their condition and therefore a victory over slavery. But the fact of belonging to a master or mistress with nearly unlimited powers inevitably rendered that victory precarious. Arrangements had to be continuously renegotiated; families risked separation at any moment due to the sale of one of their members; and in sugar plantation colonies with extremely high mortality rates, the steady replacement of the labor force with new captives from Africa fostered perpetual instability. Nonetheless, even as authorities and slaveowners continued to view them as property, slaves were collectively, over time, able to create a social and cultural fabric. They did so notably through the construction of extended family ties and community networks and the invention of cultural and religious practices and shared languages and techniques. Moreover, the diverse forms of resistance adopted by enslaved Africans and Afro-descendants fundamentally contributed to the modes of thought, expertise, artistic and spiritual expressions, and community structures that characterize the Americas today. Slavery inarguably succeeded in exploiting men, women, and children on the basis of their race, but not in annihilating their humanity.

However, in this book I am less concerned with that broad backdrop than with the particular circumstances of slaves who were able to obtain their freedom *themselves* and before abolitionism, sometimes to the extent that they constituted the majority of the population in certain regions. To understand this phenomenon, I had to consider the entirety of the continental and Caribbean Americas over a long period of time—from the early sixteenth century to 1838, when general emancipation in the British Empire set the beginning of the end of slavery in the Americas. With my focus on slaves' historical agency, I sought to reveal how countless enslaved men, women, and children managed to free themselves, against all odds, during the first 250 years of colonization, when no one in their society was envisioning, even less promoting the end of slavery. I also attempted to understand how some slaves adapted to the first challenges to the legitimacy of slavery initiated in the mid-eighteenth century and to the subsequent disintegration of the colonial order (leading to U.S., Haitian, and continental Latin American independence). I further examined slaves' action to liberate themselves and to speed up the abolition of slavery where the latter had declined after independence, as in the northern United States and several Spanish American republics. Finally, my book culminates with the general emancipation decreed by the British in 1833, effective in 1838, in which slaves' and abolitionists' actions combined to bring an end to slavery in U.K. colonies. The year 1838, thus, unequivocally stands out as the peak of a process initiated three centuries before, when slaves were alone in their struggle against slavery. After 1838, although slavery was to thrive for many years in several continental regions and Caribbean islands until its final abolition by Brazil in 1888, a new dynamic and new actors were at work, with abolitionism on the rise and now embraced by some independent governments and the imperial British power. Enslaved peoples were not alone in their struggle for freedom anymore; now they could count on important supporters.

By relying on a rich historiography, I distinguished four primary strategies through which slaves freed themselves: flight and marronage (a specific name for escape from slavery); emancipation certified by a legal document of freedom (also referred to as manumission in Roman, and subsequently Iberian and Anglo-Saxon, law); military service (for men) in exchange for promised emancipation; and revolt. I deliberately omitted suicide from my study because, though it may be considered to be the most complete form of liberation, it would have led me into more metaphysical directions.[1] I compared the four liberation strategies listed above over a period spanning nearly three and a half centuries in the Spanish, Portuguese, Dutch, French, British, and Danish colonies, as well as in countries that continued to practice slavery after gaining independence. Given that the majority of historians of slavery have concentrated on one specific strategy, period, or region, this study is therefore the first to encompass such a wide breadth of time and space. This multidimensional approach allowed me to observe the preponderance of one strategy or another depending on demographic, economic, political, and ideological contexts. It also revealed periods characterized by the proliferation of plots and rebellions, which were consistent with a particularly turbulent international context, even as other strategies of emancipation remained more consistent.

Flight and marronage, in particular, served as antidotes to slavery throughout the Americas for several centuries. This is hardly surprising—flight offered slaves a way to express their rejection of captivity and, more fundamentally, to seek salvation as human beings confronted by slavery. Marronage accompanied colonization as it developed in the American and Caribbean territories alongside the expanding slave trade. Rather than diminishing following the establishment of towns and cities and mining or agricultural domains, it increased and even became widespread during periods of war due to troop movements, the departure of slaveowners, and social decomposition. Slaves fled to cities to melt into free populations of color. They escaped to hinterlands, mountains, forests, and marshlands. They traveled from one colonial regime to the next, or one country to the next, by land, river, or ocean. Although impossible to quantify, flight and marronage allowed many slaves to obtain their freedom.[2]

Emancipation was the primary legal means through which a slave could become free. Either a slavemaster, often after his death and/or subject to additional years of service, granted a slave his or her freedom, or a slave or third party paid the master the slave's market value in exchange for his or her freedom. This emancipation was certified by a written document, a "letter of freedom," in accordance with predefined legal procedures. However, access to manumission varied greatly: while it had always been a codified right for slaves in Spanish America and Brazil, it was gradually restricted in the rest of the Americas, eventually becoming quite rare. Regardless of location, however, manumission required of the slave a long-term commitment of additional work, the ability to economize and plan, irreproachable conduct, and a support network. Though the percentage of slaves able to obtain an emancipation certificate in their lifetimes was limited, that free Afro-descendant population grew rapidly through natural reproduction, often surpassing the number of slaves in cities.[3] Even if manumission did not directly threaten the institution of slavery, it revealed slaves' full humanity and capacity to be free, thereby contributing to the abolitionist movement.

Military service in exchange for the promise of freedom was an emancipation strategy specific to the context of war and limited to enslaved men. This form of liberation already existed at the time of the Spanish conquest but attained unprecedented proportions during the U.S. War of Independence and later during the Saint Domingue revolt and the wars of independence in Spanish America. Sometimes imposed by armies in constant need of men, military service was dangerous, often entailing travel over long distances, heightened risks of hunger, disease, and death, and exposure to enemy attacks and armed conflicts. Furthermore, the slave-soldier did not automatically obtain his emancipation certificate at the end of the war but was instead forced to undergo a long procedure whose outcome was far from guaranteed. The military engagement of slaves nonetheless advanced the abolitionist cause by demonstrating their willingness to die for a homeland that would then owe them freedom and citizenship.

Revolt, defined here as the violent uprising of a hundred or more slaves, which caused destruction and/or death to whites and security forces, was the most dangerous liberation strategy and one to which few slaves resorted. Punishment in the event of failure was certain: capture, torture until a confession was extracted, followed by the torment of protracted agony, dozens of whiplashes, or sometimes sale outside the country or colony. Of course, spontaneous uprisings of small groups of slaves enraged by a foreman's abuse or collectively planning escape punctuate the history of slavery in the Americas, but they do not constitute mass revolts against the institution itself. In reality, the only mass slave revolt to definitively destroy a large element of the slave plantation system occurred in Saint Domingue's Plaine du Nord in 1791, leading to the complete and immediate abolition of slavery there in 1793. Then, between 1816 and 1831, three major revolts in the British colonies decisively contributed to the abolition of slavery by the British Parliament in 1833, which took effect in 1838. But revolts elsewhere were much smaller and only rarely succeeded in freeing one or two slave informers and a few lucky fugitives. They almost always resulted in a wave of blind repression and terror, and tougher slave codes.

In order to analyze and compare the liberation strategies used by slaves on the American continent and in the Caribbean over a period of three and a half centuries, I relied on secondary literature written in English, French, Spanish, and Portuguese, from both the Americas and Europe. My reading could not, of course, be exhaustive, but I tried as much as possible to cross-reference approaches, explore diverging interpretations, and include the most recent discoveries of a rapidly growing and constantly evolving historiography. As I explain in depth below, historians began to recognize slaves as autonomous actors of history in the 1930s, an approach that became widespread beginning in the 1980s. The resulting questions and analyses were shaped by the changing political context of the twentieth and early twenty-first centuries, which I took into consideration by separating the facts presented by historians from how they interpreted them. Due to the vast temporal and spatial framework of my study, I did not consider conducting my own archival research; however, I occasionally consulted primary sources, which warrant a few general comments.

Given the scarcity of firsthand written documents, tracing the history of strategies used by slaves to obtain their freedom while taking into account individual points of view is particularly fraught. As with all other subalterns of the ancien régime and the early nineteenth century, slaves' voices most often survived by being related or transformed by agents of the state or church, by those who owned and exploited them, and by witnesses or activists. Furthermore, among the strategies deployed, marronage, by definition, left little trace apart from brief runaway announcements placed in local gazettes by slaveowners and reports penned by slave catchers, to which archeological remains have recently been added. In contrast, emancipation had a concrete form as a written document filed and preserved, albeit unsystematically, in municipal or regional, rather than centralized, archives. That enabled in-depth studies on certain cities or provinces but rendered any systematic research on a colony or country impossible. Similarly, any methodical study of emancipation through military service would be incomplete as written records of slave-soldiers and information on their eventual manumission are inconsistent and partial. Yet revolts may be the most complex strategy to analyze, because at the time it was not necessary for a slave to physically rebel to be accused of rebellion: plotting was as serious a crime as revolting, and thinking about killing equated to killing. As a result, depending on the context, criticizing an unjust master with a few friends, discussing a possible protest, knowing a suspect, or ending up in the wrong place by chance could lead to accusations of conspiracy and rebellion. The law could detain, interrogate, and torture suspects at will, and required neither material evidence nor a confession from the accused to condemn him or her to hanging, burning, or the wheel, without a defense lawyer present. The historian's task is further complicated by the fact that many accounts of "revolts" come from the very judges who established their existence. Often the only indisputable sources of information are lists of those convicted and the punishments they received.

In addition, there are vast disparities among the written sources available in different regions of the Americas. Archives kept by the United Kingdom, France, and the Netherlands for their respective colonies, as well as archives in the United States, offer an abundance of demographic, economic, social, and political documentation. In contrast, equivalent archives from the Iberian Peninsula and Iberian America are much more modest: plantation registers are scarce, for example, and countless provincial collections have disappeared by accident or through negligence. In 1889, the First Republic of Brazil deliberately ordered the destruction of documents related to slavery in its federal archives in an effort to erase traces of the institution.[4] Admittedly, in the Americas as a whole, judiciary and notarial archives located in provincial capitals do document slavery on the regional or local level. However, these records most often contain cases brought before the law, inventories, and transactions, and reveal little about the experience of slaves in households or plantations shielded from any outside intervention. Furthermore, while historians have access to extensive literature from Great Britain and the United States, where long and virulent written debates extolled the benefits of slavery or denounced its horrors, there are relatively few such sources from the French and Dutch Antilles, Puerto Rico, Cuba, and Brazil, where illiteracy was prevalent and publications in favor or against abolition were scarce, and even less from continental Hispanic America, where the abolition process left little written trace. Starting in the 1770s, English-speaking slaves were publishing poignant poetry and autobiographies, but there were no equivalents in the Spanish-, Portuguese-, or French-speaking world.[5]

Despite those differences and difficulties, the historiography of slavery in the Americas developed throughout the continent beginning in the 1980s, in parallel with the evolution of multiethnic and multiracial American societies grappling with questions of equality and citizenship. A century earlier, Cuba and Brazil had abolished slavery in, respectively, 1886 and 1888; in the United States, the South was forced to emancipate all its slaves in 1865 following the deadliest war in the country's history; the Netherlands did the same in 1863. France and Denmark had abolished slavery in their colonies between 1848 and 1856, as had several Hispano American republics in their respective territories. In 1838, the British colonies had emancipated their enslaved population, following the United Kingdom's abolition act of 1833. Only Haiti, in 1804, had decreed an immediate end to slavery in the wake of independence, followed by Chile, Central America, and Mexico in the 1820s. The abolition of slavery in the northern United States occurred gradually, between 1777 and 1823. It therefore took over a century, from 1777 to 1888, for the enslavement of Africans and their descendants to disappear as a legal system of labor in the Americas—a testament to its scale and the adjustments necessary after its ban. In the subsequent decades, intellectuals, politicians, economists, and religious figures debated slavery and its victims in a context characterized by racial determinism and a resurgence of colonialist thinking. Barring a few activists, often descendants of African slaves themselves, these individuals rarely highlighted the role played by slaves in their own liberation, even if they did lay the groundwork for later historians.[6]

The first studies to recognize slaves as social actors in their own right appeared in the 1930s. In 1935, U.S. philosopher and sociologist W. E. B. Du Bois published *Black Reconstruction in America*, in which he highlighted the crucial role played by slaves in the civil war that abolished slavery in the United States and the brief Reconstruction period intended to integrate them into the country.[7] Pointedly Marxist analyses emerged shortly thereafter, including works by another U.S. scholar, Herbert Aptheker, on the same subject matter and on slave revolts in the United States, which destroyed the image of the passive and submissive slave,[8] and Trinidadian historian C. L. R. James, whose book *The Black Jacobins* placed the Haitian Revolution at the center of the fight to end slavery.[9] In parallel, several students of U.S. anthropologist Franz Boas published works highlighting the cultural contributions of African slaves to American societies. They included Brazilian scholar Gilberto Freyre, who, as early as 1933, theorized a "gentle" relationship between masters and slaves in Brazil in his work *Casa-grande & senzala*. A few years later, Cuban scholar Fernando Ortiz abandoned racial determinism and invented the term "transculturation" to define the process of mutual influence between Western and African cultures in Cuban society. At the same time, Melville J. Herskovits insisted on the many contributions made to U.S. culture and society by slaves from West Africa as one of several forms of resistance.[10]

During World War II, against a backdrop of pseudoscientific racism and the antisemitism of Nazi Germany's genocidal policies, the Latin American societies praised by Freyre and Ortiz were viewed as models of racial harmony. They also provided a contrast to the U.S. South under Jim Crow laws. The 1944 publication of *An American Dilemma: The Negro Problem and Modern Democracy* by Swedish economist Gunnar Myrdal, who portrayed a United States blocked by the moral contradiction between its ideals of liberty and progress and the reality of its visceral racism against blacks, prompted historians to dig into the country's slavery past to find the roots of its violent race relations. Three years later, U.S. historian Frank Tannenbaum published *Slave and Citizen*, a decisively comparative work in which he used slavery to explain why race relations in the U.S. South in the 1940s were characterized by segregation and lynching, as compared to more fluid and less violent relations in Brazil. In short, according to Tannenbaum, slavery in Brazil had been relatively mild because the Catholic Church and a Roman law–based system protected slaves, whereas plantation owners in the United States were able to make them into simple assets of production responding to the needs of a fast-growing capitalist economy.[11] Tannenbaum's thesis had a lasting impact, notably on researchers' tendency to classify American societies along a scale of racial tolerance, which often placed Protestant Anglophone America at the most proslavery and racist extreme and Catholic Latin America at the other, leaving Catholic French America in an ambiguous position. However, by adopting a legal and structural approach, Tannenbaum ignored slaves' capacity to challenge their enslavement.

The question of subalterns' agency within systems of totalitarian domination came to the forefront in the 1950s when African Americans launched an unprecedented movement against racist violence and for their civil rights in the segregated U.S. South. In *The Peculiar Institution* (1956), in a subtle response to those real-life events, Kenneth Stampp described slavery in the South as a profitable labor system though it was based on exploitation, abuse, and deplorable living conditions; however, he insisted on slaves' ability to resist by sabotaging production, and through escape and sometimes violent revolt. In contrast, Stanley Elkins, in *Slavery: A Problem in American Institutional and Intellectual Life* (1959), appeared to be going against the tide when he repeated Freyre and

Tannenbaum's arguments, claiming that slavery in the United States was much crueler than it was in Latin America. By comparing plantations in the U.S. South to Nazi concentration camps, Elkins maintained that slavery in the United States was so brutal and inhuman, and slaveholders' domination so totalitarian, that captives were stripped of their African heritage in order to be made into submissive and docile subjects.[12] A multitude of studies emerged in response to show that, far from being "Uncle Toms" and "mammies," enslaved men and women in the United States had relied on a vast arsenal of visible and other subtler strategies to survive as human beings in their own right and contribute to all aspects of U.S. culture and society.[13]

The absence of institutionalized racism and black rights organizations in Latin America allowed the myth of a "gentle" Latin American slavery to continue until the 1980s. The vision of Brazil as a land of racial harmony suggested by Freyre was extended to Spanish-speaking America, attributing more humanity to Iberian slavery than to its U.S. equivalent. In addition, beginning in the late 1950s, Latin America was shaken by the emergence of Marxist guerrillas and the establishment of military dictatorships backed by Washington. In that Cold War context, Latin American historians (at times from exile) tended to favor structural analyses, notably of dependence, over an emphasis on slaves' historic autonomy.[14] In fact, the first studies to focus on the actions of Latin American slaves were conducted by U.S. comparatists seeking to identify the factors behind the relative racial peace prevailing in Latin America (all while recognizing the existence of major socioracial disparities) at the same time that ghettos in the northern and western United States were ablaze.[15] The growing recognition of African heritages within Latin American cultures and the development of Latin American schools of sociology and anthropology interested in the links between poverty, racial discrimination, and a slavery past then prompted historians to produce more critical analyses of slavery in the region. Beginning in the 1980s, the establishment of various black organizations in Latin America and an inter-American academic dialogue strengthened the interest in the study of slaves as agents of the region's history.[16]

The historiography of slavery in the British colonies in the Caribbean and Guiana developed as they began to gain independence in the 1960s. Accession to nationhood brought with it questions about origins and ancestors, the latter in this case being primarily enslaved Africans. That trend was further reinforced by the fact that parts of those territories had been populated by fugitive slaves who formed maroon (and somewhat protoseparatist) societies beginning in the seventeenth century. The traditional British narrative that maintained that the emancipation of slaves in British colonies had been the work of London abolitionists—attacked as early as 1944 by the Trinidadian Marxist historian Eric Williams using a largely economic argument—was rejected in the early

1980s by Jamaican historian Richard Hart and the Barbadian Hilary Beckles, who argued that slaves themselves, through resistance and rebellion, had forced Great Britain to decree emancipation.[17]

As for slaveholding French America, a historiography focused on slaves as autonomous actors was slower to emerge, particularly in regard to the islands and territories still attached to France following decolonization. As in Great Britain, abolition in those regions was long identified with the French politician who signed the decree in question. Moreover, the doctrine of Republican equality temporized the study of racial discrimination and slave resistance. Marronage was again the first phenomenon to capture the attention of historians seeking to highlight slaves' actions, even in the case of Saint Domingue.[18] Early historiography on the slaves of the Dutch West Indies and Guiana was even more limited, with the exception of studies on fugitive slaves in Suriname, which gained its independence in 1975.[19] Surprisingly, though it had obsessed nineteenth-century observers, the Haitian Revolution, the only successful insurrection waged by predominantly African slaves to result in the abolition of slavery and the independence of a black nation, did not prompt its own historical field of study until the 1990s.[20] At the same time, historians of slavery abandoned national comparative studies in favor of more regional approaches or, on the contrary, more transnational ones focused on the circulation of ideas and persons, notably in relation to the Atlantic world and the African diaspora.[21]

Beginning in the 1960s, historians and sociologists of slavery, undoubtedly influenced by the social movements then upsetting the entire Western Hemisphere, from the United States to Latin America to the Caribbean, attempted to categorize and classify the actions taken by slaves to resist their condition. One of the first to do so, Jamaican sociologist Orlando Patterson, distinguished between "passive resistance," including satire, refusal to work, flight, and suicide, and "violent resistance," which he divided into "individual" and "collective."[22] U.S. historian Eugene Genovese wanted to show that a fundamental turning point occurred beginning with the era of revolutions, notably the Haitian Revolution: prior to the late eighteenth century, slave revolts had been "restorationist" (aimed at restoring the freedom of its primarily African participants); afterward, he argued, they were revolutionary, and envisaged the eradication of the institution of slavery and the establishment of a democratic bourgeois society. There would have therefore been a kind of hierarchy of forms of resistance, beginning with accommodation (considered to be passive and nonheroic) and culminating with armed revolt.[23] Yet some historians, like the Cuban Manuel Moreno Fraginals, continued to assert that the trauma caused by being wrenched from the African continent and crossing the ocean on slave ships was so intense and the dehumanization by the institution of slavery so complete that they left slaves stripped of their culture and incapable of assuming personal, economic, or familial responsibilities.[24]

As it developed, this field of studies highlighted new forms of resistance, though without refuting the distinction between violent resistance and nonviolent resistance (the latter sometimes contradictorily referred to as "passive resistance"). For most historians, violent forms of resistance consisted of marronage, suicide, murder, conspiracy, and revolt. On the other end of the spectrum, recourse to legal rights and the courts, cultural practices, religion, and any other discreet action aimed at decreasing the profitability of slavery (seduction, simulation, production delays, sabotage, theft, or inebriation) were categorized as nonviolent resistance.[25] Other specialists, such as Michael Craton, viewed slaves' African or creole origins as the fundamental explanation for their different strategies. He argued that slaves born in Africa and forcibly brought over through the slave trade more frequently resorted to armed revolt and the establishment of fugitive slave communities (maroon societies) than those born on American soil, who used more creolized forms of resistance, blending African and American elements of culture or protest.[26]

The hierarchization of forms of resistance led to a proliferation of studies of slave revolts beginning in the 1980s. The triumphant image of the male rebel slave emerged from that scholarship and became the reigning model. Some historians, focalized on that dynamic, conflated conspiracy or even the suspicion of a plot with revolt, as judges had previously done for opposing reasons. Those scholars hypothesized that if certain rebellions had not been rapidly contained and other plots denounced just before they were carried out, they could have become revolts as widespread as the uprising in Saint Domingue.[27] This idealization of the rebellious, even revolutionary slave tended to favor the masculine struggle at the expense of the feminine one and underestimate less visible forms of struggle and resistance thanks to which the vast majority of slaves survived and a minority of whom, including many women, obtained their freedom.

Yet during the same period, other historians, building on studies conducted by James Scott,[28] preferred to highlight discreet or "subtle" resistance to show that it was more effective in the long term than violent revolt, which, barring a few exceptions, inevitably led to massive, harsh, and exemplary repression.[29] Beginning with research by Deborah White, gender studies made a decisive contribution to the valorization of subtle resistance by revealing the specificities of the condition of enslaved women and the opposition strategies they employed.[30] Thanks to pioneering studies by Paul Lovejoy and, later, John Thornton, a deeper understanding of the societies, cultures, and historical context from which deported Africans emerged enabled analysis of their impact on expressions of opposition to slavery in the Americas.[31]

Introduction 11

This vast body of secondary literature served as the foundation of my study. Aware that this bibliography would remain incomplete, I attempted to compare the analyses and interpretations at my disposal without any preconceived notions. Even so, my work relies on a fundamental premise: like other subaltern classes, slaves were agents of their own history, as was incidentally recognized by judges during the trials to which slaves could find themselves subjected. Despite laws that demanded absolute submission to their masters, slaves managed to stay alive, possess a few objects, and build social links and cultural and religious traditions and even at times a family and personal project (examples include the upkeep of a personal garden, the transition from plantation slave to domestic slave, the purchase of one's freedom, and individual escape). Those acts represented a considerable victory—an affirmation of slaves' intrinsic humanity—which they would only very rarely risk destroying. Indeed, it would be a mistake to think that slaves had nothing to lose: those who wanted to win their freedom found themselves confronting serious dilemmas. Every liberation strategy carried risks, even manumission, which could be threatened at any moment by a master's ill health or bad faith. But no strategy was more dangerous than the preparation of an insurrection (plotting) and revolt, which would lead with quasi-certainty to being killed or arrested and to torture and/or a terrible death. And every slave had witnessed public lashings and executions.[32] I have therefore cautiously analyzed slave plots and revolts while paying particular attention to the repression they provoked.

My long-term comparative study of the Americas reveals, for the first time, the breadth and success of actions taken by slaves to liberate themselves. Thousands of geographically dispersed slaves were able to obtain or regain their freedom before the development of abolitionism and the era of revolutions. These extraordinary individual or collective victories over slavery by almost universally illiterate men and women challenge our conception of the history of human rights and the Enlightenment's seminal role in that evolution. They also test the centrality of revolt as a motor of history. My diachronic and cross-disciplinary analysis provides the first chronology of slave liberation strategies and reveals to what extent slaves understood the context in which they were living. From the early sixteenth century onwards, these men and women took continuous discreet or visible actions to protest their inhuman condition, choosing one strategy over another because it was the most appropriate means to obtain their freedom in a given environment.

Following an introductory section that outlines the major phases of the slave trade in relation to colonization and the evolution of the institution of slavery, this book is organized according to the changing context of the first three centuries of the colonization of the Americas. The second section examines how, within a context of expanding slavery, thousands of slaves were able to obtain their freedom, primarily by fleeing into interior regions and by buying their freedom. It demonstrates that though authorities claimed to have uncovered many plots, which they then repressed, actual slave revolts and conspiracies were few and limited.

The Seven Years' War (1756–63) disrupted the relationships between colonies and the European powers and initiated the "era of independence movements" (concurrent with the "era of revolutions") explored in the third part of this work. Slaves everywhere, in unprecedented numbers and with new urgency, quickly took advantage of the cracks that appeared in systems of domination after 1763 and which led to the independence of the United States, Haiti, and continental Iberian America. Depending on the region and period, they escaped by the thousands, embarked on a process of manumission, or enlisted in armies in exchange for eventual freedom. In Saint Domingue, the impact of the French Revolution on colonial society was such that slaves were able to launch a massive revolt that, after thirteen years of deadly fighting, simultaneously gave rise to the second independent nation in the Americas and the first to completely abolish slavery. From that point on, the institution of slavery no longer appeared unshakable, as was also indicated by its immediate or gradual abolition in several other independent territories in the Americas.

The fourth section revisits slave liberation strategies after the impact of the Haitian Revolution had diminished and the continental wars of independence had ended, and up until the definitive abolition of slavery in the British colonies in 1838. It therefore concentrates on regions in which slavery was deeply entrenched, notably the southern United States, the Antilles, the Guianas, and Brazil, and again reveals slaves' tremendous agency in accordance with their circumstances. As they pursued strategies to escape and purchase freedom that had been developing since the sixteenth century, they also increasingly questioned slavery's Christian and legal foundations. Above all, they had clearly understood that barring a new crack in the system of domination, it was useless to revolt. Aware that they were the private property of their masters, slaves realized that they could not confront the institution of slavery unless an authority superior to their masters—the king, the Bible, or Parliament—challenged the former group's power over them. When those conditions presented themselves—as in the British Empire during the first third of the nineteenth century under the influence of abolitionists—hundreds, even thousands, of slaves were willing to risk their lives revolting in order to speed up widespread emancipation.

The epilogue briefly examines slave liberation strategies as they developed during the fifty years following general emancipation in the British colonies in 1838, up to the abolition of slavery in Brazil—and in the Americas—in 1888. As much as the year 1838 had been a turning point in slaves' struggles for freedom, with abolitionism on the rise and parts of the American continent and the

Caribbean liberated from slavery, the institution still held ground in the French colonies and Spanish continental America, and the "second slavery" flourished in the U.S. South, Cuba, and Brazil. Nevertheless, as new opportunities for freedom appeared in the next decades, many slaves again actively participated in the collapse of the institution by running away, joining armies, or working tirelessly to purchase their freedom or that of a family member. This book aims to highlight the struggles of these men, women, and children.

PART I
Settings and Eras

≋ 1 ≋
The Slave Trade and Slavery in the Americas
Transcontinental Trends

Between the sixteenth and nineteenth centuries, the Christian Western Hemisphere relied on the enslavement of Africans and their descendants to varying degrees. To this end, thousands, and later tens of thousands, of men, women, and children were deported from Africa to the Caribbean and the American continent every year for nearly four centuries. In total, according to estimates by *Voyages: The Trans-Atlantic Slave Trade Database*, approximately 12,332,000 Africans were loaded onto slave ships bound for the Americas.[1] In all likelihood, an additional 8 to 10 million died during capture, marches to African ports, or the long wait in coastal depots. The slave trade initially recruited its victims in Senegambia, via Gorée Island, before gradually spreading across the entire coast of Guinea and its inland regions. During the eighteenth century, it extended into Angola and the Kingdom of Kongo, reaching as far as their vast interiors, exporting captives primarily from Elmina, Ouidah, Calabar, Cabinda, and Luanda. That region continued to supply the majority of slaves in the nineteenth century, when Mozambique, until then mainly a tributary of the Arabian Peninsula and the western coast of India, was also impacted by the transatlantic slave trade. Deported Africans therefore came from vastly different cultures, the most heavily represented being, north of the equator, the Wolof, Mandinga (including the Bambaras), Ashanti (including the Akans, called the Coromantee by the British), Gbe (Ewe, Fon), Yorubas (called the Lucumí by the Spanish), and Igbos (or Ibos), and, in the south, the Kongo and Bantus (including Landas and Mbundu), and, in Mozambique, the Makua.[2]

The forced departures of so many Africans to the Americas, which joined existing Saharan and Arab slave trades that began in the second half of the seventh century,[3] had significant demographic, economic, and political consequences on all of sub-Saharan Western Africa and Mozambique.[4] Of the 12,332,000 Africans ripped from their homeland, nearly 2 million (or 16 percent total) perished during the transatlantic voyage. Still, 10,538,000 survived the crossing to be sold as slaves in American ports.[5] Death remained a constant threat for the survivors, a large number of whom died in the year following their arrival, in ports, during travel to the mines, plantations, or households to which they were destined, and at their new places of work. During this interminable journey, millions of men, women, and children also died prematurely from maltreatment, exhaustion, hunger and thirst, disease (particularly smallpox), and despair. Some committed suicide or were killed as they attempted to rebel.[6] According to several estimates, those still alive one year after arriving in the Americas represented less than half of those who were originally captured in Africa.[7]

African survivors would nonetheless rapidly transform the demography and sociology of the Western Hemisphere. Though decimated by the slave trade, Africans far outnumbered other groups that reached the "new" continent until the 1820s: they were at least four times more numerous than European immigrants.[8] These involuntary migrants, young men for the most part,[9] adopted a variety of strategies to survive and in some instances escape enslavement. Some had sexual relations, willingly or otherwise, with persons of European and Amerindian descent, thereby accelerating miscegenation. Some within that group obtained their freedom, creating a sociracial category of "free people of color," meaning free blacks and Afro-descendants who, though subjected to considerable legal discrimination, challenged by their very existence a system of slavery based on the "race" of Africans and their American-born descendants.

Slavery affected every region in the Western Hemisphere, from North to South, Atlantic coast to the Pacific via the Caribbean. As graph 1 demonstrates, no country relied on slavery more continuously and on a more massive scale than Brazil, which imported African slaves uninterruptedly from 1561 to 1856. According to estimates by *The Trans-Atlantic Slave Trade*, 46.2 percent of the 10,538,000 African men, women, and children brought to the Americas went to Brazil. The British West Indies followed, with 22 percent of that total, half of which was represented by Jamaica alone. Next came the French Antilles, with 10.6 percent (70 percent represented by Saint Domingue), and the Spanish Caribbean, with 7.6 percent (notably Cuba, with Puerto Rico far behind). But if we add the Dutch and Danish West Indies,[10] the Caribbean islands as a whole received 41.7 percent of African slaves. The remaining 12.1 percent was brought to the non-Brazilian continental Americas: 4.6 percent to Spanish colonies, 3.8 percent to the Guianas (notably Dutch Guiana and, to a lesser degree, the British and French Guianas),[11] and only 3.7 percent to the continental colonies of Great Britain and the future United States.[12] However, that geographic distribution only accounts for slaves arriving directly from Africa, whereas some, particularly those sent to Jamaica, had been immediately reexported to Spanish and British colonies in the Americas.[13]

The slave trade was far from uniform or constant. Between 1501 and 1650, a period during which the Portuguese, until the 1620s, and then the Dutch had a monopoly on transatlantic slave imports, 726,000 African captives in total were brought alive to the Americas, primarily to continental Spanish colonies and

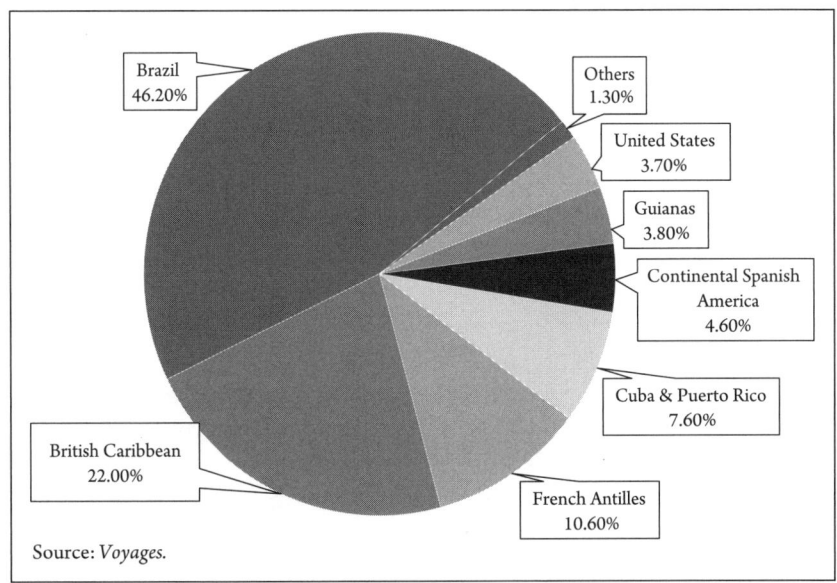

Graph 1. Destinations of Enslaved Africans Disembarked in the Americas, 1501–1866

Portuguese Brazil. From 1650 to 1775, during Great Britain and France's concurrent participation in the slave trade and the development of sugar plantations in the Caribbean and Brazil, 4,796,000 Africans were brought to the Americas. Cargos during the final 111 years of the slave trade, from 1775 to 1866, surpassed that number, delivering 5,016,000 new captives to the region.[14] What's more, that massive amount, which corresponds to half of the 10.5 million Africans transported across the Atlantic, was reached despite the influence of Enlightenment philosophy, growing recognition of freedom as a fundamental right, the transition to independence in the continental Americas, and the gradual legal abolition of the slave trade.

Graph 2 demonstrates the evolution of annual imports of enslaved Africans from 1501 to 1866. It shows that the slave trade grew continuously from 1500 to the early 1620s, a decade during which more than 17,000 Africans were imported to the Americas each year. The slave trade then slowed, with approximately 10,000 slaves arriving each year for a quarter of a century; after 1655, it increased almost continuously, reaching more than 70,000 Africans in 1755 on the eve of the Seven Years' War. Since 1766, following a drop during the war, the slave trade imported on average 78,000 captives each year until a new decline during the U.S. War of Independence (1776–81). But the decade of 1784–93 marked a climax with imports reaching nearly 91,000 Africans on average per year. From 1794 to 1824, the Haitian Revolution, the Napoleonic Wars, the abolition of the Danish, British, and U.S. slave trades in 1807–8 and the Dutch trade in 1814, and finally

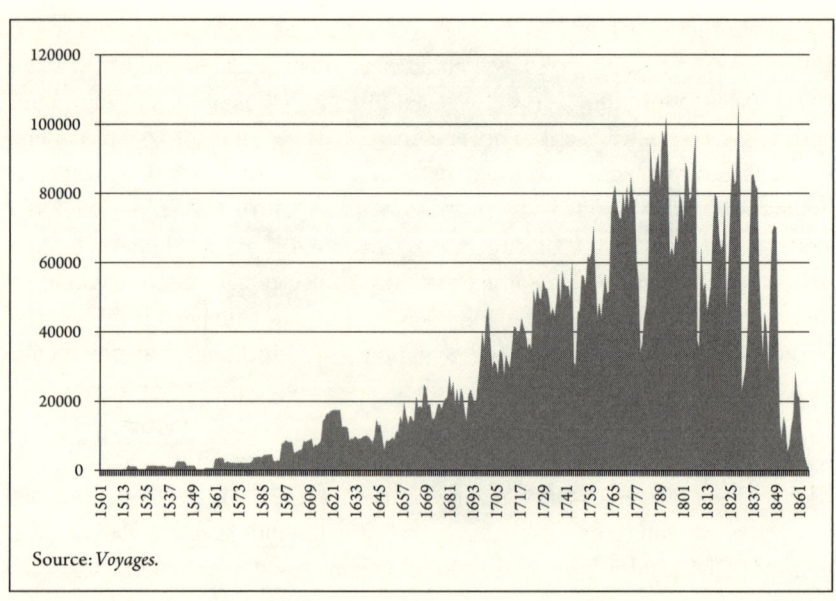

Graph 2. Numbers of Enslaved Africans Disembarked Each Year in the Americas, 1501–1864

the Spanish American wars of independence caused major disruptions to the slave trade, which nonetheless maintained on average more than 64,000 Africans imported annually for three decades. In 1825, and despite Spain's, France's, and Portugal's acceptance of a declaration relative to the universal abolition of the slave trade in Vienna ten years earlier, the importation of slaves saw a meteoric rise, once again reaching nearly 88,000 Africans per year between 1826 and 1831. In fact, the historical record was reached in 1829, when as many as 106,000 captives were disembarked, nearly all in Brazil, Cuba, and the French Antilles. From 1831 to 1859, despite the signing of new treaties banning the slave trade, nearly 54,000 Africans on average were illegally imported each year, notably by Brazil and Cuba. After 1856, when Brazil ended its contraband trade, Cuba, the last colony to continue violating treaties, imported another 148,000 captives by 1866, when the last 722 African slaves arrived on the island, marking an end to over three and a half centuries of human trafficking.[15]

Africans and their enslaved descendants contributed enormously to the development of every economic activity in American societies, from domestic service to transportation, mines to plantations, and brute manual labor to highly skilled craftsmanship, writing, and artistic creation. Slaves further represented considerable capital whose value was often superior to that of the land or buildings on an estate, and which the owner could sell, rent, pawn, use to reimburse debts, and bequeath. Slavery was a primarily rural phenomenon: in places where indigenous populations had been wiped out or were dispersed, producers of gold, indigo, tobacco, sugar, coffee, cocoa, rice, and cotton, the exportation of which made European nations and colonial and American elites rich, were most often slaves of both sexes. Many cattle breeders, muleteers, porters, rowers, and peddlers were slaves as well. Cities and small towns also had sizable enslaved populations, composed notably of women and girls performing varied domestic tasks, or working as cooks, washerwomen, ironers, peddlers, prostitutes, wet nurses, maids, waitresses, midwives, or healers. Urban male slaves served as, among others, stewards, valets, cooks, bakers, coach drivers, day laborers, construction workers, dressmakers, shoemakers, metalworkers, street vendors, horse grooms, musicians, or were assigned to military forces. Many lived with their masters, but some resided and worked independently, paying a fixed daily or weekly sum to their owners.[16] As underlined by historian Herman Bennett, not only did urban slaves play a major role in city economies, they also conferred "cultural capital" on their masters and mistresses by boosting their social rank. The more slaves, often clad in livery, were owned by an aristocratic estate, the more its owners were held in high standing by society. For large landowners living in town, slaves were simultaneously the source (via the product of their nonremunerated work) and demonstration of wealth and social status.[17]

Peru and Brazil: After the Amerindians, the Africans (1501–1650)

The first slaves reached the Americas shortly after Christopher Columbus in 1492. They were also present, alongside with free blacks and mulattos, among the conquistador armies that overthrew the Aztec and Inca Empires. From the earliest days of colonization, those slaves included *ladinos* (Europeanized slaves of African ancestry who came from the Iberian Peninsula) and bossales (non-Europeanized slaves who came directly from Africa, referred to as *bozales* in Spanish and *boçais* in Portuguese). At that time, slavery was well established on the Iberian Peninsula, particularly in the domains of domestic labor and urban craftsmanship. African slaves had supplanted their Moorish predecessors, and represented up to 10 percent of the populations of Portugal and Spain's coastal towns. But it was on the islands off the Atlantic coast of northern Africa—São Tomé, the Canary Islands, and Madeira—that, beginning in 1450, the Portuguese and the Spanish developed a sugar plantation system based on the enslavement of countless Africans that would come to characterize the Americas.[18]

Yet nothing predestined African slavery to become as important as it did in the American colonies. In fact, when the Europeans arrived, there were likely some 57 million inhabitants in the Americas as a whole. That indigenous population represented a labor force from which the colonists could have drawn at length. Incidentally, the Spanish were initially eager to enslave natives in the Caribbean, as the Portuguese did to the Tupi-Guarani on the Brazilian coast. But those populations were quickly decimated due to their conquerors' cruelty, diseases to which they lacked immunity, forced labor, and culture shock. Indigenous societies in the Caribbean and on the coast of Brazil were semisedentary and fragile, and nearly disappeared completely in the span of one century. Though the densely populated territories of the Aztec and Inca Empires were not completely depopulated, they nevertheless lost approximately 90 percent of their original populations between 1520 and 1620.[19]

The rapid and violent depopulation caused by colonization was denounced at the time by men such as the Dominican priest Bartolomé de Las Casas (1474–1566) who, after 1530, gradually persuaded the Spanish monarch to ban the enslavement of Indians. Nonetheless, the encomienda system, in which the king granted conquistadors indigenous communities from which they could extract labor and tribute, endured far beyond his royal ban of 1542. Since the second half of the sixteenth century, Spain also transformed the Inca system of tributary labor, *mita* (called *repartimiento* in Mexico), by forcing every village community to supply a quota of temporary workers to mines, plantations, and weaving mills three times a year. In parallel, authorities forcibly resettled segments of the surviving Amerindian population to *pueblos de indios* near colonial labor centers, all while forbidding them from settling in cities.[20]

By 1550, nearly every Amerindian population had become too small to form a durable labor force. At the same time, neither Spain, already strained from its vast European empire's demands for men, nor underpopulated Portugal were in a position to compensate for Amerindian demographic losses by sending colonists or indentured servants to the Americas. So the two monarchies turned to African slavery in the form in which it existed in their African island colonies and the slave trade took hold, monopolized by the Portuguese. Between 1500 and 1650, continental Spanish America and Brazil each imported a total of nearly 350,000 slaves.[21]

The main Spanish destinations were the colonies of Peru and Mexico, followed by Colombia and Venezuela, and to a lesser degree Central America and Ecuador. After a stop in Havana, Africans were sent to the ports of Veracruz in Mexico, Cartagena de Indias in Colombia, and Portobelo in Panama. Most were then taken, chained or bound, by foot and by boat, to plantation or mining regions. Those destined for Peru traveled either from Panama via the Pacific Ocean or from Cartagena via dangerous routes through Colombia's sweltering plains and the glacial summits of the Andes. The high demand for slaves in Peru was due to colonists' preference for the sparsely populated Pacific coast over the Inca center in the Andes, home to the majority of the colony's indigenous people (by then regrouped in *pueblos de indios*), and to their reticence to undertake a mass displacement of that already weakened population toward the coast. By 1555, there were 3,000 bozales in Peru, half in Lima. One century later, Peru had a total of 100,000 slaves, representing between 10 and 15 percent of the population, and most of them were concentrated along the coast. Lima counted 20,000 slaves; along with free people of color, they represented half of its inhabitants. They worked as domestic servants, porters, sellers, washerwomen, unskilled workers, artisans, seamen, and soldiers, among other occupations. Some were assigned to forced labor in bakeries and weaving mills on the outskirts of Lima, at times chained alongside convicted criminals. South of Lima, approximately 20,000 slaves labored on sugar plantations in the Pisco and Ica regions. Many were assigned to the royal navy and to gold and silver mines in the South. Slaves were also charged with raising cattle and horses, while others worked as muleteers farther inland.[22]

During the same period, Mexico (or New Spain, which stretched from present-day Florida and New Mexico to Costa Rica) had some thirty-five thousand slaves, who represented less than 2 percent of its population. As in Peru, they were employed in a large variety of sectors including domestic work, crafts, and cloth weaving, as well as gold and silver mining, but they played a less important economic role due to a slight uptick in indigenous demographics after 1600. They were, however, essential in certain regions, notably Veracruz, where they cultivated sugarcane crops.[23] Although Colombia, Venezuela, and Ecuador occupied a secondary position in Spain's American empire at the time, slaves in those regions performed production-related and domestic tasks similar to those of their counterparts in Peru and Mexico. In the Popayán region, south of Colombia, growing numbers of slaves were assigned to farms and gold mines: slavery supplemented the encomienda system (though it was illegal) until it ended at the close of the seventeenth century. Elsewhere, the Spanish pursued pearl fishing on the Caribbean coast between Riohacha and Cumaná: once they had decimated the Amerindians forced to risk their lives free diving, they replaced them with African slaves. Pearl fishing, highly profitable for the royal treasury, cost countless slave lives as well.[24]

By the 1560s, the other major destination of the African slave trade was Brazil, which imported 350,000 Africans by 1650 thanks to Portuguese and, briefly, Dutch slave ships. Lacking sizable mining operations (the gold of Minas Gerais was not discovered until 1690), and with a declining Amerindian labor force, the Brazilian coast developed slowly using the slave sugar plantation model that Portugal had tested on the African islands of São Tomé and Madeira. Whereas the Brazilian plantations of Nordeste had initially and primarily employed Tupi Indians as slaves, by 1600 half of their labor force came from Africa, and Brazil had become the world's leading sugar producer. Twenty years later, the majority of those plantations relied exclusively on African slaves and Brazil alone was annually importing more *boçais* than the entirety of the Spanish colonies.[25]

The Sugar Plantation: A New Deadly Model in the Caribbean, Brazil, and North America (1650–1775)

In 1621, the Dutch challenged Portugal's monopoly of Atlantic trade between continental America, Europe, and Africa by attacking Portuguese colonies in Africa and Asia. Their occupation of Recife and the province of Pernambuco in Brazil in 1639 and then of outgoing slave ports on Africa's Atlantic coast marked the beginning of a new and rapid expansion of slavery in the Americas. The Dutch, for example, once they entered the slave trade, incited the spread of sugar plantations in French and English colonies in the Caribbean and North America.[26] In 1641, the English also began to traffic in African captives, competing with and then surpassing the Dutch and rivaling the Portuguese who were continuing to supply Brazil with slaves. In the 1670s, the French entered the slave trade as well. Consequently, the total number of captives imported annually to the Americas increased from eighty-five hundred enslaved Africans in 1650 to seventy-nine thousand in 1775, or nine times what it had been twenty-five years earlier (see graph 2), despite a slowdown of the slave trade during the Seven Years' War.[27]

As early as their occupation of Pernambuco, the Dutch had modernized existing sugar plantations and supplanted the Portuguese in the slave trade. After being forced out of Brazil, they settled, with slaves, in the new English and French colonies in the Caribbean, notably Barbados, Guadeloupe, and Martinique, where European indentured servants were producing tobacco and indigo. Under Dutch influence, the economy of those islands switched to the model of the sugar plantation reliant on African slavery, as shown by the example of Barbados. In 1645, the island had 37,000 white inhabitants, primarily Irish and Scottish indentured servants, and 5,700 slaves. Shortly after Oliver Cromwell's invasion of Ireland and Scotland, the number of whites in Barbados swelled when thousands more Irish men and women were transported to the colony as forced laborers. But by 1680, the number of slaves had reached 38,000, while the number of whites had fallen to 17,000, only 2,000 of whom were indentured. A century later, the white population had not increased, but Barbados by then had 68,000 slaves. However, that figure masks the fact that between 1650 and 1775, the small 166-square-mile island had imported 432,000 Africans in total, or an average of 3,450 per year, whom British plantation owners exploited to death or reexported to Jamaica and other British colonies in North America and the Caribbean.[28] Sugar dominated Barbados's economy and planters its society. Guadeloupe and Martinique underwent similar though less rapid changes.

Based on those successes, the French colonized Saint Domingue (the western half of Hispaniola) in the beginning of the eighteenth century, and Great Britain, Jamaica. Vaster than the Lesser Antilles, Saint Domingue and Jamaica would become the ultimate incarnation of the large sugar colony. The colonies' best plots of lands were transformed into vast slave plantations as African captives flooded in, forming the great majority of the population, whereas free residents, either whites or free people of color, never surpassed 15 percent of the inhabitants. The number of slaves in Jamaica thus increased from 9,500 in 1675 to 193,000 in 1775.[29] Saint Domingue saw its slave population, which numbered 2,000 in 1680, reach 117,000 in 1740 and nearly 250,000 in 1775.[30] On average, each sugar plantation employed 100 slaves, and the largest ones had 200 or more, whom they exhausted at an unbridled pace. In Saint Domingue, one African in two died from maltreatment, exhaustion, disease, or undernourishment less than eight years after his or her arrival. In Jamaica, not counting new arrivals, the enslaved population declined 2.4 percent annually between 1739 and 1787. Yet this cannibalistic system of production proved profitable for planters in Jamaica and Saint Domingue, who maintained that the cost of purchasing an African captive was recouped after he or she had worked between three and seven years.[31] The system also made the French and British monarchies rich. This new type of mass rural slavery differed greatly from the diverse and more urban system that had characterized Peru and Mexico before 1650, and would gradually dominate the entire Caribbean and a portion of the continental Americas. At the same time, throughout the eighteenth century, the British, after successfully challenging the Dutch, dominated the slave trade, in which the French were by then also participating. In all, the British, Dutch, and French Caribbean islands imported 2,277,000 African slaves between 1651 and 1775—nearly half of the 4,796,000 Africans brought to the Americas during those 125 years.[32] That demonstrates the importance—and above all the human cost—of sugar and, to a lesser degree, coffee at the time.

The rapid development of sugar plantations in the French and British Caribbean coincided with Brazil's sharp increase of the importation of Africans after the 1690 discovery of gold mines in Minas Gerais. In order to meet the demands of the gold-rich region, 161,000 new captives were imported during the last decade of the seventeenth century, or twice as many as during the 1680s. The number of slaves working in Minas Gerais quintupled between 1710 and 1735, increasing from 20,000 to 100,000, before reaching 174,000 in 1786. The discovery of diamond mines in 1729 prompted another influx of slaves to the region; others became servants and artisans in nearby cities. The development of Minas Gerais led to the displacement of Brazil's center of gravity from

North to South, as demonstrated in 1763 by the change of capital from Salvador de Bahia to Rio de Janeiro, and the subsequent expansion of colonization and slavery throughout the São Paulo region. By around 1770, some 19,000 Africans were arriving in Brazil each year. Spanish colonies continued to bring in new captives as well. In Colombia, thousands of slaves joined those already laboring in the gold mines of Popayán, while others were put to work in the alluvial mines of northern Antioquia and Chocó, on the Pacific side. In Venezuela, the expansion of cocoa plantations justified the renewed importation of Africans, with the number of slaves in the colony reaching 64,000 around 1750.[33]

The eighteenth century also saw the development of slavery in the British colonies on the eastern coast of North America (the future United States of America). In total, between 1700 and 1775, the colonies stretching from Massachusetts to Georgia imported around 265,000 slaves directly from Africa, along with thousands of other captives reexported from Jamaica and Barbados. Furthermore, the number of slaves on the east coast exploded from 29,000 in 1700 to 470,000 in 1770, while the total population increased from 251,000 to 2,148,000. In 1770, there were therefore sixteen times more slaves than in 1700, and their proportion of the total population had doubled, from 12 percent in 1700 to 22 percent. However, those numbers mask a fundamental difference: to borrow the classification used by historian Ira Berlin, the British continental colonies in the South (Maryland, Virginia, North and South Carolina, and Georgia) had become slave plantation societies, whereas the colonies located in the North (Massachusetts, New Hampshire, Rhode Island, Connecticut, New York, New Jersey, and Pennsylvania) remained societies with slaves, who did not represent the majority of the labor force.[34]

Virginia's transformation into a slave society after 1675 clearly demonstrates that growing difference between North and South. In 1619, Dutch traders had sold the first Africans in Virginia to grow tobacco alongside indentured Irish and Scottish servants; some of those captives were incidentally also contractually employed and granted their freedom accordingly. During the last quarter of the seventeenth century, a convergence of factors led to the expansion of slavery in the colony: the growing difficulty of enticing European servants more attracted by the colonization of Pennsylvania, reduced mortality rates, the growth of the slave trade, and a decrease in slave prices. By 1735, the slavery-based tobacco plantation dominated the entire Chesapeake Bay region, including the Atlantic coast of Maryland and Virginia. And though planters continued to import slaves from Africa (115,000 in total between 1701 and 1775), the region also became the first in the Americas to achieve a natural growth of the enslaved population. That distinction does not mean that Chesapeake slaveowners were less abusive than their counterparts in the Caribbean or Brazil, but rather resulted from conditions that allowed births to slightly overtake deaths, notably small farms where slave families were lodged together and better sanitary conditions that prolonged life expectancy. By 1770, the Chesapeake region already had 323,000 slaves, most of whom were born there.[35]

Farther south, following its establishment in 1670, Carolina (which split into North and South Carolina in 1729) began by specializing in the Amerindian slave trade, though it was already relying on slaves from West Africa to raise cattle. Whereas English pioneers were eliminating Amerindian communities from the region, planters from Barbados, at that point saturated with plantations, settled in the colony with their slaves in order to develop indigo cultivation. They then turned to rice production, which had its American debut in Carolina thanks to techniques developed by slaves imported from the coast of Guinea, where the crop was widespread. Charleston rapidly became the main slave port in North America. As for Georgia, though it had been stipulated at the colony's creation in 1732 that it would prohibit slavery to give precedence to poor European pioneers, it attracted very few of the latter. Ten years later it therefore opened its doors to planters from other British colonies and to slavery for rice production. In 1770, South Carolina and Georgia together counted 90,000 slaves out of a total population of less than 110,000 inhabitants—in other words, a demographic profile close to that of the sugar-producing Caribbean.[36]

After 1680, African slavery spread through the English colonies north of Chesapeake. In total, more than 26,000 captives were imported to northern ports between 1663 and 1775, most arriving after 1731. Much less numerous than in the South, those later arrivals were principally engaged in port activities and domestic labor, and as artisans. In New York, the Dutch had introduced enslaved Africans since 1625 and by the English conquest in 1664, one inhabitant in five was enslaved. One century later, the colonies of New York and New Jersey collectively had 27,000 slaves, who represented 10 percent of the population. In Rhode Island, slavery developed on both shipping docks and cattle farms. In addition, the North indirectly depended on slavery in the South as its ports were making money off the trade of tobacco, rice, and indigo produced by slaves in Chesapeake and Carolina as well as of sugar from the British Caribbean.[37]

In New France, the enslavement of Amerindians preceded and largely surpassed that of Africans imported in the second half of the seventeenth century; black slave populations remained small and concentrated in domestic service. In 1689, Louis XIV authorized the import of African slaves, while simultaneously expressing reservations about the cost of their exploitation and their presumed natural unsuitability to cold climates. However, wars soon halted slavery in the region. Subsequent initiatives to import Africans were isolated and limited. In 1759, New France had approximately 1,100 black slaves (double the number of Amerindian slaves, called *panis*), who were concentrated in Montreal and a few secondary cities.[38]

Finally, the rapid rise in African slave imports between 1650 and 1775 can also be explained by the colonization of new territories, such as Louisiana and the Guianas. In 1718, the French established New Orleans. Many Caribbean planters therefore settled in the Mississippi Delta region with their slaves to grow rice, indigo, and tobacco, while also developing the barter of furs and skins with Amerindians from inland regions. French colonists even used African slaves (along with Amerindian ones) in the Illinois and Upper Mississippi regions. Louisiana had counted 1,685 slaves for less than 4,000 inhabitants in 1720, but by 1750, 4,370 of its 7,900 inhabitants were enslaved. After the colony switched from French to Spanish control in 1763, the number of slaves continued to increase, reaching 9,201 slaves out of 16,000 inhabitants in 1777.[39]

Slavery also spread along the coast of Guiana, where the Dutch, English, and French established colonies at the end of the seventeenth century, amid conflicts between the various camps. The deadly Caribbean sugar plantation model was particularly successful in Dutch Suriname. Between 1650 and 1680, a total of 16,600 Africans were deported to the colony, though the enslaved population numbered only 4,280 individuals in 1684. One century later, in 1775, the combined total of imported captives had reached 226,400 Africans. But the number of slaves officially recorded at that time was 75,000, dispersed among vast sugar or coffee plantations each with an average of 156 slaves but only a handful of whites. That massive drop can be explained by both extremely harsh living conditions, and therefore a very short life expectancy among slaves, and marronage (see chapter 3). Unlike other American colonies, Suriname had a high number of Jewish slaveowning planters, due to the Netherlands' open policy toward Jews, which was unique at that time in Europe.[40]

Cotton, Sugar, Coffee, and Chattel Slavery in the U.S. South, Cuba, and Brazil (1775–1870)

On the eve of the reforms and revolutions that would transform the Americas, colonial elites had broadly succeeded at imposing the racial enslavement of Africans and their African American descendants. During the last quarter of the eighteenth century, that socioeconomic system was reinforced by both the federalism adopted by the postindependence United States and the mercantilist reforms adopted by Spain and Portugal. Between 1781 and 1810, no less than 1,763,000 African slaves were imported to the Americas. Between 1811 and 1866, another 1,900,000 Africans joined them, including 1,145,000 destined for Brazil, 550,000 for Cuba, and 96,000 for the French Antilles, nearly all of whom were illegally smuggled into the Americas following the 1817–18 signing of new treaties banning slave trafficking. The French swelled the slave trade, dominated by the British throughout the eighteenth century, in the decade preceding the

Revolution of 1789, after which it was joined by every regional power, including the United States, before Portugal's near monopoly was restored after 1817.[41] Contrary to the demographic tendencies of the previous centuries, nearly half of African captives during this period were children, and only one-third were adult males. Slaveowners knew that human trafficking was doomed in the medium or long term and hoped to thereby perpetuate the system of enslaved labor.[42]

Following the Declaration of Independence in 1776, slavery began to diminish in the United States, initially because of the war against Great Britain. At the same time, over a ten-year period, all the northern states, except Delaware, gradually or immediately abolished the slave trade and slavery (see chapter 5), and all of the southern states, except South Carolina and Georgia, banned or heavily taxed new importations of slaves. In 1787, the slave trade issue divided the Constitutional Convention, where at least nineteen of the fifty-five delegates present (all white) owned slaves. The representatives of South Carolina and Georgia successfully fought for the international slave trade to continue unimpeded for another twenty years.[43]

Beginning in 1790, that trend was reversed: slavery once again spread dramatically through the southern United States, whose territory tripled after the purchase of Louisiana from France, the unpaid acquisition of Spanish Florida, and the annexation of Mexican Texas. The six initial southern states were joined by nine new slaveholding states between 1812 and 1850. In addition, after the invention of the cotton gin in 1793, rice, tobacco, and sugarcane were rapidly relegated to a secondary role in slave labor-based production. By 1820, cotton represented a third of exports from the United States and, by 1850, more than half. Cotton plantations dominated the entire South, from North Carolina to Texas to Arkansas. The number of slaves increased proportionally, from 700,000 in 1790 to 4 million in 1850. That rapid demographic growth was due in large part to an excess of births compared to deaths, owing to favorable climatic and sanitary conditions and the predominance of small plantations that employed enslaved families. But the importation of slaves also contributed to that growth until 1808, when the slave trade was officially abolished in the United States. Thousands of Africans arrived in Charleston on slave ships each year, enabling the South to purchase some 230,000 African captives between 1790 and 1808. Then, one to two thousand slaves were imported illegally each year until 1820.[44]

Between 1820 and 1860, however, the domestic slave trade in the southern United States took on staggering dimensions: at least 900,000 slaves were forcefully displaced to new territories during these decades. Those slaves were all either sold to other masters farther south or west, or taken to those regions by their own masters. Often chained together, the involuntary migrants traveled to their new destinations by foot or crammed into cattle cars and ship holds. Slave markets flourished at the same time. The 1850 census shows those changes clearly: at the time, a little more than half of the 4 million slaves in the South were growing cotton, 20 percent were laboring on other plantations, 15 percent were servants, and the remaining 10 percent worked in mining, lumber, industry, and construction (notably railways). The economy of the South was not alone in depending on forced slave labor; the North, where slavery had been abolished, did so as well. In reality, cotton fueled the North's weaving and textile industries before being exported in the form of manufactured goods.[45]

In 1775, the richest sugar colony was undoubtedly Saint Domingue, nicknamed the "Pearl of the Antilles." It produced half of the sugar and coffee consumed worldwide and represented two-thirds of France's external trade—and therefore considerable income for the French monarchy. That wealth was the fruit of the forced labor of some 500,000 enslaved men and women, who alone accounted for half of the slaves in the entire Caribbean. In forty years, the number of slaves in Saint Domingue increased fourfold thanks to massive importation, estimated at a total of 479,000 Africans between 1761 and 1790. Those 500,000 slaves (a majority of whom were bossales) represented 88 to 90 percent of the French colony's population, versus 40,000 whites and 30,000 free people of color. Most were exploited in sugarcane and coffee plantations, and the others in subsistence farming, domestic work, and urban crafts.[46] Unlike Jamaica, Saint Domingue's economy therefore did not rely solely on sugar but remained rather diversified.

In the 1770s, slavery also developed in Cuba, which shifted to sugarcane production due to two unpredictable events. First, in 1762, the British occupation of Havana violently impacted Cuba, up until then a colony of secondary, limited importance in the Spanish empire, except for its port, which was a vital stop in Atlantic trade. Outside Havana, the island was scantly populated and its primary export was leather. Farmers (*guajiros*) of mixed Amerindian, African, and Spanish descent cultivated subsistence products and tobacco; Cuba's thirty-two thousand slaves represented approximately a quarter of its population and worked in cattle breeding or then-marginal sugarcane farming. Over their ten-month occupation, the British imported four thousand Africans and created the first large slave sugar plantations and the first commercial links between Cuba and the future United States. After the British retreat in 1763, Spain focused on the island's military defense and sugar crop development using the model of Saint Domingue, which inevitably meant increasing its slave population. In 1789, Madrid liberalized the slave trade in Cuba, Santo Domingo (the western half of Hispaniola; the present-day Dominican Republic), Puerto Rico, and Venezuela. Two years later, Cuba already had sixty-five thousand slaves, but the number of whites and free people of color had simultaneously increased, maintaining the proportion of slaves at one-quarter of the total population.[47]

The second trigger for Cuba's expansion was the 1791 slave insurrection on the northern plain of Saint Domingue, which led to the Haitian Revolution (see chapter 6). Despite its proximity and the fear it provoked—the uprising destroyed the most profitable sugar-producing economy at the time—it allowed Cuba to become the new pearl of the Antilles. Cuba welcomed numerous refugees from the French colony, at times with their slaves, who contributed to the modernization of sugar production and introduced coffee cultivation. At the same time, Madrid prolonged the free trade in slaves by six years (while limiting it to bozales to avoid the risk of revolutionary contamination) and extended it to other American colonial ports. The results were quick to appear: in 1817, slaves in Cuba represented over a third of its inhabitants. For the first time, whites had become the minority (45 percent) within a population of 200,000 slaves and 116,000 free people of color.[48]

Even as its continental colonies were gaining their independence in the early 1820s, Spain was able to keep Cuba in its grip by allowing the island's elite to profit from sugar production while frightening it with the threat of a revolution similar to that in Saint Domingue. Despite a few fleeting crises, Cuba's economy and enslaved population continued to grow until 1841, when the island became the world's leading sugar producer, with 437,000 bozal and creole slaves out of a total of 1 million inhabitants.[49] One-third of those slaves was exploited in sugar plantations located in the center of the island, one-third in other agricultural activities, and the remaining third in various domestic, artisan, and port activities. However, unlike in the southern United States, planters in Cuba were unable to assure the natural growth of their servile labor force due to the demographic imbalance among new African captives, which was compounded by the island's deplorable sanitary conditions and the mistreatment of slaves. As a result, planters relied continuously on the slave trade (illegal since the 1817 agreement signed with London). Some 560,000 enslaved Africans were imported to Cuba between 1800 and 1850, primarily in the 1830s.[50] Between 1851 and 1866, another 188,000 slaves were brought to the island illegally.[51] Despite those purchases, by 1861 the number of slaves (born in Africa or in Cuba) had decreased to 370,000, while the population of whites and free people of color was on the rise. In this respect, Cuba continued to differentiate itself from the Caribbean sugar colony model in which slaves made up the great majority of the population. In fact, in addition to its slaves, Cuba always had a large free population of mixed and unmixed African descent, which explains the terms *clase de color* and *raza de color*, used by Cubans to blend the two categories.[52] Next, Spanish immigration increased consistently alongside the slave trade, meaning whites never represented less than 40 percent of the island's inhabitants. Finally, since 1847, Cuban planters supplemented imports of enslaved Africans by taking on Chinese laborers indentured for eight years (called coolies). In total, until 1874, 125,000 Chinese, almost exclusively men, were engaged in this way and often endured conditions similar to those inflicted on slaves.[53]

Like Cuba, Brazil, the third hub of the dramatic growth of slavery in the nineteenth century, benefited from the destruction of Saint Domingue's economy. During a first phase that lasted until Brazil's independence in 1822, sugarcane production increased rapidly, starting in the slave plantations of Nordeste. From there, sugar farming spread to the provinces of Rio de Janeiro and then São Paolo, making Brazil the second global sugar producer after Cuba. In addition, cotton production developed in the newly colonized regions of Maranhão and Pará, again thanks to the importation of enslaved Africans. As a result, the number of slaves in Brazil increased extremely fast, reaching 1,148,000 in 1823 (approximately one-third of the total population).[54] Neither independence nor the 1824 adoption of a monarchist constitution guaranteeing fundamental freedoms and equality before the law called the dependence of Brazil's economy on African slavery into question.

In fact, during the 1820s, Brazil began to transition to another major slave-produced crop dominated by Saint Domingue until 1791: coffee, which became its top global exporter. From its establishment in the Rio region until the 1880s, coffee cultivation increased continuously and spread to new areas, notably, in succession, Minas Gerais, São Paulo, Paraná, and Rio Grande do Sul. The expansion of sugar and coffee plantations depended constantly on the increase of slave manpower and therefore on the continuation of the slave trade. Until 1851, Brazil continued to import thousands of enslaved Africans each year—between thirty thousand and fifty thousand annually from 1840 to 1850—in violation of a new 1831 law intended to enforce the 1818 treaty abolishing the slave trade. Despite the lack of national censuses prior to 1872, historians estimate that the number of African- and Brazil-born slaves reached a maximum of 1.7 million in the 1840s, which placed Brazil second only to the United States, which at that time counted 2.5 million slaves.[55]

However, like their Cuban counterparts, Brazilian planters did not try to improve slaves' living conditions in order to ensure their natural growth. After 1851, the enslaved population therefore diminished rapidly both in terms of absolute numbers and percentage of the total population. But the domestic slave trade was revived as slaves from northern regions in decline were resold toward southern Brazil, which was experiencing a coffee boom.[56] Slavery thus continued to be the dominant form of labor in every exportation-linked sector. According to the first census of 1872, of the 1,500,000 slaves then present in the country (16 percent of the total population), 1,200,000 were economically active, including 800,000 agricultural workers. Among that group, one-third labored on coffee plantations, one-third on sugarcane, cotton, or cocoa plantations, and the final third in cattle breeding and its derivations or subsistence farming. The approximately 400,000 remaining slaves were most often servants or day laborers, as well as miners, artisans, market vendors, textile industry workers, or musicians, for example: 118,000 of them lived in cities with over 20,000 inhabitants.[57] Nonetheless, by 1872, free people of color had become the largest socioracial category in Brazil, with nearly 4,250,000 individuals representing 44 percent of the total population, versus 40 percent of whites.[58]

After 1775, slavery surged in other American regions, albeit on a less massive or more short-lived scale than in the United States, Cuba, and Brazil. For example, Puerto Rico, which would remain under Spanish control until 1898, saw an evolution parallel to that of Cuba, though with noticeable differences. First of all, due to mountainous terrain more widespread than in Cuba, sugar plantations could only develop in a few enclaves, notably the Ponce region. As a result, independent small farmers who settled there before the Saint Domingue revolt erupted continued to play an important role in the colony's economy. And while the number of slaves grew rapidly due to the slave trade, increasing from thirteen thousand in 1790 to fifty-one thousand in 1846, their proportion of the total population remained approximately 12 percent. The importation of enslaved Africans ceased after 1846, but the island nonetheless registered forty-two thousand slaves in 1860, though whites and free people of color constituted the vast majority of its inhabitants. Most Puerto Rican slaves worked in sugar production, in general alongside free workers. Puerto Rico was therefore far removed from the Caribbean sugar colony model, even though it supplied a considerable quantity of sugar to the United States and Europe.[59]

In decline since 1750, Guadeloupe and Martinique regained their importance to France once the colonial power lost control of and revenues from Saint Domingue. In both colonies, Napoleon Bonaparte succeeded in reestablishing slavery, which had been abolished in Guadeloupe by the National Convention in 1794 (though not in Martinique, then occupied by the British). During the Restoration, the slave trade resumed despite its official ban in 1818. In 1831, the two islands once again collectively numbered 180,000 slaves, as they had in 1789. However, their economy was less diversified than before, with slaves now primarily producing sugar, to the detriment of cotton, coffee, and indigo, major crops in the 1780s. When the July Monarchy finally abolished the slave trade in 1831, the number of slaves declined amid a simultaneous increase of free people of color, who were divided between a predominantly mulatto elite, freeborn laborers, and emancipated slaves who became independent small farmers attached to ideas of freedom and equality. On the eve of complete abolition, in 1848, free people of color numbered 72,000, versus 161,000 slaves. From 1789 to 1848, the number of whites remained stable, with less than 10,000 individuals in both Martinique and Guadeloupe.[60] Jamaica continued to import enslaved

Africans on a large scale until the early nineteenth century: numbering 193,000 in 1775, the enslaved population reached 300,000 in 1800, compared to 30,000 whites and 10,000 "coloreds" (free people of color). Thanks to the arrival of 91,400 additional captives between 1800 and the abolition of the slave trade in 1808, planters were able to prevent a reduction in their enslaved labor force, though not a drop in sugar production. In 1834, when the gradual abolition approved by the British Parliament took effect, Jamaica still had 311,000 slaves. At the same time, the number of free people of color had more than tripled to reach 35,000.[61]

On the American continent, from the end of the eighteenth century to the first few years of the nineteenth century, the Spanish colonies of Louisiana, Venezuela, and Rio de la Plata took advantage of the liberalization of the slave trade decreed by Madrid to import several thousands of slaves. Between 1791 and 1806, Buenos Aires received 109 slave ships transporting a total of over ten thousand captives from Africa and likely smuggled as many from Brazil. During this period, countless slaves were employed in domestic work in Buenos Aires: as in other American cities, they were also essential to artisan crafts and the urban economy in general. Moreover, free and enslaved people of African descent represented nearly a third of the population of Buenos Aires at the time, versus a majority of whites and mestizos (people of Spanish and Indian descent). In the neighboring pampas, many slaves were used in cattle breeding, tanneries, and farming; others were sold farther inland, as far as Chile and Bolivia.[62]

The Guianas also benefited from the destruction of Saint Domingue's economy. French Guiana imported several hundred, and possibly over 2,000, captives from Africa each year until 1829, when it attained the largest population in its history until abolition in 1848: 23,000 inhabitants (not counting Amerindians), including 19,300 slaves primarily employed in sugar production, 1,300 whites, and less than 1,500 free people of color.[63] Dutch Suriname acquired several thousand slaves each year until 1806, after which the legal slave trade ceased due to the British occupation, before resuming between 1820 and 1825 when the colony, once again under Dutch control, imported a little more than 4,000 captives in total. As a result, Suriname's population counted 49,000 slaves and 5,000 free people of color in 1830, and likely less than 3,000 whites. The British, nonetheless, were the principal importer of African captives in the region. After they seized Essequibo, Demerara, and Berbice from the Dutch in 1796, they imported a total of over 72,000 bossales until 1808 and progressively turned away from cotton and coffee cultivation to focus on sugar. When these three provinces became officially British in 1814, they reached a population of 110,000 slaves, more than all other slaveowning American colonies still held by the United Kingdom apart from Jamaica, compared to a tiny minority of whites and free people of color. At the time of complete emancipation in 1838, planters in British Guiana claimed to own nearly 83,000 slaves, for the loss of whom they were largely compensated.[64]

Thus, since the sixteenth century, proponents of slavery everywhere except the southern United States had not tried or were unable to assure the self-reproduction of their enslaved labor force and had to continue to import new captives from Africa to compensate for losses and deaths.

Slave Systems in the Americas: Similarities and Differences

Although the European monarchies that colonized the Americas did so during distinct periods and in the name of opposing Christian doctrines, they all relied on slavery and the slave trade. What's more, they all adopted a common rule dictating that slavery was a condition of indeterminate duration inherited from one's mother, not father. In other words, as in Roman law, it was the status of the womb that carried a newborn (*partus sequitur ventrem*) that defined his or her status: if the mother was enslaved, the child would also be enslaved, regardless of the father's condition. If the mother was free but the father was enslaved, he or she would be free. That divergence in filiation in otherwise entirely patriarchal societies meant that masters could rape or wed female slaves without concern for any resulting children, and even increase their human property if they owned the mother. Sexual violence committed by free men against captive women and the appropriation of their children by masters and mistresses was prevalent throughout the Western Hemisphere from the sixteenth century to the nineteenth, revealing an early fundamental similarity between forms of American slavery.[65]

At the same time, there were differences in the laws and slave codes that regulated slavery. The legislation enacted by the kings of Spain and Portugal was more demanding of masters and more humane toward slaves than British, French, Dutch, and U.S. equivalents. But they were rarely applied on the ground, due to the weakness of colonial states, the isolation of plantations, and the convergence of governors' and monarchs' interests with those of slave-owners. Similarly, in Iberian and French colonies, Catholicism imposed the evangelization and baptism of slaves, whether they were African or American-born captives, who were subsequently considered as members of the Christian community, whereas until the 1760s, and even later, various Protestant churches discouraged the Christianization of slaves for fear they would believe themselves to be free and equal.[66] In concrete terms, however, the Catholic Church in the Americas direly lacked priests outside large cities, and plantation and mining slaves only rarely encountered them. Furthermore, the Church and religious orders themselves owned slaves and tended to share the elite's economic interests. As for the treatment of slaves, those in Iberian and French colonies were subjected to punishments as arbitrary, agonizing, and humiliating as those in Protestant America.

Regardless of a slaveholder's religion and the laws governing him, working and living conditions on plantations were in general so deficient that they caused high death and suicide rates among slaves and necessitated constant replenishment of captive labor forces. In reality, factors other than colonial powers, legislation, and religion were much more impactful on slaves' lives, such as their proportion of a population, demographic makeup (sex, age, birthplace, ethnic affiliation), and work setting (large plantation, small farm, mine, factory, workshop, master's home, or autonomy with payment of a fixed wage to one's master).

That said, one consequential difference between slaveholding societies was attitudes toward emancipation and, in particular, slaves' capacity to purchase their freedom. While both processes, like *partus sequitur ventrem*, were an integral part of Roman law, they were recognized to highly varying degrees in the Americas. And that varying access to emancipation would directly affect the more or less rapid formation of a free class of men and women of African descent. From their founding, Spanish colonies were governed by laws in effect on the Iberian Peninsula. Alfonso XIII's law code of the *Siete Partidas* (Seven Divisions), inspired by Roman law and drafted between 1254 and 1265, justified slavery but simultaneously considered slaves as human beings in their own right. It deemed it legitimate for slaves to try to obtain their freedom and charitable for masters to liberate them. Slaves in Spanish colonies therefore were allowed to be emancipated or to buy freedom for themselves or their family members; at first this possibility was a privilege dependent on one's master, and gradually it became a codified right. Brazil also allowed for the possibility of diverse forms of manumission for slaves, but it was less regulated and therefore more closely tied to a master's consent.

According to Iberian laws, slaves' freedom could be purchased by the slaves themselves or by a third party (in general a family member), or could be granted by the slave's owner. In the latter case, emancipation was most often conferred following the death of a master or mistress, in his or her will, and sometimes after a series of conditions had been met by the slave, such as several years of service to another family member. In addition, slaves in Spanish and Portuguese colonies could gradually buy their freedom according to the principle of *coartación* (or *coartação*): once they had made a substantial advance payment, they obtained the transitional status of *coartados*, halfway between a slave and a free man or woman, thereby reducing the rights their masters or mistresses exercised over them. Contrary to Roman law, a slave's marriage to a free partner did not confer free status, unless the latter bought his or her enslaved spouse's freedom. The existence of manumission and coartación helps explain the rapid growth of a free population of African descent in the Iberian colonies beginning in the seventeenth century, which, despite the expansion of slavery, came to form the majority of inhabitants in regions including Panama, the Atlantic coast of Colombia and Venezuela, and certain parts of Brazil, Puerto Rico, and Santo Domingo. Even in Cuba and Brazil, during periods of massive importations of African slaves, free populations of African descent—*libres de color*—continued to grow, becoming very large, at times the majority, by the time of abolition.[67]

By contrast, British and Dutch slave plantation colonies endeavored very early on to ban manumission in order to block the demographic growth of free people of African descent, a social category that challenged the racial justification of slavery. Instances of emancipation were therefore rare, and the majority of the Afro-descended population, regardless of skin color, was composed of slaves. The practice of limiting emancipation took hold in the southern United States as slavery spread, to the extent that one's status nearly always corresponded to race: white and free versus black or mulatto and enslaved. In French colonies, the emergence of a population of free people of color resulting from concubinage between masters and enslaved women prompted the monarchy to dramatically restrict emancipation and the purchase of freedom by a slave or family members after 1685, unless the master married the enslaved mother of his children in the Catholic Church.[68]

Despite those differences in access to manumission, and consequently in the development of a free Afro-descended population, members of that group everywhere suffered from a status inferior to that of whites. Therein lies a second fundamental similarity: the entirety of the Americas was racist toward free Afro-descendants. Racial discrimination not only impacted "pure" blacks but also those of "mixed blood": mulattos (one black parent, the other white), *zambos*, *cafusos*, or *griffes* (these three terms meaning one black parent, the other Amerindian), quadroons, and quinteroons (one black ancestor, fifteen white ancestors), as well as the Iberian category of *pardos* (any mix including at least one black ancestor), all indelibly marked by their African origins.[69]

In Iberian America, colonial society was founded on the principle of blood purity (*limpieza de sangre*), which took form during the recapture of the Iberian Peninsula from Muslims. In other words, in order to be considered honorable, or be allowed to study, perform highly qualified occupations, or hold royal or ecclesiastical positions, one had to be white and, according to the language of the time, be "pure of all the bad races of Blacks, Moors, Jews, newly converted to our Holy Faith and punished by the Inquisition." This form of racism was therefore based on racial and religious heredity. In concrete terms, the Inquisition focused more on the possible presence of Jews and converts in Brazil than it did in Spanish America, where the ban on the immigration of Muslims, Jews, and converts was better respected. In the latter region, blood purity requirements applied principally to blacks and individuals of mixed African descent through a form of racism based on the inheritance of race and status (slavery). Spaniards, Amerindians, and their descendants, whether they intermarried or not, had the qualities required for blood purity. But African slaves and their descendants, even if they were free and/or partly descended from European or Amerindian ancestors, were considered to be of "impure and perverted origin" because they carried the hereditary "stain of slavery" (*mancha de la esclavitud*). All free Africans and Afro-descendants were categorized together under the degrading label of *castas* and subjected to numerous prohibitions, such as wearing luxurious or ostentatious clothes or jewelry. The most oppressive discriminations were those excluding *libres de color* from all academic training, nonmanual professions, royal posts, and the clergy. Barring a few exceptions, those restrictions confined the men and women affected to domains related to artisan work, transportation, and agriculture, and, beginning with the 1812 constitution of the Spanish monarchy, excluded them from voting on the basis of their race. Though authorities in Iberian colonies, where whites were invariably a minority of the free population, were not always able to strictly apply those royal norms, they remained in force in the Americas until the independence movements and endured in Cuba and Puerto Rico until 1876. Whereas all of independent Iberian America eliminated racial references and discriminations among its free population during the 1820s, Brazil and Argentina barred freedmen from voting until 1826.[70]

Neither British America nor French and Dutch colonies were familiar with the racial-religious principle of *limpieza de sangre*. Nonetheless, they also "racialized" the condition of being a slave and conferred an inferior status on "pure" or "mixed-blood" descendants of African slaves who were freeborn or emancipated. The colonies of those three monarchies distinguished "full" blacks from "coloreds," *mulâtres*, or *kleurlingen vrije*. During the first decades of colonization, there were few of those mixed-race individuals, and many were the illegitimate children of a white colonist father and thus could, after his death, inherit his estate if no legal successor existed. In French territories, the Code Noir of 1685 granted manumitted men and women and free *gens de couleur* equality with whites, without the hereditary "stain" of slavery. But as white colonists felt increasingly threatened by free people of color, new royal regulations situated the latter closer to slaves, notably by ordering them to carry a document indicating their free status, without which they would be considered slaves; others forbid them from having the last names of white families, subjected them to a capitation tax, and required that they always show deference to whites. In Jamaica and other British colonies, white planters managed to better defend their interests thanks to the legislative powers of colonial assemblies. At the end of the seventeenth century, discriminations against free people of color extended no further than those against all other royal subjects in England; but over the course of the eighteenth century, the colonial assemblies gradually banned free people of color from holding public employment, voting, and acquiring large estates. In the Dutch colonies, Curaçao's population of free people of color was also subjected to increasingly restrictive laws, while some within Suriname's small minority were provisionally allowed to exercise certain occupations at the end of the eighteenth century to compensate for the rapid decrease of the white population. In general, unlike free people of color in the Iberian world, those in British, French, and Dutch colonies were not barred from access to higher education in those respective metropoles, where a very small number of them were rich enough to study. In addition, across the Americas, except for the United States and some British islands, the lack of whites available to serve in local defense militias forced authorities to mobilize and arm free people of color. Nonetheless, fearful that the latter would join forces with slaves or express a desire for power, they often created units separating blacks from mulattos, which were always placed under white leadership.[71]

Since the second half of the eighteenth century, white colonial elites throughout the Western Hemisphere demanded that the distinction between whites and free nonwhites be elaborated: in general, an eighth (quadroon) or even a sixteenth (quinteroon) of African "blood" was enough to strip a free individual of his or her white status and associated privileges, as was the case with *limpieza de sangre*. Thus, in Iberian, British, French and Dutch America, as well as in the slaveowning United States, the "stain of slavery" marked slaves and free people of color alike, affecting "full" blacks as much as "mixed-bloods." Slavery was racially based and continued to affect those who were born free or had obtained their freedom.

That limitation did not stop slaves from attempting to lead a human existence, more or less discreetly, despite their status as "personal property." Some were able to win their freedom, legally through purchase or by revolting, and notably by running away and creating maroon societies within the inner frontiers of the Americas. Until the mid-eighteenth century, they did so in a context in which slavery appeared unshakable, as I explore in the following chapter.

PART II

*From Conquest to the
End of the Seven Years' War
(1501–1763)*

≋ **2** ≋

Marronage

A Risky but Possible Path to Freedom

Historically, among all social groups, flight has been the strategy the most commonly used to escape, in the short or long term, a condition judged to be intolerable or unalterable. The same is true of slaves. Most of the men and women taken in Africa undoubtedly thought of escaping at the moment of their capture, and then during their transport and confinement in coastal depots: some of those who tried to flee succeeded, individually or in groups. That is illustrated by the fact that the very term *quilombo*, or a Brazilian maroon community, has a Central African origin: it refers to warrior societies primarily composed of male adults of diverse ancestry, formed in the wake of wars, forced migrations, and famines related to the slave trade.[1] Once aboard slave ships, men, women, and children tried to escape, jumping overboard and most often drowning, while others let themselves die.[2]

Once they landed in American ports, many African captives maintained their hopes for escape and freedom. Brought to the Americas to act as a servile labor force as colonization spread throughout the Caribbean islands and along the continental coastline, they tried to flee into the hinterlands, mountains, forests, and swamp zones located near their worksites. "Petit marronage," or short-lived individual escapes, allowed slaves to enjoy a night or a few days of freedom, alone or in the company of a loved one, their children, and/or their relatives, even at the expense of a lashing or being put in stocks at their return. Some attempted to change identity and pass for free, notably women and creole slaves who blended into the multicolored populations of cities or ports and men who joined boat crews. Beginning in the 1730s, some urban runaways learned to read and write to defy the stereotype of the "uneducated slave" or to fabricate a document of safe passage or a "freedom letter."[3] Finally, by allowing runaways to survive alone or in a small group in forests and frontier zones, "grand marronage," which entailed extended flight and the transition to a free life, was a fundamental form of the fight against slavery that gave rise to maroon societies.

Those who decided to run away did so for diverse reasons: to reject a cruel and incomprehensible ordeal endured since their capture in Africa, to escape mistreatment and hunger, following a particularly unjust punishment or to avoid receiving one, to find relatives or loved ones. Slaves also ran away out of fear that their fragile survival would be threatened, notably by a master's death (mortality rates among whites were also very high),[4] sale to another estate, or the arrival of a new plantation overseer. Some fugitives wanted to do more than just escape a threat—they wanted their freedom.[5] Flight was therefore a strategy of varying intensity. It often only lasted one night or a few days, long enough for a slave to visit a family member or gain a little rest. Those episodes were frequently punished but at times tolerated by masters. The temporary fugitive slave was not seeking freedom and therefore petit marronage will not be addressed here. At the other extreme however, flight could provide a concrete way to escape slavery, by allowing runaways to blend into a free population of African descent, move to the margins of colonial frontiers, or form societies in interior regions far from whites. Grand marronage—whether urban, rural, or maritime—was a quest for freedom, which at times proved victorious.

Flight and Marronage:
Primary Forms of Revolt against Slavery

Slaves largely resorted to permanent and prolonged flight to challenge their enslavement and assert their freedom. To get a better sense of that strategy today, it suffices to closely examine the ethnic map of the Americas at the beginning of the twenty-first century: it is characterized by the existence of many communities, and even societies, whose ancestors were groups of Africans who, during the successive waves of the slave trade, escaped and successfully and enduringly settled in the vast frontier zones of the Americas, at times by blending in with uncolonized Amerindians. Located in long inaccessible border regions, those maroon communities established systems of barter and defense through which they were able to survive.

The importance of marronage, particularly in the seventeenth century, is evident in the multitude of terms invented to designate it. The words "maroon" and *marron* come from the Spanish *cimarrón*, whose semantic evolution clearly shows how colonists viewed enslaved Africans: *cimarrón* first referred to cattle that had wandered into the mountains of the island of Hispaniola, then a runaway Amerindian slave, and finally a fugitive African slave.[6] The numerous terms used to define maroon societies and their members attest to their ubiquity: *palenques, cumbes, cimarrones,* or *mambises* in Spanish; quilombos, *mocambos, ladeiras, magotes, palmares,* or *coitos* in Portuguese; "outlaw camps," "maroon settlements," "runaway" or "fugitive" slaves, "hog hunters," or "mountain negroes" in English; *boschneegers* (bush negroes) or *schuilneegers* (hide negroes) in Dutch; and *bandes marronnes* or *nègres marrons* in French.[7] Of course, many of those fugitive groups did not last long. Climates and living conditions in forests or marshlands were often unsanitary. A large number of runaways survived by looting plantations and villages as well as by robbing major roads, and sometimes they did not resist for long against the well-armed troops sent after them. Those who were captured were executed in a cruelly exemplary fashion or subjected to public whippings before being sold elsewhere. Finally, by hiding in unsettled interior regions, maroon communities unknowingly contributed to the conquest of new frontiers by indirectly serving as scouts for territories that European colonists would subsequently appropriate.

Nevertheless, even if marronage was unable to bring an end to slavery anywhere in the Americas, it weakened the institution considerably. As Richard Price writes, "Throughout Afro-America, such [maroon] communities stood out as an heroic challenge to white authority, and as the living proof of the existence of a slave consciousness that refused to be limited by the whites' conception or manipulation of it."[8] Indeed, marronage represented a constant and costly threat to authorities and slaveholders, forcing them to hire professional hunters, form militias, or bring troops from Europe to halt it or prevent its spread. Some maroon communities were recognized as autonomous and their fugitive members declared free by colonial slave authorities incapable of defeating them, representing an enormous victory against slavery. Others survived and even grew inconspicuously in frontier regions until they were gradually integrated as populations of free people of color as the state extended its control beyond existing borders—another way to combat slavery.

Marronage represented slaves' primary form of revolt until the mideighteenth century. It was a gradual, lengthy revolt that often entailed violence or "an uprising against legitimate authority" (*Webster's Third New International Dictionary*). Though differentiated at times by historians, revolt and marronage were often interlinked, one generating the other, to the extent that some revolts were in reality collective attempts at flight. Similarly, once established, maroon societies armed themselves, attacked plantations and villages to obtain certain goods, and defended themselves against all incursions onto their territory by colonial forces or slaveowners.[9] But marronage was also a liberation strategy that evolved over several centuries.

Between 1525 and 1600, the majority of African slaves who survived the Atlantic crossing were brought to continental Spanish America, meaning Mexico, Peru, and Colombia. They were mostly men, though women and children were present, imported to replace Amerindians decimated by forced labor in mines, farming and cattle breeding, construction, transportation, pearl fishing, and cloth-weaving factories. In America, as on the Iberian Peninsula, bozales were also destined for domestic work and small businesses. Slaves arrived in changing societies dominated by Spanish men, who were not numerous enough to spread their power beyond cities and their farming or mining estates. Indeed, with the exception of the most populated regions of ancient precolonial empires, the large majority of American land was not colonized and often had not even been explored by Europeans. Various Amerindian nations only thinly occupied vast stretches of land. For enslaved Africans, individual or collective flight toward these unknown territories was therefore a risky but viable option.

As a result, dozens, hundreds, and eventually thousands of bozales, including women with their children, escaped slavery by fleeing toward mountains, plains, and tropical forests, and along rivers. Countless official reports attest to this widespread phenomenon. For example, royal civil servants regularly asked their superiors for means with which to curb slave escapes, and, once those fugitives were settled in interior regions, to stop their exactions, attacks, thefts, and abductions of enslaved and Amerindian women. Since the 1520s, those demands came from the regions of Veracruz, Jalapa, and Córdoba, as well as from Oaxaca in Mexico; the island of Hispaniola; Florida; Panama; and Cartagena de Indias and Santa Marta in Colombia. As colonization spread and slavery developed, requests also came from Caracas, Coro, Lima, Trujillo, and Buenos Aires, among other places.[10]

Several examples clearly indicate that marronage was the primary form of revolt in the sixteenth century, beginning with Negro Miguel's 1553 rebellion in the gold-rich region of San Felipe, in Venezuela, where around one hundred recently imported Africans worked in royal mines. Miguel, his wife, and other bozales fled into the surrounding mountains and established a fortified camp from which they attacked the mines, enabling the collective escape of many slaves. At its peak, this maroon community numbered some 180 bozal and Amerindian men and women, who harassed the colonists scattered through the region until the Spanish were able to drive them out. Though Miguel and several of his companions were killed in combat or executed, others took refuge deeper in the mountains and continued to live at the margins of slavery's reach, eventually forming unbreakable maroon communities closely integrated into smuggling networks.[11] The gold-mining region of Zaragoza and Remedios, in Antioquia (Colombia), experienced similar uprisings in 1598 and 1607, respectively, when, according to local accounts, hundreds, or possibly thousands, of slaves assassinated their masters or foremen and hid in forests where they constructed palenques from which they continued to attack mine owners, travelers, and traders. The Royal Audience in Bogotá sent reinforcements, weapons, and ammunition to try to restore order and destroy the palenques, particularly the *rancherías de Guinea* (Guinea shanty camps), in which more than three hundred cimarrones were living off farming. The army captured an unspecified number of fugitives but was unable to eradicate marronage from the region. As piracy and smuggling developed, some maroon groups settled near the coast and provided cattle, agricultural products, and skins to privateers in exchange for weapons, tools, and money. Some cimarrones also helped the pirate Francis Drake capture a sizable royal treasure near Panama in 1572.[12]

Another example, in the Peruvian province of Vilcabamba, near Cuzco, in 1602, reveals how runaways also occasionally confronted the masters from whom they had fled. In this case, several African slaves and Indians had escaped from a gold mine and neighboring plantation on which they worked side by side under extremely harsh conditions. They formed one rebellious and multiethnic band led by an Indian, Francisco Chichima, who had reportedly meticulously prepared an attack against the Spanish, mobilizing slaves from *haciendas* and gathering supplies in the group's camp. Early on, the rebels were able to burn down an estate, kill six uncooperative Indians, and besiege some one hundred Spanish colonists. But the province's governor obtained reinforcements and in the end, the bandits surrendered with Chichima's decapitated head. Royal civil servants, *hacendados*, and mine owners continued to fear that the Africans and Amerindians they were exploiting would join forces and massacre them. But this attack remained an isolated incident for some time as rebel slaves, particularly Africans, had understood that marronage was the form of collective antislavery action best adapted to the context of an era during which colonization was still very fragmented.[13]

The Spanish monarchy tried to retaliate against slave escapes in various ways. The profusion of marronage laws and regulations reveals both the phenomenon's importance and authorities' inability to curb it. In 1520, Spain banned ladino slaves and Moors from being sent to America, accusing them of inciting bozales to run away, before advising that the importation of certain, supposedly particularly intractable, African ethnic groups be avoided. Authorities further mandated cruel and terrible punishments: fifty whiplashes followed by deprivation and confinement, a heavy weight attached to the ankle, mutilation, castration (banned in 1540), or hanging of repeat fugitives. They then encouraged that those who returned voluntarily be pardoned, considering that the fear of punishment was stopping escapees from turning themselves in. They also attempted to shift some responsibility for runaways to slaveholders by forcing them to declare any disappearances under penalty of a fine. Anyone who hid or helped a fugitive slave was then punished, whereas the individual who denounced or captured him or her was rewarded by the wronged owner.[14]

Yet those measures did not slow down escape attempts by slaves. Entire regions along the borders of Spanish-controlled zones were populated by fugitive Africans and Native Americans who had either escaped from *pueblos de indios* or had never been colonized, and later by their descendants. Consequently, the majority of the Afro-descended and zambo population that currently characterizes Panama, the inland regions of Veracruz in Mexico, and the interior Colombian-Venezuelan region situated between Valledupar, Mérida, and Valencia can trace its roots to palenques already established by the sixteenth century. The same applies to Afro-Amerindians in today's Esmeraldas region, in Ecuador, who partly descend from small groups of Africans who survived shipwrecks en route to sale as slaves in Peru. Since 1533, some succeeded in hiding in inland regions where they made contact with and often joined forces with Amerindians, creating maroon communities. By accepting the intervention of priests and converting to Catholicism, those Afro-Amerindian settlements successfully negotiated Spain's recognition of their autonomy in 1600. Only Peru avoided mass slave escapes to inland regions, as its arid coast, small cities, and Andes Mountains, densely populated by the Quechas and Aymara, were far from hospitable refuges for fugitive communities. Instead, many runaway slaves formed wandering bandit groups, notably around Lima.[15]

Unyielding Palenques and Quilombos

Large-scale marronage spread during the seventeenth century, following new arrivals of Africans destined for sugar and cocoa haciendas in all of Spain's continental colonies and in the alluvial mines along the Pacific coast of Colombia and Ecuador. The phenomenon also intensified in Brazil with the massive importation of slaves to the Nordeste coast. In addition, as piracy developed, maroon communities and Amerindian nations began to participate in smuggling networks, exchanging gold and skins for weapons and ammunition. Colonial powers continued to promulgate laws that cruelly punished runaways, but often also imposed fines on masters of captured fugitive slaves, leading many to not report escapes or claim recovered runaways. Authorities sent soldiers and militiamen against bands or fugitive camps, with mixed results. They were therefore at times forced to sign peace treaties with maroon chiefs, granting their communities territorial rights and administrative autonomy on the condition that they stop welcoming new fugitive slaves.[16]

One of the first undefeated palenques was Yanga, located in the interior mountains of Veracruz, in Mexico. Established in the 1580s by Ñanga (Yanga), a high-ranking bozal (probably Akan), who fled his master and gathered other runaways under his leadership, it lived off its own food production, raids for supply and women against neighboring haciendas, and plunder along the road between Veracruz and Mexico City. By 1608, the palenque counted approximately eighty-four men, all runaway slaves, twenty-four black or Amerindian women, and many children. Surrounded by barricades, traps, and observation posts, it boasted sixty huts, farming fields with diverse crops, livestock, and poultry. Living in constant fear of attack, half of the men were placed under the order of an Angola captain, assigned to raid and guard duties. That year, the Spanish sent a Franciscan friar to negotiate a peace settlement with Ñanga, who demanded perpetual freedom for the maroons "who fled before last September [1608]" but conceded that "those who flee after that [time] will be returned to their owners." He also stipulated that "the Captain Ñanga, who is their leader, must be governor and after him his sons and descendants." Ñanga's demands remained unanswered during nine years, during which the Spaniards launched various military attacks against the palenque, each time forcing the maroons to flee and rebuild their settlement. Eventually, in 1618 the Spanish agreed on the principal demands of the now elderly Ñanga. The palenque became a free village, later renamed San Lorenzo de los Negros. All the fugitive slaves who resided there were granted amnesty and emancipated but, in return, they agreed to detain and return any new runaway to the authorities. Using the *pueblos de indios* model, San Lorenzo de los Negros had its own cabildo (municipal council) headed by Ñanga and his sons. The village could not accept any inhabitants other than members of the old palenque and their descendants, except for a *corregidor* and a priest. The treaty was seemingly respected until the end of Spanish control.[17]

Other palenques and quilombos formed during the seventeenth century were also able to resist colonial authorities. In Colombia, Palenque de San Basilio had an outcome similar to Yanga's, even if it is often remembered in history as a blend of two palenques (Matuna and San Miguel Arcángel). In the early seventeenth century, during the rise of sugar haciendas southeast of Cartagena de Indias, hundreds or possibly thousands of recently arrived Africans fled into the Montes de María and beyond to establish numerous palenques. Among them, Domingo Bioho, who claimed to have been a king in Africa, rallied dozens of runaway men and women with whom he terrorized the haciendas around Tolú. His group continued to grow and Bioho, who gave himself the king name Benkos, and his fugitive community settled in the fortified palenque of Matuna. Spanish troops waged a long war against Benkos, interspersed with attempts at negotiation, which ended with the leader's capture and hanging in 1619.

Nonetheless, slaves in the Cartagena region continued to run away and establish palenques, even allying at times with landowners by working in their fields in exchange for tools and weapons. The governor decreed laws punishing fugitives according to the number of repeat offenses and time spent in flight: one hundred to three hundred whiplashes, ear amputation, or execution by garrote, quartering, or hanging. In 1634, following a raid against the Limón palenque, dozens of fugitive slaves were captured and judged, twenty-three of whom were condemned to a horrible death, followed by the display of their heads and limbs on the route leading to Cartagena and along certain city roads and squares.[18]

Repression did not discourage marronage, and by the end of the seventeenth century, palenques of bozal or creole slaves, Indians, *libres de color*, immigrants, and soldiers, as well as women (who had sometimes been kidnapped) and children had been formed not only to the south of Cartagena, but also in the vicinity of Santa Marta, Panama, along the Magdalena River, and in the gold-rich region of Mompox. While some runaways survived by pillaging and robbing, others joined networks of smugglers and agricultural or mine workers. Under pressure from slaveowning hacendados, the governor of Cartagena province ordered a general offensive against the illegal refuges. Some were set ablaze, like Tabacal, led by Domingo Padilla, a ladino slave on the run with his wife and children. In 1693, fourteen runaways from Tabacal, including Padilla, were hanged in the square in front of Cartagena's slaughterhouse, and Padilla's body was chopped up and his members exposed in strategic locations in order to terrify other slaves; 110 men, women, and children were condemned to one hundred or two hundred public whiplashes before being returned to their owners to be sold elsewhere. Many other fugitive slave communities suffered the same fate, which allowed hacendados to seize lands cleared by the runaways and mines they had begun to operate.

Despite that violent repression, palenques survived, including San Miguel Arcángel south of Cartagena, which was led by Domingo Criollo. Hundreds of runaways fled farther into the region's hinterlands. Finally, in 1713, one century after the deal reached by the Spanish monarchy and Yanga in Mexico, the bishop of Cartagena pressured royal authorities into compromising with some of the region's fugitives. Under his protection, the maroons of the Montes de María obtained recognition of their individual freedom and autonomy for the palenque of San Miguel Arcángel, renamed Palenque de San Basilio, in exchange for ending their attacks and sending back any new fugitive slaves.[19]

The largest maroon community at the beginning of the seventeenth century was undoubtedly Palmares, in Pernambuco in Brazil. Its establishment dates back to the 1600s and as early as 1612 the Portuguese had launched a raid against its fugitive inhabitants. In the 1630s, the Dutch occupied the province and discovered that Palmares was not a camp but a federation of villages housing at least eleven thousand runaways, half of whom lived in its two largest settlements, both of which were highly isolated and fortified. Their first attack targeted smaller villages called mocambos and ended with the massacre of approximately one hundred fugitive slaves. In 1645, the Dutch staged a second attack against the two large quilombos but found them abandoned after their forewarned inhabitants had fled farther inland. Dutch forces were therefore confined to burning down the maroons' huts and destroying their fields. A member of the Dutch military expedition was nonetheless able to report information about the Palmares community, noting that it boasted well-tended farms and was governed by a king who meted out "iron justice" to any member likely to compromise the group's safety. Despite the destruction wreaked in 1645, the federation of quilombos continued to grow, threatening expanding sugar plantations in the process.

By 1675 or so, Palmares had between eighteen thousand and thirty thousand fugitives in total, including *boçais* from diverse ethnic groups and creoles, as well as some Amerindians. They recognized the authority of a king, Ganga Zumba, and chiefs representing him at the head of each mocambo. The fortified quilombo of Macaco alone, in which the king lived, numbered fifteen hundred huts and several thousand inhabitants. In 1678, faced with the impossibility of defeating them in war, the governor of Pernambuco negotiated a treaty with Ganga Zumba that granted the *quilombolas* (maroons of the quilombos) their freedom, autonomy for their federation of villages, and use of part of the lands they occupied. But the compromise was somewhat ambiguous and an intransigent chief, Zumbi dos Palmares, rejected it, had Ganga Zumba poisoned, and took over the movement; he and his troops resisted Portuguese attacks for the next fifteen years.

It was not until 1694 that a powerful Portuguese army succeeded in storming the last fortified bastion of the vast Palmares complex. According to Portuguese sources, two hundred resistant quilombolas committed suicide by jumping off a cliff, an equal number died in combat, and more than five hundred men, women, and children were captured and sold as slaves. Zumbi and a small group of fighters were able to briefly evade capture, but the injured leader was caught and decapitated on 20 November 1695. His head was displayed in Recife to "kill the legend of his immortality." Thousands of maroons had nonetheless escaped during the years of fighting and established new quilombos in the Paraíba forests. Hundreds of fugitive slaves also created mocambos in the captaincies of Rio de Janeiro, Bahía, and Minas Gerais during the seventeenth and eighteenth centuries. Their lifestyle and economy depended in large part on their location: between 1740 and 1763, the approximately one hundred quilombolas living in Buraco de Tatú, near El Salvador, subsisted on robbery and the kidnapping of free persons and slaves on the city's outskirts, while others settled on the fringes of existing plantations.[20]

In Minas Gerais, following the discovery of gold at the end of the seventeenth century, the annual importation of new slaves increased fivefold between 1710 and 1735, ultimately reaching one hundred thousand, and simultaneously provoking the establishment of dozens of quilombos. During those two decades, the gold frenzy prompted owners to grant considerable autonomy to their slaves as long as they brought in the precious metal, but also increased their fear of revolts. Consequently, in 1719, the region's captain general announced the discovery of a vast plot by the slaves of the Rio das Mortes district's mines. Accordingly, the attack was scheduled to begin on Holy Thursday to surprise whites as they celebrated Easter, but an argument between Minas and Angolas over leadership of the revolt shortly beforehand led to the alleged conspirators being arrested and punished. In his report to the king of Portugal, the captain general congratulates himself for having unearthed and foiled what could have been a deadly plot, but also warns him of the following dilemma: "The sedition was extinguished, and the country returned to its former tranquility. However, since we cannot prevent the remaining blacks from thinking, and cannot deprive them of their natural desire for freedom; and since we cannot, merely because of this desire, eliminate all of them, they being necessary for our existence here, it must be concluded that this country will always be subjected to this problem."[21]

Indeed, in the still sparsely colonized Minas Gerais, slave flight to nearby hills and upstream of rivers was frequent, and quilombos were established almost everywhere. The largest of those was Jacuí, near São João del Rei, which housed as many as four thousand fugitives, who represented a threat to the expansion of colonial mining in the region. Even though the army launched an operation against Jacuí in 1756, the mountainous terrain and dispersal of mining and urban centers continued to facilitate slave escapes. Governors and slaveowners repeatedly complained to Lisbon about the insecurity created by runaways through attacks, thefts, kidnappings, plundering, and murders. By the end of the eighteenth century, Minas Gerais alone counted 117 quilombos and mocambos, whose members were not solely bandits—some mined gold, farmed for local consumption, or participated in smuggling networks.[22]

Marronage was such a problem in Brazil's vast territory that governors quickly adopted preventative methods such as mutilation, branding, severing of the Achilles tendon, leg amputation, and particularly cruel executions of captured slaves. They also imposed a number of restrictions on captives relating to their movements, the carrying of tools and weapons, and even kinship networks, for example by limiting the number of godchildren allowed per slave. To compensate for the absence of rural police, local authorities established private militias led by *capitães do mato* (bush captains) granted licenses to defend rural zones from attack by maroons, Indians, and anyone labeled a robber or bandit. Slave catchers practically had carte blanche to recruit men and, given the dangers and harsh conditions of their mission, often had to rely on slaves and recently freed slaves since the army did not enter forested and *sertão* regions except for coordinated attacks against the largest quilombos. Furthermore, because the *capitães do mato* were not part of the army, they did not receive military pay, but were instead paid per job, through bonuses offered by owners for the capture of their fugitive slaves and goods seized from attacked camps, some of which they distributed among their men. Slaves enlisted in those hunts by their masters were therefore offered a means to slowly accumulate the savings necessary to buy their freedom. By capturing fugitive slaves, slave militiamen could hope to free themselves; others chose to themselves become runaways. Operations by *capitães do mato* remained geographically limited and were not successful in reducing grand marronage in Brazil's inland regions. However, they forced quilombolas near cities and colonized regions to form smaller, roaming groups to avoid betrayal and capture.[23]

Maroons' Triumphs and Struggles in the Sugar-Producing Caribbean

After 1650, the rapid development of slave sugar plantations in the Caribbean islands similarly led to the establishment of numerous maroon societies following successful escape attempts by recently imported Africans or slave uprisings. Regardless of location, those maroons benefited from European colonists' still limited occupation of the area and from the existence of largely inaccessible regions in which to hide. They initially attacked plantations in order to gather food provisions and weapons and kidnap women, before gradually developing more organized communities, which proved highly problematic for colonists: maroons threatened their safety and did not hesitate to kill at times, made travel and transportation dangerous, fascinated slaves for whom they served as models, and were a heavy burden on undermanned militias and troops.

Like Spain and Portugal in the sixteenth century, other colonial powers did not know how to bring an end to marronage. At times they relied on emancipated slaves or Amerindians to pursue runaways. They also established exemplary punishments for captured maroons. Louis XIV's Code Noir, promulgated in 1685, established a progression of penalties, ranging from cutting off ears and branding a fleur-de-lis on one shoulder to cutting a hamstring and branding a slave's other shoulder, and finally to the death penalty. A similar law instituted by South Carolina in 1712 did the same, establishing punishments that ranged from flogging to branding the letter *R* on the right cheek, the removal of one ear, and then castration and the death penalty. The slave code adopted by Virginia in 1682 authorized any white person to kill any fugitive slave who refused to surrender.[24] However, those mutilations and executions proved costly to masters as they diminished their slaves' value and productivity. As a result, many ignored the legal obligation to declare escapes and tortured their slaves themselves if they returned or were captured. But even those measures were unable to slow the marronage phenomenon.

For example, in the pioneer sugar-producing colony of Barbados, African slaves and Irish indentured servants began to escape as early as 1650, hiding in caves and forests. However, the development of sugar plantations on the tiny island quickly destroyed any possibility of forming lasting maroon societies and slaves consequently turned to maritime marronage, fleeing on canoes to the small, as yet uncolonized islands of St. Lucia, St. Vincent, Dominica, and Tobago. Others joined undiscriminating merchant or pirate ships, at times forming a large proportion of those vessels' crews. Their number remains unknown, but escapes were sufficiently common for the British authorities to establish laws about maritime marronage on multiple occasions.[25]

In Jamaica, marronage spread so dramatically that the British government was forced to agree to a peace treaty granting maroons their freedom. In effect, as soon as England seized the island from Spain in 1655, slaves belonging to Spanish colonists took advantage of the transition to escape, form guerrilla units, and hide in the Blue Mountains range in the eastern part of the island. Slave revolts and escapes continued as the first English planters settled in the region, facilitated by the presence of steep, heavily wooded mountains that were hard to access and well equipped with potable water sources in several parts of Jamaica.[26] Unable to drive the maroons out, the English opted for massive importations of Africans, largely from the coast of Guinea. Numbering approximately 8,000 in 1664, the island's slave population increased from 9,500 in 1673 to 45,000 in 1703, 80,000 in 1722, and 130,000 in 1754.[27] But rebellions followed by slave escapes multiplied, strengthening Jamaica's two major maroon societies: the preexisting one in the Blue Mountains (the Windward Maroons), which expanded with the arrival of hundreds of African men, women, and children, forming an alliance of villages dominated by the bellicose personality of the priestess Nanny; and a community in the densely wooded mountains of Cockpit Country in western Jamaica (the Leeward Maroons), which was more autocratic and centralized around an Akan chief. In 1673, the first large revolt involved at least three hundred primarily Akan slaves from plantations in St. Ann parish, who murdered their masters and thirteen other whites before hiding in Cockpit Country. Several similar rebellions subsequently broke out using the same model in various provinces across the island. As elsewhere, maroons were often captured and subjected to cruel punishments intended to be dissuasive but that were ultimately unsuccessful in curbing marronage.[28]

By around 1720, the number of maroons in Jamaica had reached several thousand, and their communities continued to attract recruits from among the eighty thousand slaves then present on the island. The British redoubled their efforts to subdue them, and mobilized slaves and Miskito Indians in their operations against maroons who relied on disconcerting African tactics better adapted to the terrain. In 1734, after months of fighting, the British were able to seize the village of Nanny Town in the Blue Mountains. Hundreds of maroons fled, some of whom hid in Cockpit Country, which became the British soldiers' new target. Led by Cudjoe, who was probably born in hiding to a fugitive Akan father, those maroons opted for survival rather than risk annihilation by the army. In March 1739, following long negotiations, Cudjoe signed a peace treaty with British authorities, which guaranteed a "total state of freedom" to Cudjoe and the maroons with him who had fled their masters at least two years prior, but that obliged them to send back any runaways who joined them afterward. Other maroons had the choice between remaining Cudjoe's subjects or returning to their master in exchange for a promised pardon. Cudjoe's community was also granted six hundred hectares of land on which it could raise livestock, hunt, and grow food to sell in regional markets, though it was banned from cultivating sugarcane. It was allowed to administer its own form of justice, except for crimes punishable by the death penalty, which had to be transferred to a British court. Furthermore, it had to send any new fugitive slaves back to planters, and its men had to help defend the island by supplying a special maroon militia in case of attack. One year later, the British signed a more restrictive peace deal with the maroons in the Blue Mountains.[29] That marked the end of the first maroon war in Jamaica, but not of revolts and marronage on the island.

Slaves also formed maroon communities on other islands in the Caribbean, which did not endure as long as those in Jamaica. In 1639, in St. Kitts (at the time split between France and England), some sixty Africans, many with wives and children, fled their masters' cruelty by hiding in mountainous regions from which they continued to attack French colonists. Aware of the fate awaiting them upon capture, they built a fortified camp on the edge of a cliff. When the governor of the French part of the island sent five hundred well-armed soldiers against them and had their huts burned down, only a few were able to jump off the cliff, many were burned alive, and others quartered and their members displayed on stakes visible to the island's slaves. But new maroon groups continued to form as more Africans arrived and working and living conditions on plantations worsened.[30]

In Martinique, sparsely populated at the time, a band led by Francisque Fabulé, which numbered between four hundred and five hundred fugitive slaves, was the first to be identified in 1665 by the French governor. Once captured, Fabulé briefly helped fight against his former fellow maroons, only to escape again before being recaptured and condemned to the galleys in 1671. However, many fugitives had established small forest communities, living off farming and plundering. Marronage developed more extensively in Guadeloupe, especially in Basse-Terre, whose mountainous terrain slowed colonization. Since the 1720s, authorities attempted to apprehend the hundreds of maroons who had settled there and at times kidnapped women from nearby plantations. But though they were able to capture forty-eight fugitives, eight of whom were executed, colonial forces were largely unable to eradicate the marronage that continued in Basse-Terre until the abolition of slavery.[31] Likewise, in Saint Domingue, numerous African captives had escaped from the early eighteenth century onward, many of whom created maroon bands that regularly pillaged plantations south of Le Cap (now Cap-Haïtien). Others hid in the mountainous and at the time wooded zone along the border with Santo Domingo, the Spanish part of Hispaniola. Despite several military raids conducted between 1728 and 1749, fugitives continued to number in the hundreds, and possibly thousands, ten years later. Those maroon communities included Le Maniel, formed at the end of the seventeenth century, which resisted military attacks for several decades before finally signing a peace treaty in 1785 with the colonial governments of the French and Spanish halves of the island in exchange for promising to send back any future fugitive slaves.[32]

Before it became a large-scale sugar producer, Cuba was also home to small maroon communities of fugitive enslaved Africans situated in the mountains, notably El Portillo in the far eastern part of the island. In 1747, the Spanish colony's governor mobilized one hundred local men to destroy it. Although many maroons were able to escape, eleven adults (and two children) were captured and brought to justice. Statements by those captives, conserved in Cuban archives, notably reveal the ethnic diversity that characterized some palenques formed from the chance nature of successful escapes. They claimed to be Kongo, Carabalí, Mina, or Mandinga, and therefore survivors of the Atlantic crossing, except for one woman who called herself Jamaican. Those men and women explained that they had run away to flee a master or mistress who punished them excessively, stole their limited possessions, or had not respected a promise of freedom. They also stated that their goal was to be able to live off their crops with their families. The judge decided that if the maroons had been legally imported to Cuba, they would be returned to their master, who would punish them, but that if they had been smuggled, they would be sold at auction.[33]

In contrast, on small, flat islands such as Grenada and Antigua, maroon communities did not endure past the 1730s, when colonization and slave plantations spread across most of the region. Marronage, always heavily repressed, declined.[34] In Antigua, for example, where fifty runaway slaves had been executed on average each decade between 1722 and 1749, only ten fugitives suffered the same fate between 1750 and 1759.[35] The Moravian missionary C. G. A. Oldendorp nonetheless described the slaves he questioned in the 1760s in the Danish Leeward Islands in these words: "They follow their own irrepressible natural drives and consider any and all means of gaining their freedom to be just. To this end, they run away from their masters and flee into the mountains and forests."[36]

Transimperial Marronage and Spanish Sanctuary Policy

During most of the eighteenth century, the conflict between European powers created a new opportunity for fugitive slaves in the Greater Caribbean. As the Spanish monarchy saw its domination over peripheral territories threatened by French, Dutch, and British buccaneers and colonists, it initiated a policy of welcoming the bossales who escaped from the enemy, granting them sanctuary and freedom against conversion to Catholicism. In addition, in some areas Spain offered them land, settled them in new villages and integrated the men into local defense militias. As news of this policy spread, some slaves from non-Spanish dominions attempted to seize this chance of emancipation.

Spain's asylum policy was initiated in Hispaniola in the 1670s in response to the colonization of the island's west by the French. Its first beneficiaries were some fifty enslaved Africans fleeing their French masters, who were manumitted and settled in the new village of San Lorenzo de los Minas, near Santo Domingo, under Church supervision, paving the way for other fugitives.[37] After repeating this policy in 1680 on the island of Trinidad (then still attached to Venezuela but also coveted by the French) and granting shelter and liberty to fugitive slaves from the Windward Islands, the Spanish declared that "all blacks who came seeking faith from whichever of the foreign nations that occupy the lands of this Kingdom must enjoy freedom."[38] In the late 1680s, ten fugitive slaves from English Carolina escaped to Florida "seeking holy Baptism and the protection from Your Majesty" and were eventually granted freedom in 1693.[39] During the next decades, slaves in small groups or alone fled from French Saint Domingue to Santo Domingo; from British South Carolina and Georgia to Florida; from the Danish, Dutch, and British Leeward Islands to Puerto Rico; from Jamaica to Cuba; from British Belize to Guatemala; and from Curaçao and the Guianas to Venezuela. In most cases, the Spanish authorities decided to grant them freedom if they converted to Catholicism, while expecting them to be hard-working and law-abiding settlers.

However, when maritime maroons from the Dutch island of Curaçao crossed the forty miles of sea that separated them from Venezuela in search of freedom, they rather vanished in the hinterland already sheltering runaway communities. Yet in 1702, thirty-two of them were captured and sold as slaves by the governor of Caracas. A captain of the local militia contested their sale before the royal tribunal (*audiencia*) in Santo Domingo, advocating their rights to asylum and freedom. On the basis of the aforementioned cases, the *audiencia* ruled that all thirty-two runaways be manumitted, given land, and subjected to militia service. Venezuelan planters and authorities resisted the ruling, but in 1721 the governor finally emancipated the fugitives and settled them in the new village of Curiepe, east of the capital—an outcome that attests to the Spanish monarchy's commitment to its sanctuary policy.[40] In other dominions as well, runaways from Protestant colonies were emancipated and assigned to specific areas where they built new villages, such as San Mateo de los Cangrejos, near San Juan in Puerto Rico. Most emblematic was the village and military fort of Gracia Real de Santa Teresa de Mosé, strategically located north of St. Augustine, in Florida, founded in 1738 by decision of the governor with one hundred successful fugitives from Georgia: not only did these men contribute to build the fort and established themselves with families in the adjacent village, but they also served as militiamen against British attacks.[41]

Eventually, in 1750 and again in 1753, King Ferdinand VI, relying on the royal orders promulgated since 1680, "resolved that as a general rule from this time onward and forevermore all black slaves of both sexes who come from English and Dutch colonies in America to seek refuge (whether in times of peace or of war) in my domains to embrace our Holy Catholic Faith shall be free."[42] Slaves from Protestant colonies were fairly aware of these provisions, and some risked escaping by land or sea "under the pretext of embracing our Holy Catholic Faith" in order to obtain freedom on Spanish soil. The Spanish monarchy, for its part, saw in them an opportunity to increase the population, labor force, and defense of its borderlands, even though their numbers remain unknown.[43] As noted by historian Linda Rupert, the story of these fugitives demonstrates that occasionally "the interests of enslaved people seeking freedom intersected with the Spanish Crown's efforts to consolidate its jurisdiction."[44]

Marronage and Continental Colonization

During the seventeenth and eighteenth centuries, vast uncolonized territories on the American continent offered fugitives possible refuges. When French colonists in Louisiana wanted to develop rice, indigo, and tobacco crops employing enslaved Amerindians and recently imported Africans, they were immediately confronted by an increase in escape attempts. By 1724, an edict had adapted certain articles pertaining to marronage from the 1685 Code Noir to the new colony: the progression of punishments for fugitives was the same, but any emancipated individual who harbored a maroon risked reenslavement.

Nevertheless, the principal threat to the sparse minority of French colonists up the Mississippi River was the Native American population. Organized in nations, the Indians resisted pugnaciously against the seizure of their lands and the enslavement of some of their members by the French. As a result, the colonists increasingly feared that Native Americans attack them, in alliance with the enslaved Africans who largely outnumbered them to. Though such an alliance did not materialize on a large scale, African captives did take advantage of the conflict. Notably, during a bloody attack by the Natchez against Fort Rosalie, in 1729, which killed half of the colonists, a majority of its 280 slaves either joined the Natchez Indians against their masters or fled. More generally, however, as French colonists continued to exploit Indians and Africans, men and women from both groups unrelentingly escaped into the Louisiana hinterlands to form small and often multiethnic maroon communities.[45]

Marronage also accompanied the establishment of slavery in Britain's northern colonies, as shown by newspapers from the period. In New York, for example, slaveowners published 350 announcements about maroon slaves between 1726 and 1770.[46] In Virginia, according to a study of 1,500 runaway slave ads published in the *Virginia Gazette* between 1736 and 1800, the large majority of fugitives were creole, not African, men. Some slaves escaped to find family members, which often rapidly led to their capture, but others fled toward cities, where they could find work more easily and sometimes pass for free. A minority left Virginia for North Carolina, sparsely colonized at the time, or Pennsylvania, reputed for being more tolerant. And others fled to ports where they could sign up to be a sailor or hide on a ship, which limited the risk of being caught by their master but increased the danger of capture and resale by slave traders. Escapes were frequent enough to prompt laws for the mutilation, castration, or execution of runaways as well as monetary rewards for their capture. Similarly, the establishment of maroon communities in areas that were either sparsely colonized or not colonized at all and the protection of fugitive slaves by poor whites, either out of pity or for profit (by forcing maroons to work for them), resulted in the adoption of particularly severe laws. At the same time, territorial surveillance and pursuit of runaways required the costly mobilization of white militias.[47]

Once South Carolina had developed slavery on a large scale (by 1710, Africans outnumbered whites in the colony), slave escapes multiplied, as demonstrated, once again, by gazette ads and legislation inspired by the French Code Noir. Hundreds of fugitives settled in the marshlands and mangroves of the Great Dismal Swamp, along the Virginia border, where their recapture was impracticable.[48] Between the end of the seventeenth century and 1763, others managed to reach St. Augustine in Florida, where the Spanish authorities granted them sanctuary and freedom, as mentioned above.

It was within that context that a group of slaves near Charleston carried out the deadliest revolt in the history of the North American British colonies, called the Stono Rebellion. Because the rebellion did not prompt an archived trial or hearing, little documentation exists. Nonetheless, it appears that its leader was an Angola slave named Jemmy, accompanied by approximately twenty male followers. After gathering near a bridge over the Stono River one Sunday in September 1739, the slaves attacked a store, stole weapons and goods, and then killed two white individuals whom they decapitated before displaying their heads along the entryway stairs. The group then headed south while chanting "Freedom!" and rallying other slaves along the way, as it set houses and plantations ablaze and killed some twenty whites, including women and children. However, not every slave encountered joined the group. On the contrary, some defended their besieged masters: one in particular killed an insurgent, an act of loyalty for which he was later emancipated. The rebels, who by then numbered between sixty and one hundred, were captured at the end of the day by militiamen and planters as they celebrated their victory by dancing, singing, and playing drums. Most were killed or executed on the spot, while others fled only to be captured shortly afterward and summarily executed. Some, however, were able to reach St. Augustine and find protection under the Spanish.

Though lacking sources, historians have tried to interpret this one-day bloody rebellion. They agree that the ultimate goal driving Jemmy and his companions' saga was freedom in St. Augustine, all the more so as Jemmy and some other fugitives were undoubtedly descended from the Catholic kingdom of Kongo and therefore particularly receptive to Spanish propaganda. The rebels may have also acted because, with the resumption of the war between Great Britain and Spain in 1738, South Carolina was preparing to issue a security decree obliging all white men to carry a weapon, including to church on Sundays. According to one historian, the Stono Rebellion also had a gender dimension: through their actions (namely displaying the heads of their two first victims), march, and celebration, these men, Africans for the most part, may have wanted to affirm their masculinity and combat experience at a time when the colony was abandoning cattle breeding and logging in favor of rice plantations, thereby eliminating a gender-based division of labor. Nonetheless, even if they did spread death and fire on their way, the Stono rebels were seeking not to seize power or attack the institution of slavery, but to flee to Florida. They were therefore maroons before anything else.[49]

In South America, the slave labor–propelled expansion of mines led to increased marronage north of Medellín and south of Popayán in Colombia, on the Pacific coast of Colombia and Ecuador, and in the regions of Salvador de Bahía and Minas Gerais in Brazil, where palenques and quilombos multiplied. Throughout the entire continental Spanish empire, fugitive communities had settled in new frontier zones, illegally colonizing them in the complete absence of the state or Catholic Church. Fugitives also arrived by sea, notably making their way from Curaçao to the Coro region in Venezuela. While some communities were uniquely composed of runaway slaves, others, called *rochelas*, gathered black and mulatto fugitive slaves, Amerindians, mestizos, and even some whites who were deserters or running from the law. According to a Spanish witness in the eighteenth century, those men and women blended together so well that they "propagated an infinity of racial mixes [*castas*] difficult to verify."[50] In 1720, for example, Spanish authorities estimated that there were twenty thousand cimarrones in Venezuela; in the 1770s, they claimed that the number of *arrochelados* in the Caribbean region of Colombia alone had reached sixty thousand, or more than a quarter of the population (not counting some one hundred thousand uncolonized Amerindians).[51] Throughout the eighteenth century, in both Brazil and Spanish America, colonial armies launched costly raids to (re)conquer interior regions and resettle maroons and other fugitives in new villages placed under royal and clerical authority.[52] During that process, which was never fully implemented, thousands of runaway slaves and their descendants silently integrated into the ranks of the *libres de color*—a considerable victory against slavery, though rarely mentioned in historiography. Other fugitives advanced even farther into uncolonized hinterlands.

Outside that process of illegal colonization, the Spanish monarchy attempted to encourage the establishment of black communities in regions where its sovereignty was contested by Amerindian nations. Those involuntary recruits were at times forcibly displaced *arrochelados,* as in the Darién province south of present-day Panama, or poor *libres de color* and slaves commandeered from their masters, as in the case of Emboscada (ambush), which was created in the mid-eighteenth century in Paraguay to ensure the protection of Asunción. Abandoned by authorities, those frontier communities lived under the same impoverished conditions as palenques, but their inhabitants had legally escaped slavery.[53]

A better-known and equally significant example of grand marronage was flight by Africans brought to Dutch Suriname between the seventeenth and nineteenth centuries to cultivate sugarcane. Marronage in Suriname dated back to 1651, when the English established the first plantation on the coast of the Guianas. At that time, slaves were already fleeing into hinterlands formed of thick tropical forests and rivers and home to Amerindian communities. Slave escapes would persist throughout the following years, alongside a sporadic increase in English colonization until 1667, boosted by the arrival of Sephardic and Ashkenazi Jewish planters. That same year, the Netherlands acquired Suriname, where it continued to develop sugar plantations thanks to the massive importation of African slaves. As a result, by around 1715, the colony counted two thousand Europeans of varied origin (Dutch, French, Jewish, and German, among others) compared to a primarily Mandinga and Kongo slave population of twenty-two thousand.[54] Fifty years later, when local production expanded from sugar to include coffee, the number of slaves had more than doubled, with a large majority of them still being brought from Africa. There was barely one white for every twenty-five slaves in the Dutch colony as a whole, but on sugar plantations, which had on average 149 slaves each, the ratio white/slaves dropped dramatically.[55]

Due to disastrous living conditions, scarce security forces, and the existence of vast, unconquered interior regions, marronage in Suriname spread in parallel with the plantation system and rapidly reached uncontrollable dimensions. Groups of Africans from the same plantations initially fled south to form roaming camps near other estates, which they attacked to supplement their provisions. Those camps multiplied over time, expanding with the arrival of new fugitives or slaves (especially women) kidnapped during raids, and pushed farther south. By 1700, maroons numbered several hundred or possibly several thousand. Relying on guerrilla tactics, the so-called Bush Negroes subjected plantations to repeat attacks, which at times incited plantation slaves to rebel, kill their masters, and join runaway camps. Planters and authorities retaliated by deploying militias and military units, and even mobilizing slaves to whom they had promised freedom in exchange for destroying camps and capturing maroons. But those raids were very costly in both men and money and had limited and short-lived results. The atrocious punishments inflicted on captured fugitives were also unable to slow escape attempts by slaves mistreated on a daily basis. What's more, the Bush Negroes had a better understanding of the terrain than colonists and their troops and, with time and the increasing presence of women and children, were able to settle in fortified villages farther inland, creating three "tribes": the Ndjuka, Saramaka, and Matawai.[56] Despite food autonomy achieved through farming, hunting, and fishing, they continued to threaten plantations, either by direct attacks or by sheltering fugitive slaves. In 1757, a maroon chief stated:

> We demand that you tell your Governor and Councillors that if they do not want a rebellion they should see to it that the planters treat better the people who are their property and not leave them in the hands of directors and overseers who indulge in drinking, who punish the blacks unjustly and cruelly, seduce their wives and daughters, neglect the sick, and thus drive into the woods a large number of industrious and strong people who support you with their sweat, without whom your colony could not survive, and to whom in the end you owe your undeserved fortune to beg them for peace.[57]

Ultimately, the colonial government was forced to recognize its impotence and sign peace treaties with those three southern "tribes" in, respectively, 1760, 1762, and 1767, in exchange for their pledges not to welcome any new runaways.[58]

With escape routes to the south compromised, Suriname's fugitive slaves headed west, where they slowly formed a new "tribe" under the dual leadership of Boni, for male fighters, and Aluku, for the nonwarrior population. After several years of skirmishes, the colonial government sent fifteen hundred European soldiers and three hundred slaves under the promise of freedom and a plot of land, who decimated the maroon community and pushed its survivors toward French Guiana.[59] Nonetheless, neither this war nor the treaties signed in the 1760s brought an end to marronage, as evidenced by the creation of two additional "tribes" by fugitive slaves, the Paramaka and the Kwinti, in the colony's hinterlands. According to historical estimates, about 10 percent of the enslaved population in Suriname liberated themselves through marronage during the second half of the eighteenth century.[60]

≋ In sum, between the sixteenth and eighteenth centuries, hundreds of thousands of Africans and Afro-descendants favored marronage and the creation of fugitive slave societies, notably because those forms of revolt corresponded well to a context of gradual colonization that left immense spaces uncontrolled by authorities or slaveholders. Though militias and soldiers captured an indeterminate number of fugitives, often sentencing them to a cruel death, a great many escaped the yoke of slavery by surviving for a long time in forests, mountains, or marshlands. Groups of maroons near major towns and ports controlled the passage of men and goods to conduct robberies or carried out raids against haciendas; others joined vast mining, farming, or smuggling networks. Many others, particularly women and creoles, hid in towns where they could discreetly blend into free populations of color. Despite the proliferation of slave codes and the severity of punishments, marronage could not be eradicated. Two or even three generations later, as colonial borders advanced and mixed-race communities proliferated, those maroons' descendants were integrated into free populations and grew to represent the large majority of inhabitants of vast regions.

3

Self-Purchase and Military Service
Legal but Limited Paths to Emancipation

Like marronage, self-purchase and military service were among the strategies used by slaves to obtain their freedom beginning with the first slave ship's arrival in Hispaniola. And, like marronage, those strategies paved the way for the slow abolition of slavery throughout the nineteenth century. However, in contrast to marronage, they were forms not of revolt but rather of individual, familial, and at times community resistance that used existing legislative frameworks to escape a condition of servitude. The letter or certificate of freedom obtained by an emancipated slave was not only a legal document often carried on his or her person, but also the result of a social process at the end of which a master or judge decided that this or that slave could become free. It therefore implied an interaction between the slave, his or her master, and the authorities, during which a slave, transcending his or her condition, took initiative and foresaw a future in which he or she was free. Similarly, voluntarily military enlistment in exchange for promised emancipation showed that an enslaved man was ready to risk his life for freedom—an engagement that, at a time when armies were largely composed of mercenaries and randomly selected recruits, also proved his courage and masculinity.

In every colony, the military recruitment of slaves came as a response to the lack of local militias and soldiers sent by monarchies during enemy invasions and pirate attacks, and allowed certain captives to gain their freedom. Access to manumission, however, was much more varied and linked to historical context, existing legislation, the economic sector in which a slave worked, and whether he or she lived in an urban or rural zone. Despite the development of the slave trade and slave plantations across the Americas, huge disparities existed between slaves from Spanish and Portuguese colonies, who maintained the right to purchase their freedom, and those from British, Dutch, and French colonies, for whom that possibility grew increasingly limited and then exceedingly rare during the eighteenth century. Nonetheless, manumission, everywhere it was recognized, enabled the growth of a free Afro-descended population that slowly surpassed that of slaves once the importation of new African captives had ceased.

Planned Liberation:
Self-Purchase and Manumission in Iberian America

Numerous enslaved men and women in Spanish and Portuguese America gained their freedom through manumission or by obtaining a legal document of freedom. Derived from Roman law and revived in peninsular legislation during the thirteenth century, manumission had been extended to slaves in the Americas. Long approached solely from a legal angle, it is now well studied in its practice thanks to analysis of municipal and regional archives. In essence, emancipation could be granted by a slave's master, but it was most often the result of a process begun by enslaved men or women who purchased their own freedom (self-purchase or self-manumission) from a master or whose parents or relatives paid the required sum. Emancipation following payment for a slave's determined value was slowly codified, transitioning from a privilege dependent on a master or mistress's goodwill to an option recognized by law and exempted from sales tax (*alcabala*) in the second half of the eighteenth century. This type of emancipation could also occur progressively thanks to partial payments, a practice, referred to as coartación or coartação, which became a quasi-right and forbade masters from selling or transporting slaves who had already paid a portion of their value. By buying their own freedom or that of their family members, enslaved men and women in several regions gradually created societies in which the majority of blacks, mulattos, and zambos were no longer enslaved but free, and thus largely contributed to the erosion of slavery. However, manumission required the enslaved individual to maintain good relations with his or her owner: without the latter's consent, the slave risked being forced to pursue long and costly legal proceedings for manumission whose outcome was far from guaranteed.[1]

Despite that favorable legal framework, in reality, manumission in both Spanish America and Brazil required considerable long-term effort: slaves had to accumulate the money necessary to buy their freedom at a price agreed in advance (in principle not exceeding their market value). In several sectors of activity located in the cities, such as artisanal production, transportation, washing, cooking, street vending, and prostitution, it was not impossible for a captive working Sundays, holidays, and additional hours on top of long days in a master's service to be able to pay for emancipation after many years. For slaves living separately from a master to whom they paid a fixed daily or weekly sum, self-manumission could become a viable option when the economic context was favorable. In contrast, in rural areas, enslaved workers in farming and livestock industries were only able to buy their freedom on rare occasions by selling products they cultivated or raised, in addition to their slave duties, every Sunday. As for slaves in mining regions, access to manumission varied. In Chocó, owners did not forbid their enslaved laborers from looking for gold during their free time and in many cases accumulating enough to buy their freedom. In the gold and diamond mines of Brazil's Minas Gerais, however, masters were often opposed to allowing their slaves to do so, fearing that they would then become competitors thanks to their knowledge of lodes and production techniques. Miners' opposition to manumission was incidentally one of the catalysts of the marronage and illicit exploitation of mines that characterized that region (see chapter 2).

Due to those varied reasons, the majority of emancipated slaves was almost universally women, not because they were concubines or mistresses liberated by their white masters as historians long assumed, but because urban slavery and the activities more likely to allow for manumission were primarily feminine—in contrast to rural slavery, where enslaved men were the majority—which permitted more women than men to obtain their freedom. Another general tendency among emancipated slaves was the preponderance of American-born in relation to those from Africa, and that of mulattos or Afro-descendants of mixed ancestry in relation to "full" blacks, in part because the former groups had a better understanding of laws and local customs and were better able than enslaved Africans to benefit from patronage networks among white elites to garner support for their requests for emancipation.[2]

Parish archives also reveal that some slaves, particularly mothers, decided to buy their children's freedom rather than their own. That discovery allows historians to relativize historiography's emphasis on the phenomena of abortion and infanticide among forms of resistance by enslaved mothers who, through those dramatic gestures, wanted to spare their children and themselves a life of suffering and heartbreak while depriving their owners of additional slaves.[3] Of course, some women decided to have an abortion or kill their newborn children in that aim, as attests legislation forbidding these acts, but others did everything possible to purchase the freedom of a child born into slavery, as shown by baptism records. For example, in 1640 in Lima, an enslaved woman named María Ramos paid her mistress seventy pesos to purchase the manumission of her four-month-old daughter Inés. And in 1595, again in Lima, the slave Juana Bohio paid for her niece Lorenza to be freed. Parish registers from São José do Rio das Mortes, in Minas Gerais, similarly reveal that in the mid-eighteenth century, some children of African or creole slaves were emancipated at baptism thanks to payments equivalent to their value made by their parents or godparents (in one instance, a bozal served as payment). Though the purchase of a newborn or small child's freedom was less costly than that of an adolescent or adult, it was also riskier due to elevated infant mortality rates. Considerable effort was required from an enslaved parent to ensure that any child of theirs who survived was able to live a free life. With other familial strategies, thus, some parents first acquired their own freedom in order to then earn the money necessary for the emancipation of their children, as early as possible.[4] Baptism records also show that children born of consensual or forced unions between an enslaved woman and a white man were sometimes emancipated by their fathers, who often owned the mothers. That was the case for a sculptor and architect of baroque churches in Minas Gerais: Antônio Francisco Lisboa, called Aleijadinho, who was born in 1730 to a Portuguese father and his slave. Aleijadinho's father recorded him as emancipated at his baptism, though he did not liberate the child's mother.[5]

Enslaved couples sought to have their union sanctified by the Catholic Church more often than free common people. Indeed, religious marriage allowed them to demand the right to live together to consummate the marriage and to be better protected against forced separation following the sale of one of the spouses. Of course, the Church endorsed slavery and itself owned slaves, but at the same time it protected the legal personality of slaves and administered them sacraments just as it did to whites (although in racially separated registers). The Church therefore provided captives with a religious and normative framework on which they could base certain demands on masters disrespectful of Christian precepts. If the enslaved wife or husband died, the record of their marriage in parish registers theoretically allowed the widow or widower to obtain his or her spouse's savings or any money paid into a coartación process, although that often entailed years of a legal battle whose outcome was unpredictable. Nevertheless, Catholic marriage did not protect enslaved parents from the sale of their children to distant locations.[6] Some couples also devised family manumission strategies, resulting in one or the other obtaining his or her freedom before accumulating the sum needed to liberate his or her partner. At times slaveowners took advantage of that situation. In 1615 in Lima, for example, the draper Antón Bran had to pay one thousand pesos, half on credit, to purchase his wife Isabel's freedom, or twice as much as the average price of an enslaved creole woman at the time.[7]

Countless slaves sacrificed a significant portion of their lives to tirelessly serving a master or mistress who had promised them their freedom if they stayed with their owner until his or her death. In some cases, these were subjugated women who became concubines to their owner or one of his sons, often under force or duress, in exchange for a promise to stipulate their emancipation and/or that of their children in his will. Others were faithful domestic servants who had assisted their master or mistress through the various stages of life, including illness. But that kind of commitment made with the goal of manumission after an owner's death was not without risk, as shown by the many legal complaints brought by both slaves and masters' heirs. For example, some captives discovered at their owner's death that he or she had not included their emancipation in the will or had made it conditional on additional years of servitude to his or her descendants. Sometimes heirs contested manumissions noted in a will or wanted to reimburse any debts left by the deceased by selling his or her slaves.

Those postmortem conflicts revealed the internal contradictions of Iberian laws according to which a slave was both capital or merchandise and a human being with a moral, religious, and legal character, all of which existed in a context in which slavery was primarily a question of power and force. Furthermore, despite owners' legal obligation to care for their elderly, disabled, or sick slaves, some chose to liberate them once they had become unproductive, abandoning them to a cruel state of neglect.[8]

Enslaved individuals who obtained the status of *libertos* or *libertas* (emancipated) often remained very poor, namely because they began their free lives in debt or penniless after having spent all their savings to purchase their freedom. Many were old, having invested a considerable portion of their lives accumulating enough money to obtain their freedom or waiting for their master's will to take effect. But others were children who either left slavery at a young age or never experienced it. Some were able to overcome poverty, particularly emancipated captives who had been apprentices and later opened their own tailor or shoemaker workshops or who acquired contracts as stonemasons or carpenters; emancipated women could make a modest living through income from a tavern, a small street stand, or by renting out rooms. On occasion, those freed individuals became landowners and even acquired one or two slaves.[9]

Finally, from the late seventeenth century on, some slaves were sufficiently familiar with laws and the workings of Iberian justice to contest their treatment without overtly contesting slavery. They used clauses from the *Siete Partidas*, such as the obligation of masters and mistresses to feed, clothe, and correctly care for their slaves, educate them in the Catholic religion, and not administer excessive punishments, to denounce abuses. If mistreatment was proven to the extent that an owner was demonstrated to be unworthy of the quasi-parental role he or she was supposed to fill for his or her slaves, the latter could be purchased by another master (who thereby compensated the original owner) and, in extremely rare cases of horrendous torture that threatened public safety, the guilty master or mistress had to grant the victim's freedom and pay that victim damages for life. Such decisions were extremely rare, however, as they challenged masters' power and the social order. Indeed, Spanish archives abound with cases of slaves' abuse, injury, and mutilation, sometimes fatal, but almost all ended with the violent master or mistress keeping the property of the enslaved victim, or at most being sentenced to sell the slave. Many more cases of abuse were never brought before a royal court and remained confined to the private sphere of slaveowners.[10]

Royal slaves' long struggle in the mines of El Cobre in eastern Cuba also merits a place in the arsenal used by captives in the Americas to improve their situation and eventually obtain their freedom. As María Elena Díaz has shown, in 1670 the king of Spain seized a mining concession in Cuba, including 271 slaves whom its owner had neglected and who consequently became royal slaves. Over the next 130 years, those captives and their descendants rejected their appropriation by the king through varied methods until they obtained collective and definitive emancipation in 1800. In addition to resorting to revolt and to marronage in the neighboring mountains, they also manipulated conflicts between the governors of Cuba and authorities in Madrid in order to have their voices heard and their demands addressed. Those tenacious individuals went as far as to send a delegation to Spain on two occasions, at the end of the seventeenth century and shortly before 1800, in what was an extraordinary exploit for enslaved men and women. They were able to prove that since the king was their legal master but could not in fact ensure that their needs were met, they should be granted lands to raise food crops.

Those strategies bore fruit. Shortly after 1700, the Spanish monarchy recognized the El Cobre community as a kind of *pueblo de indios* with its own cabildo, even though nearly all of its inhabitants were slaves and Afro-descendants. Like Indians living in *pueblos*, the adult men of El Cobre had to participate in the *mita*, in other words supply a quota of temporary workers to build fortifications. However, unlike Indians, they also had to form a defense militia in service of the king. But in daily life, they had near-total autonomy: men largely concentrated on farming and women on copper mining. The population increased solely as a result of natural growth. Between 1700 and 1769, 167 slaves (predominantly men) were able to purchase their freedom through coartación; some acquired additional lands and at times one or two domestic slaves, creating significant social divisions within the community. In the 1770s, El Cobre numbered nearly 900 "slaves" without masters and 450 *libres de color*, to whom were added three or four white inhabitants (priests or royal civil servants). But in 1780, due to a combination of factors, a royal edict reprivatized the mines and consequently El Cobre's slaves, many of whom were seized by self-proclaimed owners and (re)enslaved elsewhere. The community then sent an emissary to Madrid, and in 1800, the monarchy announced the *cobreros* slaves' collective freedom though it delimited their lands and continued to impose the *mita* on them. At a time when the slave plantation system was rapidly taking hold in Cuba, that decision represented a considerable victory for those legally emancipated men, women, and children.[11]

For both Spanish and Portuguese America, quantifying the emancipations obtained by purchase, by either the enslaved or a family member, or granted by a master is an impossible task. Historians only have access to a portion of manumission registers, notarial acts, baptism records, filed complaints, and wills in which emancipations were stipulated, whereas some were not recorded. Furthermore, the countless slaves who unsuccessfully tried to purchase their freedom or that of family members also demonstrated a patient desire for emancipation. That said, according to several case studies, between 75 and 80 percent of slaves who obtained manumission in Iberian America purchased it themselves or received it thanks to payment by a relative. Methods ranged from upfront complete payments to partial loans, payments made in installments, and agreements to continue to work for a master for a set period of time. Only a minority of slaves "received" emancipation from their master during the latter's lifetime or through his will and testament.[12]

And thus slaves in Iberian America who gained their freedom through manumission, even though they represented a small portion of the enslaved population in any given year, helped to increase the number of free Afro-descendants. Many were women whose future children were also born free, in accordance with the principle of *partus sequitur ventrem*. That growth of the free population of color through emancipation troubled authorities to the extent that they began to insist that every child born before his or her mother was emancipated remain enslaved, and then, in contradiction with Roman law, that those born to a *coartada* (partially emancipated) mother be born slaves and not coartados. In farming or mining regions, in which male slaves, often bozales, outnumbered their female counterparts, populations of free Afro-descendants increased also due to marriages or unions between those men and free, Amerindian or black, women: children from those unions were neither slaves nor Amerindians subject to the *mita*.

However, nowhere in the region were *libres de color* liberated of the *mancha de la esclavitud* (stain of slavery). By the end of the sixteenth century, their numbers in Spanish colonies had increased so much that the monarchy wanted to institute a *casta* tribute, which would only apply to free Afro-descendants. But the latter effectively resisted the new tax and, in regions in which free blacks, mulattos, zambos, quadroons, and quinteroons largely outnumbered slaves and represented a significant percentage of the population, such as Venezuela and Colombia, royal civil servants were never able to collect it. Collection of the tax elsewhere was erratic.[13] As a result, thousands of slaves across Spanish continental America were liberated thanks to self-manumission (or purchase by a family member) and emancipation granted by a master. The children and grandchildren of those emancipated slaves were born free and, over time, *castas* marginalized slavery and effectively challenged the tax through which the monarchy wanted to eternally cement their ties to the slave trade and slavery.

Toward the Prohibition of Manumission in British and Dutch America

Unlike those in Iberian America, enslaved men and women in British and Dutch colonies faced increasingly tougher restrictions on manumission and self-purchase. In essence, without a legal framework imposed by colonial powers, colonists could regulate slavery much more freely than could their Spanish and Portuguese counterparts, who had to obey laws dating back to the Iberian Peninsula's recapture from the Muslim. Up until the mid-seventeenth century, enslaved Africans belonging to English colonists in Virginia or Barbados often worked side by side with Irish Catholic indentured workers on tobacco and indigo plantations. Although the majority remained the property of their masters, some Africans participated in the same contractual system as the indentured workers and regained their freedom after five to seven years. Others successfully negotiated purchase of their freedom or that of their children with their masters.[14]

Likewise, in the Dutch colony of New Netherland shortly after the foundation of New Amsterdam (future New York), slavery was not codified. In 1630, its population was composed of approximately three hundred white colonists and sixty slaves, half of whom belonged to the Dutch West India Company. Five years later, the company's slaves sent a petition to its directors in The Hague to demand a salary equivalent to that of white workers, which they obtained. Following that initial success, the enslaved workers continued to send petitions to assert their rights, notably to obtain their freedom or that of their children. They also turned to Dutch courts of law that examined their cases, thereby indicating that the judges recognized slaves' legal capacity, even if their decisions proved unfavorable. Enslaved men and women adopted Christianity, got married in churches, and had their children baptized, logically but incorrectly thinking that their children would be freed from slavery as a result. Others worked relentlessly to liberate themselves or their children, but purchasing freedom remained very costly and was resisted by slaveholders, unless unproductive captives were concerned. Manumission remained possible, however. In 1664, when the English took control of the colony, 20 percent of its 376 Afro-descendants were free.[15]

However, the subsequent increase in slave imports strengthened slavery-related legislation and prompted the majority of Dutch and British colonies to adopt slave codes (often promulgated by a colonial assembly) that limited emancipation in a draconian fashion. In Dutch Suriname, a 1733 law made all manumission contingent on the presentation by a slave's owner of an official demand and on submission of a financial guarantee to ensure that the emancipated slave never had to rely on public charity. Twenty years later, the governor of Curaçao also required that payment of a guarantee of one hundred florins (then equivalent to eighteen months' salary for a Dutch manual laborer) be made for the emancipation of an enslaved man, and half that sum for a woman.[16]

In the majority of British colonies, restrictions were introduced much earlier. Beginning in 1670, only emancipations stipulated in a will or deeds notarized by a slave's owner were authorized. These tended to primarily concern enslaved concubines of deceased masters and their children, and were sometimes supplemented by lifelong pension. Some Quakers were particularly receptive to the message of the founder of the Society of Friends, George Fox, who recommended that his followers evangelize and charitably treat their captives because they were their equals in the eyes of God. For example, Thomas Wardall, in Barbados in 1683, stipulated in his will that "certain of his slaves were to be set free, and that all the children of his slaves born after 9 April 1673 . . . were to be free on attaining thirty-four years of age, provided they were willing to be baptized in the Christian faith."[17] In very rare cases, a slave was emancipated for having played a decisive role in the protection of a white community. In 1675, for example, the Barbados Assembly liberated an enslaved woman who had reported what was then perceived to be a dangerous slave plot; in 1736, Antigua's assembly freed three captives for the same reasons (see chapter 4). But in Virginia, since 1691, any master emancipating a slave also had to pay to transport him or her out of the colony within six months and, in 1723, manumission was limited to particularly deserving slaves and made subject to approval by the governor and the colonial assembly. After 1739, South Carolina forbid emancipation by will and testament, restricting it to notarized deed alone.[18]

Those growing restrictions were also intended to combat the tendency among masters to abandon unproductive captives to public charity. By 1739, Barbados demanded that any master emancipating a slave pay the considerable sum of fifty pounds to his parish, which would then grant an annuity of four pounds to feed and care for the emancipated slave, a contribution avoided by many slaveowners. The Dutch colonies did the same.[19] Laws in New England also increasingly limited manumission by masters and demanded that they pay high fees in the event a freedman or freedwoman became destitute. Already highly infrequent, emancipation became even rarer. Even in Philadelphia, a port town with a large Quaker presence and no direct links to the slave plantation system, only ninety slaves were emancipated between 1698 and 1763, or on average one every nine months, a period during which its enslaved population increased from 213 to 1,375.[20]

Unlike slaves in Iberian America, those in British and Dutch colonies could not contemplate paying a prefixed sum for their freedom or that of a family member. The purchase of a slave's freedom did not appear in existing legislation, though in practice masters sometimes offered a kind of coartación to captives whom they did not directly need. In that case, the slave worked elsewhere for a salary and gave his or her earnings to the owner, ultimately paying his or her market value, in exchange for a deed of manumission. That form of self-liberation remained rare and impacted more enslaved men (particularly artisans considered to be more self-sufficient) than women. Moreover, it invariably depended on the goodwill of a master who could challenge the process until the last minute.[21] Likewise, denunciation of mistreatment by one's master was nearly impossible and could in no case result in emancipation. On the other hand, however, slaves did collectively complain to their master or his representatives of abuse by foremen. For example, in 1738, slaves from a plantation in Barbados set down their tools and went to Bridgetown without permission to file a complaint against their administrator before the planter's lawyers, demanding the former's replacement, more food, clothing, and free time, and that they henceforth be monitored by only two foremen, one white and one black. They agreed to return to work only after their demands had been met.[22]

The Code Noir and Restrictions on Emancipation in French America

Slaves in French colonies also faced growing restrictions on the ways in which they could obtain freedom. In 1660, emancipation and slaves' self-purchase or purchase of another captive's freedom, both entirely unregulated, depended on a master's goodwill. In the patriarchal Antilles, particularly the status of mulattos, born to enslaved African women and French colonists, was at that time considered closer to their fathers' (as free whites) than that of their mothers. But after 1675, the principle of *partus sequitur ventrem* took effect, and it became increasingly difficult for the children of enslaved mothers and white fathers to escape slavery. Furthermore, the Code Noir of 1685 attempted to end concubinage between masters and slaves, decreeing that "the free men who will have one or several children from their concubinage with their slaves, together with the masters who permitted this, will each be condemned to a fine of two thousand pounds of sugar; and if they are the masters of the slave by whom they have had the said children, we wish that beyond the fine, they be deprived of the slave and the children, and that she and they be confiscated for the profit of the [royal] hospital, without ever being manumitted."[23]

However, if the free man in question did not have a lawful spouse during his relationship with his slave, and if he married the latter in accordance with the precepts of the Catholic Church, the enslaved woman would be emancipated and the couple's children declared free and legitimate. The Code Noir did not mention rape of enslaved women by their owners, foremen, or other men, or the fate of possible offspring, as it considered slaves to be "movable property" without the right to own anything, not even their own bodies. Rape, which was widespread, nonetheless—or consequently—contributed to the birth of many mulatto slaves.[24]

The Code Noir only allowed slaves a very slim possibility to purchase their freedom or that of their loved ones since, as personal property, anything they possessed in principle belonged to their masters. They could however be emancipated by an adult master without justification, or with authorization from the latter's parents if he or she was under twenty-six years old. Finally, enslaved "children made universal beneficiaries by their masters, or named executors of their testaments or tutors of their children, will be held and regarded as manumitted," according to an article revealing that this scenario—which contradicted slaves' status as "movable property"—could occur.[25]

After 1685, with the spread of the slave trade to the French Antilles and then Louisiana, restrictions on emancipation multiplied, as they had in English and Dutch colonies. Particularly targeted by these measures were the manumissions of female urban domestics, presumably because they encouraged licentious behavior in white society. Since 1713, a decree mandated that manumissions had to be approved by colonial governors under penalty of the sale of freed individuals to the king's profit. In 1720, another decree required they be officially recorded. Progressively the French colonies imposed a tax on proprietors willing to emancipate a slave, with higher rates for the manumission of a woman than a man, and a fine on masters who freed a slave against payment (self-purchase). Whereas slaves brought to France by their masters had been declared free in the early years of the eighteenth century, a series of royal orders curtailed that avenue to freedom as well. Concubinage between masters and slaves did not cease, and among the manumitted, women continued to outnumber men, but only children of the most stable unions were emancipated by their white fathers, as the rape of enslaved women and girls was regarded by administrators and planters as a right and even a method to control and humiliate slave populations. Yet the new laws were often circumvented, as shown by the multiplication of regulations to prevent the stratagems to skirt them devised by owners and slaves. White men fraudulently emancipated children they had with enslaved women by listing them as free on baptism registries. In other cases, owners liberated slaves by selling them manumission certificates or by accepting their substitution by other slaves. Most importantly, some masters *de facto* manumitted their slaves without formal registration by listing them as *libres de savane* while keeping them as dependents. Finally, in the 1760s, new decrees subjected all acts of emancipation to a tax and governor approval and required that before baptizing a child of color, priests verify the mother's status (free or enslaved) with colonial authorities.[26]

At the same time, the condition of free people of color became more difficult. In his Code Noir, Louis XIV had granted "to manumitted slaves the same rights, privileges and liberties enjoyed by persons born free," meaning full racial equality, without the hereditary "stain" of slavery endorsed by Iberian monarchs. Following the emergence of a class of free mulattos and blacks, however, white planters and royal administrators alike challenged those provisions. Since 1694, free Afro-descendants were counted separately from whites in official censuses and regrouped under the category *gens de couleur libres*. Their rights were increasingly restricted in comparison to those enjoyed by whites, and in 1777, they were even banned from setting foot in France.[27] However, these measures could not stop the increase of the *gens de couleur libres*, mostly due to their natural reproduction and the discreet absorption of *libres de savane*. In Martinique, in 1700 free people of African descent numbered 507, or 7 percent of the free population, but in 1767 they numbered 1,814, or 13 percent of the free residents. In Guadeloupe, in the two same years, they were 239 and 1,162 *libres de couleur*, respectively, but their proportion in the free population remained below 10 percent, mostly because the number of whites multiplied fourfold. Simultaneously, in both islands the enslaved population increased sharply to reach in each of them over seventy thousand men, women, and children by 1767, showing that manumission as a path to freedom had narrowed.[28]

In Saint Domingue, the growth of the *gens de couleur libres* was even more spectacular: from 500 or 11 percent of the free residents in 1700, they rose to 2,456 in 1730, and to 6,180 or 25 percent of the free population in 1767—but during these sixty-seven years the number of enslaved people soared from some 9,000 to 220,000, reducing the proportion of the free among the Afro-descended population by half, from 5 percent to 2.5 percent.[29] This multiplication of the *libres de couleur* surpassed that in other sugar-producing islands for complex reasons. Among them stands out the fact that in Saint Domingue laws on emancipation were not toughened until the Seven Years' War, a delay that allowed for the earlier growth of a free population of color, a small minority of whom became rich slaveowning planters. With a white population in which men outnumbered women five to one until 1730, coerced or consensual concubinage (rather than religious marriage) between white men and enslaved or manumitted women was widespread. As a result, in the early decades of the eighteenth century, more mulattos were free in Saint Domingue than elsewhere in the sugar-producing Caribbean, either because they were born to an emancipated mother or because their father registered them as free at baptism: some therefore belonged to the planter class early on. Other mulattos became free at the death of their father and master if he made them universal beneficiaries. Nevertheless, still others, born of rape or a short-lived relationship between an enslaved mother and a white father, didn't escape slavery: in 1760–92, about 2 percent of Saint Domingue's plantation slaves were mulatto.[30] Manumission was thus a diverse process. As shown by 238 manumission records studied by historian Arlette Gautier in the southern parish of Nippes between 1721 and 1770, 44 percent of the manumitted slaves were concubines and mulatto children freed by white masters, but some mothers and children were emancipated by free blacks. A few were manumitted for caring for their sick master, and some purchased their freedom: a carpenter substituted himself with two male and one female slaves; an enslaved woman paid six hundred livres and an enslaved girl for her manumission. And some slaves purchased the freedom of their parent or child.[31]

Even more so than in the other French Antilles, in Saint Domingue conditions for granting manumission became harder to meet following the establishment of a tax on mulattos' manumission in 1764. This legislation also required that *libres de couleur* provide valid documentation of their freedom—and thus, if they were unable to do so, that they could be reenslaved. By implying that by default a person of African descent was enslaved, the law introduced the equivalent of the stain of slavery, which had been absent from the Code Noir. A few years later, a new regulation required masters to provide "African" names instead of those belonging to the "white race" to slaves they emancipated and to register them under these names to avoid confusion with French or Europeans. In parallel, the racial line between whites and nonwhites of all shades solidified. To their great concern, *gens de couleur libres* were increasingly labeled *affranchis* (manumitted), even though many of them were born free.[32]

Nonetheless, Saint Domingue was already distinguishing itself from other plantation colonies through a unique social phenomenon that would be critical in the lead-up to the Haitian Revolution: a large segment of its free minority was composed of Afro-descendants, many of them the children or grandchildren of slaves emancipated at the start of French colonization, and some, slaveowning planters. Even though the number and proportion of slaves in the population continued to increase at the same time, some free families of color were able to rival the white planter elite through strategic marriages and alliances.[33]

In Louisiana, French colonists relied on bossales later than elsewhere as they first imposed the slavery system on Amerindians only. The first slave ship carrying Africans arrived in 1719 and, until France conceded Louisiana to Spain in 1763, it remained a frontier colony that mirrored the characteristics of the interior regions of Iberian colonies: marronage, unions between African men and Amerindian women, and the growth of a free mixed population (mulattos and *griffes*).[34] As the frontier retreated, many of those maroons and their descendants discreetly blended into free and even "white" populations. But official manumissions remained exceedingly rare; between 1699 and 1765, only four acts of emancipation were recorded in Upper Louisiana.[35] In the 1720s, only two marriages of white men led to the emancipation of their enslaved wives and their children. Two or three free blacks or bossales emancipated for good service were able to purchase the freedom of their enslaved wives. That does not include the case of the slave Louis Congo, who in 1725 accepted a despised appointment as executioner, a role free individuals were loath to take on, in exchange for his freedom, that of his wife, a plot of land, and a ration of wine and liquor. Lacking any alternatives, the colonial council was forced to accept his demands though it never officially emancipated his wife.[36] Nonetheless, in Louisiana as elsewhere, the possibilities for manumission decreased as the plantation system spread and slave imports from Africa increased.[37]

However, after Louisiana passed from French to Spanish control in 1763, slaves were able to free themselves like their counterparts in Spanish colonies, as reveals a study by Kimberly Hanger on New Orleans between 1769 and 1779. Slaves of course continued to flee into hinterlands in search of freedom. But others quickly learned that they could legally purchase their freedom and turn to the courts if their masters refused or set a price that exceeded their market value. As a result, between 1769 and 1779, 198 slaves were able to purchase their freedom alone or with the help of a family member. Fifty of those slaves required the justice system to intercede in their favor, and this figure also reveals French masters' resistance to Spanish laws that were more favorable to slaves than French ones. In addition, 121 women and 120 children were emancipated by their masters, probably as their concubines and the offspring of those illegitimate unions, given the fact that New Orleans counted twice as many white men than white women.[38]

The Louisiana example is therefore the best illustration of the extent to which emancipation depended on legislation, in this case French and then Spanish laws, and also of slaves' aptitude to seize on the legal possibility of freeing themselves as soon as it emerged. Even if owners often flouted the law, the Iberian legal framework favorable to slaves purchasing their freedom and that of their loved ones ensured that, beginning in the sixteenth century, enslaved men and women in Spanish and Portuguese colonies could always obtain emancipation in greater numbers and proportions than those in French, British, and Dutch colonies. As a result, by the early eighteenth century, those vast territories had a free Afro-descended population that was much larger than the white one and, in places where the slave trade had petered out, much larger than the enslaved population.

Military Service and the Road to Freedom

In every slave society, armies and navies historically employed enslaved men, the most valorous of whom were rewarded, sometimes with emancipation. The colonial Americas were no exception, either during the region's conquest or the wars between colonial monarchies.[39] Bozales and ladinos accompanied the Spanish and the Portuguese when they arrived in the Caribbean and on the American continent and then during their wars against Amerindians. Some were not armed, but served as seamen, domestics, porters, pioneers, or sappers. Others, called "black conquerors" by historian Matthew Restall, carried weapons. More than one of those armed slaves obtained manumission through military service. For example, the West African Juan Garrido was originally a slave in the Iberian Peninsula before being sent on the orders of Hernán Cortés to conquer Mexico, where he was emancipated and received a parcel of land in Mexico City for himself, his wife, and their children. Sebastián Toral obtained his freedom for his role in the capture of Yucatán, where he subsequently settled and started a family. In addition to emancipation, the bozal Juan Bardales received a modest pension for his participation in the conquest of Central America. In 1533, Juan Valiente, a slave belonging to a Spaniard living in Puebla, Mexico, was signed up for campaigns to conquer Guatemala by his master. From there he joined, again at his master's behest, Pedro de Alvarado's military expedition of two hundred blacks in search of gold in Peru. Unlike many of his companions, Valiente survived the passage through the Andes. He was then integrated into the Spanish forces that set out to conquer Chile, serving under Juan de Valdivia, who named him a captain with his own horse. Valiente settled in Chile, where he married an enslaved woman emancipated by Valdivia, who also gave him land and, in 1550, an encomienda. Valdivia even tried to obtain his protégé's freedom from royal authorities, but though Valiente died a captain and an *encomendero* several years later, killed in combat by Indians, he legally remained a slave. His son, who was born free, inherited his encomienda.[40]

Since the 1550s, it was less the expanding conquest of the Americas that required military forces than the defense of ports in the Greater Caribbean from attack by English and French pirates and privateers. In particular, the sackings of Santiago de Cuba, by Francis Le Clerc, and Santo Domingo and Cartagena, by Francis Drake, forced the Spanish monarchy to act. It erected fortifications and built moats in all its port towns, which required the labor of countless slaves, and recruited residents to militias and naval guards. During the seventeenth century, confronted by increasing attacks by pirates and buccaneers of diverse origin, Spain created segregated militias of whites, free mulattos and free blacks to serve in its Atlantic and Pacific ports. During attacks, it became unavoidable to also enlist slaves to whom the monarchy promised emancipation if they distinguished themselves by heroic acts in defense of Spain's sovereignty or the lives of its subjects.[41]

Enslaved men were also employed by armies in Brazil to compensate for the lack of soldiers. For instance, the Dutch occupation of Pernambuco from 1630 to 1638 required more men to defend the Portuguese than the small white community could provide and, after much hesitation, the army called on free men of color and slaves "lent" by their masters to bolster their troops. Soldiers of African descent, whether emancipated or enslaved, numbered no more than four hundred, or less than 1 percent of the forty-three thousand slaves then present in the region. But they represented more than a tenth of the Brazilian forces, assembled into a black regiment led by Henrique Dias, the son of emancipated Africans. Among the Angola, Mina, or creole slaves sent into combat with the promise of manumission if they displayed bravery, some obtained their freedom, even if their masters ultimately had to consent to their emancipation, often after being compensated. The black regiment fought so honorably that following the victory over the Netherlands, Dias ensured that it was maintained and that all its enslaved soldiers and officers were freed. After Dias's death in 1662, the black regiment with its black commander remained an active unit in the defense of Pernambuco until the mid-eighteenth century, but the manumission of its slave recruits depended on displays of exceptional courage.[42]

By the end of the seventeenth century, the spread of marronage along the fringes of all colonized territories caused Brazil security problems more pressing than piracy. As shown in chapter 2, faced with a lack of regional police and white colonists' reticence to enlist, the search for and capture of runaway slaves was entrusted to *capitães do mato* who occasionally recruited slaves lent out by their masters as hired men. Thanks to the bonuses they received, those enslaved slave hunters were sometimes able to purchase their freedom thanks to the capture of fugitives. During the gold rush in Minas Gerais, many slaves were also recruited and armed by the pioneering colonists of São Paulo to defend the mines in their possession against rivals arriving from Nordeste and Portugal with their own slaves. Though it did not solve the problem of public order in the region, the arming of slaves by Paulistas and new prospectors provided a growing number of enslaved men a chance to buy their freedom—or run away.[43]

Similarly, the Dutch, after establishing New Amsterdam, were in desperate need of European troops to fight Indians resisting capture of their territory and repel England's hostile claims. In 1640, in addition to free men of color whom they compensated with parcels of land along the threatened frontiers, they also recruited slaves to whom they promised emancipation and occasionally land. That allowed the Dutch to create a buffer zone between white colonists and Amerindians that was defended by free and emancipated blacks. Some slaves consequently obtained their freedom, which they maintained when the region transferred to English control in 1664.[44] The recruitment of slaves conditional on promised manumission was also used to strengthen armies in the French Antilles. For instance, in 1698, during the planning of a naval attack against Cartagena in Colombia, Baron de Pointis stopped in Saint Domingue to gather reinforcements from the governor. The latter was quick to include slaves in the group and, after their victory, he granted freedom and pensions to many of them, who were then enlisted into a company of black and mulatto militiamen.[45]

In reality, however, slave recruitment across the Americas was numerically limited and unconditional manumissions extremely rare. At the same time, measures to prevent men emancipated through armed service from allying with slaves and against their former masters multiplied. Nevertheless, slaves served as soldiers in numerous military conflicts, in addition to those already mentioned:

the defense of Cuban ports against the English in the 1660s; the defense of Antigua against naval attacks related to the Franco-British wars during the first half of the eighteenth century; South Carolina's conflict with the Yamasee, Cherokee, and Creeks in 1715; Louisiana's wars against the Chickasaw and the Choctaw between 1736 and 1741; wars waged against maroons in Jamaica and Suriname; and skirmishes on the American continent and in the Caribbean during the Seven Years' War, among others.[46] Those military experiences enabled some slaves to obtain their freedom, either legally, because they were emancipated, or illegally, by deserting during campaigns and combat. In the particular case of Saint Domingue, a 1775 ordinance offered an alternative to the costly manumission tax: masters who wished to emancipate slaves without paying money could enlist them as drummers in the urban military companies or as slave-soldiers in the fugitive-slave police; after eight to ten years of impeccable service, they would be officially emancipated. White and mulatto masters quickly seized this opportunity, and after 1789 reshaped slave conscription against emancipation at fixed term to serve in their own conflicts (see chapter 6).[47]

One final example of the military recruitment of slaves, in Cuba during the Seven Years' War, reveals a new perception of the slave-soldier, whose sacrifice for the defense of a European monarch or colonial city was incompatible with enslavement. When the British attacked Havana's port in 1762, they relied on a reinforcement unit of two thousand slaves purchased in Jamaica and hundreds more from Martinique, Barbados, Antigua, and other British islands. The Spanish also depended on slaves who belonged to the king or were supplied by planters to better defend their forts, as well as on militias composed of free men of color in Havana. But because Cuba's governor feared that some of those men would defect to the British side, he bought the freedom of a dozen captives belonging to private citizens who had voluntarily taken up arms to defend Spain. Furthermore, he formed a company of a hundred slaves whom he emancipated and placed under the command of white officers, while also promising their masters monetary compensation. Granted, those captives' military service did not prevent the British from occupying the island for eleven months. But once Spanish forces were able to regain control of Cuba, the question of these one hundred or so slaves' freedom and their masters' compensation reemerged. An edict invited concerned slaves and owners to present their requests. In addition, the king of Spain authorized the island's new governor to emancipate additional slaves who had notably distinguished themselves by their courage and sacrifice, most often on the basis of their injuries. In total, 155 enslaved men were publicly declared "free of all submission, captivity, and servitude" and received certificates of emancipation. Moreover, three slaves who had been emancipated but were too seriously injured to work received a small lifelong pension; six were given the status of coartados (partially emancipated). The government compensated owners in cash or in kind (another slave).[48]

≋ Though emancipation did not challenge the system of slavery or slaveholders' property rights, it demonstrated that long before the era of revolutions and independence movements, enslaved men and women were able to pursue freedom for themselves or their families through supplementary labor and the accumulation of savings matching their respective market values. By doing so, they unknowingly foreshadowed modernity. As underlines Caroline Oudin-Bastide, they went from forced unpaid labor to working for themselves as early as the ancien régime, a time when manual labor was still considered the fate of the common people, and to a greater degree, a hereditary stain in the Iberian world. Self-purchase by slaves therefore preempted the modern conception of work as a source of progress and well-being and as a bargaining chip. It transcended Adam Smith's materialist definition, according to which "the real price of every thing, what every thing really costs to the man who wants to acquire it, is the toil and trouble of acquiring it."[49] Enslaved workers who performed additional labor for years on end to emancipate themselves were seeking to acquire not a "thing," but a natural right—freedom.

That process would further develop in the 1780s thanks to the passage of laws gradually abolishing slavery, after which more and more slaves obtained their freedom through their own means or by negotiating contracts with their masters. As for military service in exchange for the promise of freedom, it clearly responded to the lack of free men able or willing to serve in the American colonies. But it also implied a new perception of military slaves as patriots and at times heroes ready to give their lives for their king or city, rather than as personal property. Following that shift, their continued enslavement became irreconcilable with their armed service. As a result, since the 1770s, with the debut of the wars of independence on the American continent, immediate or eventual emancipation (the latter conditional on armed service) would spread. But arming slaves was also a risk as captives could turn against their masters and colonial powers. As shown in the following chapter, slaveowners lived in constant fear of slave plots and violent revolts, though few of them materialized.

≋ 4 ≋
Conspiracy and Revolt
The Most Perilous Paths to Freedom

Up until the age of revolution and independence in the Americas, slaves, like all other exploited classes, rarely revolted against their masters by killing them and destroying their places of work. When they did, it was generally in order to flee rather than an attempt to construct an alternate society that they would dominate and in which they would be free. In reality, lacking support or any challenges to the institution of slavery from other social sectors, the most radical strategy available to slaves was to escape to territories that had not yet been conquered by whites and in which they could establish maroon communities. Those fugitive groups incidentally constituted a permanent threat to several slaveholding societies due to both their ability to attract defiant slaves and their raids on plantations. In parallel, in every American colony until the 1670s, manumission represented a legal way out of slavery through which slaves could hope to gain their freedom without revolting. After that period, only enslaved populations in the Iberian colonies could conceivably hope to be manumitted in large numbers.

Nevertheless, according to many historians, the first 250 years that followed the conquest of the Americas were interspersed with conspiracies and slave revolts. This chapter shows that, in reality, many of those rebellions only existed in the frightened imaginations of colonial elites and numerous whites. European settlers and their descendants, in the minority across the region, lived in fear of an attack by Amerindians or, in the more immediate, a revolt by the enslaved Africans they were importing in growing numbers for domestic labor, construction, mines, and plantations. Amerindians could emerge from interior regions at any time, whereas Africans surrounded their masters, at times even in the intimacy of their own homes. The latter group was particularly threatening to white colonists, who ignored both their captives' language and culture but nonetheless sensed and understood their thirst for freedom. Colonists therefore felt dangerously exposed and poorly protected by troops they continually judged to be insufficient. Within that troubling context, they often transformed slaves' discreet manifestations of discontent into conspiracies that were then lumped together with revolts and cruelly suppressed. Historians had the tendency to take those accounts at face value, arguing that slaves had always been rebels driven by a desire to free themselves at any cost. Yet, a deeper analysis of those conspiracies and revolts reveals that very few of them actually materialized because enslaved men and women knew that success was only possible under exceptional conditions. Generally well informed about the existing balance of power and troop movements, they rebelled violently only when they judged that colonists were particularly vulnerable, and often only did so to flee into interior regions, rather than to destroy white society.

Crime and Punishment according to Colonial Justice

Before studying established rebellions, it is important to note that the laws of the ancien régime did not distinguish between intent and act. Conspiracy, or "an illegal, treasonable, or treacherous plan to harm or destroy another person, group, or entity" could very well be equated with revolt—that is, "an uprising against legitimate authority," as *Webster's Third New International Dictionary* defines it—even if it remained in the preliminary stages. In fact, under the ancien régime, conspiracy was as serious a crime as revolt and prompted similar punishments. Any rebellions against the legitimate authority and violations of the social or familial hierarchy were harshly punished and considered as treason. Thus, *a fortiori,* in colonies in which enslaved men and women were the property of their masters, any act or sign of resistance against their complete submission to the latter became treason. In Great Britain, in particular, between 1351 and 1828, the murder of a superior by a subordinate (a husband by his wife, a father by his child, a master by his servant or apprentice) was considered to be "petty treason" and could be punished by burning at the stake. In British colonies, slave codes reinterpreted that crime when it involved a slave: not only was the murder or attempted murder of a master or overseer by his slave designated as petty treason, but so was the murder of any white by a black individual, which always led to the death penalty. All slaves were regarded as potential traitors whose every misdeed could be interpreted as petty treason. Furthermore, in the case of a revolt or a presumed or proven conspiracy, slaves were considered to have attacked society itself, and by extension the state and the king, and therefore were charged with "high treason."[1]

Incidentally, proof was necessary in every judgment, albeit less material proof than a confession by the accused. However, suspects were presumed to be guilty, and judges were unrestricted when it came to methods of obtaining admissions of guilt. In Iberian and French colonies, accused slaves were judged in the same courts as free citizens. In Spain and its American territories, for example, the defendant's confession was indispensable in a criminal trial; ideally, it would be spontaneous, but if the defendant refused to respond satisfactorily to one or more questions, he or she could be subjected to torture, which was overseen by a judge and entrusted to a "surgeon." The degree of torture was determined by the judge, yet torture victims were considered responsible for their injuries and the loss of their limbs or life, when applicable, because they had had the opportunity to answer the questions asked, whereas royal justice sought only to obtain the truth. If the defendant later refused to repeat a confession given under torture, on the pretext that it had been violently obtained, the judge could subject him or her to torture an additional two times. Technically, documented evidence and consistent statements by two witnesses had to accompany the judge's final ruling. Depending on the gravity of the crime and the defendant's condition, the sentence could be deemed final or submitted for approval by the Royal Audience of the viceroyalty and the possibility of an appeal by either party.[2]

British and Dutch colonies established special courts of law for slaves since the 1660s, which relied on expedited trials and lacked an appeals process; when a conspiracy or slave rebellion was discovered, emergency courts were rapidly formed by judges who were often voluntary, and without juries. The latitude taken by judge-planters when quelling attempted slave plots was considerable: in 1696, the Jamaica Assembly approved a decree stipulating that, for one or more enslaved individuals, "imagining the death of a white person" was a crime punishable by death. In 1744, the same assembly confirmed that decree while specifying that the imaginary crime should be judged as "a crime of as high nature as the crime of murder, and should be punished as such."[3] Since British slave laws did not allow testimony by slaves, it sufficed for a white prosecution witness to convince the judges in order for a slave to be subjected to torture, judged guilty, and sentenced for conspiracy or revolt. In cases where there were no white witnesses, special laws could be adopted, as occurred in New York in 1741, when a "Negro evidence" law allowed one slave to testify against another, generally with the promise of a reduced punishment. Furthermore, torture served less to obtain confessions from the slave who stood accused without a legal personality, than the names of his or her accomplices. In several cases of conspiracy, the accusation, interrogation, sentencing, and execution of suspects occurred in almost immediate succession, creating a weeks- or months-long atmosphere of terror among slaves and Afro-descendants in general, and of communal vengeance among whites. Arrest would follow arrest in rhythm with forced denunciations and public executions that were as horrific as possible, followed by the public display of the heads and limbs of torture victims for weeks in public places and on plantations.[4] Throughout the Americas, a conspiracy with no material consequences and a revolt that caused death and destruction both led to a death sentence for treason.

In addition, until the 1760s, written accounts of those events were almost exclusively produced by judges, colonial civil servants, and members of the local elite. They therefore do not allow historians to reconstruct much more than the context and script of the discovery and suppression of a given conspiracy. The question of said conspiracy's existence—of knowing whether the men and women tortured, executed, whipped, or sold to other colonies were actually preparing to attack whites in order to create a new society without them, if they were simply collectively dreaming of a world in which the balance of power was reversed, or if these plans were merely the reflection of their masters' anxieties—often remains unanswered.[5]

At the same time, many isolated and local slave revolts were not reported to colonial authorities and therefore escaped historians' attention. In America, even more so than in Europe, justice was not uniform. Public servants were restricted to cities, and slavemasters and their deputies often handled criminal cases and maintained public order in a quasi-judicial but exemplary fashion by subjecting slaves presumed to be guilty to endless whippings, mutilation, detention in the stocks, the wearing of yokes, muzzles, chains, shackles, and other weights, or execution. Although the Spanish *Siete Partidas* and the French Code Noir had prohibited overseers and owners from executing or mutilating their slaves, abusers were rarely prosecuted and almost never sentenced. Moreover, forces of order and judicial representatives were not numerous or efficient enough to ensure that such laws were respected on plantations, in rural areas, and even in cities. In the British colonies, the Bill of Rights of 1689 did not protect slaves because it did not consider them individuals with legal rights, and slave laws granted great freedom to masters to punish any crime or misconduct by a slave. The first codes in effect in Barbados and Jamaica in the 1660s were limited to stipulating that owners could not kill their slaves "without reason," but if need be exempted them of all responsibility before the law. The Jamaican slave code of 1696, which remained nearly unchanged until 1788, imposed a minor punishment on masters who caused the "willing, wanton, or bloody-minded" killing of a slave but did not address the case of captives who died following excessive punishment. In 1717, a modification to the law specified that any master who "dismembered" a slave be subject to a fine.[6] In reality, as historian Diana Paton notes, the majority of offences committed by slaves were punished outside the system of law, unless they involved a conspiracy or large revolt, situations causing the loss of slaves for which the owner demanded compensation, a conflict between masters, or when a master wanted to reinforce his authority by applying a severe punishment formalized by a court of law. These observations about Jamaica can easily be extended to the entirety of the British, French, Dutch, and Iberian colonies.[7]

The image of revolts and conspiracies that therefore emerges from my comparative study takes into equal account the overestimation of plots, generally uncovered in capital cities, and the underestimation of minor rebellions that sporadically broke out in areas more or less distant from colonial administrative centers. It also takes the evolution of each colony concerned into account.

Fears and Rumors before 1700: The Making of a Slave Conspiracy Narrative

The first slave conspiracy recorded by historiography, in Mexico City in 1537, already had elements of a narrative that would be repeated in subsequent centuries and with increasing frequency since 1730. Discovered under torture before it could be carried out, the plot supposedly entailed a revolt by city slaves against whites. According to the report presented by the viceroy of Mexico, Antonio de Mendoza, to King Charles I, one of the conspirators had told him that "the blacks" had chosen their own king and decided to kill all the Spaniards in Mexico City and seize their lands with the help of local Indians. The viceroy subsequently arrested and questioned many blacks, who confirmed the conspiracy's existence, whereas the Indians interrogated seemed to know nothing about it. Mendoza also tasked spies with investigating in other cities and in mines; he asked the Spanish people to be on their guard and to arrest or kill any suspicious black individuals. At the same time, he had five Africans considered to be the leaders of the presumed plot (four men and one woman) brought to the mines and handed them over to Indians to be executed, and "with this the matter was brought to an end."[8] However, the viceroy informed the king of Spain that the conspiracy had developed because blacks and Indians closely monitored the news about the wars troubling the kingdom to the extent that, according to certain rumors, no Spanish ship would be able to reach Mexico for another ten years. The viceroy therefore recommended that His Majesty control the content of news heading for the Americas and to rapidly send a ship to Mexico to demonstrate his power.

Mendoza's report clearly demonstrates, as others too would subsequently do, how difficult it is for historians to establish the existence of conspiracies using official documents often based on statements that were obtained under torture and were intended to reassure the Spanish monarch about the zeal of his viceroys in America. This report also attests to the atmosphere of isolation and fear in which a small colonial elite was living approximately fifteen years after the defeat of the Aztec Empire. Finally, it shows that some slaves monitored the news of the day, noting and sometimes interpreting to their advantage any weakness among colonial forces in the hope of using the opportunity to improve their living conditions, even possibly, when a plot truly existed, to overthrow those in power. After 1537, Mexico gradually ended its enslavement of Indians and increased its slave imports from Africa; from the end of the sixteenth century to 1610, in particular, between two thousand and six thousand captives were brought to the Spanish colony every year, three times as many as the number of immigrants arriving from Spain. Though sold in various regions, Mexico City absorbed a large number of those bozales. As a result, slaves in the city outnumbered the Spanish, among whom fears of a slave revolt were growing. In 1608, authorities believed they had discovered a new conspiracy among enslaved and free blacks before concluding that it was merely an intoxicated Christmas celebration whose participants had shown "too much freedom and insolence" in electing and crowning a king and queen.[9]

But three years later, also in Mexico City, after two Portuguese slave traders revealed that they had interrupted a conversation during which a slave spoke about killing all the Spanish colonists on Easter Day in 1612, the government concluded that a slave plot truly was under way. The black *Cofradía de Nuestra Señora* (Brotherhood of Our Lady), one of whose enslaved members had died as the result of abuse inflicted by her master, figured at the center of the accusations. During her funeral, slaves and *libres de color* belonging to the brotherhood had publicly expressed their outrage; some protesters were arrested, whipped, and sold outside the city. Shocked by that repression, other slaves allegedly plotted an uprising. Law officials proceeded to make preventative arrests of the leaders of all the black brotherhoods in Mexico City, then, as revelations and confessions multiplied, placed the city's entire black population under surveillance and ordered countless detentions. Subsequently, every action taken in preparation for the 1612 Carnival by the *Cofradía de Nuestra Señora* and its members became suspect in the eyes of the authorities.[10] The brotherhood's election of a royal couple, composed of a free mulatto man and his enslaved wife, for Carnival was equated to the coronation of a new black power that the conspirators wanted to establish. And the funds it collected were supposedly not destined to help the brotherhood's members or finance the Carnival celebrations, as indicated in its statutes, but to purchase weapons to kill white men and pillage their homes, while keeping their wives alive. Once subjected to torture, the accused revealed a plot and weapons caches. Following an expedited trial, thirty-five of the defendants (including seven women) were hanged and their bodies decapitated and dismembered for public display; others were flagellated and sold abroad. The viceroy imposed a curfew on all free and enslaved blacks, banned their brotherhoods, limited their presence at funerals, and established the punishment for any transgressors as one hundred to two hundred whiplashes and forced labor in Mexico or the Philippines.[11] Like the plot of 1537, it is impossible to determine if, in 1612, slaves in Mexico City were truly preparing a general uprising with the goal of establishing a black kingdom. However, it is certain that, from the moment they were established, black brotherhoods provided advantageous meeting sites where recently arrived Africans, creole slaves, and *libres de color* could meet and organize in a place shielded from whites. Royal authorities consistently viewed those associations with ambivalence, both encouraging and fearing them, an attitude reflected by policies alternating between encouragement and interdiction.

On the French islands of Martinique and Guadeloupe and in Dutch Suriname, a fear of slave uprisings also developed during the seventeenth century with the arrival of new captives and the spread of marronage. As elsewhere, slave escape attempts were often accompanied by violence, though rebels did not directly attack centers of colonial power.[12] Yet it was in the British colony of Barbados that the terror felt by whites had its bloodiest repercussions. This small island, one of the first to adopt the slave sugar plantation model, was at the time the most profitable of the British colonies. In the mid-seventeenth century, its rural labor force consisted of indentured workers (who were often Irish Catholics) and enslaved Africans. Then, every year between 1661 and 1675, Barbados imported between 1,000 and 6,500 slaves from Africa, who grew to represent more than two-thirds of its population and were monopolized by a few large English owners; other marginalized plantation owners left with their slaves to colonize South Carolina.[13] The rapid expansion of the sugar plantation on this flat island had led to the destruction of nearly all its forests, making marronage extremely difficult. At the same time, authorities had restricted the possibilities of emancipation so much that it became practically inaccessible.

In 1675, a domestic slave told her master, a judge, about a conspiracy of predominantly Akan slaves to transform Barbados into an African kingdom. The plot supposedly entailed several clearly defined stages: after choosing a king, an Akan who went by the slave name Cuffee, the captives intended to burn down sugarcane fields and cut their masters' throats at each plantation, all while sparing the most beautiful white women for their own pleasure. The governor immediately declared martial law, after which some one hundred suspected slaves were arrested, including seventeen sentenced to death on the spot: six were burned alive and eleven decapitated before their bodies were dragged through the town that was the presumed center of the conspiracy and burned in its main square. Although none of the supposed conspirators had confessed, the crackdown entered a second phase called "Tony's plot," named after a slave belonging to a Jewish plantation owner (an aggravating factor at the time), who, on the stake, exhorted the other torture victims to die without giving the names of other slaves, as doing so would not spare their own lives but would further increase the number of those sentenced to death. During this phase, twenty-five more captives were executed and six committed suicide in prison.[14] Like in the cases of the Mexican conspiracies, it is impossible to distinguish what the judges believed was the planned uprising from what the suspected slaves hoped to achieve, as the former were subjected to torture and prevented by law from serving as simple witnesses or benefiting from a defense. In any case, these forty-two executions were all quite real.

Seventeen years later, in September 1692, the English elite of Barbados preemptively thwarted another putative slave uprising with renewed cruelty. In the interim, imports of African captives had increased, and the proportion of slaves in the island's population had reached nearly 80 percent. Furthermore, the white and Protestant minority was increasingly affected by the "panic of the Irish night," which spread from England after the Catholic kings Louis XIV and James II failed to reconquer Ireland from William of Orange in 1690. Rumors of attacks and conspiracies by "barbarian and fanatical" Irish Catholics circulated as far as the Caribbean, where the French and British navies were fighting each other, and blended with rumors of slave conspiracies.[15] At the end of 1691, within that anxiety-provoking context, witnesses overheard a suspicious conversation between two slaves, Ben and Sambo, which seemed to indicate the enslaved population of Barbados was preparing an uprising. Both men were arrested immediately, and a third slave, Hammon, joined them in prison. In exchange for the promise of sparing his life if he confessed his involvement, Hammon admitted to having initiated the plot and implicated Ben, Sambo, and a fourth conspirator, Samson. Shortly thereafter, a martial court condemned all three men to be hung alive from chains until they died of hunger and thirst, after which their decapitated heads would be placed on a pole and their bodies cut into pieces and burned to ashes. Samson died quickly, but the other two slaves, still alive four days after the torture began, were taken down and ordered to give the plot participants' names. Sambo died before saying anything, but Ben provided a number of names.[16]

Local judges subsequently had between two hundred and three hundred slaves from various plantations southwest of Bridgetown arrested and crammed into improvised jails and interrogated, often under torture, until an outline of the conspiracy emerged. According to the magistrates, the plotters were not Africans but creole slaves, mostly artisans, coachmen, and right-hand men who wanted to take advantage of the unrest in England and had been scheming for three years. They had supposedly planned on first killing their masters, then seizing their weapons and setting several plantations on fire, and finally advancing on Bridgetown to occupy the town's forts and burn the ships still in port. The conspirators had reportedly gained the trust of an enslaved man working in the arsenal, who was meant to provide them with powder and guns; they also hoped to benefit from the support of four or five Irish Catholics who planned to infiltrate and neutralize the militia; then the plotters intended to kill the governor and officers and take control of the island. Their goal was not to free all the slaves, but to supplant white colonists while taking their women as wives and Africans as captives, and electing one of the plotters as governor. They supposedly had had to delay their uprising several times, as they were waiting for the British navy to leave the island before taking action. Finally, the plotters had supposedly chosen fall of 1692, when the fleet was to have left for Martinique, to revolt, but the arrest of Ben and Sambo derailed their plans.[17] During the trials held for the second group of suspects, judges sentenced ninety-two additional slaves to hanging or burning at the stake and denied them burial (their bodies were cast at sea); forty-two were sentenced to castration. All slaveholders received compensation for their losses in human capital. If planters were reassured by that mass crackdown, which was also intended to terrorize their slaves, they also had to come to terms with being defended by a reduced militia from which blacks would henceforth be excluded, even as servants.[18]

The implausible conspiracies in Mexico City in 1537 and Barbados in 1675 and 1692 were not isolated incidents, though their repression was particularly cruel to slaves. As the number and proportion of captives in American societies grew, colonial powers brought new conspiracies or attempted slave uprisings to light. Sometimes, slaveowning planters themselves started rumors of such plots in order to thwart royal policies they viewed as running counter to their interests.[19]

Mutinies and Revolts through the Prism of the Slave Conspiracy Narrative

Even if accusations of conspiracies were unfounded in most cases, captives nonetheless faced worsening conditions of enslavement. Since the late seventeenth century, escape attempts and periodic rebellions multiplied, though far from cities, in new farming regions, many of which were undoubtedly quelled on the spot leaving little or no archival traces. However, as long as those sporadic uprisings did not erupt in centers of colonial power, they did not alarm elites. That was not the case when a group of slaves rebelled in New York, in 1712, at a time when the city's population was growing rapidly and had reached 5,800 inhabitants, nearly one-fifth of whom were slaves. One night in April 1712, between twenty-five and fifty enslaved men and women, armed with axes, knives, and rifles, set fire to a bakery belonging to one of their owners and attacked the whites who attempted to extinguish the blaze, leaving at least nine dead and six injured, and fled. The governor mobilized the militia and the garrison, which captured twenty-seven fugitives; six slaves killed themselves before being caught. New Yorkers convinced themselves that the rebels had been planning to reduce the city to ashes and massacre all its white inhabitants. The punishment was commensurate to that belief. Over seventy slaves were arrested and forty-three judged by five magistrates. Although eighteen were acquitted, the remaining twenty-five were all sentenced to death, five of whom were subjected to terrible torture. Among those convicted, a pregnant woman was kept alive until the birth of her baby—a slave—after which she was hanged.

Shortly thereafter, the New York legislature approved several laws that made manumission practically impossible, banned gatherings of more than three slaves, allowed masters to punish their slaves as they wanted as long as they did not kill or amputate them, decreed a slow death by torture for slaves convicted of murder, rape, arson, or assault, and excluded the small minority of free blacks from owning land. The crackdown nonetheless prompted some questions. In particular, the colony's governor was shocked by the increased number of executions, noting "that in the West Indies where their laws against their slaves are most severe, . . . in the case of a conspiracy in which many are engaged a few only are executed for an example."[20] When he made those statements, the governor was undoubtedly unaware of the repression of the two presumed conspiracies in Barbados in 1675 and 1692 mentioned above, which had led to, respectively, forty-two and ninety-five death sentences. And yet, the belief held by New York's white inhabitants that the violent rebellion of a small group of slaves in 1712 marked the beginning of a conspiracy in which they would all be massacred revealed, as was the case earlier in Barbados, how the continuous arrival of new black captives exacerbated their fear that the inhumane system of slavery would turn against them.

With the ever-rapid growth of slavery, especially after 1730, that anxiety-producing climate intensified, for multiple reasons. First, the territorial expansion of plantations increasingly limited possibilities for slaves' escape and marronage. Emancipation had also become nearly impossible in British, French, and Dutch colonies, which augmented the feeling of injustice among captives. Furthermore, with the slave trade's growth until the start of the Seven Years' War, tens of thousands of Africans were brought to the colonies each year, engendering more and more brutal exploitation that threatened slaves' survival. At the same time, whites, increasingly in the minority, constantly felt under threat. Any meeting or discussion between slaves outside the supervision of an overseer could cast suspicion on the former: white communities found songs and conversations in African or creole languages, laughter and angry shouting, funerals, dances, celebrations, drumming and conch blowing—displays typically occurring at night or on Sundays—difficult to understand and frightening. In addition, between 1729 and 1739, the monarchies of Western Europe were not waging war on the Old Continent, which translated to a decrease in armies and a certain cultural effervescence. The elites of their American colonies took advantage of that peaceful lull to gain additional autonomy and profit financially, often thanks to labor provided by constantly growing slave populations, but were also concerned about the diminution of colonial troops.

Sporadic slave mutinies and uprisings broke out in that context in Brazil,

Jamaica, Dominica, Guadeloupe and Martinique, Cuba, the Bahamas, and Virginia, among others. They generally ended in executions, whippings, and often escape by some of the insurgents toward marronage regions. Some necessitated the intervention of colonial forces, like in Tadó, in the Chocó region of Colombia, in 1728, when a few dozen slaves from an alluvial mine rebelled against abuses by their Spanish overseer, whom they killed before spreading terror in other mines, causing fifteen deaths among whites. The governor was forced to dispatch troops, whose commander lured four ringleaders with the false promise of negotiations only to execute them. The other rebels returned to their mines or disappeared into the forests as runaways.[21]

More frightening from the colonists' point of view was the Akan-led uprising that began on 23 November 1733 on St. John, one of the Dutch Virgin Islands, as it was able to rapidly spread across this tiny territory measuring less than twenty square miles, where one thousand enslaved Africans were facing two hundred whites. As a result, the rebellion revived the scenario, much feared among slaveowners, of the massacre of whites to establish a black kingdom. In this case, the rebels began by seizing the fort in Coral Bay, killing or injuring six guards, then shot off a round of cannon fire to signal their counterparts on neighboring plantations to rise up in turn. The next day, the rebels, perhaps as many as eighty, who were armed with weapons taken from the fort, had killed several whites, regardless of age or sex, and set fire to local estates. Some colonists had nonetheless succeeded in taking refuge on the neighboring Danish island of St. Thomas, from where soldiers and militiamen came to reestablish order. The latter captured several insurgents who, when tortured, confessed to an elaborate plan for rebellion: the rebels were supposedly all descended from the same Akan kingdom in which some had held high positions; guided by a royal couple, they wanted to supplant whites, while dividing the island's plantations between themselves to continue to exploit slaves of other ethnic groups; they expected Akans on St. Thomas and Tortola to rebel as well. In March 1734, despite several executions, the Danish still had not taken back full control of the small island of St. John and were forced to call on French troops in Martinique to overcome the rebels. In all, the uprising lasted six months and cost the lives of approximately forty whites, compared to two hundred slaves who were killed or horrifically executed or who committed suicide.[22]

Distorted accounts of the St. John revolt rapidly spread to Caribbean and North American ports. A Charleston gazette, for example, was quick to announce that the rebels had "massacred all the white People on that Island" and then, one week later, that a military expedition had successfully executed or "cut [the rebels] all to pieces."[23] In fact, the revolt had led to a seizure of power by slaves who may have hoped to regain the stature they once held in the Gold Coast before their kingdom was defeated and they were sold to slave traders.

Given that they were confined to an extremely small island and limited to one ethnic group, the insurgents could not resist for long. Nonetheless, the St. John uprising provided a concrete example of what enslaved rebels could accomplish and thus fostered fears of slave plots.

Incidentally, that agitated context coincided with the first questions to emerge about the compatibility of the enslavement of Africans with Christianity, in both the Americas and Europe, particularly among Quakers, who rejected all religious dogmas and hierarchical structures in favor of personal experiences with God through humanist practices.[24] Those criticisms angered slaveowners and provoked at times violent conflicts between whites, but also entered the awareness of certain slaves as a result. Some captives subsequently used those arguments to attack the institution of slavery itself, prompting rumors about the promulgation of a royal decree of general emancipation or the possibility that Christian baptism could bring about one's freedom. Whites then began to equate new forms of slave protests with conspiracies that were intended to kill them all and that therefore necessitated exemplary punishments.

For example, in 1730 in Virginia, slaves from the counties of Norfolk and Princess Ann circulated a rumor that the king of Great Britain had ordered slaveowners to free their captives once they were baptized but that masters were refusing to comply. The rumor was not completely unfounded: since 1724, the Church of England and the Bishop of London had asked planters to evangelize their slaves. In fact, in 1728, in response to slaveholders' fears, British courts had to specify that a slave remained a slave even when on British or Irish soil, and that baptism could neither liberate nor alter a slave's temporal condition. Slaves had overheard portions of their masters' heated conversations on that subject, and on the basis of that knowledge they widely speculated about the possible liberating effects of baptism. The governor ordered a first round of arrests followed by lashings, but could not stop those rumors from spreading. After the discovery of a "plot" in which slaves had reportedly chosen their leaders and were preparing to act on a Sunday while colonists were at church, four enslaved men were executed and many more publicly lashed. Undiscouraged, the slaves dispatched a free black emissary to London to request freedom from the king, but he was discovered as a clandestine passenger aboard a ship heading to Philadelphia, arrested, and led through the concerned Virginia counties to be systematically whipped in front of slaves.[25]

A similar rumor circulated among many slaves in a New Jersey county in 1734, according to which the governor of New York had been ordered by George II to free all slaves, but was prevented from doing so by his council and the colonial assemblies. Local authorities arrested some thirty suspects, who confessed under torture to having conspired during a heavy drinking binge. Each conspirator was supposedly meant to slit the throats of his master and master's sons at midnight, while sparing any women for his own pleasure, set fire to houses and barns, and take the best horses to flee to French territory among the Amerindians. After a rapid trial that linked this case to the 1712 uprising in New York and the 1733 one on St. John's Island, one of the alleged conspirators was hanged; others had their ears cut off or were whipped.[26] In both the New Jersey and Virginia cases, the colonial authorities' excessive repression demonstrated their clear understanding of the subversive reach of rumors spread by accused slaves: by framing baptism as an act of liberation for the new believer, captives revealed slavery's incompatibility with Christianity, an incompatibility also denounced by some Protestants. In addition, by claiming that the king of Great Britain had himself decreed that baptized slaves be freed, they transformed a rumor into an act of obedience to a supreme authority that was flouted by their masters. In doing so, they also attacked the legitimacy of slavery by invoking the authority of God and the king, to which even their masters were bound.

In 1735, slaves in Mexico similarly invoked a rumored royal decree of emancipation to demand their freedom in the sugar plantation region of Córdoba, southwest of Veracruz, where marronage was endemic. The triggering incident was the authorities' refusal, under pressure from the region's planters, to amnesty and emancipate runaway slaves who turned themselves in, as had taken place in Yanga. According to slaveowners, those fugitives then mobilized enslaved plantation workers and recruited a free mulatto to spread the rumor that the king of Spain had decreed the freedom of all the slaves in Mexico but that the hacendados had refused to obey. In June 1735, the slaves from one sugar hacienda rebelled, and were rapidly joined by others. In just one day, five hundred men and a few women, representing one-third of the region's captives, had abandoned their work and resorted to violence. Others arrived from neighboring districts and the number of rebelling slaves reached nearly two thousand; they set plantations on fire, destroyed haciendas and materials, stole, and killed whites. Despite the mobilization of the local militia and the arrival of reinforcements, order was not reestablished until several months later, leaving no historical record of the exact number of victims, those convicted, and the slaves who were able to join the runaways in the mountains.[27]

As the belief in a royal decree of liberation spread among enslaved populations and at times prompted rebellions, the fear of a slave conspiracy whose purported goal was to massacre whites and burn down plantations and towns to establish a black kingdom took hold in the white population. The result was a clear cycle of slave complaints and supposed plots, punctuated by a few concrete uprisings whose common denominator was a subsequent wave of repression against slaves by colonial authorities and plantation owners.

An Orgy of Fire, Blood, and Torture

Beginning in 1730, suspected plots were uncovered every year, and in various locations, in Iberian, British, French, Dutch, and Danish colonies. Therefore judges were equipped with a preexisting list of interrogation questions, and slaves had a frame of reference that allowed them to imagine their liberation—and the responses to give under torture. Though it remains difficult to establish the existence of the numerous conspiracies noted during this period, a widespread and shared context was fostering the emergence of what whites then referred to as "slaves' uncontrolled insolence."

In 1731, colonists in Louisiana unmasked a so-called conspiracy among enslaved Bambaras who supposedly planned to gain their freedom by massacring all whites and then dominate the colony while keeping non-Bambaras as slaves. Detected before it could take place, the plot remains doubtful, but its suppression was quite real, as it led to eight men being broken on the wheel and one woman being hanged.[28] Even in Montreal, in New France, the burning of a hospital and several houses in 1734 led to the enslaved Angélique, who ran away when her sale was announced, of being accused of the crime. She was hanged and her body burned, leaving the question of her guilt unanswered.[29]

The discovery of a possible slave conspiracy in Antigua, in 1736, brought colonial barbarism to its peak. According to David Gaspar, the historian who in 1985 carefully studied the plot, it was "a well-organized, islandwide affair . . . [that], had it succeeded, would have catapulted Antigua onto the stage of world history as the first territory in the slave heartland of the Caribbean in which slaves seized full control."[30] But apart from declarations by white witnesses and slaves who were tortured and trying to avoid death by confessing, there were no concrete signs of an uprising: no whites were murdered, no property was destroyed, and no hidden weapons or gunpowder were discovered. More recently, Jason Sharples's analysis of the process of accusing and imprisoning the slaves involved and how the details of the conspiracy were determined has called Gaspar's assertion into question.[31] In reality, it appears that the conspiracy was first and foremost the manifestation of magistrates' fears during a period in which the number of slaves rose from 19,800 in 1724 to 24,400 in 1734, at the same time that the white population, massed together in the small island's two ports, fell from 5,200 to 3,800.[32]

According to the judges' report, the 1736 conspiracy planned for "all the white Inhabitants . . . to be murdered, & a new form of Government . . . Established, by the Slaves, among themselves, and they intirely to possess the Island." The accused slaves had reportedly intended to begin their attack in the capital, St. John's, on 11 October, when Antigua's elite would be celebrating the anniversary of King George II's coronation with a ball. The plot's leader was supposedly an enslaved Akan named Court, alias Tackey, who had been secretly crowned king by other slaves to the sounds of drums, conches, and trumpets several months earlier. His main accomplice was an enslaved creole carpenter, Tomboy, who was meant to have taken advantage of being tasked with creating chairs for the ballroom to smuggle in cannon powder and "to blow up all the Gentry of the Island" as they danced. In the resulting confusion, three or four units of a few hundred slaves would enter St. John's via diverse points and "put all the white people there to the Sword." The rebels would then occupy several forts and arsenals, as well as all the ships in the port. They would signal slaves on the rest of the island to advance toward St. John's, "destroying all in their way."[33] The participants had reportedly prepared their takeover for months, but had been thrown off balance when the ball of Antigua's elite was postponed to 30 October. Whereas Tomboy had supposedly advised to launch the revolt no matter the cost on 11 October, Court succeeded in convincing the others to wait for the ball to take place. The conspiracy was not denounced by one of its participants: it was the slaves' growing "insolence" that shocked the island's white inhabitants.[34]

Suspicions of the plot were sparked by the shocked testimony of a white woman who claimed that during a public whipping of slaves arrested for gambling, some captives had expressed their support for the convicted individuals while referring to them as "Our Officers & Soldiers." On 11 October 1736, Robert Arbuthnot and two other justices of the peace had those slaves interrogated and ordered that one hundred whiplashes be immediately administered to them in St. John's in public view. At the same time, the magistrates sounded the alert and sent agents to search the lodgings of all the town's black inhabitants and to apprehend any suspects. Some slaves were arrested for having mocked or criticized the lashings, others because witnesses had heard them talking about gunpowder, weapons, or drums. All the imprisoned slaves maintained their ignorance about the preparation of a conspiracy, but the judges' attention focused on slaves who had mocked the whippings and those who had endured them without flinching. On 12 October, Arbuthnot interrogated a cooperative Portuguese slave named Emanuel, who stated that indeed slaves "were grown very Impudent" and gave details about the majestic clothes and the horse that Court, the conspiracy's presumed leader, supposedly owned. Testimonies by whites also accumulated against Court, to the surprise of his master, whom he had served faithfully for thirty years. On 15 October, the Antigua Assembly approved a motion "to Restrain and Curb the Insolent behavior and Tumultuous Meeting of Slaves" and designated four special judges, including Arbuthnot, to investigate the alleged plot and hold a closed-door trial. The assembly then offered monetary rewards for any denunciations that led to the arrest of suspects, on whom the judges were authorized to inflict "pains or tortures not extending to Loss of life or limb."[35]

Between 20 and 27 October, primarily on the basis of Emanuel's statements, an initial twelve slaves were publicly executed. Court, who was sentenced to quartering, had admitted to his crimes an hour after his torture began. After his death, he was decapitated, his head displayed on a high post in front of the town prison, and his body burned. The next day, Tomboy was tortured and confessed in prison that very morning. He was also quartered, but endured more than thirty-five strokes of an iron rod to his chest before dying four hours later. A third slave was subjected to the same prolonged torture. Their decapitated heads joined Court's. On 22 October, four slaves chained together were burned alive at the stake. And on 27 October, another five men were subjected to the same fate.[36] But the judges, convinced that the torture victims' confessions remained incomplete, continued their arrests. Faced with suspects' resistance, they decreed that quartering and burning at the stake were punishments "too lenitive and not Sufficiently Exemplary because the Criminals were not long enough under their Sufferings." In early November, six convicts were therefore suspended alive from iron cuffs in cages facing one another in the public square so they "cou'd see and speak to one another" "in Order to produce Discovery's" during their drawn-out deaths from hunger and thirst. One of them slipped through his cuffs on the sixth day, was resuscitated and kept in prison for one night, and was then suspended again until he died. After their deaths, all the captives were decapitated, their heads displayed in front of their plantation until they decomposed, and their bodies burned. But during their weeklong ordeal, they had provided names that led to additional arrests. On 15 November, a new wave of public executions was conducted, during which one slave was quartered and seven others burned alive. On 27 November, eight other slaves died at the stake. The judges then launched a third round of arrests and interrogations, after which they sentenced another thirteen slaves to be burned alive before Christmas. Exhausted by those efforts, which they deemed detrimental to their personal affairs, they transferred the investigation to other magistrates charged with continuing it.[37]

The year 1737 began in Antigua with another quartering, which was followed by twelve executions at the stake four days later. Detentions and public executions continued, with nine men burned alive on 15 January, eight on 18 February, and, finally, eleven on 8 March. In total, in that orgy of fire, blood, and torture, eighty-eight slaves were executed in four months, seventy-seven at the stake, six hanged alive, and five quartered. In addition, thirty-seven slaves were banned and sold in Virginia and Hispaniola. Three particularly cooperative slaves, including Emanuel, were freed for their services and given a small monthly pension. Yet no properties had been set on fire and no whites had been killed. The Assembly was then confronted with the high cost of those four months of repression: because practically every slave executed or banished, and the three acquitted and freed had been valuable artisans, coach drivers, or foremen, it was forced to compensate slaveowners for their losses. Faced with planters' refusal to accept a supplementary tax, it borrowed the money. Nonetheless, the horrendous executions had begun to shock some observers in Antigua itself, prompting one observer to write to the island's governor in January 1737: "The Burning of the Negroes, hanging them on Gibbets alive, Racking them upon the wheel, & c. takes up almost all our Time, that from the 20th of October [1736] to this Day, there have been destroyed Sixty fine sensible Negroe Men, most of them Tradesmen, as Carpenters, Masons, and Coopers. I am almost dead with watching and warding as are many more."[38]

News of events in Antigua also reached London, where a gazette questioned why Antiguans had not sold the most important conspirators as slaves to mines in Spanish colonies rather than "to put so many to Death for a Crime, which (if we may guess by what has lately come from the Press) will be deem'd a Pitch of Virtue by not a few in our Mother Nation."[39] Quite timidly, some criticisms of the barbarism of slavery started to emerge among whites in both the colonies and Great Britain.

At the same time, rumors of slave uprisings continued to circulate. In December 1736, not far from Antigua, on the western coast of Guadeloupe's Grande-Terre, the news spread that maroons were coming to free slaves, kill whites, and burn down plantations. Authorities carried out preemptive arrests, and tortured slaves confessed that a plan to revolt was in place for Christmas. Several supposed ringleaders were then hanged, but some slaves were able to flee north of Basse-Terre, where maroon bands had taken refuge. Those runaways were reported to have abducted and devoured a white child as revenge. Search-and-sweep operations led to the arrest of some one hundred suspected maroons and slaves who underwent expedited trials in early 1738. Several of them (perhaps sixteen in all) were sentenced to the wheel or hanging, and numerous others to whippings, the stocks, and hot iron branding. But according to historian Lucien-René Abenon, the repression primarily targeted the maroon bands proliferating at the time, whereas Oruno Lara, writing in 1921, suggests that the cannibalistic act was added after the fact to justify executions that many settlers considered excessive.[40] Once again, it is impossible—here and elsewhere—to know whether a plot or collective attempt at marronage, then widespread in Guadeloupe, truly existed. Two years later the Stono rebellion broke out in Virginia, in which slaves killed twenty or so whites before attempting to reach Spanish and Catholic Florida (see chapter 2), further exacerbating settlers' fears of a large slave uprising.

In that already loaded context, another war erupted between Great Britain and Spain (called the War of Jenkins' Ear by the British), which lasted from October 1739 to 1748. During that period, the white populations of port towns feared not only slave rebellions and plots, but also invasion and infiltration by external enemies. Then, during the spring of 1741, a series of thirteen fires were set in New York, the first at a military fort, the rest at stables, warehouses, and the governor's house. Widely known as the "Great Negro Plot of 1741," but also as "Saint Patrick's Plot" (in reference to the patron saint of Catholic Ireland), this major event is all the more difficult to reconstruct given that only one source remains for historians—a journal about the investigation written three years later by a New York judge to justify the large number of death sentences hurriedly handed down.[41]

Those fires had been preceded, on 28 February 1741, by the theft from a merchant of a total sum of sixty pounds. The arrest of two presumed robbers, the enslaved Gwin (also known by the name of Caesar) and Prince, prompted local judges to take an interest in a tavern belonging to a white named John Hughson. There they found a young sixteen-year-old indentured servant girl, Mary Burton, who accused her boss Hughson, his wife, and one of their renters, an Irish Catholic woman, of collaborating with slaves in fencing and other illegal activities. Two weeks later, on 18 March (the day after Saint Patrick's Day), the first fire broke out, followed by others over a period of twenty days, including four on 6 April alone. On that day, a witness claimed to have seen a slave running away from one of the fires; another said she had heard a black man, walking under her window the night before in the company of two others, laughingly shout, "Fire, Fire, Scorch, Scorch, A LITTLE,—Damn it, BY-AND-BY." The two enslaved men in question were arrested for arson, at the same time that Hughson, his wife, and their renter were arrested for trading in stolen goods. The authorities and inhabitants then began to draw parallels between the recent fires and those caused by the slave uprising in New York in 1712, which had led to the execution of twenty-five slaves, and suspicions of a new conspiracy by blacks who wanted to destroy the city took form. On 14 April, a special court was established and calls for witnesses made. Mary Burton served as the main prosecution witness in the reconstitution of the supposed plot. On the basis of her statements, the judges accused Hughson and his family of being in league with the presumed slave arsonists, in preparation for a vast plot aimed at destroying the city and killing only upper-class whites in order to construct a new society whose king would be Hughson, with Gwin and Prince established as the leaders of his "black guard."[42]

After that "discovery," magistrates ordered a first round of executions in the goal of obtaining other denunciations and terrifying New York's black population. On 11 May, Gwin and Prince were hanged without ever having confessed, and Gwin's body was allowed to decompose in a square north of the city. At the end of the month, the two slaves arrested for arson were burned alive in front of a merciless crowd. At the same time, arrests multiplied as Mary Burton had stated that five black sailors recently seized from a Spanish ship and sold as slaves in New York and a white schoolteacher believed to secretly be a Catholic priest were also involved, which transformed a New York matter into an international conspiracy fomented by Spain and the papacy. Shortly thereafter, the tavern owner, his wife, and their Irish renter were hanged, despite having denied the existence of any plot to the end, and Hughson's body was displayed next to Gwin's. In all, including the individuals already mentioned, over two hundred people were arrested in New York in 1741 and subjected to expedited trials before a vengeful public. Thirty enslaved men were executed at the stake or by hanging (including the five black Spanish sailors though they claimed to be free), four whites were hanged (the Hughson couple, their Irish female renter, and the so-called priest), and dozens of slaves were whipped or sold outside the city. A macabre detail proved quite troubling: according to witnesses, as Hughson's body decomposed, it became enormous and black, his hair curled, and his features began to Africanize, whereas Gwin's body grew smaller and whitened. Finally, when Mary Burton began to accuse several well-known white New Yorkers, the trials abruptly ceased—though she received a financial reward that allowed her to end her indentured servant contract. Some observers were then prompted to compare those events with the Salem witch trials, and criticized the New York justice system. It was to silence those criticisms and give weight to the theory of conspiracy that one of the magistrates published his journal of the trials in 1744.[43]

In brief, between 1730 and 1741, a wave of conspiracies seemed to cross the Americas, from New France to the Caribbean and to Mexico, and led hundreds of slaves to the gallows, stake, or whipping pole. Although only a handful of these manifestations of "slaves' uncontrolled insolence" involved violence and destruction, and many were likely only verbal protests, they prompted tremendous crackdowns everywhere.

The Revolts in Jamaica and Berbice in the Context of the Seven Years' War

The 1740s and 1750s were also disrupted by local uprisings and plots either proven or imagined by colonists, as well as by rumors of royal decrees to emancipate slaves. For example, in 1745, the St. David parish in Jamaica was rattled by one enslaved woman's claim that nine hundred captives were preparing to massacre all the region's white inhabitants. A few slaves did indeed rebel, undoubtedly to avoid arrest, and killed a British man and four women before escaping; they then murdered another colonist, stole weapons and ammunition, and attempted to hide in the island's inner regions. They were quickly captured, and ten enslaved men, mostly Africans, were executed, and twelve sold abroad.[44]

In 1749 in Venezuela, a rumor circulated by the black sergeant of a battalion of militiamen of color, claiming that a new bishop would arrive from Spain with a royal edict to emancipate slaves, caused a stir in the province of Caracas.[45] Elsewhere, spontaneous protest movements alarmed white communities, as in Curaçao in 1750, when, in the span of one day, slaves attacked a plantation owned by the Dutch West India Company and killed several dozen slaves and one white. In response, the governor had at least thirty-nine rebels executed and many others transported.[46] During that period, small sporadic uprisings were also recorded in Berbice, Guadeloupe, Martinique, St. Croix, and again in Jamaica.

The Seven Years' War (1756–63) would suddenly offer slaves new possibilities for liberation. The long war had major repercussions in the Americas, first in the north of the continent, and then in the Caribbean and the Guianas, which were heavily dependent on Europe and the continuing importation of enslaved Africans. The conflict slowed not only slave imports, as well as the exportation of tropical products, but also deliveries of supplies essential to those regions' populations. Slaves' dissatisfaction increased as a result of heightened exploitation and increasingly limited rations. At the same time, those enslaved men and women were hearing their masters complain that, as soldiers withdrew to fight in Europe, they were being deprived of their defenses against plantation uprisings and the threat of a sea invasion. The Seven Years' War, by visibly weakening the colonial powers, thus incited groups of slaves to take extraordinary risks, particularly in Jamaica and the Dutch colony of Berbice.

Between April 1760 and October 1761, Jamaica saw the eruption of a series of slave revolts, known collectively as Tacky's Rebellion, after one of the leaders of the initial uprising. According to a history of Jamaica published in 1774 by Edward Long, an administrator and son of a plantation owner who lived on the island from 1757 to 1769, the rebellion was a vast conspiracy involving nearly all of the island's Coromantee (Akan) slaves, whose goal was "the entire extirpation of the white inhabitants; the enslaving of all such Negroes as might refuse to join them; and the partition of the island into small principalities in the African mode; to be distributed among their leaders and head men." If not for the effective intervention by the governor, navy, soldiers, militiamen, and maroons, it would have been "more formidable than any [rebellions] hitherto known in the West Indies" due to its breadth, the secrecy behind its planning, the multitude of conspirators, and the locations it targeted.[47] For Long, responsibility for Tacky's Rebellion and its offshoots therefore fell on the Akans, viewed as particularly cruel and belligerent, the importation of whom he recommended be banned in order to avoid any new insurrections. Two decades later, the plantation owner and politician Bryan Edwards, in the first edition of his history of the British West Indies in 1793, mentioned the "very formidable insurrection of the Koromantyn [Coromantee]," which erupted under Tacky's leadership in St.

Mary parish before spreading across the island. Unlike Long, Edwards largely attributed its impetus to obeah, a form of shamanism derived from various African practices, as one of its priests had convinced the rebels that they were invulnerable to death by Europeans.[48] Based primarily on those two authors, several historians, following Michael Craton's example, theorized that barring the narrow margin of superiority held by colonial forces, Tacky's Rebellion could have been as bloody as the Saint Domingue uprising thirty years later.[49]

In 1760 and 1761, Jamaica's enslaved population undoubtedly hoped to benefit from the circumstances created by the Seven Years' War—the reduction in ground and naval forces on the island and planters' growing concerns over that insecurity—to revolt. The toll of Tacky's Rebellion was considerable. In all, rebel slaves killed sixty whites and as many free people of color or mobilized maroons and destroyed several plantations in Akan-led raids. They faced off against militias, the regular army, and British naval forces, as well as maroons who fought against them in keeping with the peace treaties they had signed with colonial authorities. In the end, the efforts taken to quell the rebellion left at least five hundred slaves dead, including those who were killed in combat or were executed more or less summarily and those who committed suicide. Some five hundred captured rebels were transported to British Honduras to work in that colony's mahogany forests. As had previously occurred in Barbados, planters were compensated for their losses in terms of both human property and land.[50]

In reality, however, this series of revolts only mobilized a small minority of the 170,000 slaves who then represented 89 percent of Jamaica's population: in total, approximately 1,500 men and women during those eighteen troubled months, or barely 1 percent of the island's slaves. The Akans assumed leadership roles because they represented a large portion of the enslaved Africans at the time and often exercised leadership functions or provided skilled labor. The uprisings only affected certain parishes on the island, in the North and later the West. Furthermore, there was no apparent coordination between the first rebellion, the true Tacky's Rebellion, in April and May 1760, confined to the northeast parish of St. Mary, and the much larger insurrection that devastated part of the western parish of Westmoreland between the end of May and August 1760. However, the third rebellion, which began in September 1760 and lasted for nearly a year, was initiated by the survivors of the Westmoreland uprising who had moved to the mountainous parishes of St. Elizabeth and Clarendon, which were more centrally located on the island. As is common in such periods of collective fear, the white minority claimed to have detected several local conspiracies linked to those revolts, which they mercilessly suppressed.[51]

The first uprising, specifically led by the enslaved Akans Tacky and Jamaica, began during Easter holidays in 1760 in St. Mary, in the island's northern region. Under their command, ninety slaves left their plantations on the night of 7 April, heading to the military fort of Port Maria, several miles away on the coast, whose sentry they killed before seizing weapons and ammunition. They then returned to the estates on which they worked, rallying three hundred new rebels along the way, and set fire to cane fields, murdered several whites—masters, estate managers, servants—and destroyed buildings and homes. Incapable of stopping their passage, the region's planters were nonetheless able to rally a few faithful slaves and alert the governor in Spanish Town, who declared martial law, mobilized the army, and ordered black maroons to send reinforcements.

One of the first victims of the crackdown by colonial forces was an old enslaved Akan, the obeah man or traditional priest identified by Edwards, who supposedly coated the fighters' bodies with a powder intended to make them invincible.[52] Then, on 14 April, a detachment of maroons killed Tacky, Jamaica, and other rebels. Tacky's head was displayed on a pole at the entrance to Spanish Town to terrorize other slaves. The maroons captured many prisoners as well, but groups of rebels were able to escape and continued to wreak havoc in the region. In May, a special tribunal convened in Spanish Town judged and sentenced several slaves from St. Mary to be executed at the stake, amid widespread rumors of morbid rituals they had performed. In parallel, on 13 April, the authorities announced they had stopped a slave plot in Kingston thanks to the discovery of a sword decorated with a parrot feather in a slave's hut. They implicated several Akans, including an enslaved woman named Cubah who belonged to a Jewish mistress and was also initiated in the practices of obeah, and whose companions had reportedly crowned her the queen of Kingston. Two weeks later, several of these accused slaves and the rebels from St. Mary were hanged in the capital, their heads thrust onto poles and their bodies burned; Cubah was sold abroad. Tacky's Rebellion and Cubah's supposed plot were contained.[53]

Nevertheless, at the end of May, hundreds of slaves revolted in the western parish of Westmoreland, spreading death and destruction in their path before regrouping in the mountains, where they thought they could defend themselves. Perhaps they had hoped to form a new maroon community, as the presence of women and children in their camps seems to indicate. However, many whites saw this new uprising as the start of the true general rebellion that slaves were believed to have planned throughout Jamaica for Pentecost, but that Tacky and Jamaica were now supposed to have launched prematurely under the influence of alcohol. Once again, the militia, soldiers, navy, and maroons were mobilized. At the same time, four new local conspiracies were thwarted in eastern Jamaica, and their alleged participants executed.

The suppression of the Westmoreland revolt was particularly widespread and brutal. In early June 1760, soldiers and militiamen massacred dozens of insurgents on the spot and, following rapid verdicts, executed dozens more by hanging, burning at the stake, or suspending them alive from chains. Many rebel slaves were able to escape however. Among those, some died from their injuries in the woods or committed suicide, and dozens attempted to discreetly return to their plantations. In July, eighty insurgents surrendered voluntarily and, in the hope of being pardoned, turned over four Akan chiefs, who were sentenced to be suspended in chains for three days, then released before being burned alive. Another leader hanged himself before being captured, and a sixth was killed by a detachment that brought his head to Montego Bay. At the end of August, with the Westmoreland rebellion seemingly destroyed, the governor lifted martial law. However, he failed to take into account the dozens of rebels who had successfully found refuge in the mountains, where they reorganized, under the leadership of an enslaved man named Simon, into several small bands that moved toward the center of the island to attack plantations and kill whites. At the same time, military troops continued to retaliate against and execute rebels, until October 1761, when order was finally restored.[54]

A detailed study of how Tacky's Rebellion unfolded thus reveals that even though the uprising lasted for several months and caused a great deal of death and destruction, it remained limited in terms of both geography and the number of participants. For that matter, in the second edition of his history of the British West Indies, published in 1794, Edwards conceded that "the revolt was not as general and destructive as that which now rages in St. Domingo."[55] As for its causes, planters and colonial administrators understood at the time that the rebellion was more due to slaves' ability to benefit from the reduction of military forces on the island during the Seven Years' War than to the presence of Akans or reliance on obeah.

Amid the uncertainty created by that war between 1756 and 1763, alleged plots and minor rebellions were also reported on Antigua, Bermuda, Nevis, St. Croix, and Dutch Guiana.[56] In addition, news of the revolts in Jamaica and their brutal suppression reached London, Boston, and other Atlantic ports, generating empathy in some circles for the African rebels courageously dying at the stake for the cause of freedom.[57]

However, in 1763, when Jamaica's colonists were celebrating having crushed the slave rebellions on their territory, whites in the Dutch colony of Berbice were facing the most serious slave revolt of the Seven Years' War period. Unlike those preceding it, the rebellion that devastated Berbice in 1763 was a true revolt, in the sense of an "uprising against legitimate authority." Though the rebels could have fled toward the maroons of Suriname, their leader attempted to establish an independent state to replace the existing Dutch colony. The revolt in Berbice was exceptionally massive, mobilizing, often forcibly, most of the 5,000 slaves then present in the colony, some 1,400 of whom worked on the sugar plantations owned by the Company of Berbice and 3,500 of whom cultivated coffee, cotton, and cocoa on the small private plantations scattered along the Berbice and Canje

Rivers. In other words, a majority of the mostly African enslaved populations in the Dutch colony, who represented 90 percent of the total, participated in the insurrection in one way or another, willingly or not. The revolt lasted as long as one year and was violent as well. Rebels murdered at least fifty of the 350 whites living in Berbice and forced many more to flee the colony. They also killed recalcitrant or innocent slaves, men, women, and children alike. They destroyed many plantations and provisionally maintained control of most of the colony's territory. This revolt, which has yet to be extensively studied by historians, was therefore proportionally much larger and more destructive than the one in Jamaica.[58]

The uprising in the Dutch colony began in February 1763 under the leadership of Coffij, a domestic and literate enslaved Akan. Launched on two plantations along the Canje River, it spread quickly, as its participants destroyed estates and killed colonists upstream of the Canje and the Berbice Rivers. Seized by panic, several white families took shelter in a plantation east of the upriver town of Fort Nassau, but insurgents surrounded and either massacred them while subjecting them to tortures reserved for slaves or enslaved them (for example, the daughter of a planter was forced to become Coffij's concubine). Other whites gathered at Fort Nassau, which they partially burned down before traveling down the Berbice River by boat to take refuge in Fort St. Andries, on the estuary, while waiting for military or naval help to arrive. Coffij, his main deputy Captain Accarra, and groups of rebels established their headquarters in what remained of Fort Nassau and seized several estates. From the beginning, Coffij communicated by writing with the Dutch governor Wolfert Simon van Hoogenheim, leaving historians his own version of events. Declaring himself the "governor of Berbice's Blacks," he blamed the uprising on, by name, several planters who were particularly cruel to their slaves, and he commanded all the colony's whites to leave the territory as quickly as possible. Van Hoogenheim chose to play for time; he did not reject Coffij's demand but claimed he had to consult authorities back home, whereas he in reality called for military reinforcements from Suriname and the Netherlands.[59]

In late March, some help arrived from Suriname, in the form of one hundred soldiers and sailors, to the great relief of the colonists hiding in Fort St. Andries. Van Hoogenheim secured the entrance of the Berbice estuary and rigged three armed boats to go back upriver with the troops, volunteer colonists, and slaves to the Dageraad plantation, six miles downstream of Fort Nassau, where he set up a fortified general headquarters. That turnaround divided the rebel chiefs, pitting Coffij, still in favor of peaceful negotiations with the Dutch governor, against Accarra, who took the initiative of attacking Dageraad, albeit unsuccessfully.[60] On 2 April, Coffij addressed another letter to Van Hoogenheim: "The Governor of Berbice [Coffij] asks Your Excellency that Your Excellency will come and speak with him; don't be afraid but if you won't come, we will fight as long as one Christian remains in Berbice. The Governor will give Your Excellency one half of Berbice, and all the Negroes will go high up the river, but don't think they will remain slaves. Those Negroes that Your Excellency has on the ships, they can remain slaves."[61]

Without demanding the abolition of slavery, Coffij went on to propose the division of the colony of Berbice, whose coastline and eastern region would be reserved for Christian whites who could continue to exploit slaves there (incidentally, in a later message, Coffij recommended that the Dutch import more slaves to replace their losses), but whose central and western regions would belong to rebels who had escaped slavery. One month later, Coffij attempted to regain general command by personally leading an attack against Dageraad, but was easily defeated. As the rainy season began in May, food became all the more scarce, and hunger and disease rampant. Coffij then reduced his demands to the governor, settling for four plantations. The insurgents also attempted to send emissaries to make contact with the maroons of Suriname, but, poorly guided, they were forced to turn back.[62]

Moreover, with worsening conditions in the rebel camps, tensions among chiefs intensified, dividing those who wanted to end all relations with white colonists and those who wanted to continue to negotiate with the governor. Those divisions also had an ethnic dimension, separating recently arrived Africans from more acculturated creoles or Africans, and Akans from other ethnicities. By fall, Atta, a recently arrived Akan, and his men overthrew Coffij, who committed suicide after having killed some of his deputies. Some groups of rebels attempted to establish runaway communities upriver only to be repelled by Amerindians allied with the Dutch. At the same time, the first boats from the Netherlands arrived in Fort St. Andries with nearly three hundred well-armed men. When Dutch military forces sailed up the Berbice River in December 1763, they were decimated, as was the case everywhere, by disease and yellow fever. But the rebels were too weakened by internal divisions and famine to effectively retaliate. As many as 2,600 surrendered, others were massacred by the Dutch troops, and hundreds were captured and summarily judged. In all, in the course of 1764, 125 men and 3 women were executed, many in atrocious ways, hung on hooks by their ribs or slowly burned after having been skinned, and all their decapitated heads were displayed on poles. Hundreds of rebels were lashed and sent back to their plantations. In total, between the rebellion's debut and end, Berbice's plantations lost some 1,700 slaves (out of 5,000). Among those, a few dozen, or possibly a few hundred, were able to escape and try to survive as runaways in the colony's interior forests. Of the 350 colonists in Berbice before the uprising, only 116 remained at the end of 1764.[63]

While the Berbice slave uprising was the largest and most serious revolt to precede the age of revolution and independence in the Americas, it also showed how difficult it was for rebelling enslaved Africans to construct an alternative society on the ruins of a plantation colony. As revealed by the depositions of several hundred "rebels" (over one-third of them women) who surrendered after February 1764 examined by historian Marjoleine Kars, most slaves were swept into the rebellion, willingly or forcibly. In many cases, the uprising split existing families, separated mothers from children, and subjected women to increased sexual abuse. As most able-bodied men were spared plantation work to be assigned to military units, the production of food and services disproportionally fell on women as well as on older men and children. Moreover, the often brutal authoritarianism of leaders such as Coffij, Accarra, and Atta, who governed as potentates and submitted "rebel" slaves to a discipline similar to that imposed under plantation slavery, proved rapidly counterproductive as it prevented the formation among followers of a broad support for the rebellion. Indeed, the brief statements taken by the Dutch from exhausted "rebels" said nothing of the hopes of freedom that many probably entertained one year before, when the uprising began. They now simply hoped to survive—even by returning to their plantations as slaves.[64]

Slave Rebellion and Slaveowners' Terror

From the late seventeenth century on, news of slave revolts and conspiracies circulated throughout the British and French colonies, as well as those established by Spain, Portugal, the Netherlands, and Denmark; plantations and mines were not spared any more than cities were. In reality, however, "slaves' insolence" rarely materialized in violent acts, despite slaveholders' fears. The only rebellions that represented a serious enough threat to necessitate a large mobilization of troops to contain them were those in Jamaica and Berbice, at the beginning of the 1760s, to which can be added the uprisings of St. John in 1733 and Veracruz in 1735. Colonial powers responded to those revolts, as well as to local mutinies, verbal protests, and unsubstantiated plots, with terror, directed primarily against slave elites. That is because, through their leadership, expertise, and professional capacities, those artisans or overseers, whether they had committed subversive acts or not, challenged the institution of racial slavery by demonstrating aptitudes that equaled those of whites. For slaveowners, they therefore had to be punished or eliminated in the vilest way possible in order to mark their exclusion from humanity.

Of course, during the ancien régime, slaves were not the only ones to endure punishments that prompted demonstrations of suffering and horror, as no social classes were immune. However, in European societies, the spectacle of executions consisted of a ritual intended to unite a community threatened by the transgressions of one of its own, whereas executions of slaves were meant to be reminders of the infallible superiority of the white and Christian "community" over the "mass" of subjugated blacks, who were largely un-Christianized (apart from summary baptisms in Catholic colonies). On sugar-producing islands, in particular, where alleged conspiracies and rebellions prompted waves of executions and lashings, the spectacle of those punishments had the double goal of terrifying slaves and reassuring small white minorities as to their right to decide who lived and who died among the immense majorities represented by enslaved populations. It demonstrated the complicity among those in power—meaning planters, the state, and white colonists—notably by moving portions of a trial from the main city to a location near plantations. The incineration or prolonged exposure of the heads and dismembered bodies of executed slaves reasserted whites' control of their human property even after death and was meant to destroy the belief among enslaved populations that the dead would return or fly back to Africa. That corporal destruction also raised the question of the fate of the torture victim's soul, feeding the belief, among slaves, that the troubled spirits of the dead visited the living. But at the same time, as stressed by historian Vincent Brown, the repetition of physical punishments and executions, reinforced by the recurrence of deaths due to exhaustion, epidemics, disease, and malnourishment, led slaves to give a new meaning to death and the afterlife in their beliefs and spiritual practices. Finally, the presence of the heads and limbs of condemned slaves in workers' daily landscape may have also reminded them of the history of the ongoing battle against slavery.[65]

Yet in mid-eighteenth-century Europe, the practice and application of justice was gradually changing. Interrogation under torture, amputation, quartering, and burning at the stake began to disappear along with the post mortem abasement and public display of executed bodies. Only soldiers and sailors continued to be subjected to immediate convictions without appeal, which were characterized by their arbitrary nature, and to sanctions meant to terrify other conscripts.[66] In that context, the cruel and interminable torture and executions of dozens or even hundreds of enslaved peoples that distinguished the suppression of slave revolts and plots, particularly in the British colonies, began to shock certain European intellectual circles. Similarly, the prolonged display of the heads and entire or dismembered bodies of executed slaves in public places, at the entrances of plantations, and along roads, recounted by travelers and royal agents, at times sparked incomprehension in Europe.[67]

The terror imposed on slaves by masters and colonial authorities began to appear more visibly, not only during crackdowns on alleged revolts or conspiracies, but also in daily life. As notions of tolerance, freedom, and equality developed among some European thinkers, slavery was called into question. Tyranny and injustice as methods of subjugation, the absence of a proportional punitive response to a wrongdoing, and the wide variety of cruel and sadistic punishments reserved for slaves all became unacceptable. Gradually, torture methods and the whip, meted out by dozens or hundreds of lashes, sometimes spaced out in time and dealt in different locales, in the goal of permanently marking bodies and terrorizing the enslaved men and women forced to watch the lashings, became weapons that would be used by slaves and abolitionists to attack the barbarism of slavery.[68] The terror waged by slaveowners began to be turned against them: it is undoubtedly not by chance that the first voices to denounce slavery emerged in London after the arrival of news of the atrocious executions in Antigua in 1736, New York in 1741, and Jamaica in 1762. The brutal suppression of Tacky's Rebellion even inspired romantic poems that transformed him into a Christian martyr who preferred the redemption or freedom offered by death to a life of servitude.[69]

⇌ At the end of the Seven Years' War, in 1763, the slave trade resumed and reached unprecedented heights, bringing dozens of thousands of Africans to American ports each year. At the same time, slave escapes and protests increased, prompting increasingly bloody crackdowns. That escalation highlighted the fundamental barbarism of slavery—and the equally fundamental humanity of those subjected to it. As we will see in the following chapters, though slaves' emancipation strategies did not change, they adapted and took on new meaning at a time when individual freedoms were beginning to be included in the demands made by a growing number of subjects of Europe's monarchies. During the age of revolution and independence, the slave fight for freedom became intertwined with a movement to break colonial chains that also challenged the chains of slavery itself.

PART III
The Age of Revolution and Independence (1763–1825)

⇛ 5 ⇚
Slaves as Actors on the Path to U.S. Independence

After the Seven Years' War, slaves in the Americas adapted previously tested liberation strategies and developed new ones in response to a broad series of transformations. Over the subsequent decades, the colonial map of the Americas was redrawn, prompting a rebalancing of power among Europe's monarchies both on the continent and in the Caribbean. Furthermore, Great Britain, France, and Spain, countries whose royal coffers had been drained by armed conflicts, were showing their desire to better control and exploit their colonies. Those upheavals, which coincided with the rise of philosophies espousing natural rights and fundamental freedoms, were the basis of the age of revolution and independence in the Americas. Every colonial system would be affected, and rivalries between Europe's colonial powers and the colonies would provide slaves with new opportunities to fight for their freedom. Military engagement in armies constantly lacking in manpower, in exchange for the promise of freedom, became a viable option for enslaved men when hostilities between colonists loyal to the tutelary monarchy and those seeking independence transformed into war. Instability as well as troop and population movements facilitated the escape of countless slaves into interior regions or toward enemy camps. At the same time, notions of independence and individual freedoms created a climate favorable to emancipation and the purchase of freedom. Attentive to any weakening of or division among slaveowning powers, slaves knew how to exploit existing tensions to advance the cause of their own liberation. As writing and Christian abolitionism developed, slaves used petitions, the publication of manifestos, and the pulpit to demand their freedom. When a European monarchy sought to reassert its authority over planters who had become too independent with rules or laws regarding slavery, enslaved peoples would collectively protest and revolt to demand an emancipation that they claimed had already been declared by the king. Henceforth in a position to combine their demands for freedom with other requests, slaves mobilized in parallel with movements that had been spreading across the continent since 1763 and would lead to the independence of nearly the entire American continent as well as Haiti.

Slaves in North America, in the British colony of Massachusetts, were the first to integrate their fight to weaken the foundations of slavery into protests by colonial subjects. In 1764, colonists in Boston launched a resistance movement, followed by armed revolt, against their colony's reduced autonomy and the imposition of new taxes by London. That process would spread to neighboring colonies ten years later before transforming, in 1775, into the first war of independence in the Americas. Following their victory over Great Britain in 1782, the thirteen British continental colonies became the United States of America and the first country to break its political subjugation to a European power. In parallel, beginning at the war's debut in 1775, thousands of enslaved peoples from those colonies sought to liberate themselves from slavery. In total, between 30,000 and 50,000 slaves of the 460,000 living in that territory resorted to one shared strategy: they ran away from their masters.[1] In other words, in the thirteen colonies, one slave in fifteen, or possibly one in nine, used the war as an occasion to obtain his or her freedom. This movement was unprecedented in terms of both scale and type, even if calling it the "largest slave uprising in [U.S.] history," as historian Gary Nash does, is inapt.[2] All those slaves resorted to flight as a strategy, but it was different from grand marronage, which entailed trying to reach uncolonized land: this was more of a vast desertion of slaves, one-third of whom were women and children, who escaped their masters to find refuge in British strongholds. This slave movement within the colonists' revolt gave a new dimension to the struggle for independence by establishing a parallel between colonists' freedom from Great Britain and that of slaves from their masters. It revealed the internal contradictions of the "American Revolution," which justified its break with the colonialist monarchy in the name of universal natural rights, even as it excluded from those same rights a segment of its population that had been reduced to the status of personal property.

Preaching, Writing, and Petitioning:
New Ways to Promote Freedom

The mobilization of enslaved peoples in the thirteen colonies during the War of Independence did not begin suddenly, but in tandem with cultural and social evolutions. When the religious Great Awakening jolted the population of the British continental colonies between 1730 and 1759, it introduced countless slaves to Christianity. Some accompanied their masters to religious services, while others slipped into white crowds to listen to revivalist preachers talk about the Bible and the redeeming Christ, conversion, and the rebirth of new believers. Those outdoor assemblies were particularly attractive to slaves: they gathered hundreds of men and women of every circumstance and color around an enthusiastic orator who painted an image of the flames of hell for unrepentant sinners and praised the benefits of a Christianity presented first and foremost as a direct and personal experience with God. If, for participating whites, the Great Awakening was a decisive moment in the process of the formation of the future United States of America, for slaves, the Christian message placed the absolute power of their masters in perspective and signified that above the latter was God, who spoke through the Bible and whose Word was the supreme authority. In other words, it offered them a hope for justice and liberation in a world temporarily run by whites. That realization was all the more radical for enslaved men and women who had been long distanced from any evangelization by their Protestant masters, unlike baptized slaves in Catholic colonies who underwent an accelerated Christianization intended to instill an obedience of God in them.

From that point on, for some Protestants, the contradiction between the equality of those baptized before God and the inequality of slavery was impossible to resolve: How could they not fear that the feeling of being equal before God would lead slaves to challenge their condition as the personal property of other Christians? If some Protestants, like Catholics, responded that temporal slavery was of divine origin and recognized by the Bible, others, notably Quakers, Methodists, and Baptists, judged that a Christian could not belong to his or her brothers and sisters before God. Those debates were closely watched by groups of slaves who extracted arguments from them against the enslavement of Christians. As a result, since 1730, some slaves in Virginia were interpreting Christian baptism as an act that would liberate the new believer, despite the decision to the contrary made by British law (see chapter 4). In parallel, the development of reading and writing among colonists inspired several slaves, who learned to read in order to understand the Bible and its teachings. They realized that their condition was not immutable, and that other enslaved peoples, like the Israelites in Egypt, had been liberated. Slaves in the North also read abolitionist texts by Methodists and Quakers that circulated throughout the Atlantic; these texts offered an antislavery and egalitarian interpretation of the Bible.[3]

After the Seven Years' War, the British colonial system was fractured, despite its acquisition of new territories such as Quebec and Florida. Of course, the growth of the slave trade, largely controlled by the British, allowed plantations to acquire African captives in previously unrivaled numbers. But the increasing demands made by London on its colonies affected their economies. The richest planters in the West Indies defended their interests from Europe, where they were living and serving in Parliament, which masked the severity of the crisis in the islands for several years. At the same time, some of those planters' enslaved domestics took advantage of their presence in Great Britain to run away and get baptized in order to contest their captivity on European soil in freedom suits supported by abolitionists. Whereas attempts by his predecessors had failed, the enslaved James Somerset, who had fled his Bostonian master in England but had been recaptured and sold to Jamaica, won his freedom in 1772, when a British court declared it illegal to force slaves on English or Welsh soil to return to America. Abolitionists and their networks in the Americas astutely announced that this decision had made slavery illegal in Great Britain, implying that any captive who made it there would be freed. In the British Caribbean and North America, several slaves subsequently applied this interpretation of the Somerset case to themselves.[4] Some fled from their masters and hid aboard ships heading to England in the hope of being emancipated there. Others maintained that the king of Great Britain had declared the general freedom of the slaves of his empire and that their continuing enslavement was illegal.[5]

Simultaneously, colonists in the thirteen continental colonies, who unlike those in the West Indies were not represented in the London Parliament, were engaged in a power struggle with Great Britain. The American movement against British tyranny thus coincided with the abolitionism emerging in both Great Britain and certain religious milieus in Pennsylvania and New England. Spreading from one Atlantic coast to the other, anticolonial and antislavery ideas influenced a growing number of slaves. From the first altercations between Massachusetts's colonists and British soldiers in 1770, enslaved peoples showed that they intended to take full advantage of tensions between their masters and the colonial government. In New England, where colonists launched the first protests against London and demanded equal treatment from British authorities, some slaves were inspired by those actions, studied the basics of law, and submitted petitions demanding an improvement in their situation and at times their liberation. Others published pamphlets and open letters or gave sermons in black churches demanding freedom. In May 1774, for example, when London imposed punitive laws closing the port of Boston, several slaves wrote to the governor of Massachusetts to condemn the fact that they were "held in a state of Slavery within a free and christian Country" even though "we have in common with all other men a naturel [sic] right to our freedoms without Being depriv'd by our fellow men."[6] Some pursued trials against their masters for illegal enslavement, at times successfully winning over jurors persuaded of the illegitimacy of slavery.[7] Relations between slaves and masters could also become violent. Small groups of slaves rebelled or were suspected of wanting to do so in New Jersey, New York, Massachusetts, Maryland, the Carolinas, and Virginia. In 1774, in St. Andrew's parish, in Georgia, six enslaved men and four enslaved women killed their overseer and his spouse and injured other whites; they then attacked two plantations, causing four deaths in all, before being arrested and convicted. Their leader and another slave were burned alive.[8]

Against that agitated backdrop, in 1770, the young enslaved woman Phillis Wheatley attempted to publish her *Poems on Various Subjects, Religious and*

Moral in Boston. Wheatley had been taken from Gambia at age seven and sold to a rich Boston family that educated her. But as few whites accepted the idea that a female African slave could write poetry, she had to prove that she was indeed the author of her collection before a tribunal of literary and religious experts. Even so, she did not find a publisher. When she accompanied her master's family to London in May 1773, shortly after the Somerset case, she met abolitionists, including Granville Sharp. Thanks to their support, she was able to publish her *Poems*, several of which revealed the importance of her conversion to Protestantism as well as of her awareness of her African origins and the implications of her status as a slave. Most importantly, she succeeded in negotiating her return to Boston in exchange for her emancipation in October of the same year.[9] In 1774, the free Phillis Wheatley published an open letter to a pastor in a Connecticut gazette, in which she thanked him for his "Vindication of [Negroes'] natural Rights." After mentioning the divine disasters resulting from the "Egyptian slavery" imposed on Israelites, she discreetly warned "our modern Egyptians" (American colonists) that "God has implanted a Principle, which we call Love of Freedom." She denounced the "strange Absurdity" in some American philosophers whose "Cry for Liberty" contradicted "their exercise of oppressive Power over others." For Wheatley, colonists' freedom was inseparable from that of their slaves.[10]

At the end of 1774, a black Methodist preacher named David, who had been educated in England, announced before an assembly of slaves in Charleston, South Carolina, that God was going to liberate his people from slavery, as he had done for the children of Israel in the hands of the Pharaoh. Threatened with death by scandalized whites, the Methodist was quickly evacuated by his white coreligionists, but his liberating message continued to spread among slave preachers.[11] David and other militants, with Wheatley, launched an antislavery movement that would last for nearly a century, until the abolition of slavery in the United States in 1865, and in which liberated or fugitive slaves played a crucial role through both trips between America and Europe and their lectures, sermons, and circulated writings. By blending the Anglo-American conception of individual rights with Christian morality, and by comparing the fate of slaves in the United States to that of enslaved Israelites in Egypt, those men and women made the Bible into a source of hope and their religious celebrations the catalysts of a collective consciousness. By demonstrating that slaves' natural rights to freedom were an integral part of human rights, they gave a universal dimension to then revolutionary principles of freedom and equality. They highlighted the fundamental contradiction of the discourse used to justify the independence of the future United States of America in terms of natural rights without ever calling the ownership of slaves into question. As Granville Sharp would underline shortly thereafter, "The toleration of domestic slavery in the [thirteen] colonies greatly weakens the claim of *natural Right* of our American Brethren to Liberty."[12]

Running Away to the British in Search of Freedom

The armed conflict began in 1775, following deadly altercations between British troops and militiamen in Lexington, Massachusetts. Shortly beforehand, Boston had obtained the support of neighboring colonies, twelve of which sent delegates to the first Continental Congress in Philadelphia to declare the British Coercive Acts illegal and establish defense militias. At the second Continental Congress, held in May 1775, delegates from the thirteen colonies, now including Georgia, decided to form a Continental Army under the command of George Washington, a rich slaveowning planter from Virginia. From London, the young monarch George III declared them traitors to the Crown and sent thousands of soldiers to subdue the colonies, where the general staff and British authorities hoped they could count on the active support of the remaining loyalist colonial population to counter the growing number of rebels enlisted in Washington's Continental Army.[13] Some British advocated the mobilization of free and enslaved blacks to support the British army, based on the positive experience of the latter's engagement during the Seven Years' War. The activism of slaves and abolitionists in New England and Great Britain rapidly prompted the British to debate the possible advantages of an uprising of American rebels' slaves against their masters in the colonies south of the Potomac, where the majority of colonists were still strongly attached to the monarchy.[14]

In effect, slaves weighed heavily on the thirteen colonies' demographics: in 1770, they numbered more than 460,000 in a total population of 2,132,000 inhabitants. Meaning that, on average, more than one person in five was kept in slavery, though proportions varied considerably according to the region and how densely it was colonized. The northern colonies (New Hampshire, Massachusetts, Connecticut, Rhode Island, New York, New Jersey, and Pennsylvania) were the most populated and represented a little more than half of the total population of the thirteen colonies (52 percent). The Upper South (Virginia, Maryland, Delaware, and North Carolina) was moderately populated, comprising 41 percent of the population, whereas the Lower South (South Carolina and Georgia) came in a distant third, with only 7 percent of the colonies' inhabitants. But it was the least populated and most recently colonized regions that had the most slaves proportionally speaking: the Lower South counted 90,000 slaves, who formed the majority of its population (58 percent). The Upper South, where the plantation system had been established at the end of the seventeenth century, had 323,000 slaves, or 37 percent of its inhabitants.

The more populated northern colonies only tallied 48,000 slaves, representing a mere 4 percent of their inhabitants, primarily in New York and New Jersey.[15] Since 1775, the entire South was impacted by British threats to make use of enslaved populations. From Virginia to Georgia, colonial elites began to fear a slave uprising at British instigation; at the same time, many enslaved men and women believed Great Britain was ready to liberate them. Within that tense climate, rumors of slave conspiracies aimed at eliminating whites and seizing power multiplied. In Charleston, South Carolina, and Wilmington, North Carolina, local authorities believed they had thwarted exactly those kinds of plots and suppressed the alleged plotters by executing and selling slaves in the West Indies and the Guianas. Throughout the region, similar rumors prompted whites to strengthen slave surveillance militias.[16]

In November 1775, the Scottish governor of Virginia, John Murray Dunmore, launched an appeal from a naval ship that would prompt the escape or desertion of slaves to a much greater degree than he had counted on. After having harassed estates owned by rebel planters all summer long, he decreed "all indentured Servants, Negroes, or others, (appertaining to Rebels,) free that are able and willing to bear Arms, they joining His Majesty's Troops as soon as may be."[17] Although Dunmore had promised freedom only to slaves who fled masters rebelling against Great Britain, his proclamation spread rapidly and was understood by many enslaved men and women as a British declaration of general emancipation. Along with news of the liberation of slaves on British soil following the Somerset case, and black evangelism based on the theme of the Israelites' departure from Egypt, Dunmore's proclamation contributed to the emergence a few months later of a small messianic movement of several enslaved preachers, including both men and women, in St. Bartholomew parish in South Carolina. They were led by a captive named George, who maintained that the former monarch George II (who died in 1760) had received a book from God ordering him to change the world and liberate blacks, and that he was now in hell for having disobeyed, but that the new king, George III, would comply and free them. Accused of conspiracy, George was hanged and his followers publicly whipped.

Outside that case, thousands of captives understood Dunmore's proclamation as a royal call for them to flee. In one week, five hundred enslaved men had joined his army, and three hundred of them would shortly thereafter be armed and ready to serve in the royal "Ethiopian Regiment," with the words "Liberty to Slaves" written on the front of their uniforms. By mid-December, the number of fugitive slaves who had joined the British side was estimated at two thousand, but many were struck down by yellow fever.[18] Other slaves fled to port cities in the North, such as Philadelphia, Boston, or New York, in the hope of blending into free African American populations or embarking for England as sailors and obtaining their freedom there. After the British army's occupation of New York over the summer of 1776, several thousand slaves—men, women, and children from the North and South alike—took refuge there, as well as in other British-held cities. A group of those fugitives was used by the British to form the first company of black sappers, followed by a Black Brigade, both under white command. The British army also employed fleeing slaves to build fortifications and clear roads, and as spies, guides, and servants. Many enslaved men supported British soldiers during their pillaging expeditions against the revolutionaries.[19] The Black Brigade attacked farms in New Jersey to seize supplies for New York while simultaneously liberating and bringing along captives.[20]

During the British occupation of New York, between 1776 and 1782, the city's African Americans contributed to social changes that were quite distinct from the narrative of the plot to kill whites that had justified the brutal repression of alleged slave conspiracies in 1712 and 1741. Slaves in New York and rural Lower Manhattan numbered a little more than eighteen thousand (12 percent of the population), in addition to several thousand free blacks. The arrival of hundreds of runaways from the South responding to Dunmore's appeal spurred many local slaves to also leave their masters to defend a British camp that offered them occasions to free themselves. In addition, some were manumitted by their owners in a surge of abolitionist sentiment. During the six years of British occupation, those African Americans—free, fugitive, emancipated, or enslaved men, women, and children—slowly formed communities in new free spaces created by the war. They met in ports, public squares, and taverns, defying restrictive slave codes. As the newspaper *New York Mercury* lamented in November 1779, "A desire of obtaining freedom unhappily reigns throughout the generality of slaves at present."[21] After taking refuge in New York, many slaves found paying jobs, got married, and had children they could record as free, for lack of a master to contest them. Often embracing the Anglican religion, they helped longtime black residents establish the foundations of the city's first African American churches, elementary schools, and associations. Others served in the British army, and some were even promoted—a considerable victory for runaway slaves.[22] That was the case for Sergeant Thomas Peters, deported from the Gulf of Guinea and first sold in Louisiana, where three escape attempts cost him whippings and iron branding before he was resold in North Carolina. In the spring of 1776, he was able to flee with his family to New York, where he was recruited as a sapper by the British and participated in several battles over the course of the war.[23]

In December 1778, the British army shifted its northern offensive to the proslavery South, attacking Georgia first, followed by the two Carolinas and Virginia, by land and by sea. In a region in which between 32 percent and 61 percent of the population was enslaved, that attack transformed the conflict between revolutionaries and the British with their loyalist allies into a triangular war whose third actor was the slaves, as noted historian Sylvia Frey.[24] Revolutionaries in the South, who, since 1775, had been struggling to keep their slaves submissive and prevent escapes through the reinforcement of surveillance militias, faced new desertions since June 1779, when the British general Henry Clinton issued a second appeal to slaves from Philipsburg. Clinton proclaimed that any slave in the service of the rebels seized by the British army would be sold to the profit of the individual who captured him, but that, on the contrary, slaves who deserted the revolutionaries to join the British side would benefit from "full security."[25]

Even though Clinton's proclamation, three and a half years after Dunmore's, did not contain the word "freedom," it galvanized thousands of enslaved peoples who interpreted it as a new promise of emancipation. Reproduced on multiple occasions by royal gazettes up until September 1779, it also sparked the rumor that fugitives would receive parcels of land from among those the British army confiscated from revolutionaries. Clinton's proclamation therefore reignited the wave of escapes and desertions that began at the end of 1775 and drove plantation slaves—men in particular, but also women and entire families—to take refuge with the Royal Army or in proximity of naval ships ready to receive them along the coast of South Carolina and Georgia.[26] The Virginian Thomas Jefferson, owner of a slave plantation, estimated that in Virginia alone twenty-five thousand slaves, including thirty from his own estate, had fled their masters to join the British army. In other words, according to his estimate, one Virginian slave in seven took the risk of trusting the British to escape slavery.[27] In South Carolina, approximately twenty thousand slaves, or nearly one-quarter of those then living in the state, defied great danger to do the same. Estimates for Georgia hover around five thousand runaways, or one slave in three.[28]

Nevertheless, British generals were reluctant to arm and integrate free or enslaved blacks into their combat troops, as some judged that such a decision risked causing a general revolt likely to inspire slaves in Jamaica, where several presumed slave conspiracies had just been thwarted at the cost of numerous executions.[29] Some officers still doubted slaves' capacity to become effective soldiers. But the British, lacking manpower, did exploit those black men and women, particularly during the occupation of New York, as a labor force to farm crops needed to feed troops, and for transportation, construction, deforestation, and ditch-digging. Other fugitives became carpenters, blacksmiths, butchers, guides, scouts, or officer valets; women served as canteen workers, washerwomen, domestic servants, seamstresses, and prostitutes, or as ammunition makers and nurses.

Ultimately, the British armed few enslaved and free blacks in the South, though they did task them with harassing deserters or terrorizing revolutionaries by participating in the looting of their properties. Nonetheless, in 1779, several hundred runaway slaves volunteered to assist the British troops under siege in Savannah, where they received weapons and were placed under the command of white officers. Several of these volunteers with a deep knowledge of the terrain proved skilled at capturing horses for the British cavalry. Fugitive slaves also served in the Royal Navy as pilots, cabin boys, and sailors. Experienced pilots guided boats and canoes through coastal waters and rivers.[30] During the last two years of the war, Great Britain was also quick to form and arm diverse, often multiracial, bands to pillage rebels' plantations in the Lower South. A cavalry unit in South Carolina called the "Black Dragoons" was particularly feared by planters, both because it incarnated the reversal of their world and because it attacked their estates and vandalized them mercilessly. The guerrilla warfare waged by the Black Dragoons was nonetheless endorsed by the British army, which paid them regularly due to the crucial role they played within the territory's interior.[31]

Yet while slaves escaping toward British strongholds hoped for emancipation, their actions failed to prompt any real challenges to the institution of slavery. In fact, even as it encouraged captives to flee their masters, the British army never sought to bring an end to the slave plantation system in the South. In order to prevent runaways from revolting, it channeled their potential for insurrection through vague promises of postwar emancipation. British forces adroitly directed the most enterprising and best-trained fugitive slaves, and therefore those most likely to be leaders, toward specialized and often noncombative roles. At the same time, they assigned most remaining slaves to tasks that varied little from those to which they were accustomed. They did not integrate enslaved or free African American men into the army corps, and would only occasionally arm a few hundred men, out of the thousands present. The army lodged those individuals separately from soldiers and gave them less food than to the troops, which made them vulnerable to disease and death. As they exploited fugitive enslaved men and women, British forces continued to dangle the possibility of their liberation. As a result, most slaves in British service probably believed until the end of the war that they would obtain their freedom.[32]

Slaves in the Liberated Territories during the War

The British policy of attracting slaves to the Royal Army with promises of emancipation embarrassed revolutionaries because it revealed the gap dividing the North and the South of the future United States. The slaveholding Virginian planter George Washington, on being named commander of the Continental Army, immediately decided to exclude all African Americans, free or enslaved alike, in order not to lose the support of southern colonists, who were less involved in the fight against Great Britain than their northern counterparts were. And yet, beginning with the first skirmishes in 1770, free African Americans in New England fought British soldiers alongside whites; one, Crispus Attucks, was even the first of five rebels to be killed by the British during the Boston Massacre. Furthermore, certain slaves, such as Peter Salem of Massachusetts, had been freed by proindependence abolitionist masters so they could fight for freedom. In contrast, south of the Potomac River, where slavery was the dominant labor system, white rebels had been opposed to including free and enslaved men of African descent in their troops from the start of the conflict, and all the more so since the presence of the Royal Navy along the coast had begun to restrict the slave trade. Dunmore's proclamation, issued in November 1775, reinforced the resistance of southern revolutionaries and also cost Great Britain the support of whites who had remained loyalist. Confronted by a wave of captives fleeing both sides to join the British army and the indiscriminate destruction and looting of various estates by British soldiers and bandits, many planters united despite their political differences to defend the system of slavery, as they all felt simultaneously attacked from the interior by their slaves and the exterior by the British army.[33]

In the North, colonists ignored General Washington's order to exclude African Americans from the Continental Army, especially after 1777, when the Continental Congress forced every state to supply quotas of soldiers, which were difficult to meet without the inclusion of free African Americans. The possibility of mobilizing slaves by promising them their freedom at the end of the war was also considered. Rhode Island was the first state, in 1778, to actually establish a black battalion of 250 enslaved men to compensate for the lack of white revolutionary soldiers. To do so, it had to provide monetary compensation to slaveowners for their human losses. The recruited captives (like many Narragansett Indians) obtained a promise of freedom and all the bonuses and other rewards offered to white soldiers by the Continental Congress. Connecticut circumvented the difficulty of recruiting whites by authorizing some men to be exempted from military service if they found an able-bodied soldier to replace them; in reality, slaves were sometimes enlisted as substitutes for their masters. In Massachusetts, revolutionary units had included free blacks alongside whites since the beginning of the war; however, when the Continental Congress established the quota of men to be provided by each state, the recruitment of slaves in exchange for promises of freedom became a necessity. Two black companies were created, including the Bucks of Massachusetts, under the command of an African American colonel, George Middleton, who fought in Yorktown in 1781. In those states, manumission via military service became an option for enslaved men.[34]

Despite the many slave defections to the British side, southern revolutionary elites did not want to reconsider their refusal to mobilize their slaves in order to meet the troop quotas demanded by the Continental Congress. In South Carolina, several counties had more slaves than whites, and it was impossible to respect said quotas without including slaves. Nonetheless, legislators consistently resisted one general's suggestions to recruit between two thousand and three thousand unarmed slaves (out of a total of over seventy-five thousand in the area), using the argument that a highly limited mobilization of captives would guarantee the support of the majority of the enslaved population for independence. Georgia also refused to recruit slaves. Unlike the Lower South, Virginia and Maryland counted a substantial number of Afro-descendants among their free populations, which made the idea of recruiting slaves more acceptable. Since 1775, more than 150 free or emancipated African American men served the rebel cause in Virginia. But Virginian legislators continued to privilege the mobilization of whites, whom they encouraged by offering a parcel of land and the choice of a slave in good health or sixty gold pounds to any white man who enlisted in the Continental Army until the end of the war. Nonetheless, as the conflict dragged on, they had to come to terms with giving white recruits the possibility of having African Americans stand in for them: some white soldiers hired free blacks, while others sent slaves to replace them.[35] Finally, though the proslavery South was opposed to the mobilization of free blacks, it did not refuse the hundreds of *libres de couleur* from Saint Domingue who made up much of the volunteer legion sent by royalist France to aid southern rebels in their fight for independence.[36]

Needless to say, the majority of the thirteen colonies' 460,000 slaves did not flee toward the British army, and even less were enlisted in the Continental Army. But they were all affected by a war that confronted them with choices often fraught with risk and particularly difficult for those with families and who had succeeded in accumulating some belongings. Besides the enslaved men and women who responded to Dunmore and Clinton's proclamations, an indeterminate but significant number of slaves decided to take the opportunity to disappear into interior regions, individually or with family members, and despite the hostility of Native American nations. Others joined runaways who had already found refuge in northern cities; others still fled to Florida, which was under British control from 1763 to 1783, to try to discreetly blend into the free population of African descent. Others set out for England, Canada, or the West Indies, even before the evacuation declared after the British defeat. Other slaves, taking advantage of the chaos and insecurity introduced to regions traversed by British troops and revolutionaries during the war, killed their owners or delivered them to the enemy. However, more than anything else, the war prompted a large exodus of southern planters, from Georgia to South Carolina, and from South Carolina to North Carolina and Virginia, and finally to Maryland. Loyalist planters headed to British Florida, notably to seek refuge in St. Augustine. On occasion, those plantation owners and their families abandoned their estates to the care of their slaves, who became masters of their fate for the first time in their lives; sometimes planters brought all their slaves with them to settle on a relative's land or uncultivated terrain; they also sometimes separated their slaves—and thus enslaved families—bringing some with them, selling others to cover the costs of moving and resettling, and relying on the rest to maintain their farmlands in the South. Those forced displacements allowed some enslaved men and women to flee. But regardless of their respective destinies, slaves were rarely spared the violence caused by the war.[37]

Indeed, in the eyes of many officers and soldiers on both sides, slaves were also personal property that could be seized, confiscated, exchanged, rented, and sold on the continent or in the Caribbean. Those who were taken during occupations often became military slaves. Forced to perform the most tiresome tasks in exchange for limited water and food, they were particularly vulnerable to fatal diseases and epidemics. What's more, troops would abandon slaves on the spot if they slowed down the company's march or threatened their supply of provisions. The royal and continental armies also used them to pay off outstanding balances or buy war materials and food, selling captives as merchandise to slave traders in exchange for cash. The possibility of being given a slave also provided incitement for whites to voluntarily enlist in armies and served as a way to reward the most valiant soldiers. Soldiers used the black men and women they had captured as slaves to be either employed in their service or sold for profit.[38]

In addition, the unrest caused by the war prompted the formation of diverse bandit groups that pillaged and resold their material and human spoils to revolutionaries or loyalists. Since 1779, more and more privateers began sailing along the Atlantic Coast of South Carolina in the goal of obtaining goods and slaves, which they sold to British vessels, slave traders, or directly to planters in the Caribbean.[39] As a result, slaves in stricken regions who had not yet fled lived in constant fear of exactions and kidnappings by loyalists or revolutionaries and by bandits, some of whom were themselves fugitive slaves.

Promises of Freedom after Great Britain's Defeat

Since 1781, the possibility of a British victory against the thirteen colonies diminished rapidly. The Royal Army, which was facing an increasingly critical situation, did not hesitate to sacrifice the captives who had allied with the British once they became a burden, as the four thousand to five thousand Virginian slaves who had found refuge in Yorktown were tragically the first to discover. During the British occupation of that port in the summer of 1781, those slaves labored under difficult conditions in the hope of being manumitted, notably on the construction of the city's fortifications. But at the end of September, when Washington's Continental Army, the Virginia troops under the command of the Marquis de Lafayette, and the French expeditionary force led by General de Rochambeau surrounded Yorktown, the Royal Army began by imposing extreme privation on thousands of slaves, many of whom died. Then, when water and provisions began to run out, the army was quick to expel those same captives and hand them over to the besieging forces. As a Hessian officer serving the British wrote: "We had used them to good advantage and set them free, and now, with fear and trembling, they had to face the reward of their cruel master."[40] Indeed, the sacrifice made by a large number of slaves did not prevent the British surrender at Yorktown on 17 October 1781. But, contrary to what the Hessian officer said, they had not been set free by the British, and many were violently taken back by their owners. Others were claimed by revolutionaries who were not their masters, compelling the Continental Army to require proof of ownership. Other slaves fell into French hands and were forcibly sent to the Antilles for sale. But because the treaty to evacuate Yorktown said nothing about fugitive slaves joining the British forces on the Royal Navy's vessels, some were able to do just that and continue to serve Great Britain.[41]

In the spring of 1782, the revolutionaries' victory over the British was assured, bringing an end to the hopes harbored by a large number of slaves who had fled their masters after 1775. Outside the cities and forts still under British control, slaves of owners who had remained loyalists were often confiscated by the Continental Army to serve as payment or reward for deserving officers and soldiers, which drove some captives to run away. The thousands of enslaved men and women—on the run or belonging to loyalists—who found themselves in strongholds in which the British had entrenched themselves, sometimes waited as long as three years to be evacuated along with the defeated forces. During that time, amid conditions of utter misery, they attempted to prove that they had voluntarily joined the British camp in order to obtain emancipation certificates, all while trying to avoid falling prey to the revolutionaries, loyalists, soldiers, bandits, and pirates fighting among themselves to take possession of those slaves. According to one of the fugitives, Boston King, who had fled his master in Charleston, the armistice "diffused universal joy among all parties, except us, who had escaped from slavery, and taken refuge in the English army."[42]

The Treaty of Paris, signed on 3 September 1783, had significant consequences for slaves who had taken refuge with the British army. Article VII of the peace treaty required that "His British Majesty" withdraw all his troops and his navy from the United States as rapidly as possible "without causing any Destruction, or carrying away any Negroes or other Property of the American Inhabitants." George Washington, aware that the vagueness of the treaty for the evacuation of Yorktown had enabled many slaves to flee hidden aboard British ships, firmly intended to ensure that the clause regarding slaves in the Treaty of Paris was respected by General Guy Carleton, who replaced Clinton in March 1782. However, the British general believed that the monarchy had to keep its "Faith to the Negroes who came into the British lines," as it was a question of "National Honor which must be kept with all colors." Carleton therefore did his best to include thousands of escaped slaves among the approximately 30,000 soldiers and 27,000 loyalists that needed to be evacuated and, for the latter, established in other British colonies, notably Nova Scotia, New Brunswick, and Jamaica.[43]

Despite the Treaty of Paris, the evacuation of loyalist strongholds in 1783 was carried out rather chaotically. It is therefore impossible to make a precise estimate as to the number of slaves who were returned to the American masters claiming them and those who left the United States after the British defeat. Historian Alan Gilbert proposes the following figures: 6,000 blacks, enslaved for the most part, evacuated from Charleston; 4,000 blacks, also primarily slaves, from Savannah; and 3,000, both free and manumitted blacks, from New York. To this total of 13,000 he adds "perhaps another ten thousand" African American men and women, free or runaway slaves, who would have left New York by land or sea before the evacuation.[44]

Finally, an indeterminate number fled to the borders of the colonized territories. In the vast region of Charleston and Savannah, in particular, slavery-based rice farming had not spread beyond marshes located near rivers and the coast, providing opportunities to hide and survive in the most inaccessible interior swamplands. Slave-soldiers also fled with their weapons after Great Britain's defeat, including some who had helped defend Savannah in 1779 and who established, with other fugitives, a fortified village in Bear Creek, located between Georgia and South Carolina, where they lived off farming and pillaging until 1786, when Georgian troops backed by Catawba Indians destroyed their huts and crops.[45]

Therefore, less than thirteen thousand slaves would have been evacuated from among the thirty thousand to fifty thousand who had escaped to join the British army. The gap between those figures can be explained by the fact that many runaways were returned to their American masters; others died in combat or from illness, hunger, yellow fever, and exhaustion; still others managed to escape abroad or were captured by privateers outside the British evacuation. In general, the fate of those who had sought refuge with the British south of the Potomac was much harsher than that of runaways north of the river. The largest slave exodus took place in Charleston, followed by one from Savannah, and in both cases, only a minority of evacuees obtained their freedom. Several thousand ended up on British Caribbean plantations, often forced there by loyalist masters. Many were held prisoner by officers of the Royal Army and

Navy, traders, or privateers who, claiming to protect fugitives from the threat of being retaken by their masters, put them on boats and sold them in Jamaica, the Bahamas, and along the Atlantic coast of Honduras and north of Nicaragua. Other runaways, to whom British generals had promised freedom at the end of the war, became the personal property of the officers they were serving or were used to indemnify British supporters.[46]

The thousands of southern captives brought to the Caribbean were joined by others from eastern Florida, which had become a safe haven for countless loyalists and their slaves during the war, and which Great Britain was forced to cede back to Spain in 1783. The treaty signed by the two monarchies gave the region's residents eighteen months to decide whether to stay or go. Of the approximately 8,000 black men and women living in the Florida territory, 1,000 were free and in all likelihood decided to stay. The fate of the other 7,000 was dependent on their respective masters: 2,500 were forced to return to plantations in the southern United States, primarily in Georgia; nearly as many were taken to the Bahamas, while 700 were sent to Jamaica, and the rest had to follow their masters or were sold in other British colonies. Amid the confusion that characterized this period, some slaves were undoubtedly able to pass for free or escape during their forced displacement. However, the majority found themselves returned to slavery.[47]

Among the thousands of blacks evacuated from southern ports, between 1,000 and 2,000 became slaves of the British army deployed in the Caribbean. In addition, the 700 Black Dragoons of South Carolina who had distinguished themselves by their conduct and military capabilities during the war were assigned, after their evacuation, to autonomous units stationed in Great Britain's Caribbean colonies, where they provided the model on which the British army would organize its West Indies troops (see chapter 9). In 1789, for example, 300 Dragoons were stationed in Grenada as pioneers, artillerymen, and cavalrymen. After additional years of military service, the majority of those slave-soldiers eventually obtained their emancipation.[48]

Incidentally, many African Americans, either runaways or evacuees from the southern United States, played a key role in the development of Protestantism, notably Baptism, among Jamaica's slaves. The first of those evangelists, George Leile (also known as George Liele, George Lisle, or George Sharp), was a slave from Georgia freed by his owner and represented one of the rare documented cases of a southern fugitive successfully escaping by sea before the Treaty of Paris. When the heirs of his former master, who was killed in the War of Independence, contested his manumission, Leile fled to Kingston aboard a boat. Because he lacked proof of his emancipation, on arriving he found employment as a servant, and after two years of work he was able to obtain a certificate of freedom. After 1784, he made a living as a carter while preaching to slaves during outdoor meetings. A few years later, his followers numbered in the hundreds, notably slaves whom he had baptized and to whom he had taught the Gospel, and reading and writing. Careful not to alienate plantation owners, Leile nonetheless established the foundations of the first black Baptist church in Jamaica, whose influence would spread rapidly after 1800 (see chapter 10).[49] As had been the case for their counterparts in the United States for a decade, Jamaican slaves began to integrate Christianity into their fight for freedom.

In contrast with the bleak future faced by slaves who had escaped to British strongholds in the South, those who fled to New York proved more fortunate. Most of them—between three thousand and four thousand men, women, and children—received a certificate from the British military attesting that they had voluntarily joined the British forces and obtained their freedom after being evacuated in 1783. Granted, the military left behind other African Americans who were taken back by their masters or to whom the British authorities chose not to grant manumission. But the British evacuation of slaves represented a veritable victory in the fight against slavery, as half of the evacuees were fugitives from the proslavery South, one-fifth were slaves escaped from New York or New Jersey, and the rest were either free African Americans or runaway slaves from New England. They were in general young adults of working age, and nearly one in three emigrated with their family. The evacuees included the survivors of the Black Brigade: forty-seven men with thirty-seven women and sixteen children.[50]

Three-quarters of the blacks who abandoned New York were transported to Nova Scotia, where they tried to build a future for themselves with their newfound freedom. Around 1,200 of those emancipated slaves established Birchtown, named after Samuel Birch, the officer who had signed their freedom certificates during the evacuation. Although the royal British government had promised them lands to colonize, they found themselves competing with thirty-five thousand other refugees, including white soldiers and loyalist planters from the South who had brought their slaves. Many therefore remained landless, underpaid, subjected to racial discrimination, and even reenslaved by employers who destroyed their certificates of manumission. Others were captured by Native Americans, who often sold them as slaves. Those men and women were therefore far from enjoying the full freedom they thought they had won. Many of them mobilized to reject that fate and sent a delegation to London to claim war compensations. That delegation met with General Clinton, who supported its request, as well as with abolitionists interested in the fate of the evacuees. But the British courts concluded that only blacks who were born free were entitled to indemnification.[51]

During its visit to London, the black delegation from Nova Scotia also encountered other emancipated slaves from New York. The Royal Navy had evacuated a few hundred African Americans to ports in Great Britain, where it left them (unlike white loyalists) without any aid. They quickly swelled the ranks of the poor in London and other cities, where their presence was noted by British abolitionists, whose cause had been reenergized by the massacre of 132 slaves on the slave ship *Zong* in November 1781.[52] The reformer Granville Sharp was particularly active: he devised a plan to send evacuees to Africa to establish a colony based on free labor and intended to bring an end to the slave trade while contributing to British commerce. Supported by British parliamentarians and financiers, the colonial project materialized in April 1787, when 411 men, women, and children left Portsmouth, south of London, for Sierra Leone, which was bombastically renamed the Province of Freedom, with Granville Town as its capital, in homage to Sharp. Half of the colonists were freed slaves from the United States, and one-fourth were whites, mostly the poor female companions of black men and colonial administrators. Those former slaves' odyssey to "return to Africa" was a massive failure: four months after their arrival, only 268 colonists remained, after surviving diseases, hunger, and conflicts with natives. In 1792, Sharp and other abolitionists launched a new attempt at African colonization from Nova Scotia; 1,192 disillusioned black loyalists, including Boston King and his family, as well as Sergeant Thomas Peters, left the North American colony to establish Freetown in Sierra Leone, under the authority of a British lieutenant. They were also decimated by disease, and weakened by internal rivalries and the frustration of once again being subjugated to British leaders and treated worse than their white counterparts.[53]

The estimate that some thirty thousand to fifty thousand slaves in the future United States fled or deserted to British forces during the War of Independence is therefore a qualified and uncertain one, given that few of those fugitives left traces behind.[54] Many undoubtedly later returned to their former masters in the South. Others were forced back into slavery elsewhere. And some died along the way. However, thousands of enslaved men and women obtained their freedom, either by their own means or because British commanders kept their promises and procured them certificates of freedom.

Freedom on the Horizon of the Northern States

Despite George Washington's reticence, the Continental Army had also enlisted many slaves as auxiliaries, at times with the promise of manumission. The question of their demobilization and emancipation, when applicable, therefore emerged after independence. And since every state was responsible for its own battalions, the fates of those enslaved men were varied. In the North, slaves who had served voluntarily or replaced their masters were in general manumitted, either after the latter's goods were confiscated, if they were British supporters, or with their consent, if they were revolutionaries; in the second case, a master could still force his slave into years of service as indemnification. A few states established additional conditions, such as New York, which decreed that only slaves who had served at least three years in the militia or the Continental Army would be emancipated. In Rhode Island, slaves had been recruited with promises not only of freedom but also of bonuses and rewards similar to those granted to white soldiers: in reality, many had to wait years—at times until 1820—to receive the pay or land due them.

Several cases illustrate the differences between states: the enslaved Peter Williams, who was initially enlisted in the loyalist camp by his master, escaped to join the Continental Army as a volunteer in 1780. After becoming the property of the state of New Jersey when his owner's goods were seized, he was declared emancipated and free of all slavery or servitude in 1784, due to his service during the war. The enslaved Briston Baker, from New Haven, served in the continental troops from 1777 to 1783, when he was manumitted by his master, undoubtedly as a reward for his service. Andrew Abner, from Connecticut, was liberated before enlisting in the army in 1777; he then served as a free black until 1780 and shortly thereafter managed to buy his wife's freedom. In the South, Virginia, which had eventually mobilized five hundred free and enslaved African Americans in order to meet the quotas imposed by the Continental Army, was the only state whose assembly attempted to compel masters to emancipate slaves who had served as their replacements during the war in exchange for the promise of freedom; however, there was no punishment for noncompliance. Virginian lawmakers directly manumitted only eight slaves for their service to the country. Among them, James Armistead, a spy in the service of the Marquis de Lafayette who had gathered information from the British that proved critical to revolutionaries' victory at Yorktown, submitted his demand for freedom along with the French general's recommendation in October 1784, but had to wait more than two years before it was granted.[55]

After independence, the gap between the North and the South in regard to slavery and the place of black men and women in society, already evident when it came to their recruitment in the Continental Army, continued to widen. Of course, the Declaration of Independence on 4 July 1776, which stated "that all men are created equal, that they are endowed by their Creator with certain unalienable Rights, that among these are Life, Liberty and the pursuit of Happiness," said nothing about slaves, slavery, or the slave trade, and therefore hid regional divergences. But by 1777, the constitutions, laws, and practices of different states, notably regarding manumission, revealed growing friction. During the Constitutional Convention in Philadelphia in 1787, slavery was an integral component of the debates. The U.S. Constitution reflected both agreements and differences of opinion. Every delegate from the thirteen states, except those from Georgia and South Carolina, opposed the continuation of the slave trade,

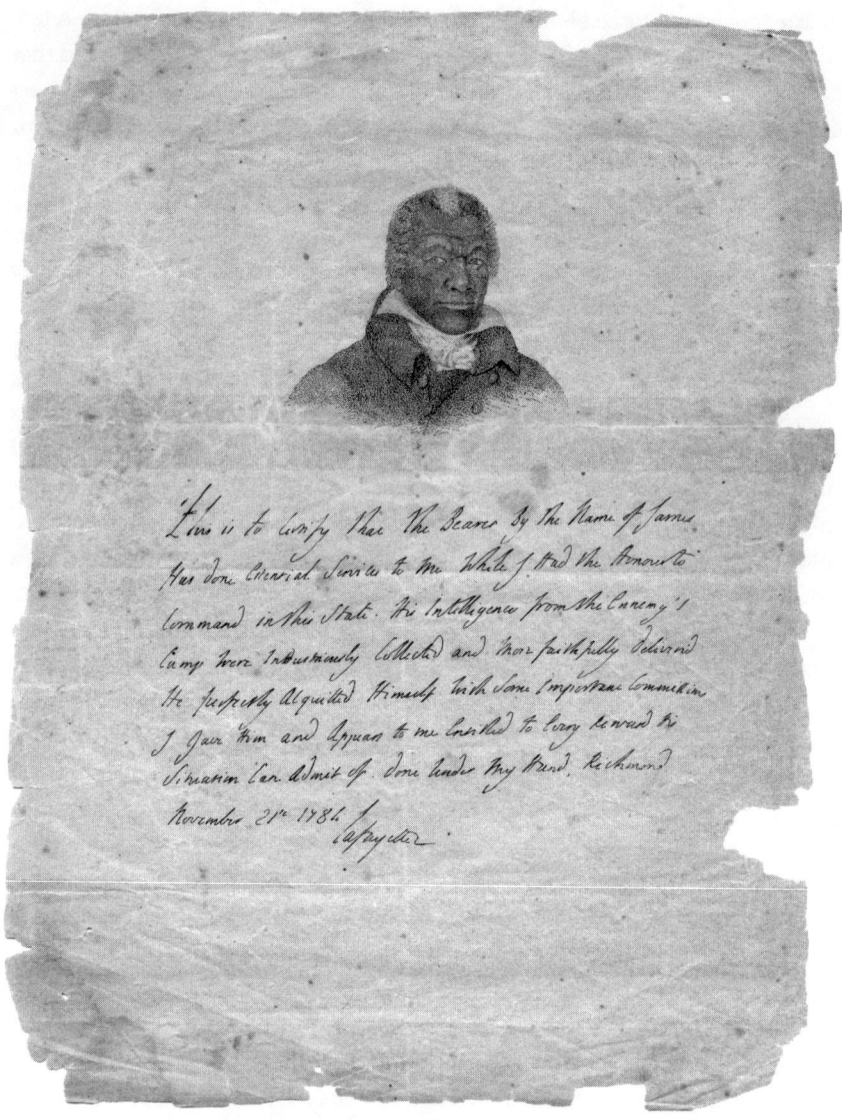

Facsimile of the Marquis de Lafayette's original certificate commending James Armistead Lafayette for his revolutionary war service with portrait after John B. Martin, 1784. (Schomburg Center for Research in Black Culture, Manuscripts, Archives and Rare Books Division, New York Public Library Digital Collections; accessed March 24, 2018)

judging it to be immoral or dangerous. The Constitution stipulated, in euphemistic terms (cited in the notes), that the slave trade could not be banned before 1808, or twenty years later, but that in the meantime a tax could be collected for "such [imported] persons."[56]

As for the institution of slavery itself, the Constitution avoided mentioning it by name. The term "slave" was nowhere to be found in the text; it was replaced by "other Persons," "such Persons," and "persons held to service or labor." The Constitution therefore did not give the federal government the right to legislate or control slavery but allowed each state to choose to conserve, develop, or ban the "peculiar institution" in the short or intermediate term. In reality, the U.S. Constitution, despite its celebration of ideals of liberty and equal rights, recognized the legitimacy of slavery throughout the country and the alleged human inferiority of slaves. One of its clauses obliged all states to send any "person held to service or labor" back to the state from which he or she had fled. In addition, northern delegates accepted a provision stating that slaves be added to the free population for the purposes of a proportional attribution of seats to the House of Representatives. But since slaves would have then been counted in determining state contributions to the federal government, it was decided that a slave would count as three-fifths of a free resident, which increased the heavily slaveholding South's representation while denying slaves status as human beings in their own right.[57]

And yet, in parallel, abolitionism was making headway in the North. More and more slaves, free blacks, and white militants had denounced the flagrant contradiction between slavery and the Declaration of Independence, with its rhetoric of freedom and equality for all. But no state in the Union moved to immediately and completely abolish slavery in the wake of 1776. When the states drafted their first constitutions, only Vermont, which had only a handful of slaves, did away with slavery in 1777, albeit in terms that allowed for the servitude of minors and adults with debts. In 1780, Massachusetts adopted a constitution that endorsed the universal principles of freedom and equality. However, it would not legally recognize abolition until 1783, a move prompted by the actions of one slave, Mum Bett, whose spouse died while fighting the British. After her mistress inflicted a serious burn on her, Mum Bett fled and filed a suit based on the constitutional article stating that all men are born free and equal. After a local court recognized her freedom as it was guaranteed by the Massachusetts constitution, Mum Bett began a new life under the symbolic name Elizabeth Freeman. Her case set a precedent and enabled the emancipation of another fugitive slave, Quock (or Quok) Walker, in 1783, bringing a legal end to slavery in the state. In New Hampshire in 1779, twenty African-born slaves signed a petition demanding that their state representatives abolish slavery. They argued, among other things, that "private or public Tyranny and Slavery are alike detestable to Minds conscious of the equal Dignity of Human Nature," but their efforts proved fruitless. Four years later, New Hampshire adopted an abolitionist constitution similar to the one in Massachusetts. Nonetheless, the state still had 158 slaves in 1790.[58]

The other northern states passed gradual manumission laws that, in actuality, allowed slavery to be prolonged for several decades. The first such law was adopted in 1780 in Pennsylvania, which had 6,800 slaves at the time. Its *Act for the Gradual Abolition of Slavery* would serve as a model for the rest of the region until 1804, and then for Spanish American republics during the 1820s. The Pennsylvania law was essentially an abrogation of the principle of *partus sequitur ventrem*, which stipulated that a newborn child's status correspond to that of his or her mother, and its replacement by the "free-womb" principle, according to which any child born to an enslaved mother after 1 March 1780 would be declared free. However, those children's freedom was relative, as at birth they obligatorily became indentured servants to their mothers' masters, whom they had to serve until the age of twenty-eight without remuneration. As such, they could be sold, rented, or passed down as inheritance; they were restricted to unskilled labor as servants or rural workers. That law therefore transformed slavery into prolonged servitude (four to five times the indenture period for a European), and its first beneficiaries were not emancipated until 1808.[59]

In 1784, Connecticut and Rhode Island also decided in favor of gradual emancipation: the former set the age at which children could obtain their freedom at twenty-five years old, and the latter at eighteen for girls and twenty-one for boys. In reality, therefore, free-womb or *post nati* manumission laws did not emancipate any slaves: they transformed the children of enslaved mothers into indentured servants for more than twenty years. Worse still, by making those girls and boys dependent on their mothers' masters, they deprived their parents of all authority over them. The northern states also legislated the slave trade in a piecemeal way. They banned the importation of new captives from Africa or elsewhere abroad first, and then from southern states, but for several years they authorized the sale of northern slaves—and even children born to enslaved mothers after the adoption of free-womb laws—to planters in the South.[60] In the states of New York and New Jersey, where slavery was an important system of labor, manumission laws would come later (see chapter 9). In addition, several northern states did not grant equal rights to free African Americans, notably the right to vote or serve as jurors in trials. The northern United States was therefore not a free and nonracist region diametrically opposed to the slave South.

Nonetheless, laws of gradual manumission accelerated the process of freeing slaves in the North. For example, Pennsylvania, which counted 6,800 slaves in 1780, had 3,760 in 1790 and 795 in 1810—a drop due to more than the impact of the free-womb law. The number of slaves in Connecticut and Rhode Island diminished rapidly after 1784 as well.[61] In contrast, in New York and New Jersey, where the process of gradual emancipation had not yet been initiated, enslaved populations remained stable between 1790 and 1800, with approximately 20,000 slaves in New York and 11,000 in New Jersey. That said, the proportion of slaves in the total population of those two states, estimated at 6.2 percent in 1790, simultaneously diminished. That was because legislators, since 1786, banned the importation of new slaves and encouraged European immigration to compensate for losses in the labor force caused by the British evacuation of several thousand blacks in 1783.[62]

In reality, many slaves played a significant role in gradual abolition by emancipating themselves. Though free-womb laws had been shaped to serve the economic interests of slaveowners for as long as possible, while also defending the principle of universal freedom, they nonetheless became catalysts for emancipation. By bringing an end, albeit over the long term, to the permanence of the institution of slavery, those laws rapidly encouraged hundreds of slaves to buy or negotiate their freedom from or with their masters. Moreover, the prospect of legal freedom allowed slaves to give new meaning to their daily lives, leaving many inclined to work more to obtain it. Other slaves or free blacks captured for sale as slaves did not hesitate to use the legal system to win or recover their freedom or that of their loved ones.

Gradual abolition also created an ideological and religious context in which it became increasingly difficult for white masters to justify owning other human beings. Some voluntarily emancipated their slaves, a decision facilitated in certain states by the lifting of the required manumission fees in cases when a freed slave fell into indigence. Employers also had the possibility of exploiting their former slaves via other forms of labor, such as sharecropping or piecework. Many slavemasters conditioned the granting of manumission on the signing of contracts engaging freed slaves to work for them for many years. Furthermore, the arrival of European immigrants in growing numbers allowed employers to place emancipated slaves in an unfavorable wage competition with the new white arrivals.[63] As a result, former captives began their lives as free men and women in difficult financial conditions and often without having completely severed their dependence on their former masters, albeit with the pride of having obtained their freedom themselves.

The process of gradual abolition also had an impact on slavery in the remaining British-controlled Canadian provinces. With the 1763 Treaty of Paris, New France had switched to British control and became the province of Quebec. Following the British legal decision in the Somerset case of 1772, colonial authorities reassured French owners that the ruling did not concern their African American or Native American slaves, who were primarily employed as domestic servants in the cities of Quebec and Montreal. But the British army's defeat by the United States marked the arrival of thousands of loyalist refugees, often southern planters with their slaves, as well as emancipated African Americans from New York. Those immigrants settled primarily in the coastal provinces of Nova Scotia and New Brunswick and north of the Great Lakes. But colonial authorities and the preestablished population in that scantly populated frontier region were opposed to slavery, for both humanitarian and economic reasons (many thought that slaves of African origin would be unable to adapt to Canadian winters and that their output would not make up for the costs of dressing, housing, and feeding them). For that matter, the new arrivals understood that the large slave plantation model was unsuited to the environment, prompting planters to attempt to resell their slaves in the southern United States and the Caribbean. The governors of those Canadian provinces would block that possibility, however, by banning the exportation of slaves. At the same time, slaves belonging to loyalist refugees seized the occasion to flee into the vast territory. Many joined communities of emancipated slaves in Nova Scotia, without arousing much interest from local authorities. As soon as they learned that the neighboring states of Vermont and New York, as well as the territory of Michigan, had decreed the immediate or gradual abolition of slavery, others fled toward Detroit, where they were considered to be free. Finally, slaves who remained to work for their masters increasingly did so for a salary, the only way to prevent flight. As a result, the total number of slaves in Canada declined rapidly and probably amounted to some fifty captives when in 1833 the British Parliament voted the Slavery Abolition Act.[64]

Southern Slaves and the Reinforcement of Racial Slavery

For slaves south of the Potomac, the postwar period offered few opportunities to obtain their freedom, except in Maryland and Virginia, where manumission was authorized between 1782 and 1808 and allowed a small but unprecedented number of captives to gain their freedom during the postindependence years. Nonetheless, not one state in the South questioned the permanence of the slavery system, which they all continued to develop without taking any steps toward gradual abolition. In the South, unlike in the North, the enslaved population increased at the same pace as the free population. However, there were differences between the states of the Upper South, such as Virginia, Maryland, and Delaware, in which some Methodists, Baptists, and Quakers actively denounced the slave trade as inhumane and slavery as incompatible with the freedoms of the republican system, and the Carolinas and Georgia, farther south, where the "peculiar institution" was only rarely contested by whites.

The first divergence between the Upper South and states farther south related to the importation of slaves from Africa or the Caribbean. During the war, the British blockade had prevented the region from importing new captives, and the evacuation of several thousand slaves alongside the British and its most loyal colonists beginning in 1783 prompted the question of whether the slave trade should resume. Virginia, Maryland, and Delaware definitively renounced the importation of slaves from abroad, but allowed for domestic trade within the United States. The Carolinas and Georgia, on the other hand, imported more than 93,000 slaves between 1781 and 1810. Thanks to the arrival of those new captives and natural population growth, the number of slaves in those states more than doubled in twenty years, going from 141,000 slaves in 1790 to nearly 340,000 in 1810.[65]

The practice of emancipation was the second issue dividing the southern states. Since 1782, Virginian lawmakers authorized slaveowners to free their slaves on the condition that they take responsibility for those who fell into extreme indigence, and by 1790, every southern state except North Carolina had revoked their decrees banning manumission. However, the application of emancipation varied considerably from one state to another. In Maryland and Virginia, manumissions multiplied, leading to the development of a small population of free African American men and women, who would distinguish themselves in a variety of trades and domains. In Virginia, approximately 15,000 slaves were emancipated between 1782 and 1808; the free Afro-descendant population grew from 3,000 in 1782 to 12,000 in 1790, and then to 30,000 individuals in 1810, which led to a rapid increase in their percentage of the population. Baptists had a strong influence over that process of manumission, notably because at the end of the 1780s, the Baptist General Committee of Virginia condemned slavery as a "violent deprivation of the rights of nature" and encouraged that the Bible to be taught to slaves. Simultaneously, some African Americans formed an autonomous black Baptist congregation, with its own pastors.[66] By contrast, the Lower South only allowed for the possibility of manumission very briefly. In South Carolina, for example, where any act of emancipation was subject to government approval, Denmark Vesey, the leader of an aborted slave uprising in Charleston in 1822 (see chapter 10), was nonetheless able to buy his freedom with money he won in the lottery in 1799. From 1801 onward, Georgia banned all owners from manumitting slaves, unless they had special permission from the legislature. Alabama and Mississippi did the same in 1805 and limited requests to masters who could prove their slaves' meritorious services.[67] The 1810 census clearly demonstrates these differences between Maryland, where free Afro-descendants represented 9 percent of the state's population (and nearly one-fourth of the population of color), Virginia, where they represented only 3 percent of the population, and the remaining states in the Lower South, where they represented less than 2 percent of inhabitants.[68]

As in Iberian America, most emancipations in the Upper South occurred in cities. Slaves could not initiate the procedure, but through their good conduct and relationships with their masters they could hope for a narrow path to freedom to open in a more or less distant future. At the same time, that slim hope favored individual rather than collective struggles against slavery, as shown by a study of three Virginia counties: between 1784 and 1806, 520 slaves gained their freedom by notarized agreement.[69] Some were manumitted by their masters, immediately or through a will; these masters were sometimes provoked by an aroused conscience rooted in U.S. independence. For example, one slaveowner justified his act by stating that he was "fully persuaded that freedom is the natural right of all men, agreeable to the Declaration of the Bill of Rights"; another justified his decision on the grounds "that God has created all men equally free."[70] Some owners emancipated their captives due to their faithful service. Even George Washington, who did not show any abolitionist leanings during his lifetime, had his will amended shortly before his death in 1799 to state that all his slaves would be manumitted after his wife's death. She preempted his wishes and, in 1801, freed the 153 slaves who had belonged to her husband.[71] This short-lived window to emancipation allowed several captives to buy their freedom from their masters, either directly or via an intermediary (namely, a free man or woman of African descent who acquired them as slaves and then freed them once reimbursed). Others obtained their freedom thanks to the intervention of a family member who was already free. In Petersburg, for example, Graham Bell, a free black, was able to buy the freedom of his five children, his brother, and three other slaves between 1792 and 1805; in Richmond, Patty Cole, a free African American woman, bought her husband on one day in 1799 and signed his act of manumission the next day "for the love and affection" she felt for him.[72]

Emancipation nonetheless remained rare for Virginian slaves, whose numbers continued to increase. Rather than dream of manumission, some sought to obtain the most autonomy possible, notably by getting their masters to rent them out or allow them to work independently in exchange for a fixed sum. Others relied on subterfuge, like an enslaved woman named Sally, in 1806, whose husband James Plummer, a free black, rented her services in order to live with her, a temporary solution that ended when her owner had the police bring her back.[73] Finally, in the wake of the recognition of individual rights, some slaves used the law to contest their abusive masters. During the decade that followed the chaotic departure of the British, whites abducted and enslaved many free blacks, taking advantage of the fact that racial slavery fostered the assumption that any man or woman of African descent was a slave. In Virginia, victims of those crimes and their loved ones could turn to the legal system, but needed to prove, using documents or white witnesses, that they were indeed born of a free mother or had been liberated by their British masters. During a dispute concerning the children of a Native American mother and an enslaved

African father, one of the judges presiding even attempted to challenge the racist foundations of slavery, maintaining that every person residing in the state should be presumed to be free: it was up to the master to prove that a person of full or mixed African descent was a slave. But his reasoning was rejected: in this case, the victims regained their freedom, but only because they could prove their free maternal lineage. Nonetheless, illegally enslaved Virginians continued to claim their freedom through the courts, successfully at times.

≋ In summary, slaves in Great Britain's thirteen continental colonies were therefore full-fledged actors in the tensions and war that led to the independence of the United States. Far from observing the political and social upheavals that marked the last third of the eighteenth century as mere spectators, many enslaved men and women attempted to take advantage of that chaos to improve their own lot and become free. The British army's calls for slaves to escape their masters, in 1775 and 1779, prompted thousands of them to flee in the hope of obtaining their freedom from the British. In doing so, enslaved men and women adapted the strategy of marronage to new circumstances—war—choosing the British camp and its king rather than the proindependence revolutionaries who exploited them on a daily basis. Involvement in the royalist side also permitted enslaved men to practice the strategy of liberation via armed service, even as the revolutionary Continental Army simultaneously excluded them, except in certain northern states. All the same, the country's newfound independence momentarily favored individual emancipation in Maryland and Virginia. In the North, the adoption of gradual abolition laws announced the slow demise of slavery, and eager enslaved men and women negotiated the purchase of their freedom. Others took an active and creative role in debates on slavery's incompatibility with Christianity, fundamental human rights, and the establishment of a representative republican government.

The 1791 slave revolt in Saint Domingue did not slow the process of emancipation begun in states north of the Potomac River, but it did have an enormous impact on the rest of the continent. The uprising marked the first time that thousands of slaves had attacked their exploiters and their plantations to demand freedom with unprecedented violence, implementing a scenario of servile revolt long feared by supporters of slavery.

6

From the Slave Revolt in Saint Domingue to the Founding of the Black Nation of Haiti

The French Revolution, even more than the process of U.S. independence, expanded opportunities for enslaved peoples to resort to liberation strategies they had already tested in the past. The revolution gradually disrupted the balance of power, not only within French society and between France and its colonies, but also within every society in the French Caribbean. The interests of slaveowners and the French state drifted apart, creating vast rifts that were quickly exploited by slaves in search of freedom. At first, conflicts between royalist and revolutionary whites and between whites and free people of color encouraged enslaved men to enlist in military service in exchange for the promise of freedom, all while allowing marronage to develop. And in August 1791, for the first time in the Americas, thousands of slaves, most of whom were bossales who had survived the Atlantic crossing, partly enacted, over a matter of weeks, a scenario greatly feared by colonial elites since the sixteenth century: the destruction and burning of work sites as well as the massacre and rape of colonists in Saint Domingue's Plaine du Nord. Thirteen years later, the scenario had played itself out: Saint Domingue's former slaves and free *gens de couleur* had expelled or killed practically all the colony's white residents, definitively abolished slavery, and founded Haiti, the first black state and the second independent nation in the Americas, after the United States.

For the first time, a slave uprising had reached a massive scale, transforming into a revolution to ensure the freedom of all the slaves of the former French colony following years of domestic conflicts and a war against Napoléon Bonaparte's armies. Through its victory over slavery and European colonialism, the Haitian Revolution would mark the social and political imagination of the Americas and Europe for decades (see chapter 7). After the insurrection of August 1791, however, the same emancipation strategies used by slaves since the sixteenth century, such as marronage and military service in exchange for promises of freedom, by then developed on a large scale, would once again ensure that the fight against slavery continued, and in fact led to the institution's abolition by France in 1794. Next, the extraordinary and uninterrupted mobilization of predominantly African slaves against French troops derailed Bonaparte's plans to reestablish slavery through a reign of terror. However, as this chapter shows, though Haiti's former slaves may have become free citizens for good by 1804, their fight to live in freedom according to their own terms was far from over.

The First Blow:
Mass Insurrection in the Plaine du Nord (1791)

The first signs of a slave uprising in the French colonies preceded news of the storming of the Bastille, appearing not in Saint Domingue but in Martinique, a small island with ninety thousand inhabitants, 83 percent of whom were slaves, 12 percent whites, and less than 6 percent free *gens de couleur*.[1] At the end of August 1789, hundreds of slaves from different plantations gathered near Saint-Pierre led by Marc, the enslaved prison warden, Jean-Dominique, a slave carpenter, and a few other enslaved artisans. The group had heard the rumor that Louis XVI had abolished slavery, but that planters were flouting his orders. Two anonymous letters had even been sent to authorities in Saint-Pierre announcing that "nous, Nègres" and "the entire nation of the black slaves united together," after long suffering, were ready "to spill [our] last drop of blood rather than support the yoke of slavery, a horrible yoke attacked by the laws, by humanity, and by all of nature, by the divinity and by our good king Louis XVI."[2] Like other slaves in British or Spanish colonies, those enslaved men and women were demanding a freedom they claimed had already been granted by the monarch through imposing but nonviolent protest.

As elsewhere, the rumor of emancipation was based on concrete facts, though Louis XVI had not sought to abolish slavery but merely to limit its brutality. According to a colonial bureau in the naval ministry: "The majority of masters are tyrants who, as it were, weigh the lives of their slaves by the output of forced labor."[3] In December 1784, the king, in order to regulate that tyranny, signed a decree that established, with corresponding punitive fines, the number of blows a master could deal to his slaves and added: "Those who mutilate their slaves will be disgraced; and those who cause them to perish for whatever reason will risk the death penalty."[4] The decree shocked planters so much that colonial administrators archived it, though some fragments of its content did reach those slaves particularly in tune to their masters' protestations. In France itself, debates about slavery and the slave trade were initiated by some critical publications and the establishment in February 1788 of the elite Société des Amis des Noirs (Society of the Friends of Blacks).[5] News of the existence of a small French coalition against the slave trade and for the gradual abolition of slavery reached the Caribbean through sailors and slaves returning from Europe with their masters. Critical texts also made their way to the islands, such as *Lettre aux bailliages* (*Letter to Bailiwicks*) by Condorcet, in early 1789, which demanded that the emancipation of slaves be added to the General Estates' agenda. In addition, travelers and seamen spread information about the growing British abolitionist movement and the gradual abolition implemented since 1780 in some northern U.S. states. Groups of urban slaves gathered to listen to and comment on any rumors or news that carried the hope of liberation, and which artisans and coach drivers brought all the way to plantations. Those publications and news items also fostered slaveowners' anger at perceived threats to their privileges, a sentiment that, in turn, would be interpreted by slaves as confirmation of their hopes.

Moreover, since the Jesuits' expulsion in 1763, the practice of sending *curés des nègres* (priests trained in France to evangelize slaves) had either proved ineffective or bore unexpected results when the clerics achieved their objectives. As was the case for Protestant missions, the religious celebrations organized by certain priests provided enslaved communities the opportunity to gather without their masters present; the dogma of the all-powerful Christian God they taught relativized the slave master's authority, and their Christian message of spiritual equality contained many contradictions with slavery itself. In Martinique, in particular, a Capuchin monk named Jean-Baptiste was popular among urban slaves to whom he spoke of freedom, even announcing, according to a magistrate, the arrival of the King of Angola accompanied by an army who would bring them back to Africa.[6] In a sign of slaves' appropriation of Catholicism, the letter, "nous, Nègres," sent to the commander of Saint-Pierre in 1789, asked the following question: "Did God create anyone a slave?"[7]

Nonetheless, the hundreds of slaves who peacefully demonstrated near Saint-Pierre in August 1789 were cruelly punished on the governor's order. Troops and a militia composed of whites and *gens de couleur* killed several protesters on the spot, before pursuing fugitives into neighboring hills, which also allowed them to capture some two hundred runaways. Soldiers harshly questioned the slaves who had remained on or returned to plantations, and a special commission of judges subjected forty or so captives to brutal interrogations. Only one suspect stated that the accused had prepared a major attack intended to begin with the assassination of white men by their servants or cooks and the rape of white women, after which the rebel slaves would have gathered to confront the governor and his security forces. All the other accused rebels said that they had assembled to march on the city in force in order to demand that the governor apply what they believed to be the king's will. But the judges chose to retain only the version of events that mentioned the massacre of whites, which allowed them to paint the protestors as bloodthirsty traitors, and therefore to torture (though the practice had been abolished in France in 1788) and execute them. Marc and Jean-Dominique were broken on the wheel, and six other protestors hanged. Thirteen enslaved men were punished with twenty-nine whiplashes each, with an additional iron branding for six of them; three were sentenced to the galleys for life, and two to witness the executions.[8] Ultimately, the protest in Martinique revealed slaves' ability to seize on any weakening of the slave regime and any dissent between plantation owners and royal authorities to assert what they believed to be their rights. It also showed slaveowners' determination to mercilessly crush any glimmers of hope harbored by their "personal possessions" of affirming their humanity.

Since mid-September 1789, the inhabitants of the French Antilles grew aware of the events of 14 July in Paris. By November, the 26 August Declaration of the Rights of Man and the Citizen, and its ideals of freedom, equality, and fraternity, had reached them. Various rumors once again circulated, including one about the abolition of slavery by the king or the state, and another about granting plantation slaves three days off per week. These provoked a wave of unrest among captives, which spread from the south of Saint Domingue to Martinique, Guadeloupe, and St. Lucia, and was repressed in "exemplary" fashion each time.[9] In Guiana, the slaves near the Approuague River, east of Cayenne, rebelled in November 1790 to demand the freedom and equality allegedly granted them by God and revolutionary France, killing five whites and one slave before they were stopped. Seven of the rebels were executed, while two enslaved men were freed and integrated into the militia for having sounded the alarm. Similar slave uprisings occurred in Guadeloupe in 1790 and 1791, both of which were also contained. Even on the British island of Dominica, between Martinique and Guadeloupe, in January 1791, captives from several plantations refused to work as long as their masters did not grant them their "right" to three or four days off a week to cultivate their garden plots.[10]

Yet when it accepted the Declaration of the Rights of Man and the Citizen, the French National Assembly did not intend to address the status of the colonies—which were quite profitable—or the rights of the free *gens de couleur*, the institution of slavery, or the slave trade. Furthermore, in Saint Domingue itself, the French Revolution's most significant repercussions were first felt not among enslaved communities, but among its white elite and free men and women of color, many of whom owned slaves. White planters, merchants, and lawyers, galvanized by the United States' recently won independence, gathered at a colonial assembly in Saint-Marc, in April 1790, to attempt to secede, while others affirmed their loyalty to Louis XVI, and a segment of *petit blancs* (poor whites) declared themselves revolutionaries. As for free men and women of color, since the fall of 1789, they made a somewhat disorganized demand for equality in the name of the Declaration of the Rights of Man, which the island's white residents fought relentlessly. Those conflicts sparked the first combats on Saint Domingue, as of August 1790, when the governor put a stop to colonists' attempts to secede, and then at the end of the year when two rich mulattos mobilized three hundred free men of color—but rejected any slave reinforcements—to demand equality before they were beaten and their leaders broken on the wheel.[11] Enslaved workers from the large sugar plantations on the island's Plaine du Nord would not revolt en masse until August 1791, in what would become the largest slave uprising in the Americas.

Reconstructing the debut of this unique rebellion is not easy, due notably to the lack of immediate sources produced by the rebels. Nonetheless, historians agree that the insurgents used conflicts between white colonists, and between whites and free people of color, to revolt, demanding that a supposed decision made in France in their favor be applied, as Martinique's slaves did in 1789. The visible reduction in colonial forces after the departure of one of the two regiments present and the disarmament of rural police in the months preceding August 1791 undoubtedly also emboldened the rebels.

Since July, slave delegates from plantations in the very center of the northern plain had met near Morne-Rouge several times to plan their uprising. The group included high-ranking slaves, notably *commandeurs* (overseers) and coach drivers who enjoyed their masters' trust while also wielding influence over the dozens of slaves on their respective plantations. The slave delegates believed that the king of France and the National Assembly in Paris had banned the use of the whip, had granted slaves three days of weekly rest, and had sent troops to force planters to comply. Yet during their planning meeting on Sunday, 14 August 1791, they decided not to wait for the supposed arrival of French soldiers and resolved instead to launch their revolt on Wednesday, 24 August. They chose that date because the colonial assembly was set to meet the following day in Le Cap (today Cap-Haïtien), where all the colony's elites and security forces would converge, giving the slaves more freedom to act. During their 14 August meeting (maybe followed by another on the 21st), the participants performed a religious ceremony that included the sacrifice of an animal and ingestion of its blood to bind and sanctify their union (later renamed the Bois-Caïman ceremony). But on 22 August, Boukman, one of the group's leaders, prematurely launched the rebellion in Acul parish, undoubtedly because some slaves, interrogated after having attacked a plantation manager, had begun to confess the imminence of an uprising.

From that point onward, the conspirators moved ahead with their revolt, which spread throughout Le Cap, under leaders who included Jean-François, Georges Biassou, Jeannot, and Jean-Baptiste Sans-Souci. Estimated at 2,000 on 23 August, the rebel slaves probably numbered as many as 10,000 (including 700 on horseback) by the 27th, and then 20,000—or possibly 80,000—one month later. By the end of September, they had burned and destroyed over 1,000 plantations (out of a total of 8,000 in the entire colony) and killed hundreds of whites, while taking others hostage. But at the same time, an incalculable number of slaves were dead—killed in combat, shot, or hanged during the indiscriminate crackdown launched by the colonial authorities of Le Cap as soon as the uprising began. Fires, massacres, and retaliatory massacres would continue for over a year, leading countless planters, at times with their slaves, to flee to Cuba, Jamaica, Louisiana, and the United States.[12]

The slave revolt in northern Saint Domingue came as an immense shock to the Americas and Europe alike. At the time, the "Pearl of the Antilles" was the most prosperous sugar colony, producing half of the sugar and coffee consumed in the world, or the equivalent of two-thirds of France's foreign trade. However, that economic success was the product of the forced labor of about 500,000 enslaved creoles and Africans in the colony, who alone represented half of the slaves in all the Caribbean islands colonized by European monarchies. It came at the price of the importation of nearly half a million captives (mostly males) from Africa between 1761 and 1790. In just the decade previous to 1791, the small French territory had imported a total of 237,000 African captives, or nearly one-third of the 768,000 new slaves then being brought to the Americas. The year 1790 alone marked an all-time high in the French slave trade to Saint Domingue: approximately 45,000 Africans were brought to the island alive, including 19,000 through the port of Le Cap, an annual record that would never be rivaled by any other port in the Americas.[13] At the same time, slaves' chances for emancipation, which had always been slim, diminished from year to year, dropping to less than four hundred cases in 1789, the majority of which involved mulatto women.[14] In order to understand how and why the uprising of 1791 occurred, it is therefore essential to grasp the human impact of those extreme figures, both from the perspective of creole slaves, bossales, or captives recently transported from Africa and from that of the planters who bought and exploited them. It is equally important to note that the ongoing importation of thousands of captive men, women, and children was due not solely to unprecedented greed among all-powerful planters, but also to the increased death rate of an overexploited labor force that constantly had to be replaced.

In 1790, the 45,000 Africans brought and sold in Saint Domingue that year joined the colony's existing 500,000 slaves, compared to only 40,000 whites (including planters and *petits blancs*) and 30,000 *gens de couleur libres* (several hundreds of whom were also slaveowning planters).[15] In 1791, another 28,000 African captives were brought to the colony, followed by nearly 10,000 the next year.[16] As a result, Africans represented a majority of the colony's slaves—and about half of its total population.[17] In other words, roughly one in two residents in Saint Domingue had survived the slave trade, originating primarily from West Central Africa (Congo) and the Bight of Benin; the majority were men, including many veterans of African wars. When the monarchic regime was about to collapse in France, and whites and free people of color began to clash in Saint Domingue, that demographic makeup would prove explosive.

The ambitions of the slaves who revolted in 1791 reflected their origins and varied perspectives. All of them undoubtedly yearned for freedom, as demonstrated by rebel groups' rejection of French promises of amnesty in exchange for voluntarily returning to their plantations and denouncing their leaders. Many among those enslaved men and women stopped demanding three free days a week, calling instead for the general emancipation supposedly declared by Louis XVI, all while claiming to fight in the king's name. Others explicitly evoked the freedom guaranteed by the Declaration of the Rights of Man, while some appealed to both the king and the National Assembly. The fact that those slaves claimed to act in the name of the king of France can be explained by three factors. First, the monarch was the only "master" to whom the slaveowners of Saint Domingue owed allegiance. Second, from the revolt's start, the Spanish king's army, in Hispaniola's eastern region, had provided aid to rebelling captives, reinforcing a perception of an all-powerful royal authority among the latter.[18] Third, many of the rebels came from African kingdoms, particularly Kongo, to which the Portuguese had introduced Catholicism at the end of the sixteenth century and where the very form of the monarchy—authoritarian or more democratic—lay at the heart of the armed conflicts in which they participated. For that matter, certain rebel groups in Saint Domingue elected or accepted the authority of a king (and sometimes a queen), a tradition going back to secret societies of "African nations" that assembled captives of the same ethnicity. However, when the uprising began, the elected kings were most often creoles, like the free black Jean-Baptiste Cap, king of Limbé and Port Mangot, who was broken on the wheel in early September 1791.[19] In addition, according to anthropologist Laënnec Hurbon, sixteen *curés des nègres*, out of the twenty-four in the apostolic parish in the island's northern region, supported the rebelling slaves, which led to the execution by colonial justice of three of them, including Father Philémon, *curé* in Limbé, who was hanged from gallows that displayed the head of Boukman, the rebel leader killed in combat in November of that same year.[20]

Confronted with colonial troops, rebels, often bossales, developed guerrilla strategies that quickly proved effective. They adapted their African military tactics to the terrain in the Caribbean and the limited means at their disposal. Organized into small groups, they preferred to launch quick-fire attacks, set traps, and then disperse rather than confront the enemy openly and in close quarters. They met French rifles and cannon with machetes, spears, and weapons they managed to steal from the enemy. Rebelling slaves thus responded to the violence of the slave plantation with an equally terrifying violence, and they did not hesitate to brutally massacre white planters, their overseers and their families. Granted, not every slave in the northern plain rebelled, and some defended their masters,[21] but for a majority of those enslaved men and women, even if they could not imagine where their rebellion would lead, the momentum driving the destruction of slavery, and its symbols and settings, overcame the fear of torture, the gallows, and the wheel. For them, slavery had never been a "patriarchal" and "civilizing" institution, and they had every intention of destroying it in its every form.

From January 1792 onward, rebel slaves in northern Saint Domingue had to simultaneously confront colonial forces, militias of whites and *gens de couleur*, and troops slowly arriving from France. Thousands of them had undoubtedly already been killed, or died in battle or from hunger and disease. Several of their leaders had been arrested and executed. But thousands more had, in fact, obtained their freedom by killing and expulsing their masters and could no longer be subjected as they once had been. Nonetheless, unbeknownst to their followers, the rebellion's main creole leaders, Jean-François and Biassou, tried to negotiate a deal with the colonial assembly, which was meant to result in several hundred rebels being amnestied and emancipated in exchange for the liberation of all white prisoners, even as other insurgents were to be reenslaved. Worse still, once the white captives were freed, the assembly broke its promise and refused to emancipate a single rebel under the pretext that such a move would legitimize the violent antislavery uprising. The battle resumed and the rebels' demands became more general. In July 1792, Jean-François, Biassou, and a third leader sent a declaration to the colonial assembly stating that "men are born free and equal in rights" and that their natural rights included "resistance to oppression," using phrasing more evocative of the U.S. Declaration of Independence than the French Declaration of the Rights of Man and the Citizen. From that point onward, they demanded "general liberty for all men retained in slavery" and a general amnesty before surrendering their weapons.[22]

Military Enrollment and Marronage in Western and Southern Saint Domingue

The situation in western and southern Saint Domingue was equally complex. Since the end of the Seven Years' War, immigration of French citizens to the region had increased. And like free men and women of color, many of the new immigrants had settled in areas unconducive to growing sugarcane; instead, they established coffee plantations that each employed between twenty and forty slaves. Before the rebellion in the northern plain even broke out, in January 1791, slaves had gathered in Port-Salut, near Cayes, to organize a protest demanding the three free days a week supposedly decided on by Louis XVI, but local authorities discovered their plan before it could be carried out and punished the participants. A precarious calm was then restored, and in August the slaves in those regions did not join the massive uprising in the North. However, since 1790, western and southern Saint Domingue had been destabilized by the triangular conflict between whites in favor or against the French Revolution and free people of color fighting for equality. None of those three camps was concerned with the plight of slaves, but, given their meager forces, each would enlist hundreds of enslaved men to reinforce their ranks, while promising them their freedom after several years of military service. Very quickly, however, those long-term promises were not enough to ensure slaves' support, and in February 1792, revolutionary colonists attempted to rally maroon bands through proclamations of amnesty, while free men of color mobilized slaves by promising them their immediate freedom.[23]

As a result, slaves on the battlefield ended up fighting one another in order to win their individual freedom, all while risking their lives to serve the interests of whites or *gens de couleur libres*, which were often contrary to their own. In the case of slaves enlisted in the service of free men of color, the former (whether they were black or mulatto, creoles or bossales) were in reality fighting so that *gens de couleur*, who were often their masters, could have the same rights as whites. As shown by a tragic episode near Port-au-Prince between September 1791 and March 1792, free men of color were ready to sacrifice slave combatants whom they had recently emancipated in order to ensure their own equality, without any consideration of their shared African ancestry.

In fact, during their negotiations with whites on the application of an initial and very limited decree of equality adopted in Paris in May 1791, which only applied to free Afro-descendants born to free parents, *gens de couleur libres* first agreed to demobilize the two thousand enslaved men they had armed and send them back to their plantations, and to submit the three hundred they had already emancipated to eight more years of service in the Port-au-Prince militia before they could actually become free. Then, even as the recruits protested against that violation of promises made them by free men of color, the latter once again ceded to the whites' demands and agreed that the three hundred freedmen be deported to British Honduras. The deportees were then chained and transported by boat to the coast of Nicaragua, no doubt for sale as slaves, but in March 1792 the British governor rejected them and sent them back to Port-au-Prince, still in chains. Local authorities then transferred them to another boat and charged *petits blancs* with killing them and throwing them into the ocean, leaving the survivors on board to die of hunger, a tragedy that deeply marked the collective memory of slaves in the region.[24] At the same time, however, in western and southern Saint Domingue, the conflict between whites and free *gens de couleur* allowed many slaves to flee their work sites, at first to join one of the two enemy camps, and later to disappear into nearby wooded hills, a strategy of collective marronage that would continue to be used for a long time. Consequently, in March and April 1792, in the Cul-de-Sac plain, between ten thousand and fifteen thousand rebel slaves, many of them Africans, formed an army led by an insurgent named Hyacinthe, and laid waste to the surrounding plantations before dispersing into hard-to-reach encampments.[25]

When all the island's free Afro-descendants—that is, blacks, mulattos, and quadroons, whether they had been emancipated or were born of free parents— learned that the National Assembly had adopted the decree of 4 April 1792 that granted them equality and citizenship, they stopped fighting and became defenders of the republican regime. They then turned to disarming the slaves who had supported the belligerents and convincing runaways to return to work on plantations, including their own at times. Whites did the same, even as divisions remained between republicans and defenders of the ancien régime. As for the slaves who had taken advantage of the unrest to enlist or flee, they were far from ready to abandon their hope of freedom. Several bands of rebel slaves took refuge in the South and established new marronage camps, particularly in a mountainous region called the Platons. In July 1792, two of their leaders, Armand and Martial, attempted to negotiate with planters, proffering their return to work in exchange for their freedom and that of three hundred combatants, three free days a week for every slave, and a whip ban, but not for the general abolition of slavery, in contrast to Jean-François and Biassou in the North. Those demands were nonetheless an important step toward the end of slavery, as they transformed slaves into part-time workers and eliminated the symbolic and concrete mark (i.e., scars left on the skin) of the master's absolute power: the whip. But planters refused to make any concessions and asked government forces to chase the rebels from the region. In response, hundreds of other slaves fled plantations and wreaked havoc across the region of Cayes.

The governor then sent new troops against the rebels, which included a regiment of *libres de couleur* under the mulatto leader André Rigaud. The operation failed, however, prompting the rebels to demand the emancipation of the four thousand to five thousand runaway slaves hiding in the Platons, as well as rights over the land they were occupying.[26] Negotiations resumed, with the participation of Rigaud, who had just been promoted to an officer in the French republican army, but whom the rebels did not trust. When he offered to grant seven hundred insurgents their freedom, a group of them accepted, while the rest refused to believe Rigaud and remained with the thousands of fugitives in the Platons. Over the following months, hundreds of slaves from the South and West continued to abandon their plantations and flee to the Platons, which became home to a true maroon society despite the dispatch of fresh recruits from France to subdue them. By the end of 1792, the rebelling slaves had destroyed more than one-third of the plantations in the South and killed a similar proportion of white colonists and mulattos. The entire plain south of the Platons had been destroyed and its white residents had fled to the city of Les Cayes or left the colony.

The Kingdom of the Platons, as it was called by rebels, numbered between ten thousand and twelve thousand men, women, and children. According to historian Carolyn Flick, its social organization reflected the aspirations of those who had survived the terrifying universe of plantations, often after having endured capture in Africa and the Atlantic crossing. Its thousands of rebel-maroons had established several encampments, each with eight hundred to nine hundred huts, cultivated fields, food reserves, and emergency shelters. They had constructed observation posts and pits for protection and, like maroons in previous centuries, launched raids across the region to collect livestock, weapons, and munitions and to recruit new fugitives. At the same time, the entire South was impacted by the uprising, as many slaves still on plantations had more or less stopped working.[27]

Slaves' Struggle for the Abolition of Slavery (1793–1794)

In September 1792, the arrival of six thousand French soldiers and civil commissioners appointed by the National Convention modified the balance of power but was unable to reestablish peace in Saint Domingue. The envoys from France first sided with free men of African descent, who claimed to be defending the French republic that had granted them equal rights. However, they lost the support of conservative white planters, many of whom left the colony for regions that were more stable. At the same time, runaway or recalcitrant slaves continued to refuse to return to work on those plantations that remained operational. The two commissioners sent from France, Léger Félicité Sonthonax in the North and Étienne Polverel in the West and South, were Jacobins in favor of giving rights to free *gens de couleur*. But though they may have been opposed to slavery in principle, they first wanted to reestablish order and resume production, and consequently sent French soldiers and free colored troops against the rebel slaves. Those well-armed forces killed countless insurgents and destroyed their camps and plots of farmed land, forcing some of the survivors to return to their plantations, though many maroons were able to avoid capture.

In the South, the Kingdom of the Platons was the very antithesis of the French Republic and represented an alternative society that the commissioners wanted to destroy at any cost. To that end, Polverel mobilized two thousand soldiers and slaves with the promise of freedom. Approximately two hundred of those slaves, placed under the orders of Jean Kina, recently emancipated for exemplary military service, would play a crucial role in the suppression of the rebel kingdom.[28] Faced with such a broad deployment, the insurgents could not

Burning of Le Cap, 1793. (Frontispice of *Saint-Domingue, ou Histoire de ses révolutions* [Paris: Tiger, 1820])

win by force of arms. In early 1793, Armand and Martial gathered the leaders of the maroon camps and ordered them to disperse in small groups into the inland mountains. Others, particularly women, children, and the elderly, surrendered to French troops, who massacred every last one of them. Similarly, fugitives who decided to return to their plantations were brutally punished or executed by planters who did not hesitate to display their dismembered heads and limbs to terrify remaining slaves. Nonetheless, more than three thousand insurgents, including Armand and Martial, remained on the offensive between the Platons and Macaya, resolved to never fall under the yoke of slavery again.[29]

Shortly after Louis XVI's execution in January 1793, revolutionary France went to war with the British and Spanish monarchies. The latter allied with Jean-François and Biassou in the North, along with thousands of slaves still in rebellion. Two new uprisings simultaneously erupted, the first launched by slaves in the Cul-de-Sac plain, and the second by maroons in the Baoruco Mountains, on the southern frontier with Spanish territory.[30] The situation worsened when Polverel and Sonthonax promulgated a decree limiting masters' rights over their slaves, following which they lost the support of the remaining white planters. In addition, in the port of Le Cap, sailors, soldiers, and *libres de couleur*, backed by rebel slaves released from prison, faced off in the name of one side or the other, then pillaged and set the city ablaze, forcing thousands of colonists into exile.[31] With Le Cap on fire, and lacking enough French troops to reestablish order, the two commissioners announced, on 21 June 1793, that all "black warriors" who would "fight for the Republic" would be free and enjoy "all the rights belonging to French citizens."[32] That promise of freedom and equality as citizens to enslaved men who enlisted in the republican army was a first in the history of the Americas: in addition to making military service a method of emancipation, it erased all racial discrimination by granting full citizenship to recruits.

The first to respond to the commissioners' offer were three thousand members of rebel maroon bands from the hinterlands of Le Cap, led by the African Pierrot. But a large number of slaves, many of whom had been rebelling for nearly two years, remained distrustful. In the North, Jean-François and Biassou and their thousands of insurgent slaves continued to serve the king of Spain, who since May had promised them land and freedom for themselves and their families in exchange for their military support. And in June, Toussaint Louverture, himself a creole and former elite slave turned emancipated owner of a small plantation, also sided with the Spanish monarchy. In fact, following Louis XVI's execution, many rebel leaders doubted that France, now incarnated not by a king but by the unpredictable institutions of a republic in full revolution, could honor the promises of emancipation made to soldier-slaves. In July, Polverel and Sonthonax were forced to make another effort to demonstrate their good faith: they declared that slave combatants would obtain not only their own freedom, but that of their wives and children as well. In western and southern Saint Domingue, where the Spanish did not directly threaten the commissioners' power, many slaves, notably the intransigent maroons of the Platons and the Cul-de-Sac region, responded favorably to the offer of military service on behalf of the French Republic in exchange for the promise of collective emancipation.

The massive surge of slaves to the commissioners' side had an indirect consequence, as it transformed some *libres de couleur* into enemies of the French Republic that had granted them equality one year earlier but that was now depriving them of their captive labor force. Those tensions were compounded by the efforts of pro-Spain royalists to break the recent alliance between slaves and the French commissioners by promising the former freedom and land. Polverel had the conspirators captured, but that measure did nothing to restore domestic calm or stop attacks by Spain and Great Britain. At this stage, the revolutionary commissioners hoping to keep Saint Domingue under French control had no choice but to rally the enslaved majority of the population to defend the colony against its internal and external enemies. To do so, they had to abolish slavery and grant all slaves the freedom they demanded, first in the North on 29 August, then the West on 4 September, and finally the South on 31 October 1793.[33] In other words, it was rebel slaves themselves who wrested the concession of abolition from Sonthonax and Polverel.

A few months later, on 4 February 1794, the National Convention in Paris voted that "the slavery of the Negroes is abolished in all the colonies. In consequence, it decrees that all men, without distinction of color, domiciled in the colonies, are French citizens and will enjoy all rights guaranteed by the constitution."[34] This decree was revolutionary in two ways: not only did it liberate all slaves in French colonies without compensating slaveowners, but it also confirmed the equality and citizenship of all. In France, where the abolitionist movement had expanded from the Société des Amis des Noirs to several Montagnards, the decree prompted modest festivities, supervised by authorities lauding the French motto "Liberty, Equality, and Fraternity."[35]

Freedmen's Resistance to Labor Codes

In Saint Domingue, slaves quickly grasped that, in reality, the abolition declared by French commissioners between August and October 1793 only brought about a partial end to slavery and was far from offering freedom as most of them had imagined, forcing enslaved men and women instead to work on plantations or enlist in the army. The decree abolishing slavery adopted by the National Convention in February 1794 did not change that. In fact, Sonthonax and Polverel intended to encourage the resumption of the exportation of sugar and coffee produced by the African and creole *nouveaux libres* (newly free).[36] Their labor codes therefore compelled "cultivators," as former plantation slaves were renamed, to work six days a week, for which they were paid a quarter of the plantation's output, after taxes, according to a distribution system that corresponded to the worker's rank and gender, with women receiving less than men despite performing identical tasks. The commissioners also reduced the size of the garden plots in which workers had been able to grow their own provisions and sell the surplus in local markets. Though the whip was officially banned, the stocks, prison, fines, seizure of one's production, and the galleys were used to punish transgressors, defiant workers, and troublemakers.[37] The idea of distributing emigrated colonists' property to cultivators, suggested by Polverel in 1793, was never implemented.[38]

This regulated version of freedom was quite far from the complete one envisaged by the *nouveaux libres* or even the version that included three rest days for plantation workers, which had supposedly been approved by the king in 1789 and rumors of which had regularly sparked rebellions. For freed slaves, those highly sought-after three days represented a chance to focus on cultivating their own provision grounds, on which they could grow food and raise pigs and chickens to eat or sell at local markets, access the wood and water in surrounding areas, circulate freely, and, more profoundly, be masters over themselves and a significant portion of their time. The gap between *nouveaux libres*' expectations, especially those of Africans who had not been born within the slave plantation system, and the commissioners' was therefore substantial.

Refusals to work, escapes, and complaints multiplied among cultivators—especially among women, who protested being paid less than men for identical work now that, with the army's recruitment of men, a large portion of plantation production relied on them. Unequal conditions were another source of contention, as certain estate masters and overseers (now no longer called *commandeurs* but *conducteurs*) as well as their disciplinary methods had not changed, to the great discontent of former slaves who accused them of violating the emancipation decree. Elsewhere, new managers had difficulty forcing their workers to obey them, to the point that the commissioners gave the latter the choice between working six days a week in exchange for one-quarter of their production, or five days in exchange for merely one-eighth. Despite the imbalance between the two reward systems, many cultivators collectively opted for the two days off, which, in their minds, was preferable though seemingly less profitable. Others moved onto abandoned plantations that they reorganized so that the best land was dedicated to food production. *Nouveaux libres* everywhere used communal areas, like woods or pastures, for their own benefit, appropriated a portion of products intended for exportation, and used goods left behind by exiled colonists. Many cultivators fled to maroon communities established after 1791, which had never been completely dissolved. This informal economy did not correspond to the idea that the commissioners and the National Assembly had regarding the emancipation of slaves, but by supplying cultivators and local and regional markets, it was undoubtedly what ensured the survival of the colony and its troops between 1793 and 1800.[39]

Toussaint Louverture rallied behind revolutionary France in May 1794. He was even harsher than the revolutionary commissioners when it came to former slaves. When he began to wield power in 1796, Louverture told cultivators protesting their new conditions that they needed to work hard in order to thank the French government for having granted them their freedom and to show that they deserved it—without mentioning that it was in fact the slave uprising that had forced France to abolish slavery. Shortly afterward, the former black slave Jean-Jacques Dessalines, then Louverture's faithful right-hand man, and Rigaud moved to militarize farm work. In the South, Rigaud went so far as to rent abandoned plantations to members of pre-1794 slaveowning *gens de couleur*. Almost everywhere, army officers, many of whom had been slaves, and Dessalines in particular, took advantage of their new power to seize plantations. In 1798, when Louverture called on former white planters to come back and take over sugar production, those who returned sometimes found their plantations in the hands of the new black military elite or their former overseers.

Once established as the colony autocratic governor, Louverture imposed iron discipline on its inhabitants, purporting to be defending their freedom. His *Règlement de culture* (Agriculture Code) of October 1800 subjected cultivators to the same rules governing soldiers: leaving one's plantation without a permit was equivalent to desertion, and disobedience to treason. In February 1802, Louverture signed a decree banning farmers from individually or collectively buying the small plots of land available near plantations.[40] Granted, his constitution of July 1801 maintained that "there can exist no slaves in [Saint Domingue] territory, where servitude is forever abolished and all men are born, live and die free and French." Moreover, "every man, whatever his color, has access to all types of employment." At the same time, though, the constitution transformed the plantation (*habitation*) into a fundamental institution of the new society, akin to the family: the plantation owner was meant to be like a father to any farmers or laborers, who were equated to his children. Though the cultivator had a clear right to a portion of the harvest, he or she was forced to labor tirelessly to get the colony's agricultural production on track. In other words, although *nouveaux libres* were free in principle, they had to work full time as cultivators—the price of their freedom. A constitutional article even stipulated that "agricultural workers essential to the revival and expansion of agriculture shall be brought to Saint Domingue" and charged the governor with "taking suitable measures to encourage this increase in the labor force," which looked much like a willingness to resume the importation of slaves.[41] In November 1801, Louverture took another step toward the militarization of society, obliging all the island's inhabitants to carry security cards, a measure that his government did not have the means to enforce but that was representative of his desire for absolute control. And indeed, in 1801, exports of sugar, coffee, and cotton saw a considerable uptick in relation to 1795 levels, though they remained largely inferior to the quantities recorded in 1789.[42]

The militarization of farming developed by Toussaint Louverture sparked distrust and rebellion among many of the *nouveaux libres* already stinging from the regulations implemented by revolutionary commissioners and who saw their hopes for three days off a week once again disappearing. Some even suspected that Louverture wanted to reestablish slavery, based on the return of the whip to plantations in the form of the liana and his inviting exiled white planters to return. The *nouveaux libres*, notably women, who were often more numerous in the fields, increased their resistance efforts. By 1800, young men and women who had never experienced slavery at its peak, except briefly during childhood, had grown up against a backdrop of revolt and the mobilization of their elders, as well as the disorganization and war that followed abolition; they were therefore ill inclined to forced labor, even when ordered by a black governor who looked like them. Strikes increased, despite crackdowns. Cultivators did not hesitate to destroy their work sites or kill their new superiors. A lot of men enlisted in the army to escape the plantation and hoped to become, in their turn, military oppressors. Many continued to rely on the old strategy of marronage, either by hiding with their families in largely inaccessible regions or by forming bands that lived off pillaging and benefited from the reigning instability. Others still, particularly in the devastated plain of Le Cap, were able to form communities of autonomous farming families on the ruins of former plantations. They drew from their experiences with garden plots attached to slave plantations to develop food crops and raise livestock that provided subsistence and were also sold in local markets. Some cultivators, as demonstrated by the ban passed by Louverture in February 1801, allied to buy land together. At the same time, they openly asserted their culture, language, and syncretic religious practices (already known by the name of Vaudoux), which had been nourished by the continuous arrival of new captives from various regions of western Africa until 1791. Those practices, notably "nocturnal assemblies and dances," were sufficiently widespread for Louverture to view them as subversive and ban them via decree in January 1800.[43] As for the articles of Louverture's 1801 constitution pertaining to religion and "mores," they appear to have served as warnings against popular lifestyles, stipulating "the only religion to be publicly practiced is the Catholic, apostolic, and Roman religion" and forcing each parish "to provide for the upkeep of the faith and its ministers." Those articles also protected the "civil and religious institution of marriage," outlawing divorce and favoring the rights of legitimate children.[44] The imposition of militarized labor and Catholic cultural norms would subsequently alienate a number of cultivators and former urban slaves under Louverture's regime.

The Maroon Bands, Spearheads of Bonaparte's Defeat

The *nouveaux libres*' resistance to Louverture's dictatorship took diverse forms. Existing maroon bands often refused to dissolve or surrender their weapons. That tenacity was particularly characteristic of Africans who had been waging guerrilla warfare since 1791. Although there are few sources documenting the lives of those rebel groups, some historians have attempted to reconstruct them. As a whole, though the uprising of August 1791 was well planned by elite creole slaves, the insurgents lacked military experience, unlike a large number of Kongo, Yoruba, or Igbo bossales, among others. In addition, Africans from the same nation or ethnic group, though dispersed across several plantations, often joined forces through secret societies, a by-product of the law banning Africans of shared origin in the French Caribbean from associating with one another.[45] Those characteristics explain the widespread participation of Africans in the insurrection of 1791–92, followed by their resistance to the new "free" labor codes beginning in 1793. While some of those men became soldiers in the large armies organized on the European model and led by the creoles Jean-François, Biassou, Rigaud, Louverture, and Dessalines, others continued their fight in autonomous rebel units. Several bands assembled fighters from one primary ethnic group, which would then impose its strategies and chosen leader (and possibly language of communication) on the others. That was the case for the small army led by Macaya, a runaway originally from Kongo, as were most of his followers; the three-thousand-man unit led by Dieudonné, also from Kongo; and the group formed by the Yoruba leader Alaou. Other bands indiscriminately gathered former enslaved creoles, Africans, and runaways under the command of a black or mulatto leader. Though Jean-François, Biassou, and Louverture all often complained that they were unable to control these undisciplined bands, they each recognized their aptitude for waging war. According to historian John Thornton, tensions between rebels in Saint Domingue led to the development of a two-tiered military system: above, large armies led by well-established leaders recognized in France, and below, a number of small units under the command of autonomous chiefs who periodically renegotiated the terms of their support for military troops.[46]

However, in 1802, when Napoléon Bonaparte, sixteen months after seizing power in France, sent General Victor-Emmanuel Leclerc to wrest control of Saint Domingue from Louverture, the "maroon bands" were the only ones to resist from the beginning. In February 1802, Bonaparte's brother-in-law arrived in the colony with an armada of fifty ships transporting twenty-two thousand soldiers and twenty thousand sailors.[47] His plan consisted of four stages: first, rally several black generals to his cause by assuring them of his peaceful intentions; next, attack and defeat Louverture, Dessalines, and Henri Christophe[48] to deprive the *nouveaux libres* of their principal leaders; third, disarm all the men in the existing troops and bands; and, finally, send those men back to work on plantations and deport all the black or mulatto generals regardless of their political engagement. After that, slavery could be reestablished—an objective to which Leclerc only admitted after several months.[49] In order to gain international support at a time when European powers were also facing off in the Caribbean, Bonaparte presented Leclerc's expedition as a crusade of civilization against the rise of black barbarism in the Americas.[50]

At first the four-stage plan seemed feasible. Before his departure, Leclerc had enlisted the participation of mulatto commanders banned by Louverture, such as Rigaud and his second-in-command, Alexandre Pétion, who was in France. Of course, black generals initially joined forces to oppose his arrival in Saint Domingue. Christophe had Le Cap evacuated and burned down; other cities endured the same fate. His troops and those under the command of Louverture and Dessalines violently resisted the arrival of French soldiers, notably inflicting 1,500 deaths and a humiliating retreat on Leclerc's forces on Artibonite plain. However, Leclerc was quickly able to take advantage of the colony's internal conflicts, and the junior chiefs rallied to his army. Bonaparte sent reinforcements from France and, in mid-April, Christophe, in all likelihood concerned about the effects of the recent signing of a peace treaty between Great Britain and France, negotiated his surrender to Leclerc. Shortly thereafter, Louverture and Dessalines also admitted defeat, along with the majority of their men. In May 1802, therefore, it seemed that Leclerc had accomplished the first part of his plan. And though his French troops had been decimated by fighting and yellow fever, he would henceforth be able to rely on "indigenous" troops led by black generals to continue his mission.

However, the "maroon bands" that Louverture and his allies had never been able to control refused to give themselves up, and with the cultivators' support they harassed the French. At that point, it had already been over ten years since the slaves from the Plaine du Nord had revolted, and nearly as long since many of them had refused to return to their plantations. The rebel commanders included Sans-Souci, Macaya, Sylla, and Petit-Noël Prieur in the North, Lamour Dérance and Cangé in the West, and Toussaint Jean-Baptiste, Gilles Bénech, Goman and Jean Panier in the South. They were primarily Africans, and each had at least a few hundred followers and sometimes camps to shelter their families and provisions. They continued to resist because they sensed that slavery would be restored and distrusted both the French and creole, mulatto, and emancipated black leaders, all of whom wanted to militarize agriculture. The tenacity and courage of those maroon bands was notably put to the test after Louverture's deportation in June 1802, when Dessalines and Christophe became the main executors of Bonaparte's design. In fact, Dessalines proved so deft at using troops to execute "all the most odious measures" ordered by Leclerc that the latter praised him as "the butcher of the blacks," and another French general as "the cultivators' scarecrow."[51]

Yet Leclerc failed to implement the other stages of his plan. First of all, though he was able to neutralize and then successively deport Louverture and Rigaud, he could not do without Dessalines, Christophe, and other black and mulatto commanders and their "indigenous" troops, whom he needed to compensate for the heavy losses among French troops despite the arrival of reinforcements from France. Consequently, he was not only forced to abandon his plan to eliminate the black generals, but in fact had to reinforce and therefore legitimize their power. Finally, even with their cooperation, the task of disarming *nouveaux libres* and rebels in maroon bands proved impossible. The disarmament prompted the mistrust and later open resistance of a population increasingly convinced that the final goal of the Napoleonic operation was the reestablishment of the slave plantation system. "Indigenous" men and officers began to divert weapons to be either hidden or given to rebel bands, while others joined those same groups. The reduced French army demonstrated a growing suspicion of the "indigenous" army, and was quick to inflict terror and summary justice on creoles and bossales who were ready to die rather than return to slavery.[52]

By October 1802, Leclerc understood that he could not implement the fourth stage of his plan, meaning sending soldiers of the "indigenous" army back to their plantations and deporting their black and mulatto military leaders. Faced with defections and the risk of a general uprising of the population, he launched a war of extermination. "We must destroy all the blacks of the mountains—men and women—and spare only children under twelve years of age. We must destroy half of those in the plains and must not leave a single colored person in the colony who has worn an epaulette," he wrote to Bonaparte at the time.[53] French units carried out multiple massacres, killing black rebels and loyalists alike. In one month they imprisoned nearly four thousand "indigenous" soldiers on boats before throwing them overboard in shackles. At the same time, news from France confirmed Bonaparte's racist and proslavery schemes: he passed decrees reestablishing the slave trade and banning blacks and mulattos from entering the continental territory of the Republic without special authorization, amid rumors of the reestablishment of slavery in Guadeloupe.[54]

The first "indigenous" general to turn against Napoleonic France with his men was Pétion, also in October 1802. Dessalines and Christophe followed suit with their troops. In November, Leclerc died from yellow fever. His second in command, General Donatien Marie Joseph de Rochambeau, another veteran of the U.S. War of Independence, took command of the army and alienated the last remaining defenders of France in Saint Domingue through his unrestricted use of terror and torture against blacks. For example, he employed dozens of dogs that had been trained to chase cimarrones in Cuba, which he distributed to his regiments while specifying: "I don't need to tell you that no rations or expenditures are authorized for the nourishment of the dogs; you should give them blacks to eat." He also terrified the populations in cities by publicly feeding live blacks to the famished dogs.[55] Those atrocities temporarily united many of the island's inhabitants—blacks and mulattos, creoles and Africans, *nouveaux* and *anciens libres*, cultivators, runaways, and members of "indigenous" armies or "rebel bands," who though primarily men also included women and children at times. They too used cruel and terrifying methods against whites still in the territory and against a French army whose troops dissolved under the combined effect of attacks, massacres, and diseases. Of the tens of thousands of soldiers and sailors sent to Saint Domingue between January and June 1802, 50,000 had died. Thousands more were no longer able to fight. Furthermore, in May 1803, Bonaparte had sold the vast Louisiana territory to the United States for 60 million gold francs to try to compensate for the debts caused by this war.[56] Battles and massacres continued for another six months, costing tens of thousands of human lives. Of the 40,000 whites in Saint Domingue before the August 1791 uprising, nearly all had disappeared, been massacred, or gone into exile. Many of the colony's 30,000 *gens de couleur libres* had also left the island, while others had been banished and thousands had died in combat or been exterminated. Of the 500,000 enslaved Africans and creoles, at least 100,000, mostly men, had been brutally killed or had perished as a result of Leclerc's expedition. In 1805, the total population of Haiti was estimated to be a mere 380,000 inhabitants, or a decrease of nearly one-third in comparison to 1790, though historian Philipp Girard posits a drop of 50 percent. Moreover, the proportion of women to men was nearly three to two, and the army absorbed between 15,000 and 37,000 men. As a result, most of both plantation labor and subsistence farming relied on women.[57]

Following the French defeat at the Battle of Vertières on 18 November 1803, Rochambeau surrendered to Dessalines, who triumphantly entered the city of Le Cap. Napoleonic France abandoned its "Pearl of the Antilles" to its former slaves and *gens de couleur libres*. Renamed Haiti, Saint Domingue became the second independent nation in the Americas and the only one to have irreversibly abolished slavery. From the slave perspective, this victory was enormous: by using different combat strategies and their demographic strength, they had forced revolutionary France's commissioners to declare their freedom in 1793, which was reinforced by the decree abolishing slavery in every French colony in 1794. Ten years later, those former slaves definitively expulsed Bonaparte's troops and the last French slaveowners from the territory. The thousands of rebel men, along with women and children, in the "maroon bands" as well as the thousands of soldiers led by "indigenous" generals had clearly demonstrated their rejection of forced plantation labor. With independence, they would gain the certainty that slavery could never be imposed on them again. However, the internal conflicts that arose during the thirteen years of war had not disappeared, not even during the united front against Leclerc and Rochambeau's army.

The Meaning of Freedom for the New Citizens of Haiti

Since 1791, free *gens de couleur* and slaves, renamed *anciens* and *nouveaux libres* following abolition in 1793, had not been fighting for the same goals. These two major social categories, already divided under the ancien régime, continued to split apart, as demonstrated by certain episodes previously described in this chapter. Most notably, beginning in 1794, the militarization of agricultural work, culminating with the iron discipline imposed by Louverture in 1800, made cultivators, whether they were creoles or bossales, hostile to the new leaders. In reality, the postemancipation overseers considered the *nouveaux libres* to be an exploitable workforce requiring military discipline, meaning the whip or the liana, as during the slavery regime. At the same time, Louverture and his deputies launched a merciless—though inconclusive—war against resistant maroon bands harboring plantation fugitives.

Those tensions, exacerbated by over ten years of fighting, were fully revealed during the decisive months between June and October 1801, when several leaders, nearly all Africans, refused to rally behind General Leclerc. According to anthropologist Gérard Barthélémy, "Leaders of band like Sans-Souci, Sylla, Macaya, Petit-Noël Prieur, and Lamour Dérance were the only ones to maintain dissidence alive" and saved the uprising.[58] When the creole generals Dessalines, Christophe, and Pétion finally turned against a France that was once again racist and proslavery, rebel leaders refused to yield to them. The creole generals then waged a war within the war against Bonaparte's troops, which was intended to eliminate or marginalize the rebellious chiefs and their bands. For example, Dessalines had Petit-Noël Prieur and Lamour Dérance killed; Christophe tracked Sans-Souci and his followers before trapping them and having them slain.[59]

Among all the chiefs of the "maroon bands" who, since the summer of 1802, foiled Bonaparte's plan to restore the ancien régime to Saint Domingue, the creole and mulatto Cangé was the only one to be included among the signatories of Haiti's Declaration of Independence on 1 January 1804.[60] The others cosigners, led by Dessalines, had all collaborated with Leclerc at some point. No African survivors of the slave trade were included among them, but a few signatories had been plantation slaves in their early lives. The majority were mulattos, sometimes from families of slaveowning planters and educated in France. That meant they had opposing interests, which would lead to internal divisions. Nonetheless, on a grimmer note, they all agreed on the necessity, already demonstrated by Louverture, of building a nation in which former African and creole plantation slaves and their descendants would continue to be marginalized and exploited by the new military and mulatto elites. Dessalines's proclamations and constitution failed to mention Africa entirely: the general announced that he had "avenged America"; the 1805 constitution renamed Saint Domingue "Haïti" or "Hayti," a Taino-Arawak word that had supposedly been the name of the island before Christopher Columbus's landing in 1492 and stated that, regardless of their skin color, "the Haitians shall hence forward be known only by the generic appellation of Blacks."[61]

But how did these "Blacks," many of them former plantation slaves born in Africa, live? Granted, the Imperial Constitution of 1805 confirmed that "slavery is forever abolished" in its second article. But it allowed Haitians few liberties beyond freedom of religion. It split the territory into military districts and spoke of "respect for the chiefs, subordination and discipline." The Haitian was meant to be "a good father, good son, a good husband, and especially a good soldier," and "must possess a mechanic art." Agriculture had to "be honored and protected." Property was "sacred," but "all property which formerly belonged to any white Frenchmen" (the last French citizens remaining in Haiti were massacred or expelled on Dessalines's orders) was confiscated by the state, after which no white could acquire land within the territory. Conferring unlimited power on Emperor Dessalines and his minister of finances and the interior, the constitution instituted a system of militarized agriculture similar to that sought after by Sonthonax and Polverel, and later Louverture, though it did introduce a new actor: the Haitian state, as incarnated by a military dictator.[62]

However, less than a year and a half after his imperial constitution was approved, Dessalines was assassinated, and Haiti's new elites continued to be divided over ways to incite or force cultivators to produce sugar and coffee for exportation. The country generals (for many blacks living in the North) favored a regime reminiscent of Louverture's, with land belonging to the state, for which they would act as managers and for which cultivators would be paid with a small portion of their crops. The *anciens libres*, primarily mulattos in the West and South, typically preferred a system of private property that allowed them to conserve their estates and acquire new lands that would be farmed by poor laborers or sharecroppers. Until the end of the 1810s, those differences resulted in a divided Haiti, with a northern kingdom under Henri Christophe (who became King Henri I of Haiti) and a southern republic led by Alexandre Pétion (named president for life in 1816). Dispersed throughout the territory, illiterate and penniless men and women cultivators (the latter were often widows and raising children on their own) were in no condition to formulate a collective counterplan against the island's new elites. On the other hand, many did fight to keep their plantation-adjacent garden plots. A large number settled in particularly steep interior regions where sugarcane and coffee plantations had failed to take hold. During the war these areas had been controlled by "maroon bands"; those men and women grew food crops, raised chickens and other animals, and produced goods for markets and their own needs, just as they had while enslaved.[63]

Though the experiences of former slaves who became Haitians had been harsh, in 1805 they in all likelihood were living under conditions similar to those of a large number of poor free men and women in Iberian continental America—and far from the deadly brutality of the slave plantation. Nonetheless, whether they belonged to the large farmer majority or the small military and urban elite, every Haitian was facing a world of unprecedented hostility. They paid an exorbitant price for their victory over slavery and Napoleonic France. For over twenty years, France refused to sign an armistice with the newly independent nation and continued to threaten Haitians with invasion as long as exiled colonists were not compensated for their losses. As King Henri

Christophe's outraged secretary told the English abolitionist Thomas Clarkson in 1819: "What rights, what arguments can the ex-colonists then allege to justify their claim for an indemnity? Is it possible that they wish to be recompensed for the loss of our persons? Is it conceivable that the Haitians who have escaped torture and massacre at the hands of these men, Haitians who have conquered their own country by the force of their arms and at the cost of their blood, that these same free Haitians should now purchase their property and persons once again with money paid to their former oppressors?"[64]

Yet that was what France wanted. With threats of aggression made as soon as the colony gained independence, it compelled Haitian leaders to resume exports of tropical products to be able to import weapons and maintain countless troops in a state of alert, at a time when they should have been rebuilding a country devastated by thirteen years of war. France also ensured the new nation's diplomatic isolation, while delivering it into the diktats of U.S. and European merchants. Finally, after northern and southern Haiti were reunited, in 1825, the king of France Charles X sent fourteen ships armed with hundreds of cannons to force Haitian president Jean-Pierre Boyer to sign a peace treaty on French terms, meaning payment of compensation of 150 million gold francs and trade advantages for France—whereas Bonaparte had sold the vast territory of Louisiana to the United State for 60 million gold francs. Even though that sum was reduced to 90 million gold francs in 1838, Haiti would continue to gamble its future by paying it off in installments until 1888.[65]

The punishment was undoubtedly commensurate with the outrage felt by French leaders. However, from 1791 to 1804, the slave uprising in Saint Domingue and its transformation into a liberation war panicked rulers and slaveowners in a large portion of the Americas as well; at the same time, the Haitian long revolutionary process fostered hopes for freedom among servile populations. Those years were therefore interspersed with slave revolts and conspiracies that showed the extent to which the question of maintaining slavery had become central in American societies.

≡ 7 ≡
The Shock Waves of the Haitian Revolution

The massive slave insurrection in northern Saint Domingue in August 1791 took both the Americas and Europe by surprise. Yet the uprising did not truly represent the "unthinkable," to borrow an expression from anthropologist Michel-Rolph Trouillot, given that fears of a planned slave revolt entailing the destruction of centers of production and the murder of whites had haunted colonial elites regularly since the discovery of a presumed conspiracy in Mexico City in 1537.[1] In reality, the truly "unthinkable" came with the outcome, thirteen years later, of the process begun in Saint Domingue in 1791: the Haitian Revolution—visible proof, in other words, that former, often African, slaves could defeat Napoléon Bonaparte's army, abolish slavery for good, and declare the independence of a European colony. Between 1791 and 1804, and afterward, news of the events that had transformed Saint Domingue into Haiti circulated widely across a Western Hemisphere already agitated by imperial wars and privateer attacks, prompting diverse interpretations and rumors.

This chapter focuses on how the Haitian revolutionary process impacted the liberation strategies used by enslaved peoples in the Americas during the two decades that followed the uprising on the Plaine du Nord in 1791. To what extent did the general revolt in Saint Domingue and the resulting definitive abolition of slavery and establishment of an independent black nation favor, in the minds of enslaved men and women in the rest of the Americas, armed rebellion over other liberation strategies? In other words, was the revolutionary process that wreaked havoc across Saint Domingue a decisive turning point that prompted other slaves to resort primarily to insurrection to gain their freedom, following the model of their counterparts in the former French colony?

To answer those questions, this chapter examines the many slave rebellions and conspiracies recorded in the wake of events in Saint Domingue between 1792 and 1811. In particular, it aims to identify movements that were clearly inspired by the Haitian process in terms of objective—the general emancipation of slaves—and strategy—a massive slave insurrection involving destruction and/or violence against whites and security forces. Namely because during that period, announcements of slave uprisings and conspiracies, at times coordinated with free people of African descent, multiplied nearly everywhere, from Cuba to Curaçao, Virginia to Louisiana, and Venezuela to Brazil. David Geggus, for example, counts no less than sixty rebellions and plots outside Saint Domingue, while highlighting that, in fact, very few were revolts aimed at the general emancipation of slaves.[2] Many movements only mobilized one or two dozen slaves, others were limited to enthusiastic discussions or nonviolent protests by men and women hoping for freedom, and others still only existed in the imaginations of frightened whites.

Of all those revolts and conspiracies, the only extensive slave rebellion overtly linked to the one in Saint Domingue occurred in Curaçao in 1795. However, if slaves elsewhere only rebelled rarely or in small numbers, it was clearly not because they did not desire their freedom, but because they understood that the local and international conditions in which they lived were unfavorable to revolt. As chapters 8 and 9 will show, they continued to resort primarily to flight, manumission, and military service, when and how the context allowed.

After its 1804 victory, the Haitian Revolution had indisputable repercussions on enslaved peoples across the Americas: it broadened their perspectives and revealed that slavery was not an indestructible institution. But Haiti, at that time divided between an imperial North and a republican South, threatened by a French invasion, and ostracized by all nations, could not back the slaves rebelling in its name. At the same time, its very existence gave substance throughout the region to the age-old narrative of the slave plot to destroy a colony and exterminate its whites. As a result, leaders everywhere, and whites in general, remained on the lookout for "another Haiti," which lead to unprecedented waves of repression.

French Colonies' Slaves in the Turmoil of the Haitian Revolution

The first slaves to be affected by revolutionary events in Saint Domingue were those in other French colonies, notably Guadeloupe, as news of the massive uprising in the Plaine du Nord in August 1791, and then of the abolition of slavery by Sonthonax and Polverel two years later, spread. Captives would attempt to benefit from the conflicts dividing whites, pitting royalist planters against poor republicans who had allied with free *gens de couleur*, to have their enslavement somehow mitigated or be recruited by the opposing factions in exchange for a promise of emancipation. After Louis XVI's execution and France's declaration of war in early 1793, Great Britain embarked on a largely successful campaign of invasion of the French Antilles with the support of counterrevolutionary planters. But in February 1794, the abolition of slavery by the National Convention in Paris changed the balance of power. Though it reinforced slaveowning planters' determination to oppose the Republic, it also allowed republican France to mobilize the slaves they had just emancipated to defend its colonies, whereas the British monarchy was primarily relying on European troops rapidly decimated by yellow fever. Great Britain nonetheless continued its military offensive with the support of French proslavery planters, which, despite failing in Saint Domingue and Guadeloupe, succeeded in Martinique and St. Lucia, which it occupied from 1794 to 1802.

In Guadeloupe, the period 1791–93 had seen an increase in slave imports from Africa, as planters attempted to profit from the losses suffered in Saint Domingue. They also reinforced their surveillance of slaves, who represented 85 percent of the island's 107,000 inhabitants, in order to prevent any protests. But amid the split between royalists and republicans, some planters took the risk of mobilizing and arming enslaved men to support their cause while promising the latter emancipation. At the beginning of 1793, the arrival of revolutionary commissioners on the island exacerbated those conflicts and encouraged defenders of the ancien régime to call for British intervention. An atmosphere of paranoia resulted, characterized by the circulation of diverse rumors, notably the idea that "since a liberty tree had been planted, there should be no more slaves,"[3] which were in all likelihood spread across plantations by a few recently emancipated men and women. At the same time, republican whites feared that royalist planters would mobilize some slaves and segments of the small, predominantly poor minority of free *gens de couleur* (3 percent of the island's inhabitants) against the Republic to facilitate a British invasion. But the planters themselves also feared that *libres de couleur* would ally with slaves. To prevent that scenario, a few plantation owners claimed that republicans would brand the face of every slave so that he or she could not pass for free, a rumor that prompted gatherings of slaves railing against free blacks and mulattos.[4]

Yet the first slave uprising in Guadeloupe contradicted all those rumors, clearly showing slaves' capacity to adapt their strategies to the context at hand. On the night of 20 April 1793, some two hundred slaves from different plantations in Trois-Rivières, south of Basse-Terre, used weapons provided to them by royalists to fight republicans to in fact turn against their royalist masters and kill twenty-three whites, including men, women, and children. Led by Jean Baptiste, a slave driver, the rebels claimed to have acted on their own initiative, as "citizens and friends" trying to save the Republic from a royalist plot orchestrated by planters backed by Great Britain, which allowed them to maintain that they had acted as defenders of their country and to therefore hope to avoid punishment and even be granted emancipation. According to a witness, "Some poorly armed black slaves [*nègres*] told us that their masters wanted to make them march on the city in order to exterminate the patriots, their wives and their children, but that, as they wanted to stand for the republic, they killed their masters and mistresses, and after making this statement, they shouted 'Long Live the Republic.'"[5] As historian Frédéric Régent notes, those slaves sought emancipation more than anything else. Given how political conflicts in Guadeloupe were evolving, they had judged that by presenting themselves as defending the colony against Anglo-royalist threats, they had a greater chance of obtaining their freedom by voluntarily surrendering to security forces than by fleeing into the hinterlands.

Subsequent events proved the insurgents right, in part. Whereas republican authorities still fully recognized the legality of slavery at the time, they adopted an ambiguous position in response to the deadly slave uprising. On one hand, they acknowledged the validity of slaves' accusations against royalist whites (some of whom were their masters) and ordered proceedings against the latter; on the other hand, they imprisoned the rebels during their investigation and, doubting that the insurgents had acted without external manipulation, increased surveillance on all plantations. At the same time, a decree stipulated that any slave who reported a conspiracy against the Republic could be rewarded with "civic emancipation."[6] However, the two hundred rebels from Trois-Rivières did not benefit from the edict and were still prisoners when the British attacked Guadeloupe in April 1794, when historians lost track of them.[7]

On 25 August 1793, not long after the Trois-Rivières massacre, a second sizable revolt erupted in Sainte-Anne, south of Grande-Terre. In this case, the insurgents included free *gens de couleur* and over one thousand slaves, whose demands differed: the former wanted inheritance rights for illegitimate children, while the latter sought freedom. It appears that in the beginning, free people of color had recruited slaves to protest alongside them, but that the latter quickly appropriated the movement to demand immediate freedom for all. The overwhelmed free leaders then attempted to negotiate with the mayor of Sainte-Anne for the emancipation of a few slaves in exchange for the majority's return to their plantations, warning him that without this concession, three thousand captives would soon revolt. Yet neither the mayor nor the governor of Guadeloupe considered the deal, opting instead for an immediate crackdown of a revolt that, in their eyes, risked following the Saint Domingue model. Although the rebels had not killed anyone, troops received the order to capture and imprison the main participants and send the rest back to work. On 27 August Saint-Anne's white residents removed eight free men of African descent from prison and rapidly lynched them, and shortly thereafter the governor ordered summary judgment passed on seventy-nine slaves: twenty-nine were shot, ten imprisoned, five whipped in public, and thirty-five acquitted. In the following months, varied measures allowed authorities to force slaves into obedience, while others facilitated emancipations by removing a burdensome tax on the latter, perhaps with the aim of making the process of manumission more accessible.[8]

The power dynamics changed in early 1794, with the imminence of a British attack on the island. Guadeloupe's governor understood that without slave reinforcements his troops could not resist the invasion and therefore decided to form an infantry corps of five hundred enslaved men. At the same time, in Paris, the National Convention was approving the abolition of slavery in the French Antilles. But after conquering Martinique, the British seized Guadeloupe in April 1794 without encountering much resistance—that is, until June, when Paris sent Victor Hugues to take back the island, subdue the royalists, and implement abolition with the same limits as those already established by Sonthonax and Polverel in Saint Domingue: restricted freedom for slaves who would either become soldiers fighting for republican France (for able-bodied men) or plantation cultivators under tight discipline.[9] Those new black soldier-citizens (representing 2,500 of the island's 4,600 troops) contributed to the British defeat at the end of the year. At the same time, Hugues, given full powers, applied a regime of terror backed by the guillotine to Guadeloupe's entire population, including royalist planters, revolutionary free *gens de couleur*, and emancipated slaves. The many cultivators who refused the militarized plantation system and resisted through marronage, violence, and more discreet tactics faced execution, prison, or deportation if caught. With the arrival of news of Sonthonax's expulsion by Louverture in 1797, the *nouveaux libres* intensified their protests against the labor system and called for whites to be forced out of the island, as in Saint Domingue. But in Guadeloupe, political power remained in Hugues's hands until he was recalled for abuse of power at the end of 1798, and the republican army harshly repressed all autonomous movements involving *anciens libres* or cultivators.[10]

Nonetheless, since 1797 privateering became an alternative to the army or militarized plantation work for *nouveaux libres*, who joined privateer boats by the hundreds, which resulted in women performing an even greater proportion of the agricultural work on plantations. In effect, Hugues had launched a vast maritime campaign to destabilize the Greater Caribbean, which blended piracy with propaganda about revolutionary ideas of freedom and equality. More than one hundred boats operated by Guadeloupian privateers participated in naval attacks targeting British or neutral vessels and seized spoils large enough to compensate for the decline of Guadeloupe's sugar economy. Three years later, a brigade chief estimated that there were more than two thousand *nègres marins*, meaning former slaves who had become privateers receiving a small portion of the spoils, which many would use to purchase land. Privateering also led some *nègres marins* to participate in the lucrative slave trade when they seized a slave ship or a boat whose crew included free or enslaved blacks: they would then resell the human cargo and black sailors as slaves. But privateering could also backfire, notably when the enemy took their ships and the *nègres marins* were at best made prisoners and at worst considered to be slaves and sold as such.[11]

In French Guiana, the abolition decree of February was officially enacted on 14 June 1794 and welcomed by slaves with festive dancing. At the same time, the commissioner in charge of the colony attempted to curb marronage and establish procedures to pay the new plantation cultivators. But from the start, in this territory of barely 12,500 inhabitants (86 percent slaves, 10 percent whites, and 4 percent free *gens de couleur* in 1789, not including Amerindians), *nouveaux libres*' freedom was regulated, notably by the repression of vagrancy. From 1794 to 1799, transfers of officials prompted by the changing whims of the revolution in France provoked rumors of the reestablishment of slavery that went hand in hand with whispers about the landing of Portuguese from Brazil, at times instigated by counterrevolutionary whites. According to Lieutenant-Colonel François-Maurice Cointet, a Jacobin who ran the colony between November 1794 and April 1796, fears of a return to slavery were so pronounced among cultivators that "a large movement developed in several parishes. The new citizens, highly worried about their freedom, rushed to grab weapons to defend themselves. That readiness is undoubtedly commendable in its objective: it should prove to those detractors of blacks, to the enemies of their freedom, that they know how to keep their word and perish rather than return to slavery." At the same time, Cointet demanded that the *nouveaux libres* disregard the rumors and stop "gathering tumultuously," and ordered that whites cease dreaming of a return to the "old order of things." And the Guiana Assembly voted to adopt a decree punishing the diffusion of false news of the reestablishment of slavery with prison sentences.[12]

In April 1795, following a new incursion by Portuguese slaveholders and to the great dismay of some planters, Cointet formed a battalion of *nouveaux libres* in Cayenne, both to reassure those men that abolition was permanent and to better defend the Republic. But since the beginning of the year, the colonial assembly, which only included three nonwhite deputies, had been vocally criticizing the colony's financial ruin since the end of slavery. As early as February, it voted an agriculture Code, and in August it prohibited poor families from settling on subsistence farms, which contributed to the spread of famine. Then, in December, the assembly decided to requisition cultivators on state-controlled plantations. In essence, as soon as slavery was formally abolished in Guiana, white planters attempted to undermine its abolition, leaving cultivators with good reason to worry about their future.

Shortly after the assembly's decision to requisition cultivators on 27 January 1796, Cointet announced that he had foiled a massive plot involving emancipated cultivators and a few whites whose goal had been to start several fires in

Cayenne to attract its white residents, then seize the city's fort and gunpowder magazine, and finally assassinate the governor and several high-ranking figures and military leaders to take power and declare Guiana's independence. In actual fact, on that day some rebels had simultaneously attacked a few republican guard posts near Cayenne and injured five soldiers, including three whites, before breaking into the homes of several citizens, whom they assaulted. The army, the battalion of *nouveaux libres* created nine months earlier, and the national guard retaliated and were able to subdue the rebels immediately. After an expedited trial, nineteen defendants (including five whites) were sentenced to death, and fifteen were executed: thirteen former slaves and their alleged leaders—Hector Ménénius, the only *nouveau libre* elected to the colonial assembly, and a white gunsmith named Dubart (the four other whites had their death sentences commuted to deportation). According to historian Yves Bénot, in one of the rare studies of French Guiana during the revolution, though it clearly appears that the groups of former slaves who attacked soldiers on 27 January 1796 had acted to protest the increasing militarization of agricultural labor, the existence of a plot to seize power involving whites remains questionable.[13]

In Martinique, following the brutal 1789 crackdown on hundreds of Saint-Pierre's slaves who had demanded the implementation of Louis XVI's supposed emancipation decree (see chapter 6), the rumor that three free days per week would be granted spread along the east coast. But royalist planters quickly subdued any and all slave protests. By the end of 1792, they had retaken control of the island and, in February 1794, they facilitated the British occupation, which lasted until 1802. As a result, the revolutionary decree of abolition was never applied in Martinique and, confronted by slaveowning planters under the protection of the British army, slaves prudently avoided any signs of rebellion.[14]

St. Lucia was a different story entirely. Since 1791, its slaves had taken advantage of conflicts between royalist and republican planters to join maroon communities in the dense forests of the inland mountains of the small 238-square-mile island. When the British army arrived in April 1794, some slaves were already aware of the abolition decree of 4 February, and a growing number of them fled toward the hinterlands, where they were joined by republican soldiers. Runaway slaves and fugitive soldiers gradually formed a "French army in the woods" of some six thousand men led by two French soldiers, Kermené and Sabathier Saint-André, who, with the help of Victor Hugues in Guadeloupe, waged a guerrilla war against the British. By June 1795, they had almost taken back the entire island from British troops by rallying more and more slaves and by spreading news of the decree abolishing slavery among those who had not joined their camp.

Ten months later, Great Britain was forced to send eleven thousand men, including several hundred black rangers, to lead what they called the Brigand

War. The general in charge promised to pardon rebels who surrendered with their weapons, but soon recognized "that men after been told they were free, and after carrying arms, did not easily return to slavery and labour."[15] At first he attempted to convince planters that more humane treatment would draw slaves out of the woods, then, given the ineffectiveness of those measures, opted for a policy of pursuing and mercilessly executing rebels as well as destroying the provision grounds cultivated by plantation slaves who secretly fed them. Nonetheless, the maroons and fugitive soldiers, though by then lacking outside support, would not abandon their open resistance to the British occupation until Hugues's recall and Bonaparte's coup of 18 Brumaire.

Two figures provide an idea of the number of slaves involved in the "French army in the woods": whereas St. Lucia had 18,400 slaves (out of 22,000 inhabitants) in 1790, by 1799 only 14,000 remained (despite imports of African captives). Of those 4,400 fewer slaves, many—primarily young men—had died in combat, been executed or deported, others had fallen prey to hunger and disease due to the destruction of garden plots; however, many were still alive and had successfully moved to the mountains or fled by sea. For that matter, several slaves who had become "soldiers in the woods" were integrated into a British regiment intended for combat in Africa, in a reversal of allegiances that spared them a much-feared return to plantation life.[16]

The Nouveaux Libres' Struggle against the Restoration of Slavery in Guadeloupe and Guiana

After the 18 Brumaire coup, the *nouveaux libres* and new citizens of 1794 saw slaveholding planters regain influence in both the colonies and Paris up until 1802, when their worst nightmare became reality: Bonaparte reestablished slavery, the slave trade, and the Code Noir. First, with the law of 20 March 1802, the First Consul decided to maintain slavery in the colonies returned by Great Britain after the Treaty of Amiens, meaning Martinique, Tobago, and St. Lucia. Then, in areas where the abolition decree of 1794 had been implemented, Bonaparte, aware that overtly restoring slavery would provoke uprisings among blacks, sent his generals and thousands of soldiers to preemptively neutralize any opposition.

Former slaves everywhere resisted or rebelled. Those in Guadeloupe confronted a plan for military subjugation similar to Leclerc's ambitions for Saint Domingue, but which would in this case eventually succeed. In September 1801, Admiral Jean-Baptiste Raymond de Lacrosse implemented a policy to deport all the island's black soldiers who were considered dangerous, as well as resistant cultivators, to other parts of the Lesser Antilles, Guiana, France, and even as far as Madagascar. Some among the *nouveaux libres*, sensing that their advances were fragile, set out to obtain proper certificates of freedom, which were more reliable in their minds than the 1794 decree of general emancipation. However, the majority of those men and women did not see that the island's new administrators were starting to dismantle what they thought were permanent gains. As few cultivators had been bossales, strategies of marronage and guerrilla warfare were rarely used—the contrary of what occurred in Saint Domingue.

In May 1802, when Bonaparte sent General Antoine Richepance with 3,500 men to disarm all the blacks and mulattos still among the troops and reestablish slavery in Guadeloupe, part of the island's population was initially incredulous. Then creole officers, white, mulatto, and black, split over the best way to react to the disarmament and the sidelining of the most republican leaders. For example, one of them, the mulatto Martinican captain Magloire Pélage, allied with Richepance, whereas another mulatto from Martinique, the lieutenant Louis Delgrès, led hundreds of still armed black soldiers to escape to Basse-Terre. A number of cultivators, panicked by the idea of a return to slavery, went along with them under the slogan "To live free or die!" Some creole whites also joined Delgrès's movement and helped draft a manifesto intended for "the entire universe," which justified "resistance to oppression [as] a natural right," borrowing from the U.S. Declaration of Independence. In all, the rebels included some three thousand trained soldiers and nine thousand cultivators, men and women armed with machetes, pitchforks, and sticks, who faced off against French troops sent by Richepance and backed by Pélage and his men.

After a few victories, the rebels lost the initiative and dispersed into bands in southern Basse-Terre. But lacking a collective resistance strategy, some found refuge in the mountains while others burned down plantations and killed civilians. Among the insurgents, a mulatto woman named Solitude advocated for a merciless war against whites. As for Delgrès, he seized Fort Saint-Charles as a base for his soldiers and officers, and refused to negotiate unless guaranteed that slavery would not be restored. Rapidly surrounded by the army, he and his men were able to escape and divide into two groups intending to set all of Guadeloupe aflame.[17]

The first group of resistance fighters was composed of four hundred soldiers and dozens of men and women cultivators, and intended to stir up Grande-Terre. It headed for Pointe-à-Pitre, setting fire to plantations and rallying new followers on the way, before retreating to an unguarded fort near the port, where Pélage and French soldiers would wipe them out—killing 675 men and women and taking 250 prisoners who were all publicly shot. Over the following days, the rebels' leader killed himself, and his head was displayed in Pointe-à-Pitre. Solitude was executed after giving birth to her child. As for the second group, composed of several hundred insurgents led by Delgrès, their goal was to maintain Basse-Terre in a state of rebellion. Those resistance fighters headed for the mountains of Matouba, south of La Soufrière volcano, where small rebel bands were still active. They turned a plantation protected by two ravines into their headquarters, but did not have enough force to survive a siege by Richepance's troops. After a period of resistance that cost the lives of many French soldiers, they collectively committed suicide in May 1802 while holding hands and shouting "No slavery! Long live death!" As a French officer noted at the time, "The fanaticism of liberty" had once again driven more than five hundred men, women, and children to die rather than become slaves again.

Up until his death in September from yellow fever, Richepance would continue his reign of terror with hangings and deportations intended to definitively eradicate the spirit of freedom and equality in Guadeloupe. Lacrosse succeeded him with just as much cruelty and determination. He considered that every person of African descent was by definition a slave unless he or she could prove a free status prior to 1794; any black or mulatto man who had served in the republican army had to be killed or banished—and even the faithful Pélage was arrested and deported after having carried out his repressive mission. Code Noir policies were reestablished, and free men and women of African ancestry were stripped of their French citizenship. In all, ten thousand men and women, or nearly one-tenth of the island's population, were likely massacred, executed, or deported in the name of reestablishing slavery and racial inequality. Even so, cultivators and former slaves continued to resist, either by hiding out in the mountains or by attacking plantations. A new rebellion erupted near Sainte-Anne in October 1802 when cultivators, supported by free men of color and three whites, killed twenty-three whites before marching on the city with the intention of restoring revolutionary-era laws. Lacrosse and his men were able to stop the rebels, whom they punished and subjected to exemplary tortures: between eighty and one hundred insurgents were hanged or burned alive; one of the white rebels was broken on the wheel and then burned alive, whereas the two others died, at least one by suicide, before enduring the torture to which they had been sentenced. Lacrosse then ordered the formation of white militias charged with hunting down the remaining fugitives and terrorizing the cultivators into returning to slavery. Nonetheless, small rebel groups were able to survive far from plantations.[18] And though planters tried to compensate human losses by importing a total of twenty-five thousand new African slaves by 1830, Guadeloupe would never recover its pre-1789 sugar production.[19]

The reenslavement of the men, women, and children emancipated in 1794 in Guadeloupe was therefore primarily the result of a vastly uneven balance of power. Granted, even when revolutionary France introduced immediate abolition in 1794, it had simultaneously charged its colonial commissioners with implementing control and discipline to ensure that the system of plantation production was not destroyed, which facilitated the work of Bonaparte's generals. Several additional factors explain why Guadeloupe's *nouveaux libres* were subdued, unlike those in Saint Domingue. First of all, they were predominantly creoles (80 percent), whereas in Saint Domingue, Africans represented the majority of the island's captives, many of whom were recent arrivals with military experience. Before 1794, most of Guadeloupe's free population was white, with only 18 percent of free *gens de couleur*, whereas in Saint Domingue nearly one free person in two was black or mulatto, including many rich, educated planters who played a decisive role after October 1802.[20] Second, Guadeloupe's slaves had, of course, never revolted on a massive scale, like those on the Plaine du Nord in 1791, or created strongholds, after 1792, of thousands of runaways who refused to disarm after the abolition of slavery. Richepance and his 3,500 men therefore had an easier task than Leclerc and Rochambeau did when facing Saint Domingue's bossales. In fact, the leaders of the great Guadeloupian rebellion of 1802 came from the ranks of the French army, whose strategies they employed, and were ill qualified to challenge Napoleonic troops with disconcerting guerrilla tactics. Furthermore, none of those leaders came from the island's small pre-1794 minority of free people of color. Delgrès, in particular, was a mulatto born free in Martinique and a career soldier. In the final moments of his resistance, he systematically led his men toward military forts, which the French were then able to surround, rather than mountains propitious to marronage.

As for Guiana, the other colony still in French hands after 1794, Victor Hugues was charged with restoring slavery there after having previously abolished it in Guadeloupe. In early 1800, he arrived in Cayenne on the First Consul's orders, and his first act was to demand that the city's domestic servants and workers provide proof of their employment and force cultivators to live on their respective plantations. He then reestablished slavery, as specified by an 1803 decree: all slaves emancipated after 14 June 1794 "could not benefit from freedom until they had reimbursed their personal value and that of their children to their former masters."[21] Hugues had slaves' huts and family farms systematically destroyed. By using the same repressive methods employed in Guadeloupe during the Revolution, he accomplished his mission of restoring the ancien régime for Bonaparte. The majority of the island's previously emancipated men and women conceded, but between 1,200 and 3,000 of them (or between 10 and 29 percent of the 10,430 slaves recorded in 1788) fled into inland forests. Some were caught and brutally killed, including Simon Frossard in 1808, whose head was then displayed in Cayenne, but many others formed small runaway communities.[22] While the reestablishment of slavery in 1802 encountered strong resistance from the populations of Guadeloupe and Guiana, it was facilitated by the lack of protests in France, where no popular abolitionist movement had formed. The 1794 abolition of slavery had been announced as much due to the need to mobilize enslaved men against the British threat as to humanist convictions. But both that revolutionary decision and the one to restore slavery went unnoticed by a majority of French people.[23]

The Great Slave Revolt of Curaçao (1795)

The most direct and violent repercussions of events in the French Antilles would be seen in Curaçao, during a rebellion that erupted in August 1795. A few months earlier, the establishment of the Batavian Republic in the Netherlands under the aegis of revolutionary France had sparked a rumor that the 1794 French decree abolishing slavery would be applied—not illogically—to the colony of Curaçao, still ruled by a Dutch governor. The island council attempted to stem "the insolence of blacks and mulattos" by restricting their movements and gatherings. But on 16 August, slaves on a plantation at the western end of the island refused to work. Two days later, those from two neighboring plantations rebelled under the orders of named Tula (or Toela), an enslaved cultivator, and Bastiaan Carpata, an enslaved overseer who also had ties to Louis Mercier, a slave from the French Antilles. In another sign of Saint Domingue's influence on the revolt, Tula took the last name of Rigaud, in reference to the mulatto general André Rigaud, while another rebel took the name Toussaint. They headed toward the island's center, rallying slaves and stealing weapons along the way. The number of insurgents grew and, after two days without violence, they began to burn down planter estates and killed a white man after tying him to the tail of a horse and dragging him. By 19 August, the rebels likely numbered 2,000—including men, women, and children—out of Curaçao's total population of 12,000 slaves, primarily creoles, 4,000 whites, and 3,000 free people of color.[24]

The Dutch governor mobilized troops by land and water to prevent insurgents from gathering support from more western plantations. At the same time, he sent a priest who spoke the local creole dialect (Papiamento) to negotiate their surrender in exchange for a general pardon, which Tula refused, declaring, according to the priest: "We have suffered enough. . . . We want our freedom. The French slaves have been emancipated, and Holland, conquered by the French, should follow." The army's commander sent emissaries on two more occasions but, despite their earlier defeats, the rebel chiefs refused to capitulate. On 30 August, the army began to take back western Curaçao and gradually pushed the insurgents to the island's northern tip. There the rebels had only three possibilities: attempt to resist, surrender, or jump from the rocks overlooking the sea. Many of them, gripped by panic, threw themselves into the water; dozens were massacred on the spot by soldiers and militiamen. A thousand turned themselves in, and several hundred of these were sent back to their plantations after their ears were mutilated to show their participation in the revolt. Some 250 rebels were jailed and judged, but Tula and Carpata managed to escape. On 4 September, the first four rebels found guilty were hanged; one week later, eight convicted slaves, including one woman, were executed, hanged, strangled, or broken on the wheel, and their bodies thrown into the ocean. Tula and Carpata were soon arrested, and interrogations, tortures, and convictions multiplied, leading to a total of twenty-nine death sentences, carried out over seven days. Tula and Carpata were subjected to a long, agonizing torture on the wheel after having their faces burned; their heads were then displayed on poles. Mercier, more talkative during interrogations, was hanged, as were the majority of the twenty-six other rebels sentenced to death.[25]

Authorities in Curaçao continued to worry: rebels remained active in the island's hinterlands and the hundreds who had been returned to their masters had now known armed freedom. The island's rulers therefore boosted their surveillance measures, while simultaneously enacting a slave law that attempted to limit abuses by masters. The new regulations banned planters from making slaves work on Sundays and holidays and restricted authorized punishments; it also obliged slaveowners to feed, house, and adequately clothe captives. Furthermore, after the 1795 revolt, Curaçao stopped importing slaves from outside the colony and, on the contrary, exported some to the Caribbean and the Guianas; slavery and the plantation system declined rapidly on the island. But though the 1795 rebellion contributed to that decline, it did not accelerate the emancipation of slaves, as neither the French nor the British, the latter of whom successively dominated Curaçao until 1816, nor the Netherlands challenged the institution of slavery, which the Dutch would only abolish in 1863.[26]

The Spanish Código Negro of 1789: A Short-Lived Reform

The Haitian Revolution reverberated across Spanish America as well, though its impacts are difficult to discern without taking a brief step backward. The slave trade had declined in importance in Mexico and central and southern Spanish America after 1760. By the end of the eighteenth century, most Afro-descendants in those regions were free. Slaves represented a minority of the population, as domestics in cities or regrouped on plantations or near mines, and few of whom were African survivors of the Atlantic crossing. Aware of those realities, slaves knew that any insurrection without the support of *libres de color* or Indians was destined to fail. And in fact, self-purchase and marronage remained less dangerous paths to freedom. After the Seven Years' War, the reforms introduced by the Bourbons to make their colonies more profitable provoked resistance movements among free populations regardless of race and Amerindians, which transformed into larger revolts in certain regions. Although rebels had not placed the abolition of slavery at the center of their demands, slaves often joined those movements or benefited from the resulting disorder to flee or request their freedom themselves.

During the 1781 revolt of the *comuneros* in Andean Colombia, for example, against a strengthened royal Spanish administration and the creation of new taxes, hundreds of partisans from local communities who marched on Bogotá did not present any demands concerning slaves. Only one *comunero* leader of modest background, José Antonio Galán, recruited landless free men of color and slaves when he expanded the revolt to Antioquia province's gold-rich northern region and freed eighty-one slaves employed in a mine owned by a Spaniard. Incidentally, creole slaves from the province took advantage of the situation to plan a march on Santa Fe de Antioquia to demand that the provincial governor and the cabildo implement a royal decree that they believed would liberate all of the province's five thousand slaves. Denounced before their march began, several slaves were arrested and imprisoned, though their final legal fate remains unknown. Nonetheless, their interrogations reveal that, had they been able to carry out their plan, they would have offered paying an annual tax to the king "like they were Indians" and to work for their former masters in exchange for a daily salary; if the governor had refused their proposal, they would have then threatened to establish a palenque while also paying the Indian tribute. In this case, as in 1730 in Virginia and 1789 in Martinique, the protesting slaves displayed their loyalty to the king and legitimized their demands by claiming to be carrying out the monarch's charitable decision. Rather than asking for their freedom, however, they demanded a status identical to that of Indians, perhaps because they believed that this request would be more acceptable while still improving their situation.[27]

The largest rebellion to come out of the Bourbon reforms was launched in November 1780 in Upper Peru by José Gabriel Condorcanqui, also called Tupac Amaru II. Stemming from a local revolt against a corregidor's abuses, it spread rapidly across the Andean region from Cuzco to Lake Titicaca. In order to gain the support of vast segments of the population, Condorcanqui and his followers recruited not only Indians but also mestizos and zambos, and at the end of the year, the number of rebels had in all likelihood reached fifty thousand. Furthermore, in mid-November Tupac Amaru posted a "Proclamation to the citizens of Cuzco so that they desert the *chapetones* [Spaniards] and free the slaves." He called all to join him, "even if they were slaves to their masters with the added benefit that they will be freed of the servitude and slavery to which they were subjected."[28] His goal was undoubtedly to swell the insurgent forces while making the Spanish feel they were vulnerable even in their very homes, where they employed enslaved domestics. However, in May 1781, royal troops gradually took back control of the Andean region. Condorcanqui, his family, and his collaborators were arrested, judged, and cruelly executed in Cuzco's main square. Slaves were included among the hundreds of rebels who were massacred, imprisoned, or summarily executed in the wave of repression that slowly ended the uprising, showing that some had responded to Tupac Amaru's proclamation. For that matter, his offer to free slaves was one of the many charges used by Spanish justice to justify his death sentence.[29]

By the late 1780s, the Bourbon reforms aimed at developing the Spanish colonies in the Caribbean basin through the expansion of slavery. In 1789, shortly before the French Revolution erupted, the king of Spain, Charles IV, signed two seemingly contradictory measures to that effect. He first liberalized the slave trade to Cuba and other colonies. However, on 31 May, he also promulgated an "Instruction on the education, treatment, and occupation of slaves," better known as the Código Negro of 1789, which protected enslaved men and women from abuse by their masters in all of Spanish America. In reality, the Código Negro was an attempt to prevent abolitionist ideas from emerging on the Iberian Peninsula, but first and foremost, to preclude the formation of a class of omnipotent planters disrespectful of their king, by clearly limiting masters' rights over their human property at the same time that the slave trade resumed.[30] Those measures would have unexpected repercussions within the revolutionary context that followed.

Madrid's liberalization of the slave trade was only ever fully implemented in Cuba, where the number of slaves doubled between 1774 and 1792, when it reached 84,600. After the 1791 uprising in Saint Domingue, the island also saw the arrival of thousands of refugees from the French colony, often with their captives. In 1804, Cuba counted 180,000 slaves in total, or 36 percent of its 504,000 inhabitants. Furthermore, in addition to slaves, the island had sizable communities of *libres de color*, who represented approximately 20 percent of Cuba's population. Of course, Cuba was far from facing the explosive demographics of most sugar-producing colonies, but by the end of the eighteenth century its population contained fewer whites than Afro-descendants. It was therefore in Cuba that Spanish authorities and creole elites most feared the influence of the revolution in the French Antilles, and where they also most sought to fill the void left by the destruction of the slave plantations in Saint Domingue. In 1791, the liberalization of the slave trade also led Spain to eliminate its asylum policy, which had granted freedom to slave refugees from Protestant territories if they converted to Catholicism (see chapter 2), out of fear of retaliation.[31]

The 1789 Código Negro included a long list of duties masters owed their slaves, borrowed for the most part from the *Siete Partidas* of 1256–65, but gathered for the first time in a separate document. The list mandated that owners evangelize their slaves and ensure they respected the precepts of Catholicism, feed and clothe them like "free day laborers," take care of them even when old or unproductive, provide adequate lodging, and monitor them for transgressions of Christian morality. In addition, the code stipulated that slaves had to be employed principally for agricultural labor, which was to occur from sunrise to sunset, while allotting them two hours for their personal use. The physical punishments that overseers and owners could inflict on undisciplined slaves were limited to twenty-five blows with a soft instrument that would cause neither bleeding nor serious contusions. The Código Negro also forced estates that relied on slave labor to undergo commissioners' annual inspections. Any owner or boss who neglected or mistreated a slave was to be punished with a fine or even, in cases of extreme cruelty, the sale of the abused slave to another owner or manumission. In exchange, slaves had "to obey and respect their masters and overseers, to fulfill the tasks and jobs that are assigned to them in conformity with their means, and to venerate them as heads of the family."[32]

In areas where slavery was not the dominant labor system but coexisted with peonage, tenant farming, salaried labor, and unpaid Indian labor, the Código Negro strengthened existing practices such as slaves purchasing their freedom or that of their kin, and emancipation granted by one's master. It also encouraged slaves who were horrifically mistreated, particularly in cities, to denounce abuse and torture by their masters or mistresses if able to do so. But in regions whose economy depended primarily on slave labor, enslaved men and women benefited little from the Código Negro, which ultimately angered their masters. In Havana, Caracas, Louisiana, and Santo Domingo, many slaveowners demanded that the king repeal the law. They argued, often with the backing of their governors, that if they were to obey the code's injunctions, they would no longer be able to produce the crops enriching the royal treasury. How could they make slaves work without dangling "the threat of the whip always raised above their backs"? How could captives be kept in their inferior positions and prevented from running away after "having lost absolute fear"? How could sugarcane be gathered if slaves only worked from sunrise to sunset? In short, according to slaveholders, "literal application [of the Código Negro] would destroy a large part of the settlements in the Indies."[33]

The Impact of Saint Domingue's Revolt on Spanish America

The successive eruptions of the French Revolution and the slave insurrection in Saint Domingue played in favor of slaveowning planters in Spanish America. In March 1794, shortly after France abolished slavery, the Spanish Crown opted for discretion: it decided to stop enforcing the Código Negro in its colonies but would not announce the law's revocation for fear of creating resistance among slaves, already stirred up by news of the turmoil in the French colonies. Spain thus counted on slaveholders to exercise prudence and treat their slaves in an "incomparably gentler" way than elsewhere in the Americas.[34] Despite its desire to populate its colonies, the Spanish monarchy only welcomed those planters fleeing Saint Domingué with their slaves in Cuba, Louisiana, and a few outlying areas, for fear that the latter would "contaminate" local populations with ideas of liberty and equality.[35]

That discretion did not prevent news from circulating or inspiring hope among slaves. The contradictory measures taken by Madrid between 1789 and 1794 regarding the Código Negro created confusion and generated diverse rumors in its colonies, on the basis of which small groups of slaves mobilized. As in Saint Domingue in 1791, the most recurrent rumor was that of a royal edict abolishing slavery, which local authorities and the province's elite were supposedly hiding. That was founded on slaveowning planters' protests against the Código, which were mixed up with news of revolutionary France's promulgation of decrees establishing the equality of blacks and abolishing slavery. Nonetheless, local conditions and the balance of power on the ground limited slaves' room to maneuver: there was no region of Spanish America in which the concentration and demographic weight of slaves allowed them to envisage a massive uprising without the support of other social sectors.

That explains why the French abolition of 1794 only inspired one major uprising to exclusively involve slaves, in Boca Nigua, near the capital Santo Domingo, in the Spanish part of Hispaniola, in 1796. In other Spanish colonies, slave mutinies were quickly quashed after their inception, while, in numerous cases, simple unrest among slaves was interpreted as a conspiracy or revolt by particularly nervous elite classes. As a result, the attempted insurrection that would be the most brutally crushed in Spanish America, in Louisiana in 1795, was denounced before it even began, once again demonstrating the absence of a link between the gravity of slaves' actions and the cruelty of governmental repression.

The slave rebellion that broke out in 1796 in Boca Nigua occurred within a tense atmosphere, rife with rumors, often spread by visitors from the French part of Hispaniola, about the conflicts troubling Saint Domingue and the decrees abolishing slavery there. Granted, Santo Domingo had never developed the typical Caribbean slave sugar plantation; its slaves were outnumbered by the free white and Afro-descended populations, and divided among small haciendas and villages.[36] But ever since Spain ceded Santo Domingo to France with the Treaty of Bale in July 1795, rumors had spread that "slaves finding themselves in Spanish possessions would be indiscriminately freed from the moment [the Spanish possessions] passed to the [French] Republic."[37] Slaves' impatience grew, even though in reality Santo Domingo would remain under the authority of its Spanish governor until 1799.

The 1796 revolt did not erupt by chance on the largest plantation in the Spanish colony, in Boca Nigua, which had two hundred slaves, most of whom were

African men. Although historians only have access to the version recounted by the Spanish governor who crushed the rebellion, it appears that one of the triggering factors was intensifying resentment among slaves after two of them died at the hands of their white overseers. Launched one Sunday evening by the plantation's enslaved driver, Francisco Sopo, the rebellion initially involved six Kongo slaves, including one carter, Antonio, and his wife, Ana María. After stealing weapons and materials from the sugar plantation stores, they mobilized dozens of slaves and plundered buildings, taking goods and food. The following night, they elected Antonio and Ana María as their king and queen, and feasted before continuing to other plantations, where they rallied slaves "to the sound of freedom and to the elimination of whites," according to the governor.[38] But in the meantime, Sopo had abandoned the rebellion to help his master flee toward the capital. There, the latter alerted the governor, who quickly sent troops and local militias to chase the rebels to nearby hills, where they took refuge. Six slaves and one soldier were killed in the fighting, and one hundred slaves were captured and given expedited judgments at the end of November 1796. Sopo (despite his defection), Antonio, Ana María, and four other plotters were hanged, decapitated, and dismembered. The majority of the other rebels, except for four who were found innocent, were sentenced to up to one hundred whiplashes and irons to be worn on their necks and ankles for ten years.[39]

According to the governor, the insurgents had wanted to replicate events "in Guarico [Le Cap, in Saint Domingue] and in the rest of the French part." They supposedly had connections to emissaries of the black creole general Jean-François and wanted to draw most of Santo Domingo's plantations into their uprising. That explains why the governor took extreme security measures to prevent any signs of solidarity among slaves and *libres de color* during public executions and whippings. Despite his fears and accusations of links to Saint Domingue, the Boca Nigua uprising did not inspire any imitators, though slavery did decline rapidly in the colony. In fact, Toussaint Louverture was the first to decree abolition when he arrived in Santo Domingo in January 1801, after the departure of Spanish authorities, while imposing the same militarized agricultural labor system as the one in Saint Domingue. The following year, French troops sent by Bonaparte to take back Hispaniola reestablished the legality of slavery in Santo Domingo, but were unable to slow its decline before being expulsed in 1809. In 1822, the Haitian president Jean-Pierre Boyer definitively abolished slavery in the former Spanish part of the island, without indemnification to slaveholders, as a prelude to Santo Domingo's twenty-two-year annexation to Haiti.[40]

In several other Spanish colonies, it is clear that Saint Domingue's revolutionary course inspired and motived slaves, as indicated by short-lived mutinies that followed rumors of the abolition of slavery and exchanges of enthusiastic commentary about the French Antilles. But though colonial rulers continued to suspect slaves of plotting general uprisings, unrest very rarely translated into violence. In Puerto Rico for example, the Spanish governor announced that he had uncovered a slave uprising inspired by events in Saint Domingue, scheduled for 15 October 1795 in the province of Aguadilla, which had few slaves, in the island's northeast region. Although no concrete incidents emerged, the governor used the opportunity to implement emergency measures.[41] In Cuba, the Spanish governor and creole elites had become particularly fearful of the influence of the French Caribbean after whites became the minority in relation to free and enslaved Afro-descendants, and whites and *libres de couleur* arrived by the thousands with their slaves to seek refuge from the turmoil in Saint Domingue. Rumors circulated that mixed the Spanish monarchy's contradictory measures with the French decrees of liberty and equality and claimed that the king of Spain had passed an edict abolishing slavery, supposedly hidden by authorities and Cuban elites. Slave protests broke out accordingly, with insurgents demanding forcefully, though nonviolently, a freedom that they believed or alleged had been already granted by Charles IV. A notable example occurred in the Cuban province of Puerto Príncipe, when, in July 1795, seven enslaved creoles from a hacienda locked their master up because he refused to grant them their freedom, and then attempted to rally slaves from neighboring plantations to march on the province's capital and demand their emancipation, without killing or destroying property. In that case, the governor of Cuba did not resort to expedited justice, and three years later, ten of the accused were still in prison awaiting trial. In June 1798, a new munity broke out in the province, and this one entailed violence: twenty-five captives from several small sugar plantations killed three overseers with machetes and set a farm on fire. According to confessions extracted from the insurgents, if their revolt had not started prematurely, it would have involved a large number of participants whose goal was to liberate slaves, kill white men, and capture white women. In all, the judges prosecuted twenty-three slaves, including sixteen bozales. Twenty of them were convicted: three Kongo leaders were hanged, twelve endured whippings and were sent to the galleys, and the rest were sold outside Cuba.[42]

Also in Cuba, another alleged slave conspiracy inspired by Haiti was uncovered beforehand in 1806 on a plantation in Güines, in Havana Province after denunciation by three Kongo captives. According to them, the plantation's slaves had been preparing a plot which would have entailed revolting against their masters and marching on Guanabacoa while killing whites on their path, and settling in the town's fort "in total freedom . . . like in Guarico [Le Cap]." The governor immediately ordered an investigation that led to the arrests of three slaves: the creole Francisco Fuertes, Estanislao, originally from the French Antilles, who inspired his companions to dream of revolt and freedom by claiming to have participated in the Haitian Revolution, and Mariano Congo, who was betrayed by his compatriots. More concretely, however, as in Boca Nigua in 1796, the plantation slaves were driven to envisage rebellion by the exhausting exploitation and atrocious punishments to which they were subjected. In effect, shortly beforehand, five of their comrades had died from blows and punishments they received and a sixth committed suicide after a series of abuses. By planning to act "like in Guarico," the enslaved workers dreamed not only of escaping the hell of plantation life but also of living in a world in which they would be liberated from their white exploiters. Although the three presumed leaders never enacted their plan, the confessions extracted from them led to several additional arrests during an investigation that lasted for more than a year and undoubtedly prompted several convictions. Thanks to those measures, the governor could tell the region's white inhabitants that a bloodbath had been averted.[43]

In 1795, Spanish justice would pass a particularly severe judgment on presumed conspirators, who never actually rebelled, in Pointe Coupée province in Louisiana. Indeed, though the alleged Pointe Coupée revolt remained at the discussion stage, it prompted the cruelest crackdown in Spanish America during revolutionary events in Saint Domingue, once again demonstrating that imagining a crime was as serious as committing it. The affair began in mid-April 1795, when two Tunica Indians alerted the Pointe Coupée authorities of the imminence of a slave revolt in the province. At the time, Louisiana was a colony underexploited by Spain, which had obtained it from France in 1763. Even as New Orleans grew, Pointe Coupée province, some ninety miles north, numbered two thousand mostly French white inhabitants, numerous free *gens de couleur*, and seven thousand slaves working on sugar plantations spread along the Mississippi River, along with many Indians and maroons who controlled the hinterlands. Despite the distance, news of the revolt in Saint Domingue, the abolition of slavery in the French Antilles, and the war between Spain and France reached Pointe Coupée, where it worried whites but nourished slaves' hopes for freedom.

After hearing the Indian women's claims, the Spanish governor ordered local law enforcement to search every plantation and to arrest and interrogate every suspicious slave. A plot scenario materialized under torture: the captives from one plantation had reportedly planned to revolt while their master was absent, steal his weapons, and burn down his estate to attract neighbor planters, who they would then kill while sparing their wives. The plotters then supposedly planned to go from estate to estate, destroying properties, rallying new rebels, and killing whites and reticent slaves. Although no revolt took place, much less any violence or destruction, sixty-three people were charged: fifty-six slaves, three free men of color, and four whites. Their trials took place on 8–19 May 1795 and resulted in the hanging and decapitation of twenty-three slaves; the remaining defendants were sentenced to banishment or sale in other colonies. The governor had the heads of the hanged men displayed on pikes in various locations in Pointe Coupée. Spain banned Louisiana from importing new captives, first from French territories and then from Africa. Yet the conspiracy's discovery did not lead to a profound change in relations between French planters and Spanish authorities. The former were too attached to their autonomy from a weak state to agree to finance the governor's proposals to deport dangerous slaves or to form a militia to better monitor plantations and pursue runaways. In fact, those kind of changes would not occur until the beginning of the nineteenth century, during Louisiana's brief return to French control, followed by its sale to the United States by Bonaparte in 1803, when sugar and cotton plantations multiplied in the territory, exploiting an ever-growing number of slaves.[44]

Whereas those protests only involved slaves, other plots and revolts were led by free men of African descent or Indians but included the participation of slaves who made their freedom one of the rebels' demands. Those multiclass and multiethnic movements, emerging from a context of social tensions exacerbated by revolutionary events in Saint Domingue, rarely involved a concrete plan to seize power and were often thwarted by governments before any tangible action was taken. It is therefore difficult to know whether there were slaves among their initiators, whether they acted in coordination with other social groups because they knew their numbers were too small to act alone (except in a few sugar-producing regions of Cuba), or whether they were compelled or obliged to join those movements.

The brief rebellion in Coro, Venezuela, in 1795, which involved some four hundred insurgents, including free and enslaved men and women of African descent, was probably the most important multiclass movement to develop in Spanish America in the wake of Saint Domingue. However, available sources have not yet allowed historians to clearly define its organization or plan, or to establish the number and role of slaves who participated, particularly since the military forces that quelled it massacred a large number of suspects without recording any information about them. In a region in which nearly half of the population was composed of *libres de color*, versus 30 percent Indians, 14 percent whites, and 12 percent slaves, it appears that rebels were primarily free farmers of mixed African descent of the sierra, who were joined by several dozen slaves. Their motivations were diverse, ranging from resistance to an abusive tax collector, defense of lands they were cultivating from the growing claims of creole hacendados, and a new demand for respect from free men and women of African descent. The spread of revolutionary ideas from the French Antilles along the coast of Venezuela and growing complaints among Coro officials regarding the lack of troops to defend it also contributed to creating the idea, in some minds, that a regional uprising was possible, at a time when many were losing patience with various administrative measures that in their minds had failed to assert what they considered to be their rights.

On 10 May 1795, José Leonardo Chirino (or Chirinos), a literate zambo born of an enslaved father and an Indian mother, and his accomplices gathered near a hacienda south of Coro, armed with sticks and machetes, before attacking the estate belonging to Chirino's employer, a rich creole merchant, whom they killed before burning down other haciendas and murdering two other whites. At the same time, they called on slaves, *libres de color*, and Indians to join them on their march on Coro. They demanded "the law of the French," meaning a republic, racial equality, slaves' freedom, removal of taxes and tributes, and the elimination of the white aristocracy. If Chirino's leadership role is clear, that played by José Caridad González, one of the many Kongo fugitive slaves from Curaçao who obtained their freedom in Coro thanks to the Spanish monarchy's asylum policy before 1791, and who was meant to have launched a simultaneous revolt in the town of Coro, is less certain. Nonetheless, by 13 May González and other emancipated men from Curaçao had been imprisoned for attempting to steal weapons, after which he and two of his men were killed in a so-called escape attempt, while several others were sentenced to transportation or the galleys. Meanwhile Chirino's rebels in the sierra were unable to resist the forces sent against them by the provincial authorities. Despite promises to pardon any rebels who surrendered, on 15 May the commander of Coro had twenty-four insurgents decapitated on the spot, and one week later, twenty-one others were executed after a semblance of judgment. A few rebels managed to escape and undoubtedly joined maroon communities in the hinterlands. Chirino was able to hide for three months before being denounced. He was judged in Caracas for high treason and sentenced to hanging on 10 December 1796. His head was placed in an iron cage atop a pole, while his hands were sent to Coro for public display, one at the town's southern entrance and the other near his employer's hacienda. His wife and their children, all of whom were slaves, were sentenced for sale separately in other provinces.[45]

Although the Coro rebellion included slaves among its participants, it cannot be equated to a slave uprising, as it was primarily a movement driven by free men of African descent who were eager to incorporate slaves' demands for freedom.[46] Incidentally, even though the revolt occurred three months before the massive slave rebellion on the neighboring Dutch island of Curaçao, it does not appear to have had an impact on the latter; it was, however, a response to changing conditions in that coastal region east of Caracas, while also being symptomatic of the intense circulation of ideas in the Greater Caribbean. Its suppression illustrates the intransigence of the Venezuelan elite in regard to demands by the free and enslaved populations of African descent. Thus, for Venezuela's slaves, emancipation and marronage and the establishment of palenques in still largely unregulated hinterlands remained the best ways to gain their freedom.

Other planned multiclass revolts in Spanish America either never passed the discussion stage or were merely demonstrations of dissatisfaction incorrectly interpreted as plots by leaders on high alert. For example, in 1799, the governor of Cartagena de Indias, on the Caribbean coast of Colombia, reported having barely avoided the launching of a conspiracy involving a black sergeant and his black militia men, a few bozal and creole slaves, and slaves from Saint Domingue illegally sold to officers stationed in Cartagena. According to the governor, the plotters had hidden weapons and munitions (which were never found) for the purposes of an uprising during Holy Week. They had supposedly been planning to assassinate him, occupy several forts, and then massacre all white residents and pillage the port city. Yet one day before the plot could be carried out, it was reported to the governor by a pardo (of mixed African ancestry) corporal whom the conspirators had attempted to recruit along with his militia unit. Six French slaves and a few local slaves were immediately arrested. The former maintained that they were free but had been illegally captured and sold as slaves. The Spanish judge dismissed the accused's claims of freedom: he considered them first and foremost to be dangerous slaves who had participated in rebellions in the French Antilles and was equally concerned that they had been brought to the province in violation of the royal decree of 1791 authorizing only the importation of bozales to Cartagena. Two enslaved suspects managed to escape and set fire to a nearby hacienda, but one week later the governor deemed that the arrests had "not caused the slightest sign of unreasonableness or discontent among the remaining blacks . . . entertained [sic] in their respective occupations." He nevertheless asked for additional troops from Spain to protect the Caribbean Coast, because its "dull" population could easily "become corrupted by the detestable maxims of liberty and disobedience" spread by revolutionary France.

The accused black sergeant and military slaves from Cartagena requested trials by military tribunal, as permitted by law (the *fuero militar*), but in May 1799, royal authorities uncovered a new putative conspiracy, this time in Maracaibo, on the Caribbean coast of Venezuela. Two mulatto French captains, their Afro-descended crew, and a second lieutenant of the city's pardo militia were accused of planning to "introduce [there] the same system of freedom and equality that has reduced to total ruin . . . the French ports of the island of Saint Domingue." Madrid demanded that the defendants from Cartagena and Maracaibo be rapidly judged and executed and that all slaves be subjected to heightened vigilance. Although the ultimate fate of those charged remains unknown, tensions increased shortly thereafter, when royal functionaries began to imagine that the presumed plots were part of a vast revolutionary plan that also encompassed Santa Marta, Riohacha, and as far as Santiago de Cuba, with the support of Wayúu Indians from the Guajira Peninsula and the French consul of Curaçao. Nonetheless, no concrete revolt ever erupted in this vast and scantly colonized region, where marronage remained an option for slaves.[47]

Gabriel Prosser's Conspiracy and the Louisiana Revolt: Two Movements Unrelated to Saint Domingue

As slavery declined in Curaçao and continental Spanish America, it rose dramatically in the southern United States. Between 1791 and 1812, the number of slaves in the southern states continued to increase, due both to natural growth rates and to the importation of African captives (see chapter 5). The total slave population in the South went from 650,000 in 1790 to more than 1,100,000 in 1810.[48] Slaves were increasingly employed in the new production of cotton, though many continued to farm rice, tobacco, and sugarcane or work as domestic servants, transportation workers, or specialized artisans. At the same time, in the majority of the northern states, the enslaved population was shrinking following the adoption of laws that gradually abolished slavery, as well as due to emancipations. New York and New Jersey were the only states where slaves still numbered in the thousands.[49]

As in Cuba, the Haitian Revolution contributed to the development of slavery in the southern United States. Shortly after 1791, planters from the ravaged French colony had begun to seek refuge in the southern states, bringing slaves with them, notably to South Carolina and Virginia. Residents of those states welcomed the refugees with a mix of empathy and distrust—they feared the pernicious influence of slaves who had experienced revolution firsthand. Stories about the "horrors of Saint Domingue" abounded, as did rumors of conspiracies. In addition, authorities tended to link certain rebellious acts by one or more slaves to one another, creating the impression that they were part of a dangerous interstate network. For example, in August 1793, the interception of an anonymous letter by a "Secret Keeper" mentioning the enlistment of thousands of men prompted fears that a slave revolt with nationwide ramifications was about to erupt in Charleston. Various incidents involving slaves residing anywhere between Albany (New York) and Georgia were interpreted as links in a vast conspiracy with connections to the French Antilles. The arrival of religious practices from Saint Domingue, such as voodoo, further amplified some state officials' concerns.[50]

It was against that backdrop that, on 30 August 1800, Pharaoh and Tom Sheppard, two slaves from Richmond, Virginia, warned their master that a conspiracy involving dozens or possibly hundreds of slaves would begin in town that very night before spreading across the region. According to historians who have studied a detailed transcription of the defendants' coerced statements, the documents indicate that, in this case, the slaves had in fact been conspiring to liberate themselves for several months. Gabriel's conspiracy, named after its primary organizer, Gabriel Prosser, a literate enslaved blacksmith, included his brother Salomon and several other enslaved artisans who recruited supporters at their work sites and social gatherings such as ceremonies at black Baptist churches, funerals, and Sunday barbecues. The conspirators secretly transformed spades and other farm instruments into swords and lances and gathered munitions. Well aware of the regional political situation, they were counting on taking advantage of divisions among white Virginians, between Thomas Jefferson's Democratic Republicans and John Adams's Federalists, as well as of the limited number of troops and militias in the town and surrounding areas during the summer of 1800.

Their plan was to meet on Saturday evening 30 August on the outskirts of Richmond, and then divide into three groups: the first group would enter the town after midnight to set buildings in the east on fire, while the other two would arrive from the other side to seize weapons from the arsenal and take the governor hostage. Next, after killing any whites who came to extinguish the fire, they would take power and abolish slavery. Although it is impossible to know the exact number of slaves involved, it was probably high, around five hundred or more. Nonetheless, two unpredictable events doomed the conspiracy to failure: as mentioned previously, two plotters revealed the plan to their master that Saturday morning; and that evening, a violent storm flooded the entrances to the city, forcing Gabriel to delay the attack until the following day. In the meantime, militias had begun to patrol the area, preventing slaves from meeting. Over the following weeks, more than one hundred slaves were arrested and between mid-September and mid-November, seventy-two were judged in court for conspiracy and insurrection. Among them, forty-four were found guilty: twenty-six or twenty-seven were hanged on Richmond's main square, the others either deported and sold or pardoned by authorities. Gabriel, who managed to escape, would finally be arrested, judged, and hanged in October 1800. Pharaoh and Sheppard, who had betrayed their comrades, were rewarded by emancipation and a monetary reward.[51]

In addition to those figures, documents pertaining to Gabriel's conspiracy provide important information about its participants. All the plotters were creole, and some had witnessed the United States' journey to independence. Several were literate and enjoyed considerable economic and geographic autonomy because they worked independently for a master to whom they paid wages, moving between urban and rural areas and from one estate to another on foot, horseback, or by boat. In a region in which free or enslaved African Americans represented between 50 and 60 percent of the population, they played an active role in the capitalist development of Virginia's farming economy. It was therefore not by chance that some chose the word "business" to secretly refer to their plot. Moreover, interrogations show how the main plotters recruited supporters and which arguments they used to try to arouse their enthusiasm, dissipate their fears, and convince them to themselves recruit new followers, all while minimizing the risk of leaks or betrayal.

The suspected conspirators did not invoke an official abolition decree hidden by slavery supporters, as had been the case in Louisiana and Curaçao and during the Haitian Revolution, but some did refer to Bible passages on the enslavement of the Israelites and their exodus from Egypt (a recurring theme since the 1770s), which they regarded as parallel to their own fate. Others more violently announced that they wanted to fight or kill whites to gain their freedom, although some recruiters specified that they would spare women and children, or Quakers, Methodists, and the French, as they were opposed to slavery; some plotters indicated that any blacks who did not join the rebellion would also be killed. Unlike other conspiracies characterized by the inclusion of women and the election of a king and queen, Gabriel's conspiracy was based on the Bible, masculine fraternity, and individuals' fundamental right to freedom. For that matter, Gabriel had planned to write the words "death or Liberty" on the rebels' white silk flag. One of the plotters maintained on the gallows that "he had nothing more to say in his own defense than 'what General Washington would . . . had he been taken by the British and put to trial': he had 'adventured [his] life . . . to obtain the liberty of [his] countrymen, and . . . [was] a willing sacrifice in their cause.'" Other rebels were less political and claimed to have been motivated by the thought of being able to seek revenge for repeated abuses and "to kill whites."[52]

Yet the documents also reveal that apart from Gabriel and two or three confidants, all the slaves involved had doubted the conspiracy's success. Some suspected plotters swore that they had indeed been contacted by the leaders, but had wanted to see if "the business progress[ed] well" before compromising themselves. Others, frightened, attempted to reason with the conspirators but did not inform on them. In all likelihood, many measured the slim chance of the plan succeeding against its real risks: death, torture, sale as slaves to a distant plantation or in the Caribbean—in other words, the destruction of the small sphere of autonomy and family life that they had been able to build through patience and sacrifice. Still, the records of Gabriel's conspiracy do not explain why Pharaoh and Sheppard decided to denounce their comrades twelve hours before the uprising was meant to begin—unaware that a storm would prevent it from occurring on the night of 30 August. Arrested and interrogated two days later, the two enslaved men again informed on their friends without explaining their motives: Did they become frightened at the last minute? Or did they want to protect themselves in case the "business" went sour, though without giving up the chance to join the uprising if it succeeded? They undoubtedly knew that their betrayal would lead to the deaths of at least the primary leaders; they may have been hoping to save their own lives, but could not have anticipated that their betrayal would be rewarded by freedom.

Indeed, several of the slaves caught up in Gabriel's conspiracy were living in Richmond, where, like enslaved artisans in Spanish colonial cities, their skilled trades allowed them to live with their families without their owners' immediate supervision. For them, participating in the conspiracy was a choice with extremely serious consequences. Local authorities and whites generally reacted by meting out exemplary punishments, although once Gabriel Prosser was captured and executed, they did not attempt to punish other slaves who had likely been involved. Subsequently, enslaved Virginians continued to talk about liberty and revolt, and plot rumors circulated once again, notably before Easter in 1802, though no rebellion occurred in the region.[53]

By contrast, in 1811, several hundred slaves did in fact revolt in Louisiana, just before the territory was integrated as a state of the Union. Only a recent object of study, some historians consider it to be the "largest slave uprising in the history of the [independent] United States," due to the number of slaves who lost their lives as a result.[54] However, its immediate and brutal suppression means that few documents remain, making it difficult to reconstruct the revolt and understand the rebels' goals. At the time, Louisiana was under the command of a governor charged with preparing its entrance into the United States. The first national census of 1810 counted 34,111 whites, 34,660 slaves, and 7,585 free people of color in the region. One year earlier, in 1809, 10,000 refugees from Saint Domingue—whites, *gens de couleur libres*, and their slaves, all undoubtedly marked by the violence they had witnessed or experienced firsthand—had arrived in the territory, expelled from their first asylum in Cuba after Bonaparte's invasion of the Iberian Peninsula.[55] At the same time, planters from southern states were moving to Louisiana with their slaves. That wave of new arrivals worried the free men and women of African descent who had settled there during Spanish colonialism and who feared to be marginalized by the migrants and subjected to the racial segregation practiced in the slave South. At the same time, French Louisiana's former white residents, still unsettled by the 1795 aborted Pointe Coupée conspiracy, worried about losing their rights to the benefit of the newcomers. Tensions were therefore high within that changing and rapidly growing population.

Between 8 and 10 January 1811, during festivities celebrating Epiphany as well as the end of the harvest, dozens, or possibly hundreds, of slaves from sugarcane plantations situated along the Mississippi River northeast of New Orleans revolted. The uprising appears to have been planned well in advance, notably by Charles Deslondes, an enslaved mulatto whose mistress rented him to other planters, which allowed him to move along the banks of the Mississippi and meet numerous slaves, including Kook (or Kwaku) and Quamana (or Kwamina), two Akans who had arrived in 1806. As a group, they had supposedly planned to seize weapons that had been stored by the militia at the plantation of one of Deslondes's employers, and gradually rally support from slaves on the plantations downstream of the Mississippi, destroying estates and killing whites, until they reached New Orleans, some thirty miles to the south, where a simultaneous rebellion would have begun. However, the first stage of the plan was a failure: on 8 January, the rebels found the weapons depot nearly empty; after brutally assaulting the plantation master and killing one of his sons, they headed toward other estates, some on horseback but most on foot, armed with machetes, pitchforks, and axes. Organized into a military column behind the riders, the insurgents marched to the sound of drums, waving flags, and rallied other creole and African slaves along the way, whether they were willing or not. They set fire to houses and plantations, and left another victim: a planter, killed with an axe.

However, many whites had the time to flee toward New Orleans, where they alerted the government. Ten hours later, at nightfall, the rebels, by then numbering between two hundred and five hundred, stopped a dozen miles from the capital, which they planned to attack the next day. They were rapidly ensnared by the troops dispatched against them and by a local well-armed militia that surprised them and killed many, leaving "a great carnage." Some insurgents were spared and captured, while others were able to escape into nearby swamps, though many were often caught shortly thereafter. Considered to be the leader by planters, Deslondes was taken from prison during a lynching that saw him mutilated, burned, and then shot. The other imprisoned slaves were rapidly judged in ad hoc courts composed of planters, and at least twenty of them, including Kook and Quamana, were executed. Their heads were displayed on pikes along with those of the slaves killed by the militia and placed along the path they had taken and in the city of New Orleans. Some eighty slaves were considered to have been forced to participate in the revolt and were sent back to their masters. At least a dozen managed to disappear into the hinterland. With a death toll of about one hundred slaves killed during the crackdown, versus only two whites killed by rebels, the Louisiana uprising of 1811 was indeed the deadliest revolt for slaves in the history of the United States. It also stands out due to the exceptional capacity of its creole and African leaders to mobilize hundreds of slaves despite differences in origin, culture, status, and color. However, none of its participants came from the French Antilles and the revolt does not appear to have been influenced by the Haitian Revolution.[56]

Slaves in Brazil and the British Colonies

News of the slave uprising in Saint Domingue also reached Brazil and, starting in June 1792, the governor of Pernambuco voiced his concerns to Lisbon about the arrival of French agents spreading revolutionary ideas of freedom and equality, which could incite slaves to revolt against their masters. But in all of Brazil's provinces, slaves continued to gain their freedom through marronage or self-purchase. The slave insurrections and conspiracies that broke out or were uncovered in the region of Salvador de Bahia between 1807 and 1814 were linked to quilombos or asserted a Hausa identity (Hausa is the Islamized region encompassing present-day northern Nigeria and southern Niger; see chapters 9 and 10). In reality, the Brazilians inspired by the revolutionary events in the French Antilles were not the slaves, but the free black and mulatto inhabitants who mobilized for racial equality, notably with the Tailors' Revolt, uncovered in Bahia in 1798.[57]

In the British West Indies, as well, free people of color were more likely than the slaves to organize to gain rights similar to those decreed by the French National Convention. However, when the free mulatto slaveowning planter Julien Fédon launched a revolt in Grenada in March 1795 to bring the island under French control, countless slaves joined him. Acting in contact with Victor Hugues in Guadeloupe, Fédon built on the growing frustrations among the free people of color and the divisions existing within the small white minority to form a multiclass and multiethnic movement that attacked British rule behind the banner of "Liberty, Equality, and Fraternity." Indeed, Grenada had been a British colony only since 1763, when France was forced to cede it to Great Britain after the French defeat in the Seven Years' War. (France recaptured it in 1779–83.) As a result, many in the island's population identified with France rather than Great Britain. Its three thousand whites were split between British and French, and among the latter after 1789, between royalists and republicans; its two thousand free people of color, most of them francophone, tended to side with revolutionary France, especially after the 1792 decree of racial equality; and many of its thirty thousand slaves were looking for opportunities to improve their condition or free themselves. Thus, Fédon managed to rapidly recruit some 7,200 men, including between 4,000 and 6,000 slaves, against British plantations and strongholds. To face them, the British had to bring troops from Europe and mobilize Grenadian slaves into a newly created Corps of Loyal Rangers. At the same time, many slaves took advantage of the turmoil to escape alone or in families. Although neither side openly promised freedom to the enslaved belligerents, slaves fought against slaves over sixteen months in what ended up being a devastating war that destroyed lots of plantations. Furthermore, Fédon's Francophile rebellion and its repression cost the lives of one thousand free people of color and whites and seven thousand slaves, who died of hunger or disease, fell in combat, or were executed after Fédon's movement was defeated in July 1796. In other words, almost one out of four enslaved persons, and one out of five free individuals, died in the Grenada uprising in what was to remain the deadliest rebellion in the British Empire until its abolition of slavery in 1838.[58]

In other British colonies, enslaved populations avoided open rebellion. In Jamaica, which neighbored the French colony, captives rejoiced at news of the August 1791 revolt on the Plaine du Nord, which was brought by sailors or French refugees and their slaves. Some Jamaican slaves quickly composed songs glorifying the rebels of Saint Domingue, leading planters to condemn the sudden "insolence" of their captive labor force. Then came rumors, in December 1791, that slaves were preparing a Christmas rebellion, though no such revolt disrupted the end of the year festivities. Twelve months later, free mulattos from Kingston, undoubtedly inspired by the gains obtained by French free *gens de couleur*, submitted a petition asking that certain racial discriminations be lifted, though slaves themselves did not mobilize. A similar appearance of calm reigned in other British islands and Guiana, though they all had explosive demographics, counting more than 80 percent of slaves versus a minority of Europeans and free people of African descent. At the same time, between 1791 and 1800, the British colonies were beating their own records of African slave imports: more than 300,000 (over half of whom were destined for Jamaica alone) out of a total of 764,000 Africans for the entirety of the Americas during that decade.[59] Planters remained uninterested in encouraging their captives' natural reproduction, as they considered that investment in a new captive was recuperated after seven years, all the more since the fall in French demand had led to a reduced price for bossales.[60] For slaveholders, arbitrary use of terror continued to be the best antidote for revolt. As the British historian Bryan Edwards wrote in 1793 in his account of the British West Indies, "In countries where slavery is established, the leading principle on which the government is supported is fear: or a sense of that absolute coercive necessity which, leaving no choice of action, supersedes all questions of right."[61]

Besides terror, though, other factors explain the lack of revolts in most British colonies after 1791—with the remarkable exception of Grenada. First of all, enslaved peoples had a keen understanding of the context in which they lived. If they revolted, it was generally because they observed significant weaknesses in the colonial and slave system dominating them, as was the case in the thirteen continental British colonies after 1776 and the French colonies after 1789. Until the 1800s, however, those internal divisions did not exist in the British West Indies, where the unity of the white population, particularly planters, remained stable (except, again, in Grenada). Next, as historian David Geggus notes, the presence of considerable military forces (including cavalry troops in

Jamaica) prevented any local uprisings from spreading.[62] Even when, in 1795, the British mobilized its armed forces against maroon communities with which the monarchy had signed peace treaties, such as the one in northern Cockpit Country in Jamaica and the one in St. Vincent, to prevent them from acting as a bridgehead for revolutionary France, only a few dozen slaves from the two islands allied with maroons, despite Victor Hugues's appeals from Guadeloupe, calling for the chains of a tyrannical Great Britain to be broken.[63] Moreover, even in Great Britain, abolitionists, who had begun to speak out against the slave trade in the 1780s, kept quiet after the revolution in Saint Domingue; the Royal Army and Navy had been able to occupy the French colonies where they maintained slavery without prompting abolitionists' criticisms. Without allies in Great Britain, and in the absence of rifts in the system of colonial domination, enslaved peoples on British islands knew that an attempt at rebellion would lead them to certain death.

In addition, traditional liberation strategies were increasingly unavailable: marronage territories were shrinking, manumission was for all intents and purposes banned, and emancipation via armed service, though promised by Great Britain to slaves in the thirteen continental colonies during the U.S. War of Independence, became impossible after 1791. In fact, in light of events in Saint Domingue, planters and administrators in the British West Indies grew more systematically opposed than ever to the presence of blacks in the Royal Army, whether they were free or even slaves charged with the vilest tasks, for fear that they would organize a revolt against the sugar colonies' white minorities. Nonetheless, maroons who had reached peace treaties with Great Britain, and whose efficiency and speed in mobilizing was well-established, continued to act as reinforcements in times of crisis. But given the impossibility of recruiting enough soldiers on the ground and in Great Britain to serve its growing needs, the Royal Army turned to a new type of recruit: slaves coming directly from Africa. Between 1795 and 1808, His Majesty's army bought a total of 13,400 young slaves in Africa for the purposes of turning them into organized soldiers in special units, the West India Regiments, despite protests by planters predicting disastrous consequences for the colonies. In 1798, twelve of those regiments had been formed, each with one thousand African soldiers led by British officers. Those twelve thousand slave-soldiers represented one-third of the British troops stationed in the region.[64]

Their position was precarious and ambiguous. As Africans in colonies whose enslaved workers were primarily creoles, they were doubly isolated by their culture and military role. Trained and armed, they remained slaves and property of the king, subject both to the army's laws and to those governing racist slave colonies. They could kill whites in combat, but did not have the right to testify against whites in court. They lived in constant fear of having to work on plantations or of being captured by the enemy or privateers for sale elsewhere. Those fears meant that slave-soldiers rarely revolted, except in cases when they were persuaded that they were going to be sent to plantations. Governed by iron discipline, they even defended slavery in the Caribbean at times, and some became impressive soldiers fighting the maroons of Cockpit Country and the "French army in the woods" in St. Lucia.[65]

After the British Parliament voted to abolish the slave trade beginning in 1808, the Royal Army could no longer purchase slaves from Africa to make them into soldiers. But like their predecessors, the new recruits were far from voluntary: they were illegally enslaved men that the Royal Navy had confiscated from contraband slave ships, and "emancipated" before integrating into regiments as "apprentices," alongside black soldiers from French and Dutch colonies occupied by Great Britain. The Mutiny Act of 1807 ensured their loyalty: it declared the immediate emancipation of some ten thousand military slaves serving in the West India Regiments, but simultaneously forced them into lifelong service as soldiers of His Majesty. Unlike enslaved men who enlisted in the armies of Iberian monarchies and revolutionary France at the same period, those in the British army had the status of "emancipated," though they could not exercise their freedom, even after many years of service.[66]

The Haitian Revolution: A Turning Point?

News of the revolution in Saint Domingue and revolutionary France's abolition of slavery in 1794, followed by reports of Haiti's military victory and independence, produced shock waves across the Americas. But although the news was enthusiastically welcomed by countless slaves, it did not produce the broad slave insurrections feared by so many masters and rulers. The territory the most disrupted by those events outside Saint Domingue was undoubtedly Guadeloupe, where thousands of slaves emancipated in 1794 revolted against Bonaparte's attempt to reestablish slavery in 1802 and resisted the French army for several months. By the time Napoleonic troops withdrew, almost 10 percent of the island's population had disappeared—most massacred or deported, a few hidden in the mountains. In St. Lucia as well, hopes aroused by the French abolition decree prompted the armed resistance of thousands of slaves against the British occupation beginning in April 1794, during which the island lost 20 percent of its slaves. But among the other rebellions examined in this chapter, only those in Curaçao and Coro, in 1795, and in Louisiana, in 1811, spread significantly and mobilized hundreds of participants. Of those three uprisings, only those in Curaçao and Louisiana were essentially slave revolts. At the same time, small mutinies broke out in various regions but were suppressed before they could spread. Several conspiracies, real or presumed, were also quashed early on following denunciation or betrayal and ended in the arrest, torture, and at times execution of dozens of slaves, for example during the supposed Pointe Coupée plot in 1795 or Gabriel Prosser's conspiracy in Virginia in 1800.

Among those events, Saint Domingue's influence was notably visible in the revolts of St. Lucia, Curaçao, and Coro, during which rebels invoked the 1794 "law of the French." It was more indirect elsewhere and associated with the arrival of refugees from Saint Domingue or expressed via slaves' threat to "do as in Saint Domingue"; sometimes it only existed in the imaginations of rulers haunted by their fear of "another Saint Domingue." Indeed, the latter tended to interpret any demonstration of slaves' discontent as a gestating plot and were quick to sentence suspects to the scaffolds, with or without confession or other evidence. For example, the twenty-three slaves from Pointe Coupée executed in 1795 had never rebelled and possibly had not even met with that intention. On the contrary, the twenty-six or twenty-seven slaves hanged with Gabriel Prosser in Richmond in 1800 had probably planned a major revolt, but were wiped out before it could begin. The scale of repression was therefore not in relation to the reality of the crime; rather, punishments could be disproportionally cruel to terrify slaves or deliberately indulgent to minimize slaveowners' losses.

Nonetheless, the rarity of large-scale revolts after 1794 does not mean that the Saint Domingue insurrection had little impact on slaves. Those who were aware of it clearly understood its revolutionary character. But when looking around them, those slaves also grasped that in their own circumstances revolt or conspiracy would be deadly. The greatest lesson they retained from Haiti was that the institution of slavery was neither unchangeable nor invincible. Amid the troubled backdrop of the age of revolutions, many attentively followed the legal changes upsetting their owners, like the Spanish Código Negro, the French abolition of slavery, gradual emancipation laws in the northern United States, and the ban of the slave trade by Great Britain and the United States. More and more slaves used legislation and natural rights as the basis for denunciations of their masters' abuses and torture or for attempts to obtain emancipation for themselves and their family members. Furthermore, after 1794, protests during which slaves claimed freedom they believed to have been decreed by the king or the government, but hidden by their masters, multiplied.

≋ Beginning in 1810, the wars of independence waged in Spain's continental colonies following the Napoleonic invasion of the Iberian Peninsula would provide slaves in those territories with new occasions to free themselves. Thousands of them fled or found themselves without masters, while others enlisted in rival armies in exchange for promises of emancipation.

≋ 8 ≋
The Wars of Independence in Continental Iberian America
New Opportunities for Liberation

Bonaparte's invasion of the Iberian Peninsula in 1807–8 disrupted relations between the kings of Portugal and Spain and their respective subjects on both sides of the Atlantic Ocean. At the same time, as had occurred in 1776 in the British colonies and in 1791 in Saint Domingue, enslaved peoples in Brazil and in Spanish viceroyalties were beginning to hope that the changing relationships between their king and their masters would lead to their liberation or an improvement in their condition. But although the Spanish king's abdication and the Portuguese king's escape to Brazil immediately cast doubt on Europe's relationships with its colonies, the institution of slavery was not a central part of those debates. That did not, however, prevent rumors of emancipation from circulating among slaves who would renew attempts to gain their freedom.

The King: Protecting Slaves from Colonial Slaveholders?

In 1808, when the emperor Dom João arrived in Brazil with his court and administration—in total, forty ships transporting between ten thousand and fifteen thousand people under the protection of the British navy—false claims that he was going to end slavery spread widely. According to witnesses, slaves in Rio de Janeiro chanted: "Our master has arrived. Slavery is over!"[1] Those hopes were likely inspired by the fact that the Portuguese monarchy had decreed in 1761 that any African who reached Portugal would be declared free, and later, in 1773, that children born to enslaved parents would be free, which amounted to a gradual abolition of slavery. When the emperor came to Brazil, some slaves believed, not illogically, that he would implement the laws in effect in Portugal. But those decrees did not affect slavery as a system of labor, and most importantly, João VI did not extend them to his territories in Africa, Asia, and the Americas.[2]

As a result, the Portuguese monarchy's move to Brazil had very little impact on the slaves' condition. While many peninsular refugees were shocked by the violence of Brazilian slavery, others rapidly grew accustomed to buying and exploiting captives. Rio's population more than doubled in ten years, reaching eighty thousand inhabitants in 1815, due in part to the arrival of thousands of enslaved Africans imported annually. In response to those changes, the city's new intendant from Lisbon tried to prevent the excesses of slavery by imposing controls on the slave market and public whippings. João VI himself expressed his indignation at the cruelty of certain slaveowners, notably by intervening during a lashing he witnessed. Some slaves began to hope once again that the emperor would become, if not their liberator, at least their protector. Several used their day off to visit the royal palace and submit individual petitions denouncing their masters' abuses and requesting emancipation. That movement gained such traction that the intendant of Rio decided to imprison the petitioners until their individual cases were resolved in order to protect them from retaliation by their masters. Although the outcome of their requests remains unknown, those initiatives demonstrate that enslaved men and women were willing to use the slightest opportunity to try to win their freedom—peacefully and legally if possible.[3]

Outside Rio, the Portuguese emperor's temporary move to Brazil did not change slaves' daily life. Likewise, João VI's return to Lisbon in 1821, followed by the empire of Brazil's declaration of independence, made by his son Pedro I in 1822, only marginally impacted slavery and the slave trade. Every year until 1850, tens of thousands of enslaved Africans continued to flood Brazilian ports, constituting the majority of the country's labor force. Existing slave laws were not changed. For that matter, since Brazil's separation from Portugal did not entail a true war, the new nation did not resort to recruiting enslaved men, as had been the case in the thirteen British colonies and Saint Domingue, nor did it offer its slaves additional ways to obtain manumission. Only one particularly combative episode, in the province of Bahia in 1822–23, enabled a few enslaved men to be emancipated when the Portuguese occupation of the port city of Salvador forced Brazilians to enlist free blacks and mulattos to reinforce their meager troops. Some slaves then escaped their masters to enlist while claiming to be free, while others were forcibly conscripted though neither the army nor Pedro I promised them emancipation. The number of those slave-soldiers, though difficult to determine, remained quite low. Nonetheless, the question of their status emerged after the separatists' victory, as their forced return to plantations threatened to create problems. Brazil's new authorities therefore resolved to emancipate all the former slaves while keeping them as conscripts and compensating their unhappy owners.[4]

Unlike Brazil, Spanish America's road to independence was long and violent. The abdication and then internment in France of the young King Ferdinand VII led to the tricky question of which form the government should take in the king's absence. In several viceroyalties, Spaniards and white creoles gradually divided into royalists and autonomists, and later royalists and separatists or republicans (proindependence). For many slaves, the king remained a merciful and protective figure, whereas the infighting elites were often the masters from whom they wanted to liberate themselves. At the same time, separatists' discourse comparing Spanish colonialism to slavery and demanding that the chains of servitude be broken fostered slaves' hopes for freedom. When tensions between royalists and republicans transformed into civil war in several regions, new occasions for emancipation became available to enslaved men who joined one side or the other of the conflict, while the resulting disorder favored flight attempts for slaves regardless of gender. As a result, in every Spanish continental colony, the institution of slavery weakened and the captive population decreased, particularly as, with the exception of Río de la Plata, most of them had stopped importing bozales two decades earlier.

Slaves' Liberation in Rebelling Mexico

By the time Ferdinand VII abdicated, Mexico's enslaved population had dropped to ten thousand out of a total of 6 million inhabitants (approximately 10 percent of whom were free Afro-descendants).[5] Those slaves were primarily concentrated in the Chilpancingo region, southeast of Mexico City (in the modern-day state of Guerrero), as well as in Veracruz and its interior regions of sugarcane plantations. Since 1810, in response to the creation of aristocratic juntas of creoles and peninsulars to govern Mexico on the king's behalf, a large popular movement emerged, led by the priest of the town of Dolores, Miguel de Hidalgo y Costilla. In his first proclamation in October 1810, Hidalgo, wielding a flag bearing Our Lady of Guadelupe, claimed to be Christian, Catholic, faithful to King Ferdinand VII, and opposed to the ungodly ideology of the French Revolution. He added: "The political freedom we are talking about entails that every individual be the sole owner of the work produced by his or her hands." He spoke out against exploitation, incarnated according to him by the *gachupines* (Spaniards), whom he felt should be nonviolently expelled from the country. Then, on 19 October, Hidalgo published a decree abolishing slavery, which he considered to be fundamentally opposed to divine law: "I warn all those who own men and women slaves that they must immediately ... set them free, grant them the necessary freedom documents (*escrituras de alahorria*) with which they can ... do all that free people do" or risk death sentences and confiscation of their belongings. Hidalgo also banned the sale of slaves and eliminated the tributes imposed on *castas* (free Afro-descendants) and Indians.[6] One month later, in his government plan, Hidalgo confirmed the absolute freedom of all slaves and the elimination of all tributes. He further declared equality between all individuals: "No one will be distinguished by his position, and we will all be called Americans." After Hidalgo's arrest and execution by royalists in 1811, the priest José María Morelos replaced him as the head of the revolutionary movement. Morelos would go on to declare Mexico's independence while confirming his profound adherence to Catholicism. Both the first draft of Mexico's 1812 constitution and the "Feelings of the Chilpancingo Nation," written under Morelos's supervision in 1813, reaffirmed the total abolition of slavery and caste distinctions.[7]

Unfortunately, historians have yet to take much interest in the impact of those declarations of freedom on Mexico's slaves. Studies that attempt to evaluate the socioracial composition of the revolutionary armies formed by thousands of farmers, day laborers, artisans, mule drivers, miners, plantation workers, and other men and women, often in families, who followed Hidalgo and then Morelos mention blacks, mulattos, and zambos, but not slaves, perhaps because the latter considered themselves free at that point.[8] Unlike other proclamations, such as that made by Lord Dunmore in the United States in 1775 or those made by French revolutionaries in the Antilles in 1793, or those by separatists in Venezuela or the Río de la Plata (examined below), the abolition decreed by Hidalgo and then Morelos was unconditional. All enslaved men, women, and children would thereafter be free, without being obliged to fight in the army or continue to work on plantations.

Furthermore, for nearly two years, Morelos's troops controlled the territory south of Mexico City, where many of the country's ten thousand slaves were living. That was where, in Chilpancingo in 1813, revolutionaries held their first congress and Morelos ordered intendants and magistrates to "set free" all men and women still enslaved. Undoubtedly, some of the region's remaining slaves seized that opportunity to gain their freedom, both by calling for the decree's application and by joining the thousands of Indian, white, mestizo, and Afro-descended rebels active at the time, while others remained at the service of their masters. Morelos also sent emissaries to the sugar plantations in Córdoba, southwest of Veracruz. Countless slaves responded by swelling the ranks of disorganized rebel bands to the point that planters were forced to form militias to defend their estates. After royalists executed Morelos at the end of 1815, many revolutionaries accepted their offer of amnesty, which temporarily brought an end to the popular separatist movement. But because the amnesty did not grant freedom to fugitive slaves, some chose to hide out in nearby mountains, living off pillaging and small subsistence crops, out of the reach of planter patrols.

When Mexico gained independence in 1821, its constitution did not put an end to slavery, but at the time fewer than three thousand men, women, and children were still enslaved. Morelos's former lieutenant, Vicente Guerrero, would be the one to definitively abolish slavery in Mexico in September 1829, during his short-lived presidency of the republic. That abolition formalized a freedom already won by many fugitive slaves as they fled during the previous two decades of unrest and war. Yet Guerrero was not able to impose it in Texas, which was being colonized by settlers from the United States, who brought thousands of slaves from Alabama and Georgia with them to establish cotton plantations.[9] Nonetheless, the abolition of slavery in Mexico, which had been one of the first beneficiaries of the slave trade in the sixteenth century, joined that decreed by Central America in 1824 (see chapter 9)—meaning that all the Afro-descendants living between Upper California and the territory south of the Rio Grande and Costa Rica would henceforth be free citizens.

Venezuela's Slaves: The Quest for Freedom in the Service of the King

Unlike in Mexico, where a large segment of the lower classes were involved in the anti-Spanish front spearheaded by the priests Hidalgo and Morelos, the separatist movement in Venezuela was led by elite creole owners, which tended to drive free and enslaved Afro-descendants to the royalists' camp. On the eve of the continent's independence wars, Venezuela had approximately 60,000 slaves out of a total population of 900,000 inhabitants, over half of whom were free blacks and pardos (of mixed African ancestry), while whites remained a minority. Those slaves were primarily concentrated in the vast province of Caracas, which was rich with cocoa plantations and where social tensions had been exacerbated after the suppression of the Coro revolt in 1795. Incidentally, southern and eastern Venezuela were controlled by rebellious indigenous nations, while the country's interior remained scantly colonized and harbored between 24,000 and 30,000 maroons living with fugitives from other social groups in tenacious communities, many of which had existed for several generations.[10] But that marginalized population was not seeking to reverse the colonial status quo to which it had adapted.

It was Caracas's creole elite, composed of the merchants and slaveowning planters who had contested the Código Negro of 1789 and opposed any gains for free people of African descent, who declared Venezuela's independence on 5 July 1811. The republican constitution that those separatists adopted at the end of the year established a selective voting system based on wealth and education, which allowed for the exclusion of most free pardos and blacks. As for slavery, no new legislation improved the lots of the country's many enslaved men and women, and the constitution limited itself to banning the importation of new captives—in part to earn the goodwill of Great Britain, which had abolished the slave trade as of 1808—but without affecting Venezuelan planters who had already ceased to import new slaves. As a result of those measures, Caracas's republican elite lost all support from slaves and many *libres de color*, whom royalists were then able to court. In certain coastal regions, such as Barlovento, located east of the capital, rural slaves began to revolt against their masters, while invoking obedience to the king and his supreme authority. Allied with free pardos, they attacked separatists' haciendas with the backing of royalists.

At the same time, other Venezuelan cities rose up in the king's name, launching a civil war whose main concern was regional interests, not independence. The arrival of a new Spanish governor, Juan Domingo de Monteverde, in early 1812 strengthened royalists' control over several provinces. Thanks to vague promises of equality, they ensured the loyalty of black and pardo militias and won the backing of many *libres de color*. They were also able to channel some slaves' resentment and hopes for freedom into their cause—defending the king. Many slaves, some with their wives, responded favorably to a call for mobilization against the "usurpers" made by Monteverde's agents and priests in separatist-dominated regions, notably on the cacao-producing coast stretching from Barlovento to Valencia, as it confirmed their trust in the Spanish monarch as their ultimate protector while legitimating their desire to turn against their masters. Numerous slaves thus mixed claims of defending the king with defiance against their owners and overseers and fled plantations, leaving death and destruction in their wake, and thereby contributing to the First Republic's surrender in July 1812. Although royalists were then able to compel the majority of rebelling slaves to return to their plantations, hundreds of fugitives joined the maroons in the country's hinterlands. Furthermore, royalists had unleashed a spirit of revolt against the colonial social order that would rapidly surpass them.[11]

Indeed, in 1813 separatists attempted to establish the Second Republic, and Simón Bolívar declared "war to the death" on the Spanish in order to unite proindependence Venezuelans in spite of sociracial differences. However, following that declaration, the war entered a lethal phase for the civilian population, which fell victim to two rival camps. In addition, the fact that Bolívar belonged to the slaveholding planter elite limited his ability to persuade free Afro-descendants and slaves, especially given that his main approach to the latter consisted of tracking fugitives and those who fought alongside royalists. Bolívar also had to contend with José Tomás Boves, an Asturian innkeeper and cattle dealer, who assembled a people's army of free pardos, blacks, mestizos, poor whites, Indians, and slaves, all ready to fight the separatist elite in the king's name in the territory's vast southern cattle-breeding plains. On the eastern coast of Caracas, Francisco Tomás Morales, a shopkeeper from the Canary Islands, and now Boves's second-in-command, recruited from Venezuela's lower classes and mobilized slaves. Another of Boves's lieutenants, Francisco Rosete, also a Canarian shopkeeper, attempted to rally slaves in the Tuy Valley, who represented the majority of inhabitants southwest of the capital. Many enslaved men, sometimes with women and children, fled to join royalist troops; others were enlisted by masters loyal to Spain. In February 1814, bands of slaves led by Rosete attacked the small town of Ocumare, where, according to reports received in Caracas, they raped, mutilated, and killed more than three hundred inhabitants. Bolívar responded by harsh repression against "bandits and fugitive slaves" and the execution of hundreds of Spaniards La Guaira. The "war to the death" period deeply affected civilians in both royalist and separatist strongholds as they fell prey to the invading faction. Residents in villages and towns were subjected to plunder, assault, and rape, and slaves, regardless of gender, were sometimes kidnapped for the assailants' use or for sale. In July 1814, royalists toppled the Second Republic, forcing hundreds of separatists, including Bolívar, into exile. However, that royalist victory, obtained thanks to the mobilization of Venezuela's lower classes and slaves led by Boves and his lieutenants, threatened to create a socioracial war. From that point onward, slaves were no longer content to only attack republicans, but also targeted aristocrats and planters still loyal to Spain.[12]

That development coincided with Ferdinand VII's return to the Spanish throne. Against all expectations, the king reestablished the absolute monarchy and wanted to forcefully restore its sovereignty and the colonial order across the simmering American continent. He eliminated the regent's council that had run the kingdom's government from Cádiz during the Napoleonic occupation, declared the Cortes (Parliament) illegal, and annulled the Spanish monarchy's constitution that the latter had adopted in 1812. He also dispatched ships and men to reconquer the American colonies that had seceded. In February 1815, the Spanish general Pablo Morillo arrived in Caracas at the head of a "pacification" expedition of more than ten thousand soldiers. With separatists temporarily beaten or exiled, Morillo did not try to recruit slaves but, on the contrary, put them back to work on plantations. Nonetheless, those who had joined royalist troops were granted concessions: royal decrees manumitted men who presented a certificate from their military superior attesting to their service and military exploits. Several slaves, such as Ramón Piñero and Juan Nepomuceno, submitted documented requests and obtained their certificates of freedom. Morillo also made concessions to slaves mobilized by separatists who turned themselves in: he incorporated them into his army with the promise of emancipation after a certain number of years of service, all while compensating their respective owners if they were royalists. The enslaved recruits still loyal to the Republic were less lucky: as had occurred during the U.S. War of Independence, Morillo's army seized them as enemy property and often resold them to Cuba. Nonetheless, in the sparsely colonized Venezuelan territory, the Spanish reconquest remained largely incomplete and countless slaves recruited by Boves, Rosete, and Morales formed maroon bands living off pillaging and stealing.[13]

The temporary recapture of Venezuela by Spain therefore did not call slavery itself into question, though it did weaken the institution by rewarding some slaves with manumission and by reducing the number of enslaved men and women in the territory. It also deeply scarred the separatist white aristocracy, for whom the first phase of the independence struggle looked much like a "race war" or "another Haiti" pitting it against *libres de color* and slaves. Even though both royalist and separatist troops had in fact been multiracial, Simón Bolívar, in particular, never relinquished his distrust of pardos and slaves, whom he suspected of secretly wanting to kill all whites.[14]

Simón Bolívar and Slavery

In 1816, the Venezuelan war of independence entered a new phase, first led by Manual Piar, a mulatto originally from Curaçao, who established the core of the liberation army in western Guiana. Because Spain's military presence was accompanied by growing abuses, popular resentment escalated, and more and more men who had once fought under Boves (who died in combat at the end of 1814) joined the separatists' ranks, attracted by the leadership of another cattle merchant, José Antonio Páez, barely literate and of modest origins but white. When Bolívar returned from exile in August 1817, thanks to an expedition supported by the president of Haiti, Alexandre Pétion, he attacked Piar, and not Páez, to establish himself as the republicans' supreme leader. He had Piar accused of planning a conspiracy aimed at establishing a *pardocracia* (a dictatorship of pardos) and had him shot in the name of the equality "of colors" in October 1817 in front of hundreds of mestizo and Afro-descended fighters. During his exile in Haiti, however, Bolívar had secretly agreed with Pétion to abolish slavery in the territories he would liberate. His statements on the subject remained ambiguous: though he had declared "the absolute freedom of all slaves" in his first, short-lived expedition from Haiti in 1816, he subsequently specified that men aged between fourteen and sixty who did not enlist in the separatist army would condemn themselves, and their wives and children, to continued enslavement. And though Bolívar enlisted a dozen of his own slaves in his army, he did not liberate the others in his possession. In any event, more and more enslaved men joined the liberation army: some were sent by their separatist masters, others were forcibly conscripted as troops moved through, whereas others enlisted after running away from their owners, such as José Ambrosio Surarregui, who fled to Cumaná in 1817 with the explicit goal of obtaining his freedom.

The resumption of war and its expansion across the territories of Venezuela and Colombia exacerbated pressure on their respective populations to supply royalist and republican armies alike with food, cattle, men, and money. When Morillo's "pacification" army attempted to take back Colombia at the end of 1815, it mobilized slaves on its way, often forcibly taking them from their masters, notably on the Caribbean coast and in the Cauca region. Those slaves were primarily used as porters, camp servants, and for clearing and constructing roads, but also sometimes in combat. Then, as separatists made headway in

Colombia, they aggressively competed with royalists to recruit slaves by force or with promises of freedom. In 1817, repeating his Venezuelan tactic, Morillo offered freedom to any armed slaves among separatist troops who deserted to join the king's cause, while also promising to compensate their owners if they were confirmed royalists.[15] In Cauca province, largely hostile to Spain, he even decided to create a battalion of slaves to whom he promised emancipation. As a result, separatists accused him of emptying haciendas to form bands intended to massacre republicans. In fact, officers in both camps enlisted numerous slaves to replace soldiers who were succumbing to disease and injury, dying, or deserting at an unbridled pace. But neither royalists nor separatists challenged the institution of slavery itself. Indeed, the Spanish monarchy boosted slavery in its faithful colony of Cuba. As for Colombia's separatist creole elite, it demonstrated, during debates at the 1819 Congress of Angostura, the predominance of powerful slaveowning planters in its ranks: the majority of delegates agreed not to make any decisions that would weaken slavery, against the advice of Bolívar, who remained convinced of the imminence of a collective slave revolt modeled after Saint Domingue if the congress did not decree complete abolition.[16]

Since 1820, the two camps, both in need of soldiers, unceremoniously recruited free and enslaved men alike. In order to fight royalists in southern Colombia and farther south in Peru, Bolívar required that thousands of slaves be mobilized to compensate for his heavy human losses and increase his armies' ranks from twenty thousand to thirty thousand men in two years.[17] Ever pragmatic, he made three arguments to justify the conscription of slaves. First, there were military reasons: slaves were strong men, used to working hard, and ready, according to Bolívar, to die for freedom. Second, demographic reasons: if free men were the only ones to fight and die for their country, there would be a dangerously high number of slaves at the end of the war. And third, political reasons: it was "madness in a revolution of freedom to pretend to maintain slavery," as they did in Saint Domingue after 1789.[18] But in 1820, Bolívar would only obtain a portion of the thousands of slaves he demanded. On the one hand, the republican government in Bogotá did not dare require owners of slave plantations and alluvial mines to supply the requested recruits, for fear of losing their support for independence. On the other hand, since Bolívar and his deputies had practically eliminated all references to freedom in their discourse, enslaved men themselves demonstrated little enthusiasm for the idea of abandoning their families and risking their lives by heading to unknown regions in exchange for a vague possibility of manumission. From then on, Bolívar no longer hesitated to forcibly recruit hundreds of men, which nonetheless failed to satisfy his growing needs for able-bodied soldiers. For example, among the slaves supplied by the provinces of Cauca and Antioquia, many were not fit for combat or were quickly rendered useless by diseases and injuries, even as others compensated for the lack of food by stealing. Most significantly, however, many deserted to join the fugitive bands flourishing as the war progressed.[19]

Moreover, in regions that had remained on the fringes of Spanish colonization until the end of the eighteenth century, some slaves, *libres de color*, and Indians mobilized to defend the king, whom they viewed as their bulwark against the appropriation by separatist landowners of the territories harboring them. That was notably the case for the inhabitants of the Patía Valley, in southern Colombia, where maroons and other runaways had formed the palenque of El Castigo around 1750, giving rise to small rural communities that subsisted by family farming and cattle raiding. When Bolívar's troops arrived, those illegal settlers and fugitives launched a long guerrilla war in support of royalists from the town of Pasto. They only gave up their resistance in 1822, after Pasto was seized by separatists, to avoid massacres and the destruction of their villages.[20]

More generally, since 1820, royalists began to accumulate defeats, prompting shifting allegiances. Sensing a separatist victory, experienced slave-soldiers among the king's troops voluntarily joined the republican side to ensure they would be freed at the end of the war. For example, José de Jesús Malpica had initially followed Boves in Venezuela, which had undoubtedly also allowed him to settle scores with his separatist master, but as of 1821, he served as a volunteer in a separatist unit, a fact he later used to claim his freedom. At the other extreme, some enslaved men chose a strategy of nonengagement. They avoided all conscription and throughout the war sought to preserve the autonomy they and their family had acquired on the estate of a master at war or in exile, all going into hiding when troops approached. Enslaved men and women from the auriferous mines of the province of Micay, on Colombia's Pacific coast, continued to work and produce gold between 1811 and 1824, which allowed several of them to legally purchase their freedom.[21]

The broader question of slavery resurfaced in 1821 during debates held by the Cúcuta Congress on the constitution of the republic of Colombia (including modern-day Venezuela and Colombia). The creole planter aristocracy had become even more influential by that time, and Bolívar stopped asking delegates for the complete abolition of slavery, as he had in 1819, settling instead for freedom to be granted to children born to enslaved mothers (the free-womb principle), which, according to him, would allow for "possessive," political, and natural rights to be reconciled. However, the congress did not heed Bolívar's request: the 1821 constitution guaranteed equality and tacitly abolished racial discriminations against free Afro-descendants but did not mention slavery. Slavery was addressed in a separate law of gradual manumission that did little to change the condition of slaves in the new republic. Only those who reached the age of sixty would be declared free, though they would not receive any support in their old age. Furthermore, the children of enslaved mothers would henceforth be born free (the "free womb" demanded by Bolívar), but only once they reached adulthood and on the condition that they had served their mother's master well up until then. As in the northern United States, that arrangement meant those children's education and care were entrusted to said master, thereby preventing their parents from filling that role. The law banned the importation of slaves to the republic, but authorized a variety of transactions in the territory, including the sale of prepubescent children within the province where their parents resided. It also called for the creation of juntas charged with buying the freedom of the most "honest and hardworking" slaves through an inheritance tax. But few juntas were actually formed, and when they were, they did little: from 1821 to 1827, they freed at most three hundred slaves in Venezuela and Colombia combined. In addition, after 1821, enslaved men no longer had the possibility of gaining emancipation by joining the army. They would have to be authorized or designated by their masters to enlist and do so without the promise of eventual freedom.[22] Nonetheless, the number of slaves decreased in both countries. In Colombia, it dropped from 70,000 men, women, and children in 1810 to less than 46,000 out of a total population of approximately 1,200,000 inhabitants in 1825, and in Venezuela from 60,000 slaves in 1810 to 42,500 out of 900,000 inhabitants in 1830.[23]

The loss of one-third of slaves during the fifteen years of unrest and war that led to independence can be partly explained by escapes and self-purchase by slaves, as well as natural deaths among an aging captive population. But the decline also resulted from the war itself, which caused massacres, violent raids, and long-lasting sieges during which civilians, above all the poor, and among them the slaves, died of hunger and epidemics. The war also forced some slaveowners into exile, at times taking their slaves with them, whereas slaves confiscated as enemy property were sold abroad. Altogether, the decline of the enslaved population was only marginally due to the decrees abolishing slavery issued by Bolívar and to the emancipation promised to army veterans. Granted, the congress of Cúcuta declared the absolute and irrevocable freedom of any enslaved individuals who had been emancipated by republican authorities and reenslaved by the Spanish when the latter took back the territory, but excluded any men or women who had been liberated by royalists "out of hatred of independence."[24]

As for enslaved men recruited by republicans and promised emancipation, they would face a new struggle to obtain certificates of freedom at the war's end, when they were required to supply attestations of service from their officers, a process complicated by the latter's distance or absence. Though some were able to obtain the needed document when they were decommissioned, others had to persevere for some time before receiving it. In the meanwhile, many clashed with their former masters, who demanded either their reenslavement or payment of their market value. That drove the enslaved Venezuelan José Ambrosio

Surarregui, mentioned above in relation to his 1817 enlistment, to protest against reenslavement in 1829, maintaining that "a man who defends the sacred right of his country's freedom with his blood and his life should no longer be able to be a slave." Those who could start a new life as freedmen received military pay inferior to that given other soldiers, despite a postwar economic crisis affecting the entire population. In addition, at the congress of Cúcuta, delegates rejected a suggestion to give the most deserving emancipated slaves a few plots from among the land abandoned by the Spanish and the monarchy, arguing that they did not belong to "the best class of people." Then the republican government adopted laws against fugitive slaves and vagabonds allowing them to be sentenced to convict labor in the army or navy, which led to many abuses against emancipated slaves and free Afro-descendants.[25]

Slave Recruitment and Manumission in the Río de la Plata

In the viceroyalty of the Río de la Plata, slaves and *libres de color* played an important role from the very beginning of the independence struggle. At the end of the eighteenth century, well before the massive immigration of Europeans would transform its demographics, the port town of Buenos Aires only numbered 25,400 inhabitants, including 6,650 Afro-descendants, three-quarters of whom were probably enslaved. Between 1788 and 1807, 27,000 bozales were imported to the Río de la Plata, a process that peaked between 1803 and 1806, when between 3,300 and 4,700 captives were brought in annually—more than at any other moment in the region's history.[26] Consequently, the number and percentage of slaves, often African-born, in the city grew. Increasingly they also worked in agriculture and cattle ranches in interior regions.

As in its other colonies, the Spanish monarchy had entrusted a large portion of the defense of the Argentine coastline to free blacks and mulattos organized into racially separate militias. Though those militiamen were unable to prevent a first British occupation of Buenos Aires in June 1806, they chased out the British six weeks later, thanks to slave reinforcements. Realizing the role played by slaves in that victory, the city council of Buenos Aires promised that in the future it would liberate any men who distinguished themselves in combat against any invader. During a second attempted British invasion in 1807, hundreds of enslaved men enthusiastically responded to calls to defend the city. Driven by the prospect of freedom, they were a key factor in the *porteño* victory. But when the time came to deliver on its promise, the town council announced that it was out of funds and that no emancipations could be granted without compensating slaveowners. It therefore prioritized emancipating slaves who were disabled or rendered unproductive by the fighting, who also received a small pension. The fate of the remaining slave-soldiers depended on chance: the town council organized a "freedom lottery" and committed to buying some twenty winners. In order to sign up, candidates had to obtain an attestation of merit from the officers under which they had served; widows of slaves killed in combat, bearing their husbands' certificates, could also participate in the random draw. An impressive number of slaves—688—met the conditions required to participate. The "freedom lottery" took place during a grandiose ceremony attended by royal, church, and military authorities and many of the city's inhabitants. The militias and armed forces were present as well, in part to prevent any disorder. The viceroy and his officers announced, undoubtedly for good measure, that they would pay to liberate forty-five additional slaves, bringing the total to seventy. The lucky winners were cheered but not truly liberated as they were immediately assigned to a military unit as soldiers. While the losers did not revolt, several continued for months to demand what they considered to be their rightful freedom, on the basis of substantiating documents.[27]

During the wars of independence, the mobilization of slaves became systematic in the Río de la Plata. After having successfully expulsed the viceroy from Buenos Aires in May 1810, the creole elite formed an autonomous government and then cruelly suppressed a royalist conspiracy (forty-one executions in 1812, though an enslaved men named Ventura who reported the plot was given freedom and a pension). As elsewhere in continental Spanish America, until Ferdinand VII's Spain attempted to win the region back in 1815, the Río de la Plata was beset by a civil war in which subregions faced off under banners proclaiming loyalty to the king, autonomy, or independence. In order to monopolize external trade and consolidate their power against both Spain and neighboring provinces, Buenos Aires's creoles had a growing need of troops, which could not be supplied by the free male population alone.[28] By June 1813, a few months after adopting a free-womb law and banning the importation of new slaves (in part, as in Venezuela, to win Great Britain's goodwill), the government decided to recruit enslaved men to form a special battalion. Far from relying on slaves' willingness, however, the decree ordered owners to present their slaves to a commission that would select men whom it would buy in advance for the army in proportions meant to protect slaveholders' private property and ensure the local economy continued to function. The purchased slaves were incorporated into the army under the status of *libertos* (freed), but would not obtain their freedom until after five years of service.

Between 1813 and the end of 1814, 1,015 slaves were mobilized in that way to form the Seventh Infantry Battalion. In 1815, following the start of Spain's reconquest, separatists decreed that, henceforth, all enslaved men between sixteen and thirty years old belonging to Spaniards would be enlisted as *libertos*, but would only become free one year after the end of the war. After a vain attempt to similarly requisition creole owners, the republican army ordered

Spanish citizens in Buenos Aires province to procure it four hundred additional slaves or their equivalent in silver in order to form a new cohort. Confiscations from Spanish owners enabled the creation of the Eighth Battalion, composed of 1,059 *libertos*. In total, among the 2,000 or so enslaved men conscripted into the two battalions, 149 were recently imported Africans.[29] Not all of them had been supplied by their masters: some had fled, claiming to be free, and often in the company of their wife and children; others had been released from prison to serve in the army; still others—free or enslaved—had been captured and forcibly conscripted. Moreover, in December 1816, every one of Buenos Aires's 2,500 able-bodied enslaved men was incorporated into the city's militias without acquiring the status of *libertos*. Those slaves continued to work for masters who had to regularly lend them out for training exercises—but they were unable to obtain their freedom after the war.[30]

The leading separatist general in the Río de la Plata, José de San Martín, established a training camp for those *porteño* slave-recruits in Mendoza, a region with over four thousand slaves employed in cattle raising and agriculture. With the goal of forming an army of ten thousand slaves, San Martín continued to demand large numbers of male recruits from Buenos Aires, as well as from Cuyo, Mendoza, and Córdoba, but the actual troops fell far short of his target, especially given the fact that desertions were on the rise as many conscripts fled hoping to pass for free. At the same time, some enslaved women also joined the camp, either as companion of an enslaved conscript, or to escape their owners and try their luck in the army as laundresses, nurses, cooks, or seamstresses, hoping to be freed for their services later. Other enslaved women were the private servants of officers, such as María Demetria Escalada de Soler, the personal slave of San Martín, while some were kidnapped or confiscated from the enemy and became military slaves possibly subjected to sexual abuse. Slave women in San Martín's army, as in all other separatist or royalist armies, represented both an additional burden as they slowed down the movement of the troops and needed food and shelter, but also a contribution as they performed many essential daily duties. Incidentally, the forced or voluntary conscription of so many able-bodied enslaved men in the Río de la Plata during the war shifted much of the work due to slaveholders, both in the countryside and the cities, to enslaved women, who on top were left alone in charge of their family. Nonetheless, at the end of 1816, San Martín was able to form an army of 4,000 soldiers and 1,000 auxiliaries, 40 percent of whom were *libertos* who could reach the ranks of corporal and sergeant. After leaving Mendoza in early 1817, the emancipated slaves from the Seventh and Eighth Battalions of the Army of the Andes played a crucial role in the liberation of Chile in 1818. However, nearly half of those men (the women's fate is unknown) lost their lives or were seriously injured in battles with royalist troops.[31]

Chile itself had a mere 5,000 to 6,000 slaves out of a total population of 380,000 inhabitants and, by 1811, the junta of creole autonomists that had taken power declared the gradual abolition of slavery (ending slave imports and "free womb"). At first, it did not envisage recruiting slaves for the army, though it did form a segregated battalion of free blacks and mulattos, called *Infantes de la Patria* (Infantrymen of the Fatherland), that some enslaved men were able to join by pretending to be free. According to one royalist, three hundred slaves in Santiago had pooled their money to hire a lawyer who, acting on their behalf, asked the separatist junta to grant them their freedom if they enlisted to defend the country: they reportedly even protested, armed with knives, to ensure they were heard, prompting authorities to have several of them arrested. When fighting with royalists who came from Peru intensified in 1814, Chilean separatists began to enlist slaves, whether they were fugitives, confiscated from the enemy, or supplied by their masters, in specific units curiously named *Ingenuos de la Patria* (Freeborn of the Fatherland) within the *Infantes de la Patria* battalion. Slaves conscripted by Chilean republicans were therefore doubly segregated, on one side from whites and on the other, from free mulattos and blacks. Chile eventually fell under Spanish control during the reconquest, until troops led by General San Martín, including the Seventh and Eighth battalions of emancipated fighters, successfully relaunched the independence movement in 1818.[32] In Chile, after liberating the country, San Martín wanted to reproduce his policy of recruiting enslaved men by promising them freedom to replenish his troops in preparation for the invasion of Peru, but only succeeded after offering 150 pesos per slave to Chilean owners. Finally, in August 1820, nearly 5,000 men, including 2,000 Argentinian and Chilean *libertos*, were transported by boat from Valparaiso to Pisco, south of Lima.[33]

In fact, Peru remained loyal to Spain, except for some separatist guerrillas in the hinterlands. Spanish and creole elites, still marked by Tupac Amaru's rebellion thirty years earlier (see chapter 7), were not divided like their counterparts in the rest of continental Spanish America; their main problems in terms of security were the marronage and banditry rampant in the areas surrounding Lima and Indian unrest. Independence was therefore imposed on them from the outside, starting with San Martín's armies. After landing in Pisco, his troops marched on Lima by way of the coastal region of sugar plantations and vineyards, which employed a large portion of Peru's ninety thousand slaves, and seized dozens of men to expand their ranks. Other slaves fled their masters to join those troops in the hopes of gaining their freedom by serving as scouts and spies. In response, royalists recruited slaves as well to confront the invaders and compensate for defections: in order to win slaves' loyalty without losing the support of their masters, they announced that the conscripts would be freed after six years of military service and that their owners would be compensated each slave's value at the time of his conscription. At the same time, a large number of slaves, alone or in families, took advantage of the confusion to flee as far as possible from plantations and both armies.

In July 1821, conscious of the rapid degradation of the social order, San Martín made his triumphant entrance to Lima. Shortly thereafter, he declared Peru's independence, while detailing his policy regarding slaves: all fugitives had to return to their masters; all those who belonged to royalists or exiles had to turn themselves over to the army, after which the men would be enlisted with a promise of eventual emancipation. For enslaved women, the promise was indirect: as of 12 August 1821, all infants born to an enslaved mother would be free. In early 1822, the separatists in power in Lima tasked a commission with drafting hundreds of slaves, borrowing the recruitment model of the Río de la Plata in 1813, but the results were limited due to resistance from hacendados and slave escapes. A few months later, royalists took back control of the capital; San Martín renounced his role as the independence leader in favor of Bolívar, and both sides abandoned all plans to enlist the region's enslaved men.

When Bolívar began the final phase of the war in Peru, he was counting primarily on Colombian and Venezuelan troops that he controlled personally and was determined to first win the war in the country's Andean interior before attacking its Pacific coast. And in fact, in 1824, the battles of Junín and Ayacucho, won by troops coming from the north with the help of the region's multiracial *montoneras* (guerrillas), marked the end of Spanish domination in Peru and throughout South America. Many of the victorious soldiers were *libertos* from Venezuela and Colombia dispersed across different units, but few came from Peru. Nonetheless, the war helped reduce the number of slaves in Peru from nearly 90,000 (40 percent of whom were concentrated in the province of Lima) in 1812 to 50,400 out of a total population of 1,325,000 inhabitants in 1825, or a drop of 40,000 slaves in thirteen years. As in Venezuela and Colombia, that decrease in Peru can be explained by the halt of importations and natural aging, combined with the effects of the war, such as abnormally high mortality rates and the departure of slaves forced to follow their masters into exile. One of the most notable causes, however, was the thousands of slaves who took advantage of the chaos of war to escape and settle elsewhere. But among the 50,400 men and women still listed as slaves in Peru in 1825, many had benefited from the high prices generated by the war to begin to accumulate the savings necessary to purchase their freedom in subsequent years.[34]

The fate of slaves who had voluntarily enlisted to fight for the king of Spain or for independence with the goal of liberating themselves and their families was far from certain—the emancipation promised them at the war's debut was visibly often a ploy. Sometimes authorities refuted their own decisions in order to exploit those soldiers as much as possible while continuing to regard them primarily as slaveowners' private property. For example, in 1810, during the siege of Montevideo, still loyal to Ferdinand VII, the separatist government of Buenos Aires supported General José Rondeau's plan to emancipate royalists' slaves who would flee their masters to join his army. Many slaves responded to the general's call, such as Francisco Estrada, who joined the troops in Buenos Aires with his wife and child, and even obtained a certificate of freedom for himself and his family members. But in 1812, during negotiations with royalists, authorities in Buenos Aires agreed to the demand of Montevideo slaveholders that their dispossessed slaves be returned to them. Like many others, Estrada and his family were sent back to his master, who punished them harshly for escaping; he then submitted several demands for justice in Buenos Aires in order to be able to "defend my freedom and that of my wife," without ever receiving a response. The *porteño* government also broke its own laws by extending the amount of time *libertos* had to serve in the army to gain their freedom or by making that freedom subject to new conditions. Numerous *libertos* were systematically remobilized after having completed their years of service: for example, members of the Eighth Infantry Battalion who had survived eight years in the Andean campaign, from Chile to Ecuador, were immediately reenlisted on their return to Buenos Aires in 1824. Finally, in 1825, Buenos Aires decreed that the five to six years of military service necessary for a slave to be truly free would be counted, not beginning with his enlistment, but with his purchase from his master, allowing authorities to prolong, and at times double, the time served in the army. In addition, those who had been able to obtain their letter of manumission were continually at risk from laws against vagabondage targeting the lowest social classes and authorizing the forced recruitment of so-called vagabonds and idlers.[35]

Despite all those pitfalls and a republican elite largely in favor of slavery, many enslaved men saw military service as a way to obtain, while risking their lives, their deepest wish: freedom. Not only did they not resist army conscription, but some fled their masters to enlist. Enslaved women, following their husbands or on their own, also joined the army to work in diverse capacities. However, as masters could easily denounce them for that tactic, some slaves fled to other provinces to pass as free and join the army. And even then, enslaved men and women were not safe from being reclaimed by their owners, as was the case for Domingo Antonio, from Córdoba, who was spared reenslavement thanks to his fellow soldiers, who collectively helped buy his freedom. Incidentally, the mother of a slave abused by his master set a precedent when she used an article of the Código Negro authorizing mistreated slaves to solicit purchase by another master willing to do so: she proposed that the army purchase her son for integration into a *liberto* battalion, a method that would become legal practice. *Liberto* soldiers also saved their meager wages to buy their family members' freedom.

Finally, the many demands for manumission submitted by slave-soldiers—and by a few enslaved women—to the state from the start of the independence process showed that they considered their emancipation to be a right justified by their military service. Of course, it is impossible to know how many slaves were actually integrated into the Río de la Plata army, how many died or fled over the war's duration, how many were recuperated by their masters, and how many truly became free. Two figures are revealing, however: of the 2,000 *libertos* who left Buenos Aires with San Martín in 1816 to fight in Chile, Peru, and Ecuador, only 150 returned in 1823.[36] As in other former Spanish possessions, the number of slaves in the Río de la Plata decreased between 1810, when they numbered approximately 30,000 out of a total population of 310,000, and the postwar period, though no statistics exist to quantify that decline.[37]

By contrast, in Chile the slave survivors of Peru's liberation did not have to fight for long: in 1823, when there were roughly 4,000 slaves remaining in the country, the Senate decreed the total abolition of slavery. Despite the executive's Director Supremo attempts to block that decision with measures to protect and indemnify masters, at the end of the year the Chilean constitution confirmed unconditional abolition, making Chile the second American nation to be liberated from slavery, after Haiti in 1804 and before Central America in 1824. Of course, abolition did not signify immediate autonomy for emancipated slaves; a majority of them continued working for their former masters, and some men were conscripted into the army, though they would henceforth be free and their children would never know slavery. The announcement of the liberation of all of Chile's slaves spread rapidly to Argentina, especially as a clause in the Chilean constitution stipulated that any foreign slaves who set foot on national soil would be declared free the day following their arrival. Argentinians who were still enslaved therefore attempted to cross the border to gain their freedom, but in April 1824 authorities in Mendoza province asked Chile to prevent slave escapes in the region. Chile complied by decreeing that any "slave from neighboring states who fled with the sole goal of obtaining freedom granted by the Chilean government will not legally set foot on the Chilean territory." Subsequently, the Chilean government applied that reinterpretation of the constitution to all slaves arriving by land or sea, whether they came from Argentina, Peru, or even the southern United States. Its defense of slaveowners extended far beyond neighboring states, and up until the U.S. Civil War, Chile agreed to send fugitive slaves back to their nation of origin by claiming they were deserters or illegal immigrants.[38]

Slave Conspiracies and Revolts in the
Loyal Spanish Caribbean

While the wars of independence offered slaves in Spain's American continental colonies occasions to gain their freedom, enslaved populations in Puerto Rico and particularly in Cuba were contending with the intensification and expansion of slavery: a little more than 3,000 Africans were imported by Puerto Rico between 1810 and 1825, compared to a total of over 180,000 by Cuba during the same fifteen-year period, with a peak of nearly 26,000 in 1817. As a result, by 1817, almost 40 percent of Cuba's inhabitants were slaves, and people of African descent, both free and enslaved, outnumbered whites despite heavy immigration by Spaniards and royalists fleeing the wars of independence on the continent.[39] Within that changing demographic context, many Cubans and Puerto Ricans were closely observing events in Spain, Mexico, and South America. In the spring of 1811, during the Cádiz Cortes sessions, a rumor about an abolition decree began to circulate in the two islands. As was often the case, it was not completely unfounded. In fact, in Cádiz, a Mexican delegate had suggested gradual abolition (an end to the slave trade coupled with a free-womb law), whereas a Spanish delegate had proposed solely abolishing the slave trade. Though those suggestions, immediately challenged by a Cuban delegate, were quickly dismissed, they alarmed slaveholders in colonies that had remained loyal to Spain, and their slaves overheard their shocked reactions.

In Puerto Rico in particular, during Epiphany celebrations in 1812, several slaves came to believe that the island's governor was hiding the existence of a decree of general emancipation. That false rumor was amplified by the arrival of a royal navy that some interpreted as the Cortes wanting to apply the decree by force. In various villages around the capital of San Juan, enslaved men and women assembled and refused to work, claiming to be free; others threatened to spill blood as in Saint Domingue if they were not immediately liberated. The governor chose to quell the rumor with arrests and public whippings and authorized all whites to capture any suspected black individuals, free or enslaved, and bring him or her before the courts. By the end of the month, at least twenty-six men had been accused of conspiracy and rebellion. None were executed, but several were sentenced to dozens of whiplashes and sale outside the island. Others were returned to their masters after being acquitted or to be punished by them as they pleased.[40]

In Cuba, the unrest was much more serious. Planters there had been able to transform the island into the leading global sugar producer, replacing Saint Domingue, thanks to the forced labor of slaves imported from Africa by the thousands every year. Cuban society had become a slave society, in which *libres de color* were increasingly lumped together with slaves. In January 1812, slaves on several plantations revolted, beginning in Puerto Príncipe, followed by Bayamo, Holguín, and finally Havana, leaving twenty whites dead and significant destruction behind them. According to their interrogations, the slaves had revolted because their masters refused to respect a supposed royal decree abolishing slavery, which some said came from the king of Spain, and others from the Cortes, the king of Great Britain, the king of Kongo, or even the king of Haiti (due to Henri Christophe's recent crowning). Nearly all of the incriminated slaves were convinced that their emancipation was imminent, based on news and rumors of the tensions between Christophe's kingdom and Alexandre Pétion's republic in Haiti, the first separatist uprisings in Venezuela, and the Cádiz Cortes debates. The investigation also revealed the existence of vast networks linking *libres de color* in the island's cities with creole and bozal slaves on plantations. More worrying still for authorities was the presence among the uprising's leaders of free, artisan, and literate blacks, who were often members of defense militias and active in cabildos de nación, mutual aid associations that gathered Africans and their descendants of shared ethnicities.[41]

José Antonio Aponte, a free black sculptor, was revealed to be the main instigator of the 1812 uprisings, prompting them to be named "Aponte's conspiracy," and a book of his drawings became a major piece of evidence of the alleged plot. Although no historian has found the document to this day, it contained dozens of images that Aponte described in detail to his interrogators, seemingly without being subjected to torture. The book showed plans of Cuban cities and military garrisons, battles in which black soldiers were defeating white ones, portraits of Aponte's ancestors, and drawings of the king of Spain, popes surrounded by high-ranking black dignitaries, and Ethiopian kings—in other words, a military, religious, and political world in which blacks were dominant. In addition, many of the accused claimed to have seen Aponte with portraits of heroes of the Haitian Revolution.[42] On that basis, Cuban authorities determined that Aponte and his companions were preparing to take power, like blacks in Saint Domingue, and began a vast crackdown. A total of 381 people were arrested, mostly slaves, many of them Africans. They were nearly all black, and thirty or so were women. Their trials led to thirty-four executions by hanging, including Aponte, followed by the display of their heads in public places. Nearly two hundred people were sentenced to prison terms or public whippings, often followed by the wearing of irons.[43] But black and mulatto militiamen continued to ensure the military defense of Cuban ports, in all likelihood because there were not enough whites willing to serve in the militia.

In 1814, Ferdinand VII's return to the throne inaugurated a period of close collaboration between the monarchy and its two faithful slaveholding possessions in the Caribbean. Beyond planters, large swaths of those societies benefited directly and indirectly from the growing success of slave-produced agricultural exports. Vague hopes for independence among liberal circles or for freedom among slave were therefore quickly quashed. In Puerto Rico, for example, in July 1821, Bayamón district attracted authorities' attention following a report that slaves were on the point of revolting. The so-called "Marcos Xiorro conspiracy," after the bozal who reportedly masterminded it, followed a script already seen many times before, beginning with slaves rebelling on several plantations, taking the small town of Bayamón, crowning the creole elite slave Mario, slaughtering whites, and finally capturing San Juan thanks to reinforcements sent from Haiti by its president, Jean-Pierre Boyer. Nothing happened, but many slaves were arrested and interrogated, leading to the execution of Mario and one other slave, but Marcos Xiorro and others were returned to their masters for punishment.[44]

In the following years most thwarted slave plans in Puerto Rico involved attempted escapes, not revolts, until accusations of a conspiracy in July 1826 shook the Ponce region, whose sugar industry was growing rapidly and whose enslaved population had tripled between 1812 and 1826. Once again, four slaves told their master of a plot in which the bozal coach driver Antonio Congo had incited them to participate. Brought in for questioning, he gave the names of thirty accomplices, who were quickly arrested. Their plan had supposedly been to start an uprising in the guise of a *bomba*, a ceremony including chants and a dance to drum rhythms. The plotters would have taken advantage of the occasion to set fire to sugarcane fields to attract firefighters and militiamen while they attempted to take weapons from the barracks in the neighboring town to murder whites, plunder stores, and seize power. Although no protests or violence had occurred, one month later Antonio Congo and nineteen other suspects were executed, three enslaved men were sentenced to ten years of convict labor in Cuba, and sixteen others were forced to watch the executions. The four informants were emancipated and received a small monetary reward. Shortly thereafter, the island's governor passed a slave law that extended masters' powers and dramatically limited slaves' movements and free time.[45]

In Cuba as well, fears of a slave uprising grew in the 1820s, with the arrival of thousands of enslaved Africans every year to work on sugarcane, coffee, and tobacco plantations. Several revolts and mutinies erupted, showing the capacity of Africans of diverse origins to unite against their masters, though they were more reactions to administrators' violent excesses than planned movements. Rebels were rapidly subdued by troops sent against them, and before they could recruit other nearby slaves. Those periodic revolts could have heavy human costs, however. For example, in 1827, fifty-seven slaves from a coffee plant farm in western Cuba revolted against the brutality with which they were treated, murdered their overseer, and spread regionwide until a militia of planters ended the rebellion, costing the lives of twenty-three slaves: five shot, and eighteen hanged in what was officially recorded as a group suicide.[46] Even at the height of slavery in Cuba, as in Jamaica previously, revolt may have been a way to assert one's humanity for some slaves, but it did not lead to freedom, except for those men and women who were able to flee into impenetrable marronage zones—and sometimes for those who denounced alleged plots.

⇛ The processes of independence triggered after the Napoleonic occupation of the Iberian Peninsula therefore had profound repercussions on slaves in the American colonies of Spain and Portugal. Many of them hoped those changes would bring them their freedom. In places where wars eventually led to independence, as in continental Spanish America, armies on both sides conscripted thousands of enslaved men, hundreds of whom obtained their emancipation as a result. More numerous, however, were the enslaved men and women who took advantage of local unrest to run away and settle far from their owners as free citizens. In effect, the decrease of a third, and at times half, of the slave populations in all the new republics between 1810 and the 1820s was partly due to slaves' desire to liberate themselves through flight or manumission. The institution of slavery was weakened by war and then by laws of gradual abolition that banned the slave trade and promoted the free-womb principle. But war and manumission laws instituted a fundamental difference between enslaved men and women: whereas the first could gain freedom—and thus citizenship—through their military sacrifice for the new republic, women were still regarded as vessels, not as mothers with parental rights on their new babies. Indeed, slavery remained a component of most republics until the 1850s, as only Chile, Central America, and Mexico would abolish slavery entirely in the immediate wake of independence.

For Brazil's slaves, however, both during the Portuguese court's move to the colony and following an independence won without major armed conflicts in 1822, laws did not become any more lenient, and the empire's economy relied increasingly on the slave trade and slavery. Similarly, in the two islands that had remained loyal to Spain—Cuba and Puerto Rico—slaves' situation worsened with the rise of the sugar plantation and the massive importation of enslaved Africans. In fact, in all the American regions in which slavery was still practiced, even in places where wars of independence had led to the establishment of republics and the slave trade had been banned, marronage and self-purchase remained enslaved peoples' primary means to obtain their freedom.

PART IV
Defending Slavery versus Abolitionism (1800–1838)

≋ 9 ≋
Marronage and the Purchase of Freedom
Old Strategies in New Times

Between 1770 and 1825, revolutions and independence wars disrupted relations between colonists and Europe, leading to power vacuums and waning control over territories, both of which aided enslaved peoples in their quests for freedom. In Great Britain's and Spain's continental colonies, conflicts between loyalists and separatists and the population displacements that they generated enabled thousands of slaves to flee their masters, buy their freedom, or enlist in armies in exchange for promised emancipation. Nonetheless, only slaves in Saint Domingue, who constituted the vast majority of the population, were able to carry out a massive uprising—after which they merged the battle against Bonaparte's France with the fight against his attempts to reestablish slavery— and win their freedom.

After the wars raging across the Americas ended, the weakness of new states, instability, and poverty continued to enable some slaves to escape, at the same time that others attempted to buy their freedom. In the northern United States and the former Spanish colonies in South America, laws of gradual abolition took two to three decades to bring an end to slavery, during which many enslaved men and women decided to liberate themselves by their own means. However, in both the southern United States and Brazil, as well as in the Guianas and the Caribbean, planters sought on the contrary to bolster slavery, first through massive importations of new African captives, and then, in places where the slave trade was banned as of 1808, by more profitable management. Africans continued to be forcibly brought to the French Caribbean, Cuba, and Brazil until 1830, and in these last two countries until midcentury. Incidentally, the year 1829, with a total of 106,000 African men, women, and children brought alive to the Americas, marked the peak of that odious trade's history.

The ongoing influx of African captives accompanied individual or collective escapes and endemic marronage in certain regions. Where possible, slaves attempted to gain their freedom through legal means, by obtaining a certificate of emancipation. The liberation rhetoric of the independence movements, awareness of the 1789 Spanish Código Negro, and the spread of gradual abolition models adopted by several U.S. northern states and South American republics undoubtedly all provided slaves with legal references on which they could base their demands and fight back against their masters' abuses.

Flight: An Almost Impossible Path to Freedom in the U.S. South

In the United States, the abolition of slavery by some northern states and the climate favorable to manumission that emerged after independence encouraged many slaves to run away, even though since 1793 the Fugitive Slave Act defined any aide given to a fugitive slave as a federal crime and stipulated that an escaped slave could also be captured in states that had abolished slavery. In several cities in the North and the Upper South, the free population of African descent increased rapidly, due not only to natural growth and emancipations, but also to the discreet arrival of fugitive slaves who hid there by passing for free.[1] In the hinterlands of the Carolinas and Georgia, marronage spread following those states' importation of more than ninety-three thousand African slaves between 1781 and 1810, two-thirds of whom were imported right before the slave trade was banned by the Constitution.[2]

The Great Dismal Swamp, on the border between Virginia and North Carolina, continued to shelter between one thousand and twenty-five hundred fugitive slaves, alone or in families (the latter sometimes composed of a single mother and her children), who lived primarily through hunting, fishing, and gathering. However, some of those runaways occasionally worked in the timber industry, which, since the end of the eighteenth century, operated from February to June. Teams of slaves would be sent to cut down trees in the region to make planks and clapboards. Those slaves, rented out by their owners to logging companies, were paid by the job after their food costs and a fixed sum for their masters were deducted. Maroons were also hired under similar conditions, which benefited all parties involved. In other places as well, individual runaways or families of fugitives settled near farms where they worked in exchange for small monetary sums, food or clothes, and, above all, for their employer's silence. Though fragile, those arrangements were undoubtedly more bearable than slavery, demonstrating that for many runaways, the key to survival was discretion, not isolation.[3] Other maroons, organized into almost exclusively male armed bands, survived by stealing and pillaging. They largely depended on what they could obtain from plantation slaves, willingly or otherwise, whom they did not hesitate to attack and rob. As a result, relations between maroons and slaves were often tense and could lead the latter to participate in raids to track and capture the fugitives who were threatening their livelihoods, notably in the coastal region of Charleston in the early 1820s.[4]

The War of 1812 between the United States and Great Britain led to more slave escapes from southern plantations. As had occurred during the U.S. War of Independence, the British army appealed to slaves to fight at its side by promising them emigration and cultivatable land (though it did not mention granting their freedom this time). And when the warring nations made peace, fugitive slaves once again faced an uncertain future, as in 1783. Though many were recaptured and punished by their masters, over 3,600 runaway slaves in total, from Maryland, Virginia, North Carolina, Georgia, and Louisiana, were transported out of the United States by the British between 1813 and 1815. Most were taken to Halifax, in Nova Scotia, and the rest to Bermuda and other Caribbean islands. Though emancipated, those men, women, and children nonetheless encountered many difficulties. Nearly all of them came from plantations and were therefore illiterate and unskilled, and their arrivals in large numbers coincided with that of European immigrants. In Canada, individuals sent to colonize interior regions were poorly welcomed by loyalist blacks who had settled there in the 1780s. Furthermore, the plots of land given them were small and the soil far from fertile. Thus, they typically remained together near cities in an attempt to survive off of the meager rations distributed by the colonial administration. The slave-soldiers recruited by the British in 1814 in Chesapeake Bay to form a corps of emancipated colonial sailors had better luck. At the end of the war, the British army sent them, with their families, to Bermuda first, to build an arsenal, and later transported them to the island of Trinidad, where in 1816 they settled as independent farmers on cultivable lands in what would become the "Meriken" (American) Company Villages.[5]

During the War of 1812, some slaves fled Georgia to establish maroon communities in northern Florida, still under Spanish control, where they lived alongside Seminole Indians. Forewarned of a U.S. military advance on their land, they constructed a fort in Prospect Bluff, near the Apalachicola River, at the prompting of Great Britain, which provided them with weapons and munitions. After the British evacuation, some four hundred black and Indian warriors, as well as women and children, remained in the "Negro Fort," which had a village and food crops and continued to attract new fugitive slaves from Georgia until it reached at least one thousand inhabitants. Planters considering the stronghold a threat to the security of their plantations obtained federal intervention. In 1816, the U.S. Army and Navy, backed by Creek fighters, attacked the fort and killed at least 250 of its occupants and took many survivors to distribute them as slaves to planters in the region. A few groups of maroons and Seminoles were nonetheless able to escape to the swampy forests of Florida's hinterlands and into Tampa Bay. As Anglo-Saxon, slave-based colonization spread in the territory, those "black Seminoles" had an increasingly difficult time surviving, and when Spain lost Florida for good in 1821, many fled to Cuba, Mexico, and Haiti. Yet Florida remained a land of refuge for maroons, thanks to a terrain—forests crisscrossed with waterways and unfavorable to colonization—that was particularly attractive to runaways, until a second war launched by the U.S. Army against blacks and Seminoles in 1836–42 decimated both groups.[6]

Elsewhere in the rapidly expanding South and West, frontiers offering refuge to runaways were constantly being pushed back, making marronage more and more risky. The United States' appropriation of Indian territories to create Kentucky, Tennessee, Mississippi, and Alabama, as well as its purchase of Louisiana from Bonaparte in 1803, prompted waves of colonization by planters from the Old South, who brought their slaves with them. During the 1810s, 120,000 slaves from southern coastal states, largely young adults and men, were forcibly displaced or sold to cotton planters who settled in the new territories, in a trend that would continue until 1840. For those slaves, displacements meant that families were ripped apart and separated; but they also at times offered possibilities for escape, especially because the new regions were characterized by an absence of state control over vast lands, bayous, forests, and waterways conducive to smuggling and marronage. The fugitives, most often referred to as "bandits" in documents, established small mobile communities bordering Mississippi's riverside plantations and hinterlands, where they remained in contact with slaves and some white colonists. Some took refuge with Cherokee, Creek, or Choctaw nations west of the river, but because those communities practiced slavery, a few runaways found themselves captives once again.[7]

Slaves still tried to escape by sea. They hid aboard foreign ships, often thanks to the help of black sailors, so often that in 1822 South Carolina adopted a law forcing all boats docked in its ports to lock up their black crews until departure, a measure subsequently imitated by other slaveowning states. Furthermore, flouting the Fugitive Slave Act of 1793, slaves from the South fled to northern cities in growing numbers, hoping to blend into the free black population. But prior to the development of an abolitionist movement in the 1820s, African Americans in the North were too isolated to be able to effectively protect runaways from slave hunters and a court system that in most cases sent them back south. Other fugitives made it all the way to Canada, along whose border they established new communities, like the one in Amherstburg, on the Canadian side of Lake Erie, where they helped develop tobacco farming. Those escapes were perilous, as shown by the example of Josiah Henson, who fled Kentucky with his wife and four children in September 1830: they crossed the Ohio River thanks to a boatman friend, then found themselves in a free state but still at risk of being arrested and returned south, until six weeks later, when they reached the banks of Lake Erie; from there smugglers brought them to Canada. For those who fled south, Mexico, which had abolished slavery in 1829, at that time also guaranteed the freedom of maroons who sought refuge on its territory.[8]

The Continual Reinvention of Marronage in the Caribbean and South America

In territories that remained under British control, the abolition of the slave trade in 1808 meant that planters would do anything to keep the slaves in their possession, though that did not lead them to improve the latter's living conditions. They instead attempted to prevent slave escapes and destroy existing maroon communities. However, the many fugitive slave announcements published by newspapers, some for runaways who had been missing for several years, clearly demonstrate that captives everywhere continued to escape from cities and plantations alike. Although fugitives were predominantly men, women fled as well, at times taking children with them. Skilled slaves, such as artisans or servants, tried to pass for free and live off their occupation or trade in a city far from that of their masters; other, less well equipped runaways became day laborers or raiders. Historian Gad Heuman notably mentions the case of Appea in Barbados in 1815, described by a runaway notice as a confident and very dangerous man in his fifties, with several scars and a piece of his ear missing due to fighting, but who had survived for over a year by going from estate to estate and "drawing the figure of negroes on paper."[9] Some slaves fled by sea, such as seven enslaved sailors from Jamaica who, in 1817, managed to divert the boat on which they were serving to southern Haiti because its new constitution agreed to consider any black or Indian who came to settle there as a Haitian.[10] For that matter, in the most recently occupied colonies, like British Guiana, inland regions offered runaways even greater possibilities to establish partially self-sufficient maroon communities, with their own agricultural production, which continued to attract fugitive slaves.[11]

In French colonies in the Caribbean and Guiana, the reestablishment of slavery in 1803 and the ongoing importation of enslaved Africans—sixty-eight thousand between 1815 and 1831—also translated into a resurgence of marronage, both in uncolonized interior regions and near ports rife with smuggling and vagrancy.[12] In Guiana, for example, between twelve hundred and three thousand former slaves emancipated in 1794 escaped the brutal repression ordered by Victor Hugues and entrenched themselves farther inland. In the 1820s, the army launched antimarronage raids, which often ended with arrests and public executions. But the maroon Pompée, on the run since 1802 and captured with five others in 1822, was given a royal pardon that spared him a death sentence. However, his wife and two other fugitive couples taken with him were executed in Cayenne. Many other runaways were able to survive semi-independently in the forests by cultivating cotton, rice, and yams with tools taken during flight and selling their farming products to intermediaries who then resold them at markets.[13] The mountains of Basse-Terre continued to shelter fugitives in Guadeloupe as well. Some communities were formed when slavery was reestablished, but others had endured for decades, like the northeastern Kellers camp, established in 1776 by captives who had survived a shipwreck and which had subsequently become a network of small hamlets of huts still in existence in 1832.[14] Given the constant need for manpower, slaves would often abandon their plantations for another one with a more lenient master, who would discreetly hire them as paid *libres de savane* or *libres de fait* (de facto free); others fled toward ports where they easily found employment with ship captains, transporters, or smugglers unconcerned with their employees' origin. In addition, at the end of the 1820s, "amelioration of slavery" orders in the British colonies impacted the rest of the Americas. Slaves in the French Antilles and Cuba attempted to flee by sea toward colonies controlled by the British monarchy. Following the 1833 British act abolishing slavery, a considerable movement of slaves wanting to emancipate themselves took form in Martinique and Guadeloupe and, by the early 1840s, some five thousand of its participants had fled to Antigua, Barbados, and other small British islands, where they were warmly welcomed by planters in constant need of cheap labor.[15]

On the continent, former Spanish colonies that had maintained slavery after independence had to contend with marronage as well. Years of war had weakened their economies and social structures, and their populations were often impoverished. Many men and women, including slaves on the run or abandoned by exiled or missing masters, set out in search of a job and a roof. In Peru, in the area surrounding Lima, some fugitives formed thieving bands, while others chopped wood that they then sold to slaves for resale in the capital. If caught, maroons were ordinarily assigned to bakeries that served as jails.[16] In general, the governments of those new republics addressed poverty with antivagrancy laws that, though rarely enforced by ineffective security forces, unfairly targeted Indians and Afro-descendants. However, the fact that slaves were largely outnumbered by *libres de color* allowed some of them to surreptitiously blend into the free laboring population in cities or recently colonized areas.[17]

Whereas the decline of slavery in Hispanic South America facilitated marronage, in the Antilles that remained loyal to Spain, the continuing importation of enslaved Africans for expanding plantations encouraged the practice. Cuba in particular, which imported 350,000 slaves between 1791 and 1830 (on average 8,700 per year), saw marronage take lasting hold. In the island's western and central areas, fugitives tried to hide among the free people of color living in cities, build temporary camps, or form marauding bands. In the mountains north of Trinidad and especially those in Oriente province, cimarrones established truly autonomous communities. In 1796, Spanish authorities published a new law regarding the capture of runaways. Groups of *rancheadores* or professional slave hunters and their terrifying dogs would henceforth conduct monthly patrols in regions suspected of harboring palenques and maroon bands. Other units composed of amateur slave hunters and soldiers did the same, and slavemasters were required to advise authorities of any slave escape immediately. *Rancheadores* were encouraged to bring maroons back alive by a system of payment per slave that increased with the total number captured: ten pesos per slave for a group of six to eleven cimarrones, eighteen pesos per runaway for any group surpassing twenty-one—figures that reveal the extent of the phenomenon. Slave hunters could also seize maroons' belongings, but had to burn down their huts, barns, and crops.[18]

Even though Cuban *rancheadores* and their dogs had an unrivaled reputation in the Caribbean, as confirmed by the fact that the governor of Jamaica resorted to them in 1795, as did General Rochambeau in Saint Domingue in 1802, they were unable to completely eradicate the palenques in Cuba's Oriente. New measures adopted there in 1814 attempted to respond to their proliferation. Local militias, each composed of twenty-five slave hunters, were established in threatened areas and their leaders obligated to submit raid reports. *Rancheadores* were now paid not according to the number of maroons captured but by the distance between the location in which the cimarrones were captured and the militia's point of departure. The total number of fugitives captured increased, but the number of huts burned down was in general ten to twenty times greater, indicating that the majority of maroons were able to flee before slave hunters arrived.[19]

In Brazil too, the resurgence of the slave trade went hand in hand with increasing marronage. Brazil's importation of enslaved Africans totaled 1.6 million between 1791 and 1830 (an average of forty thousand slaves per year), notably young men from the Gulf of Guinea. Many had been taken prisoner during the Muslim expansion in that region before being sold in the transatlantic slave trade and therefore had combat experience. Amid that continuing influx, slave escapes multiplied, as did quilombos and mocambos in Brazil's vast hinterlands, to the point that authorities stopped intervening unless maroons were directly threatening plantations or inhabited areas. The phenomenon was particularly notable in Bahia province, whose sugar production had resumed after that industry's collapse in Saint Domingue. In both the city of Salvador and its surroundings, 40 percent of the population was composed of slaves, two-thirds of whom were born in Africa. In the Recôncavo, quilombos had spread as far as the underbrush separating sugarcane plantations, villages, and small towns. Even when military forces managed to destroy certain quilombos and capture or kill some of their occupants, they were unable to eradicate them because maroons would successfully escape and create other settlements, which welcomed new fugitive slaves in an endless vicious cycle.

Conspiracies, revolts, and marronage sometimes blended together, for example when runaway communities offered conspirators places to prepare and hideouts, as well as emergency refuges. In concrete terms, near Salvador de Bahia, networks linked groups of urban slaves to mocambos, bandit groups, and larger quilombos spread throughout the region's hinterlands. As a result, a conspiracy among Hausa slaves (originally from a vast region including Niger) discovered in Salvador in May 1814 was able to rely on teams of porter slaves from the city and on quilombos (see chapter 10). Shortly beforehand, 250 maroons had attacked plantations to recruit slaves, leaving dozens dead and causing major destruction before being subdued. Regardless of whether they were composed of one particular African ethnic group or included emancipated slaves or free people of color, these movements involving slaves and quilombolas demonstrated the capacity of a servile population constantly reinventing itself to detect and penetrate the uncontrolled cracks in slave societies.[20]

In addition, dozens of quilombos continued to exist and form in Pernambuco and Minas Gerais, where some fugitive slaves exploited gold and diamond mines whose products they sold via smuggling networks. In the province of Rio de Janeiro, slave escapes increased in parallel with the growing slave trade, creating an outlet for revolt: fugitives, primarily African-born men, hid in the capital's poor neighborhoods, nearby forests, Rio's bay, along the Atlantic coast, or deep in the hinterlands. Although their number cannot be estimated, it was high as, in 1826, Rio's main prison listed 925 inmates detained for flight, even as the majority of fugitives remained on the run and often unreported by their masters. Many of those maroons lived in near self-sufficiency and bartered with intermediaries; others worked secretly for employers happy to look the other way; others still stole from and attacked travelers and convoys. In short, few maroons were completely isolated from society. But genuine quilombos did form that each gathered dozens of runaways, including women and families, in Tijuca, Santa Teresa, and Corcovado near Rio.[21]

As colonization spread to Brazil's interior, the vast region of Amazonian forests along the Trombetas River, northeast of Manaus, also began to shelter a large number of fugitives in the early nineteenth century.[22] Around 1820, some of those runaways joined forces under King Atanásio, an officer's slave, who had deserted with forty or so slave-soldiers. Governed by Atanásio's iron discipline, the quilombolas grew manioc and tobacco and harvested cocoa that they sold in the Amazonian port of Óbidos. Far from living in autarky, they were in contact with merchants, other quilombos, and Amerindian communities as far away as Suriname. The Trombetas quilombo increasingly attracted fugitive slaves, prompting the government to launch several retaliatory raids, though the army would not destroy the community until 1827, when it numbered some two thousand inhabitants. Atanásio, imprisoned along with other runaways, managed to escape and rebuilt another maroon village with survivors and new fugitives.[23]

Indeed, slaves continued to establish quilombos or escape to cities throughout the nineteenth century.

Manumission in the United States: The North versus the Slave South

As shown in chapter 5, in the United States, the rhetoric of individual freedoms present in the 1776 Declaration of Independence led Vermont to abolish slavery in 1777, followed by Massachusetts in 1783. The other northern states adopted gradual emancipation laws, following the 1780 Pennsylvania free-womb model. The last states to do so were those that had the greatest number of slaves according to the 1800 census: New York, with 20,343 slaves (or twice as many slaves as free blacks and 3.5 percent of its total population), and New Jersey, with 12,422 slaves (or three times as many enslaved as free African Americans and 6.9 percent of the state's population).[24]

As in Pennsylvania, the emancipation law adopted by New York in 1799 only applied to children born to enslaved mothers after 4 July of that year, all while forcing them to serve their masters without remuneration until the age of twenty-five for girls and twenty-eight for boys. In 1817, New York passed a second, more lenient gradual abolition law, which stated that all slaves born before 4 July 1799 would be emancipated on 4 July 1827. The law also lowered to twenty-one the required age for the manumission of free-womb children born after 31 March 1817, but not for those born between 4 July 1799 and 31 March 1817, meaning that theoretically, slavery would remain legal in the state of New York until 3 July 1845, when the last boy born to an enslaved mother before 1 April 1817 would be twenty-eight.

Among the northern states, New Jersey maintained slavery the longest: it did not adopt a gradual abolition law until 1804, at the same time that it banned free blacks from entering the state. As a result, until the early 1820s, the majority of African Americans living there were slaves. In addition, New Jersey's free-womb law was highly damaging for enslaved mothers and advantageous for their owners as it allowed them to turn the children born after 4 July 1804 over to county trustees of the poor. Trustees could then place those children with their former masters, who received a monthly subsidy of three dollars until the age of twenty-one for girls and twenty-five for boys. Masters therefore benefited both from state subsidies and unpaid work performed by the free-womb child. Incidentally, slaveowners in New Jersey could also sell their slaves to the South until 1818.[25]

However, though gradual abolition laws allowed masters, in principle, to keep ownership rights over their slaves for several more decades as well as access to their unpaid labor, they also accelerated the emancipation process: by the sole fact of bringing an end, albeit a very distant one, to slavery, those laws offered an alternative to flight for slaves who wanted their freedom—the negotiation of a contract for eventual emancipation. Hundreds of slaves resorted to that strategy, or else sought to buy their freedom or that of their loved ones. In New York, by the early nineteenth century, many enslaved adults had committed to work a certain number of years after which their masters would liberate them, sometimes on the additional condition that they paid him or her a sum of money.[26] For those captives, that was the best way to end their enslavement themselves. Other cases show how liberation strategies were family-oriented. For example, in 1818, the free black carpenter Thomas Charnock emancipated his sixteen-year-old son George, whom he had purchased in 1809 as a slave in Charleston, South Carolina. Charnock had the act of emancipation include an long declaration, in which he stated his desire "to release from the galling chains of slavery (the bane as well as the disgrace of a free Country) and to liberate, manumit and set free the said George and to permit him the free and unrestrained exercise of those rights to which nature's God entitles him but which through the tyranny of wicked men and the influence of unjust laws he has been practically ignorant of." Charnock thus used his son's emancipation as an opportunity to condemn slavery and underline his determination to free him by using four synonymous verbs to express himself, before declaring his son entirely capable of living off his own labor following the education and professional training he had received in New York schools.[27]

Thanks to many individual acts of manumission, by 1820 the number of slaves had decreased by nearly half since 1800 in the two states, with 10,078 slaves in New York and 7,557 in New Jersey. Ten years later, in 1830, New York only had 76 slaves left. But slavery had not yet disappeared from the Northeast, which still counted 2,787 slaves, 2,254 of whom were in New Jersey and 403 in Pennsylvania, though the latter had been the first state to adopt a law of gradual abolition half a century earlier.[28]

While the liberation of slaves and conditional emancipation were spreading in the northern regions where slavery remained legal, since the 1800s slaveholding states in the South were drastically limiting, or once again completely outlawing, slave emancipations. Maryland and Virginia, which had favored manumission after independence, ended the practice when Gabriel Prosser's 1800 revolt in Richmond and news of the Saint Domingue revolution alerted whites of the growing presence of free people of color in their communities (see chapters 5 and 7). Furthermore, at the end of 1805, Virginia passed a law banning any slave emancipated after 30 April 1806 from staying in the state for more than twelve months, at the risk of being resold as a slave. The reaction of slaves yearning for freedom was quick in coming: whereas the maximum number of emancipated slaves in one year, between 1800 and 1805, had been seven, between January and April 1806, thirty-three slaves were able to record their manumission in Richmond alone, often thanks to payments by relatives who were already free.[29] In the Lower South, manumissions practically ceased, and the few slaves who were still emancipated were immediately expelled. Even in Louisiana, by then a state in the Union, lawmakers wanted to erase the possibilities of emancipation allowed by the Código Negro applied during Spanish rule (1763–1803). In 1807, they banned the coartación and manumission of slaves less than thirty years of age. But they continued to authorize payment of wages to slaves working on Sundays, as much due to their fear of unrest as to their awareness of the economic gains that such labor represented. The average number of manumissions per year in Louisiana dropped from 114 between 1793 and 1802 to seventy-six during the decade after 1807, as the number of enslaved peoples increased with the arrival of planters from the United States who brought their slave labor force with them. In 1830, though, Louisiana was one of three states in the South, along with Delaware and Tennessee, that continued to allow slaves to purchase their own freedom.[30]

Lawmakers in the majority of southern states, except for Louisiana, also banned slaves from working in exchange for payment during their free time, in order to limit their possibilities of emancipation. Nonetheless, captives managed to thwart those liberticidal laws by being fictitiously purchased by free people of color. In Petersburg, Virginia, out of the sixty-nine free black slaveholders listed in 1827, only seven exploited their captives for labor and were not solely masters on paper. In South Carolina as well, the fictional purchase of slaves by free blacks became a disguised substitute for emancipation: in Charleston, a rich black family thus "possessed" nine slaves who had paid for their own purchase; the Episcopalian church of St. Philipp owned over a hundred under the same conditions.[31] Although it is impossible to determine the number of slaves able to secretly emancipate themselves in the southern United States, it was not insignificant and showed that, at a time when ideologists wanted to justify slavery by blacks' supposed inferiority, the latter could indeed provide for themselves once free, but also that slaves succeeded in performing enough supplementary work to accumulate and pay the equivalent of their monetary value.[32]

However, those hidden manumissions did not change the demographic reality of the Lower South, where laws and practices alike were aimed at building a racist society dominated by white slaveowners and in which all African Americans would be enslaved. According to the 1830 census, approximately half of the populations of South Carolina, Georgia, Alabama, and Mississippi were composed of slaves, whereas free blacks represented less than 1 percent. Even in Florida, long under Spanish control and a refuge for slaves fleeing Georgia, only one Afro-descendant in twenty was free in 1830.[33] In reality, in the Lower South, being of African origin was almost always synonymous with being enslaved. As a result, free blacks were most often considered as and treated like slaves, and therefore sought at any cost to rebuild their lives in the North, in a less oppressive state.

Self-Emancipation and the Decline of Slavery in Hispanic South America

Among Spain's former colonies, only Chile, Central America, and Mexico abolished slavery following independence in the 1820s. While the rest also adopted republican systems, they maintained the institution of slavery, favoring the protection of private property—even that of other human beings—at the expense of the freedom guaranteed by their constitutions.

Guatemala abolished slavery in 1824 because the vast majority of its population was Amerindian and continued to be forced to pay tributes and perform unpaid labor. Slavery was therefore a marginal form of labor there, limited to domestic servants in cities and to farm laborers on some estates, notably those belonging to the Dominican Order, whose largest sugar hacienda had several hundred slaves. But as early as the eighteenth century, the majority of Guatemalan Afro-descendants were free and of mixed-race; among those who were enslaved, some did not hesitate to hide out among relatives in order to pass as free. In cities and even on some plantations, slaves received small earnings that they were occasionally able to save to purchase their freedom or that of their partner or child. Thus, when the general emancipation of slaves was announced in Guatemala in 1824, only fifty adults and eighteen children arrived in the capital to demand their freedom certificates. Even though other slaves were undoubtedly unaware of the decree or unable to travel, manumission only affected a small number of Guatemalans.[34] As for Chile and Mexico, their wars of independence were responsible for destroying an institution already on the wane, and the general emancipation of slaves in 1824 and 1829, respectively, most likely concerned no more than a few hundred individuals.

In the rest of Hispanic America, where slavery would endure until the mid-nineteenth century or later, the stakes were much greater. In Venezuela, Colombia, Peru, Bolivia, Paraguay, and the Río de la Plata, captives not only were servants and symbols of prestige in cities, but they also worked in exportation sectors (gold, cocoa, sugar, maté, livestock). As in the United States, many delegates of postindependence constituent assemblies were slaveowners and only envisaged abolition in the long term, even though they were not opposed to manumission as it had existed under the Spanish monarchy. For that matter, again as in the United States, they were careful not to mention slavery in their constitutions, as it violated fundamental human rights, addressing it instead in separate laws, grandly called manumission laws. Inspired by legislation first adopted in Pennsylvania in 1780, the latter generally decreed the freedom of children born to enslaved mothers starting on the date said laws were enacted; banned the importation of new slaves; granted freedom to those who reached the age of sixty; and stipulated the creation of manumission juntas to purchase the freedom of the "most deserving" slaves from their masters. In reality, however, although theoretically freeing the newborn, the laws also obliged free-womb children to serve their mothers' masters until adulthood, which had negative impacts on enslaved families, as they entrusted the training and care of those children entirely to their mothers' owners, who henceforth held all "parental" rights over them, including to separate them from their families and dictate their futures. Slaves age sixty and more could easily become destitute once emancipated. In addition, republican elites formed very few manumission juntas, and on the occasions when they did, those committees were low on funds and therefore emancipated only a small number of slaves. That did not prevent authorities from celebrating those emancipations during grandiose patriotic ceremonies that highlighted the generosity of a republic to which the few newly manumitted individuals would henceforth owe unfailing obedience.[35]

For the enslaved populations, therefore, independence and the establishment of new republics changed nothing. The manumission laws did not increase masters' duties toward their slaves, nor did they restrict their rights over them, even when abuse could cause severe injuries or death. The republican laws did not provide new options for manumission beyond those existing during the colonial era, whether it was the purchase of a slave's freedom by him- or herself or by family members, in one payment or by installments (coartación), or at the end of an additional period of captive labor. Other slaves continued to gain their freedom from their masters, through wills or contracts, often following a preestablished period of unpaid work that benefited the master or his descendants. As a result, both before and after independence, slaves living in the city were better able to purchase their freedom than those working in haciendas were, and women more so than men, because they tended to work in urban areas.

As analyzed by Christine Hünefeldt in her study on Lima and nearby sugar plantations between 1800 and Peruvian abolition in 1854, some enslaved couples developed family strategies to gain their freedom, starting with the sanctification of their union by the Catholic Church, as before independence. Next, experiences varied, but often the wife was liberated first, as women had more possibilities for autonomous work than their husbands did. For example, an enslaved woman could seek to move from the hacienda to the city by becoming a slave at her master's urban residency or being bought by another master. She would temporarily leave her husband and any children and devote great effort to gain her own freedom, and then that of a child old enough to be able to work in the city, followed by the freedom of her spouse and their other children. But it was rare for a couple or family to gradually emancipate all its members, given the many obstacles and unforeseen factors present. In particular, purchasing the freedom of children born before the free-womb law created significant dilemmas: though the price of manumission of a newborn or young child was comparatively low, the risks (due to high rates of infant mortality) and costs of feeding and caring for him or her were high; indeed, those costs could halt the gradual liberation of the entire family. As a result, some parents decided to leave their children in the care of a master during early childhood and pay more for their manumission once they could contribute to the family earnings. All those plans remained precarious, however, and dependent on economic fluctuations, the health of the family members and their master, and the latter's goodwill. As many slaves who went to court to contest their continuing enslavement learned, oral promises of emancipation counted for little: they needed a written document and witnesses of high social status attesting to their market value, existing payments in the case of coartación, or emancipation on a master or mistress's death.[36] For that matter, it was not rare for slaves to borrow all or some of their value from a third party. While that method certainly accelerated their emancipation, it also rendered it more fragile. When a manumitted slave was unable to reimburse his or her lender, he or she could be reenslaved and, in the event of premature death, the consequences for his or her spouse or family could be serious.[37]

Although independence did not bring concrete change in the lives of slaves born before the adoption of free-womb laws, it transformed their perspectives: they had the knowledge—shared by their owners—that slavery would be abolished one day. That certitude encouraged more and more enslaved men and women to take charge of their futures and obtain emancipation themselves. At the same time, some masters attempted to retain the capital represented by their slaves, which on occasion meant willingly emancipating them in exchange for payment. In parallel, masters had increasing alternatives to slave labor: peonage, sharecropping, wage systems, Indians' labor tribute. The number of slaves in the South American republics inevitably diminished, and not only because captives died and were not replaced by new imports (except by smuggling, notably in Argentina, Uruguay, and Peru). It also decreased because a growing number of slaves were buying their freedom or that of family members, contributing to the institution's rapid decline.[38] Nevertheless, until the 1850s legislators resisted abolishing slavery.

From Restriction to Endorsement:
Manumission in the British, Dutch, and French Colonies

When the British Parliament banned the importation of slaves in its colonies as of 1808, it did not attempt to improve the conditions of slaves working there, trusting that planters would do so themselves to preserve their labor force.

Protector of Slaves Office, Trinidad, by Richard Bridgens, 1838.
(Courtesy of the Yale Center for British Art)

Manumissions continued to be subjected to drastic restrictions imposed in the previous century and were therefore extremely rare (see chapter 3). Only in 1816 did the colonial assemblies of Jamaica and Barbados reduce manumission taxes for fear of London interventionism. Yet the British government, under pressure from the abolitionist lobby, waited until May 1823 to recommend that emancipations no longer be conditional on masters paying a deposit or annuities guaranteeing the future needs of the emancipated slave so that he or she did not become destitute and dependent on the community.[39]

The island of Trinidad, which Great Britain seized from Spain in 1797, was the only colony directly administered by the Crown in which, since July 1824, London implemented an "amelioration of slavery" policy that included a manumission component inspired by Spanish regulations in effect on the island until the end of the eighteenth century. That legacy was reflected in the distribution of its 35,270 inhabitants in 1810: though its slaves, who counted 26,000, represented 75 percent of that total population, that percentage was the lowest among all the British colonies in the West Indies, whereas the proportion of its 6,300 free people of color, 18 percent, was the highest, leaving whites averaging 7 percent of the population. With the new law enacted by the Crown, slaves could buy their freedom or that of a family member in exchange for payment of their market value; in cases of litigation over the price between a slave and his or her master, a "protector of slaves" would intervene to reconcile the parties.

At first, between July 1824 and December 1827, emancipations increased in

Trinidad, which recorded 588 manumissions in total, 409 of which were purchased by slaves in a wave of enthusiasm, versus a total of 388 manumissions, 167 of which were paid for by slaves, during the previous three and a half years. But that number subsequently dropped again, notably because the sums demanded from slaves to purchase their freedom were larger than those applied during the sale of slaves. The case of the eighteen-year-old domestic servant Pamela Munro, in 1826, clearly shows the abuses committed by slaveholders and the limits on the extent to which slave protectors could intervene. When the girl's mother wanted to buy her daughter's freedom, Pamela's master estimated her value at 261 pounds—three times the average price of manumission—due to her age and exceptional attributes. Her mother then demanded arbitration by a protector whose only suggestion was to replace the girl with another slave with similar qualities, indirectly condemning her to her fate. For that matter, even though measures to ameliorate slavery were intended to facilitate emancipations paid for by slaves, they also included a ban on Sunday labor and markets to encourage Protestant evangelization, which considerably limited the ways in which slaves could earn the money needed to emancipate themselves. Nonetheless, in 1830, the number of free people of color in Trinidad had more than doubled, with 16,000 individuals representing 38 percent of the island's population, while the number of slaves had dropped to 22,750 (54 percent). However, natural growth was a larger factor behind the rapid increase of the free population of color than emancipations.[40]

Based on its experience in Trinidad, the British government applied its measures to ameliorate slavery to all the colonies under its direct rule in the form of the Consolidated Slave Act of 1826. It also required from colonial assemblies in the more autonomous colonies of Jamaica, Barbados, and Antigua to reform their slavery laws to incorporate those improvements, but legislators there were able to reduce London's reach. Generally speaking, colonial assemblies respected the order to adapt their Slave Acts to include manumission paid for by slaves and the appointment of a slave protector to arbitrate disagreements with masters. But planters renamed that first stipulation "compulsory manumission" to clearly show that they considered it to be a violation of their rights over their human property. They also set the value of slaves wanting to liberate themselves at very high prices and delayed the nomination of protectors or else appointed men favorable to their interests.[41]

As had been the case in the northern United States, those manipulations of the law compelled some slaves to develop long-term liberation strategies, notably by first getting themselves purchased by a free individual of color whom they gradually reimbursed by working off their debt until they attained the sum needed for their fictional owner to record their emancipation. Manumission consequently remained out of reach for the large majority of slaves in British colonies. Nonetheless, at the end of the 1820s, when abolition began to appear inevitable, the number of emancipations increased, although sizable differences between colonies remained. According to calculations by historian Barry Higman, in 1834, the lowest annual rate of manumissions—1.4 per thousand—was recorded in Britain's most populous colony, Jamaica, which had over 310,000 slaves, versus 4.9 per thousand in Barbados, second in terms of slave populations. The Bahamas, which counted 10,000 slaves and had never developed a sustainable sugarcane industry, had the highest rate of manumission in all the British colonies—11.4 per thousand or 1.1 percent, the same as in Brazil.[42]

In the Dutch colonies, manumission was regulated by slave codes similar to those in effect in British colonies prior to 1816, but in the absence of a popular abolitionist movement in the Netherlands, slaves' voices long remained unheard. In Curaçao, slavery declined rapidly after the 1795 slave uprising and the subsequent end to the importation of African captives (see chapter 7). The large sugar plantation model had failed to spread across the island's entirety and was gradually supplanted by small farming properties that employed few slaves. In fact, a large portion of Curaçao's slaves worked in cities as servants, artisans, or day laborers in connection with international trade. By the 1800s, some were living autonomously, earning their own money, and paying a preestablished weekly sum to their masters. Like their counterparts in the Iberian world, they sometimes managed to accumulate the sums necessary to buy their freedom. Indeed, enough did so that authorities decreed that they could only benefit from their civil rights (notably equality before the law) two years after being emancipated. In effect, by 1817, free people of color were much more numerous than whites, and by 1833 they also largely outnumbered slaves.[43]

In Suriname, in contrast to Curaçao, the slave plantation model predominated; slave conditions were particularly harsh and the possibilities of emancipation highly limited. After 1779, the slave trade had remained constant, bringing in several hundred, and even as many as five thousand, Africans every year until 1802, before declining and then ending six years later. Then, in the early 1820s, four thousand captives were once again brought to the Dutch colony, despite the Netherlands' 1814 ban on the trade.[44] Restrictions on manumission multiplied due to elevated death rates among slaves and their uncontrollable propensity for marronage. In 1788, the Surinamese Court of Justice imposed heavy taxes on emancipation certificates: fifty florins for women and children under fourteen years of age, and one hundred florins for men over fourteen who had the option of serving for three years in the militia if they could not pay the new levy. Because the new tax was announced several months before being implemented, some slaves hurried to obtain their emancipation as soon as possible. In 1804, in response to the slave trade's decline, the amount of the aforementioned tax was multiplied by five for men and by ten for women who would henceforth have to pay five hundred florins to obtain the long-coveted attestation of freedom, which led to a new surge of manumissions before the increase took effect. Of course, emancipations in Suriname remained very rare in terms of the proportion of slaves impacted, but far from negligible for a slaveholding colony doing everything to prevent captives from obtaining their freedom. Though manumissions were most often granted by a slaveowner during his lifetime, the purchase of freedom by a slave or his or her family members was not unprecedented, albeit always contingent on a master's agreement. In most cases, slaves obtained their freedom as a result of long negotiations with their masters, based on their day-to-day interactions and a slave's good service, which favored women who were essential servants in masters' households. And since women were the ones who passed their status on to their children, the total number of free Afro-descendants in Suriname went from 3,075 in 1791 to 5,041 (or double the white population) in 1830.[45]

In the colonies in the Caribbean and Guiana that remained under French rule, the reestablishment of slavery and the slave trade in 1803 meant the suppression of all related legislation that had been adopted after 1789 and the return of the Code Noir of 1685. All slaves emancipated by the 1794 decree lost their freedom and found themselves enslaved once again in 1803. All the decrees granting equality and citizenship to free *gens de couleur* and especially to *nouveaux libres* in 1794 were also repealed. In short, since 1803 every black and mulatto individual was assumed to be a slave unless he or she could prove a pre-1789 emancipation. Slaves who possessed a manumission certificate from their master dated after 1789 had to pay a tax of 1,200 francs in order for their freedom to be confirmed, without which they would be reenslaved. All duly emancipated Afro-descendants faced discrimination and racial segregation and were henceforth banned from entering France (until 1818); those emancipated outside the French empire were given three months to leave or risk reenslavement.[46]

French legislation reintroduced several antimanumission measures previously implemented following adoption of the Code Noir: a ban on the emancipation of concubines and an obligation for priests to verify the free status of the mother of a nonwhite child before baptizing him or her as free, for example. Since 1805, marriage, adoption, recognition of illegitimate children, and shared inheritances were only allowed between whites, in order to prevent slaves from obtaining their freedom through those channels: marriage between a free man or woman of color and his or her slave no longer allowed one to liberate the other. Manumission would only be authorized if a slavemaster waived his rights and by payment by a slave or a third party of his or her market value; in all cases, the slave also had to pay an increased emancipation tax, which ranged between three hundred and five hundred francs. Nonetheless, it seems clear that some slaves emancipated by the 1794 decree had managed to save enough to officially obtain their freedom once and for all, given that, in Guiana, during the first year after slavery was reestablished, 274 men and women (out of a total of 357 manumissions) bought their freedom or that of a relative.[47]

When the British occupied Martinique and Guadeloupe between 1810 and 1814, they loosened restrictions on manumission, undoubtedly to weaken planters' positions, as they waited another fifteen years to do the same in their own colonies. Great Britain also reintroduced willed emancipations (banned under Bonaparte), regulated the status of freed slaves who had foreign emancipation certificates, and facilitated manumissions paid for by slaves. In total, during the occupation, some one thousand slaves were able to obtain their emancipation, to the great displeasure of French slaveowners. After the British left, planters tried to revive the sugar economy and, with Paris's agreement, imported thousands of African captives every year until 1830. At the same time, French governors attempted to once again limit manumissions by making it illegal to free slaves under thirty years of age and by increasing emancipation taxes.[48]

Yet despite all those restrictive laws, free populations of color in French colonies only continued to grow. In reality, by 1803, thousands of men and women emancipated in 1794 were refusing to become slaves again and adapting to being *libres de savane*, whereas planters, conscious of the difficulty of reenslaving those men and women, tried to replace them with bossales. In addition to flight and marronage, slaves resorted to diverse stratagems to free themselves without having to pay the high manumission tax, which alone represented earnings from several years of work. The most frequent case entailed slaves asking their owner to initiate the emancipation process: the master would then relinquish ownership rights over his slave with a notarized act, but neither party subsequently performed the long and costly administrative steps that led to an official act of manumission. The slave would settle for a certificate of the waiver granted by his master (who kept the slave listed in his records but mentioned the relinquishment of ownership rights), while behaving as if he or she was free. Those *libres de fait* also tried to make their free status official when recording the baptism of a child or the death of a parent. That tactic was so widespread that in 1818 the governor of Guadeloupe required that an emancipation certificate be presented during the registration of every birth or death of a free person of color and ordered the destruction of the official manumission title belonging to an emancipated individual who died without leaving any descendants, in order to prevent later falsifications.

Despite those precautions, slaves continued to illegally obtain their de facto freedom through falsified purchases, wills, and other manipulations of notarized documents, as shown by the flurry of decrees echoing legal restrictions on emancipation in the French Antilles. More and more Afro-descendants were classified as "so-called free," *libres de fait*, or *libres de savane*—a category that grouped legally enslaved men or women working independently, as well as children and unproductive slaves abandoned by their masters. Slaves' thirst for freedom was so great that in the early 1830s, according to historian Josette Fallope, Guadeloupe had a total of fifteen thousand *libres de savane*, equaling in number its legally recognized free population of color.[49] In Martinique as well, the free or so-called free Afro-descendant population increased and surpassed the white one. Faced with that demographic reality and in the wake of the July Revolution, King Louis-Philippe published a series of orders in 1831 that reestablished free people of color's civil rights, which had been stripped by Bonaparte, and made manumissions easier by removing burdensome taxes. As a result, the number of official emancipations soared, in part thanks to the regularization of so-called *libres*. That increase was the most dramatic in Guadeloupe, where the number of manumissions rose from 479 in 1831 to 3,190 in 1833. It was multiplied by four in French Guiana and by two in Martinique. That legislation, which coincided with the halt of the slave trade and the stagnation of the white population, also marked a rapid increase in the number and relative influence of the *gens de couleur libres* across the French Antilles. In Martinique, for example, both the number of free Afro-descendants and their proportion of the island's population doubled between 1831 and 1835, when they accounted for one-fourth of inhabitants. Moreover, beginning in 1833, slaves in French colonies accelerated their demands for abolition in light of the process launched in the British Caribbean.[50]

The Purchase of Freedom in the Slave Societies of Cuba and Brazil

In Cuba and Puerto Rico, as well as Brazil, the institution of slavery was only occasionally questioned by elites who further developed slavery through the unrelenting importation of African captives. In Cuba, however, despite the intensification of the slave trade, the purchase of freedom continued to offer a way to escape slavery. Although no detailed study exists on manumission in the largest island in the Caribbean before 1865, it appears that, on average, between 1790 and 1880, for every four slaves sold in the markets of Havana, Santiago, and Cienfuegos, one slave obtained freedom, almost always through purchase from his or her master. Though manumission remained more accessible in cities than on plantations, some enslaved workers did not hesitate to steal pigs, chickens, or cereals to sell and thus earn the money needed to buy their freedom, while others participated in smuggling networks that brought British fabrics to Cuban markets, for example. Between 1790 and 1850, importations of African captives to Cuba were so large that more bozales than creoles emancipated themselves. Slaves often used the coartación system to change their status, as it allowed them to pay their market value (fixed at the first payment) little by little, in stages, going from slave to coartado and finally *liberto* or emancipated. As a British traveler evocatively noted in 1820, the slave engaged in coartación bought his freedom "by knocking off his chain link by link."[51]

In Brazil as well, where slavery was the dominant labor system until 1860, the slave trade grew so dramatically following the Saint Domingue uprising that it changed the patterns of manumission. The country's northeast region absorbed one-third of the 976,000 *boçais* who arrived between 1810 and 1830, when its sugar production resumed. Even so, the southeast appropriated two-thirds of those captives to respond to the demand for slaves in Rio de Janeiro, where sugar plantations were spreading, and São Paolo, where coffee farming and cattle raising were beginning to develop. Furthermore, the continuing influx of enslaved Africans led to a growing distinction between African-born and creole slaves, and between blacks and mulattos, though the price of freshly disembarked *boçais* remained low, allowing their purchase by even those of modest means—and even by other enslaved men and women.[52]

As was the case in Hispanic America, manumission—paid for by a slave or granted by a master—had been institutionalized in Brazil since the sixteenth century, but it still depended on an owner's agreement. After 1800, emancipations increased in both absolute and relative figures, annually allowing, on average, a percentage of the enslaved population ranging from 1 to 1.5 percent to earn its freedom—or ten times greater than in Jamaica during the same period. That growing rate of manumission was all the more remarkable given that between 1800 and 1830, Brazil's population doubled, increasing from approximately 2 million inhabitants to 4 million, all while continuing to maintain nearly four out of ten inhabitants in slavery, thanks to the importation of *boçais*.[53] Based on those figures, some historians see emancipation as an essential outlet within Brazil's slaveowning society, without which uprisings would have multiplied. Hope of manumission undoubtedly prevented slaves from rebelling, but there were other, equally important avenues of escaping enslavement, like flight and marronage throughout a vast and partially colonized territory, in which it was practically impossible to organize a widespread uprising. In addition, the constant arrival of new slaves (primarily young men and adolescents from West Central Africa) was making Brazilian society more fluid. Finally, following independence, Brazil's imperial constitution of 1824 granted equality to free people of color, born free or emancipated, which may have provided additional motivation to enslaved men seeking to legally emancipate themselves.[54]

The doubling of Brazil's enslaved population between 1791 and 1830 due to mass importations affected the demographic profile of emancipated men and women in cities along the Atlantic coast.[55] Of course, since *cartas de alforria* were not filed with provincial governments but dispersed among municipal establishments, in-depth studies, like historian Mieko Nishida's examination of Salvador de Bahia, have focused on specific locations. That city's population also nearly doubled after 1775 and reached 65,500 inhabitants in 1835. Thanks to the continuous importation of slaves, captives (two-thirds of whom were African) represented 42 percent of the population in both 1775 and sixty years later; however, in that interval, the percentage of free people of color increased from 22 percent to 30 percent while that of whites decreased. Free people of color were therefore the only segment of the population to increase in number and proportion, due to their natural growth, the arrival of migrants (and undoubtedly many fugitive slaves) from rural regions, and emancipations that were growing faster than the city's enslaved population.[56]

Moreover, though the Brazilian-born slaves who emancipated themselves in the first third of the nineteenth century continued to outnumber Africans, the gap between the two groups decreased over time, as did that between men and women: in 1808–9, the ratio was thirty-nine men for every sixty-one emancipated women; in the early 1830s, the ratio had narrowed to forty-eight versus fifty-two. At the same time, the majority of manumitted creoles began to be composed of blacks, rather than mulattos or pardos. The most prominent difference between creole and Africans was the mode of emancipation. During the first few decades of the nineteenth century, half of liberated Africans bought their freedom, versus only 20 percent of creoles, who were most often emancipated by their masters without payment, though sometimes on the condition that they continue to work for a certain period of time without compensation. Finally, 5 percent of Salvador's slaves born in Brazil had their emancipations purchased by their mothers, fathers, or other relatives, which proved nearly impossible for Africans. To remedy that, the latter adapted African tontines to their new needs and created collective savings associations in which members paid dues cosigned by notches on a stick with their names. After reaching a certain sum, they could borrow the remainder to purchase emancipation. Men and women also obtained manumission through substitution: they saved the money necessary to personally buy, in all likelihood with their masters' permission, one slave from among the thousands of relatively cheap *boçais* unloaded every year. They could then train that slave to take their place with their master, which would allow them to obtain their *carta de alforria*.[57]

Those differences between Brazilian and African slaves clearly reflected each group's ability to adapt to changing contexts: creoles who had grown up in Brazil and often worked as servants in their master or mistress's households had more occasions to build the trusting relationships indispensable for emancipation by one or the other than Africans. But among the *boçais*, women stood out due to their particular aptitude to acquire the necessary capital to buy their freedom, notably as peddlers and market vendors, such as those portrayed below; their success was made all the more remarkable by the fact that more African women

Black women selling angu (corn porridge), Brazil, ca. 1820. (Jean-Baptiste Debret, *Voyage Pittoresque et Historique au Brésil* [Paris: Firmin-Didot, 1834–39]; courtesy of the Miriam and Ira D. Wallach Division of Art, Prints and Photographs, New York Public Library Digital Collections; accessed March 24, 2018)

were able to liberate themselves than their male counterparts, who represented the majority of imported *boçais*. Similar trends emerged in Rio de Janeiro and the small port of Santos, near São Paolo, during the same period.[58]

≋ Despite the changes caused by wars and the independence of most territories on the American continent, in every state or region in which slavery had not been abolished, slaves, whether they were Africans or creoles, plantation or mine workers, artisans or servants, continued to use flight as a way to gain their freedom. The opportunities to do so varied considerably: the existence of a nearby uncolonized frontier and, increasingly, of a free population of color that had come to outnumber slaves undoubtedly boosted the chances of success. That was notably the case in Brazil and Spain's former colonies. At the same time, in several regions, including French colonies, authorities eventually adapted to the presence of *libres de savane* and maroons who contributed to the informal economy without directly challenging the system of slavery. In the United States, more and more slaves escaped from Virginia and Maryland toward northern cities where they hoped to blend into small communities of free African Americans; farther south, however, the strengthening and expansion of racial slavery to the detriment of the establishment of free black populations rendered marronage nearly impossible.

Manumission and the purchase of freedom also remained highly dependent on circumstances. Those practices grew in areas in which they were facilitated by the law. In particular, the adoption of gradual abolition laws by the northern United States and Hispanic republics allowed an increasingly large number of slaves to emancipate themselves as the institution of slavery declined. In British colonies, pressure from the abolitionist movement at home and, since 1830, the sense of the nearing end of slavery, encouraged slaves to buy their freedom. Emancipation purchased by a slave or granted by one's master also became more accessible in French colonies as the possibility of reenslaving *libres de savane* dwindled. In general, in every society that stopped the importation of new captives and authorized manumission, the free population of color increased rapidly and often became the majority of the free or even total population. Even in Brazil and Cuba, which remained large importers of African captives, emancipation expanded to the point that new trends emerged, notably Africans' capacity to buy their freedom in proportions similar to those of enslaved creoles. Only the southern United States kept the door to manumission resolutely closed in the goal of creating a racist, slaveowning society with free whites on one side and blacks—the overwhelming majority of whom would forever remain enslaved— on the other.

Very few slave uprisings disrupted slaveholding regions in the Americas after 1815 because enslaved peoples understood the risks. It was therefore not by chance that the three largest uprisings over the subsequent fifteen years occurred in Great Britain's colonies: they could both rely on the abolitionist movement that had led to the end of the slave trade and give it renewed momentum by demanding the total and immediate emancipation of every slave in British America.

≋ 10 ≋
Revolts and Abolitionism

At the same time that the Congress of Vienna was ending conflicts between empires in Europe and the Americas, a new kind of uprising erupted in the British colonies, between 1816 and 1831. Claiming to act in the name of reforms from the British Parliament and liberating Christianity, enslaved men and women revolted in numbers never before seen in that region to demand their emancipation. Their rebellions coincided with the growing conflict pitting British slaveholders against the royal government, which allowed captives to glimpse an alternative authority to planters, on which they could base their claims and demands for freedom. In that particular context, hundreds, and possibly thousands, of slaves proved ready to risk their lives to rebel in the name of freedom in Barbados in 1816, Demerara (British Guiana) in 1823, and Jamaica in 1831. Quelled with massacres and dozens of executions, those insurrections revealed the inhumanity of the institution of slavery and its methods of repression to an enlarged British public audience. They radicalized abolitionism in Great Britain, and slaves and abolitionists, each helping the other, brought an end to British slavery in 1838.

In contrast, during the same period, firmly proslavery regions in the French and Dutch Caribbean, Brazil, Cuba, and the southern United States experienced only sporadic revolts, attempts at violent escape, and a few proven or suspected conspiracies, which were almost always punished with the same degree of cruelty. In effect, slaves in those territories were well aware of the context in which they lived and the existing imbalance of power. Like their counterparts in British colonies, they were facing militias and security forces ready to destroy them. But most significantly, they knew that they could not liberate themselves from slavery unless a king, a state, or a substantial portion of lawmakers with power over their territory challenged that institution.

Isolated Revolts in the French Caribbean and Brazil

In the French colonies in which slavery had been reestablished, the most noteworthy revolt occurred in the coffee plantation region of Carbet, in Martinique.

In the middle of an October night in 1822, some thirty enslaved men attacked their masters, stole their weapons and victuals, and then recruited participants from neighboring dwellings. By daybreak, they had killed two whites and injured seven others, including a woman, before encountering a group of policemen. Believing they were dealing with military troops sent to subdue them, they fled into nearby forests. Shortly afterward, 1,500 men, drawn from security forces, militias composed of whites and free men of color, and the army, surrounded the area in which the fugitives had hidden. They gradually captured insurgents who, interrogated on the spot, confessed that their intention had been to seize the city of Saint-Pierre and "kill all whites," according to the habitual scenario. They provided the names of their leaders and the rebels who had killed the two masters and injured the others (a crime equivalent to murder). The revolt's presumed instigator, the mulatto slave Jean-Louis, was captured four weeks later, together with another rebel who killed himself by jumping off a cliff. The search for suspects continued in nearby plantations and in Saint-Pierre, leading to the arrests of hundreds of men and women.[1]

In the end, sixty-seven slaves were tried by the Martinican justice system. Despite the use of torture, the special court formed to judge them was unable to obtain information about potential accomplices in the rest of the island, be it among the *libres de couleur* or men sent by Haiti, as they suspected. The judges delivered twenty-one death sentences, seven by axe decapitation after cutting the defendant's right hand off and fourteen by hanging; ten sentences of lashing (including to two women), iron branding, and the galleys for life; five sentences of lashings alone; and sixteen minor penalties. Fifteen defendants were acquitted. Every slave in Saint-Pierre and Carbet had to attend the executions during a ceremony monitored by militias, troops, and a warship. Organized with the goal of permanently terrifying the audience, the punishments lasted three hours, beginning with lashings and ending with decapitations. The bodies of those sentenced to death remained on display for several hours before being thrown into a mass grave. Incidentally, the decapitations of the Carbet rebels were far from isolated incidents in Martinique. Shortly beforehand a special court had been established to eradicate a "sect of poisoners" among slaves and sentenced dozens of defendants to beheading on the chopping block between 1822 and 1827. Furthermore, one year after the executions in Carbet, the island's white aristocracy—the *béké*—attacked the *libres de couleur* in what became the affair of Cyrille Bissette, who was sentenced to the galleys for life for publishing a brochure advocating racial equality and the gradual abolition of slavery. White planters in Martinique, an island under British occupation when abolition was first decreed in 1794, were fiercely attached to their privileges and quick to mobilize against any demands by enslaved and free people of color, at a time when the latter were becoming more numerous than whites in the free population.

Faced with *béké* entrenchment, more and more free people of color, following Bisette's example, demanded the abolition of slavery.[2]

The July 1830 revolution in France gave new hope to slaves and *gens de couleur libres* that profound reforms would finally be promoted. It simultaneously alarmed *békés*, who were also dealing with the decline of the sugarcane economy amid Europe's emerging beet sugar production. It was against that tense backdrop that, on the night of 5–6 February 1831, the gallows used to execute slaves in Saint-Pierre was destroyed. A rumor circulated that a slave had been walking around that evening with a dead cat and a sign reading "Long Live the Cat," while another one claimed that someone had placed a banner with the words "Liberty or Death" on a fence. On the night of 9 February, again in Saint-Pierre, fires destroyed sugarcane fields and four neighboring homes. Authorities immediately announced a state of siege; the army and white militias organized a general raid during which they arrested 260 people. Forty-nine of them, including two whites, were accused of conspiracy and brought before a criminal court. The crackdown was merciless: twenty-two slaves were sentenced to death for rebellion and conspiracy and executed on 19 May 1831. One of the two white defendants, a plantation administrator, was sentenced to prison for complicity because he had tried to defend his enslaved workers when security forces arrived; the other white defendant was a liberal colonel who reportedly was in contact with the incriminated slaves. According to historian Lucien-René Abenon, the events were so complex and the repression so brutal that the conspiracy could well have been created by colonists anxious to maintain their absolute control over their enslaved labor force.[3]

In Guadeloupe, the "island's revolutionary element [had been] decapitated," as historian Josette Fallope notes, by the massacre or deportation of ten thousand slaves ordered by Richepance in 1802 (see chapter 7). Planters imported twenty-five thousand bossales between 1815 and 1830 to replace dead and fugitive slaves. In that climate, authorities believed they had discovered plots with links to revolts then under way in Martinique, but only one rebellion was recorded, in 1827, when Africans recently brought to a plantation in Port-Louis attempted to escape before being caught.[4] In French Guiana, as previously seen, resistance to slavery manifested primarily through marronage.

In the independent Brazilian empire, revolts and conspiracies, proven or otherwise, were concentrated in Bahia province between 1807 and 1835. In 1800, Bahia had four hundred thousand inhabitants, and its capital, Salvador, fifty thousand, twenty thousand of whom were slaves, in their majority African-born young adults. Until the mid-nineteenth century, slave ships brought thousands of captives to the province each year, including many Muslims who had been sold following the wars ravaging Africa from northeast Nigeria to Sudan: they were often literate and referred to collectively as Hausas, a term that masked their internal differences. In 1807, authorities in Salvador, worried about the Hausas' activities, discovered and quashed a first conspiracy supposedly being planned in the port city with two executions and ten sentences of 150 whiplashes. However, the Bahia government was less troubled by the presumed scheming among Salvador's slaves than by their connections to their counterparts on plantations in the Recôncavo and *quilombo* fugitives, an alliance that could lead to widespread revolt. And in fact, in 1809, some three hundred Hausa and Yoruba maroons from a Recôncavo *quilombo* attacked the town of Nazaré das Farinhas, joined by hundreds of slaves from Bahia. Rapidly mobilized troops from Salvador and militias intercepted the slaves en route and inflicted a heavy defeat to the Recôncavo rebels: several of the slaves died, and eighty-three men and twelve women were imprisoned; although their ultimate fortunes remain unknown, small groups of rebels were able to escape. Authorities and planters were therefore on high alert.[5]

For that matter, other rebellions and conspiracies in Bahia province revealed that slaves collaborated among themselves—whether they were in cities or plantations, fugitives in quilombos, or creoles or from different African ethnic groups—and at times allied with free people of color: revolt and marronage were often intertwined. That was the case for an uprising in the fishing port of Itapoá just outside Salvador in February 1814, which involved 250 enslaved men led by a Hausa preacher. Crying "Liberty!" and "Death to whites and mulattos!" they set fire to several homes and killed some whites, mulattos, and slaves who refused to follow them. They then headed for Recôncavo's fazendas to recruit other slaves, kill, and set fires before being stopped by cavalry that massacred fifty or so rebels, arrested several dozen others, while the remaining insurgents committed suicide or managed to escape. Expedited trials led to the execution of at least four rebel leaders, countless whippings, and twenty deportations to Angola. In March and April, other violent incidents involving Hausas broke out in various locations in the Recôncavo and All Saints Bay. Then, in May 1814, a Mina woman reported preparations for a large conspiracy including enslaved and emancipated Hausas in Salvador and its surroundings. The governor convinced several slaves to infiltrate the conspirators, and those spies uncovered plans for a revolt on St. John's Day, after the sugarcane harvest, coordinated by gangs of porters and intended to spread across the entire sugar-producing region as far as the quilombos. Barrels containing arrowheads and wood to make bows and arrows were discovered and dozens of plotters arrested, whose fates remain unknown.[6] Two years later, new revolts erupted in the Recôncavo, causing occasional fires and the deaths of whites or slaves who had stayed loyal to their masters. In the majority of cases, planters appealed to local militias to subdue the insurgents, who were most often executed outside the law, rather than being sent to stand trial in Salvador. In 1821, slaves from a sugar plantation in the district of

Ilhéus, south of Salvador, refused to work, stole tools, and disappeared into the surrounding areas to form a *quilombo* that would not be destroyed until 1828.[7]

Brazil's short war of independence, in 1822–23, created anxieties among whites in the Bahia region that slaves would use the conflict between creoles and the Portuguese as an opportunity to liberate themselves. In response, captives spread the rumor that the king of Portugal had abolished slavery but that Brazilian slaveowners were refusing to comply. And slaves in the sugar-producing region of Cachoeira sent a petition in 1823 demanding that Bahia's representatives in the Cortes grant them their freedom. Because that rumor was being debated by several groups of slaves in the area, local authorities feared that they would revolt "like on the island of Saint Domingue." They believed they had uncovered conspiracy plans, and quashed local mutinies before they spread. The most serious threat came from an attack against patriot troops stationed north of Salvador, led by two hundred slaves who were probably being advised by the Portuguese then occupying the city, in December 1822; it was brutally suppressed by the French general Pierre Labatut, commander of the Brazilian pacification army, who had fifty-two rebels executed and many others whipped in the greatest string of executions in the history of slavery in Bahia.[8]

After independence, the Recôncavo was once again disrupted by various small revolts, undoubtedly prompted by disorganization in the region and the departure of some troops to Uruguay. Faced with growing instability, and the destruction and occasional deaths caused by that unrest, planters obtained reinforcements of the military presence in the region, but neither revolts nor acts of violence committed by quilombo maroons ceased. In 1830, the city of Salvador was rattled by a new kind of attack. Around twenty slaves seized knives and sabers from downtown stores, then, soliciting dozens of other slaves along the way, went to the slave market where they liberated recently arrived Africans, while killing those who resisted. They next attacked a police station and killed a soldier before the police and crowd joined forces and lynched some fifty of the rebels. That incident showed slaves in Salvador the great risk involved in revolting in the middle of a city without preestablished connections that would allow them to escape toward the Recôncavo plantations and quilombos.[9]

Finally, the cycle of Muslim revolts in Bahia province came to an end in 1835 with the suppression of the Malê (Muslim) rebellion, studied by historian João Reis. That movement likely included hundreds of conspirators, organized into a vast network of enslaved and freed men of color, many of whom were Muslim, linking Salvador to nearby villages, plantations, and quilombos. Anticipated by the governor thanks to an informant, the Malê revolt began hastily during the night preceding the last Sunday of January 1835, which was also Ramadan Laylat al-Qadr (night of destiny). Between four hundred and six hundred men participated in the rebellion: they were all enslaved or manumitted West Africans already well settled in Brazil, of diverse ethnic origin but united by the Islamic faith practiced by the majority of them. Their plan was to mobilize a large segment of Salvador's twenty-two thousand Africans and regroup at a plantation in the north before rallying other African-born slaves from the Recôncavo with whom they had been in contact, possibly in order to seize the port city. However, the governor had time to alert the police, the militia, and the army, meaning at least fifteen hundred armed men. An "every man for himself" scenario emerged among the rebels, who fled toward the countryside or threw themselves into the sea. The fighting that followed resulted in fifty insurgents killed or drowned, dozens of arrests, and nine dead among civilians and security troops.[10]

All of the 308 suspects brought before the law were African-born (except for one creole), 65 percent of whom were Yoruba and 10 percent Hausa; the remainder belonged to other ethnic groups from western and central Africa. Many were young men without families, who were connected via work. Most importantly, 37 percent had been emancipated and were therefore particularly competent men who had survived since capture in Africa and succeeded in obtaining their freedom in Brazil. According to statements coerced from some of the accused, the plotters had wanted to "kill whites," a recurring theme in most slave conspiracies. Yet the details reinforce this plot's originality. Several of its leaders were literate spiritual guides, some participants wore long white boubous, and amulets and Koranic verses were found on the dead bodies. The Malê revolt of 1835 was likely intended to unite Africans from different ethnic groups under Muslim leadership and against the white, creole, and mixed-race Christian world of Bahian slavery.[11]

During the hunts and raids that followed 25 January 1835, soldiers at times beat innocent individuals to the point of death. But suspects were entitled to trials that respected due process (especially in comparison with those held in the French and British colonies described in this chapter). Four men (three enslaved and one emancipated) were sentenced to death and shot, as no hangman volunteered to hang them. At least forty-five men, including two freedmen, endured several hundred whiplashes (at a rate of fifty per day), while others were sentenced to years of convict labor. Furthermore, in May, a first lot of 154 Africans, including a handful of women, and nearly all of whom had previously managed to manumit themselves, was deported to the western coast of Africa, followed by a second group of two hundred. To prevent other revolts, the province of Bahia instituted rules imposing strict vigilance and new restrictions on enslaved and freed Africans. Shortly thereafter, other provinces adopted similar laws.[12]

The slave trade continued to strengthen slavery in Cuba as well, but slaves, often mindful of the Haitian Revolution, were less isolated from events like the abolition of the slave trade by Great Britain and the United States than their Brazilian counterparts. Nonetheless, between 1815 and the early 1830s, revolts able to mobilize more than small groups of slaves were rare and rapidly contained. A "freedom" uprising near Havana in 1832 mobilized nearly every one of a coffee plantation's 375 slaves (mainly Yoruba). But after damaging nearby property, they were caught and punished.[13] In reality, Cuba's slaves were aware that despite support from some *libres de color* living in cities, they could not count on the power held by planters and colonial authorities to weaken. For that matter, pressure from British abolitionism did not reach the island until the end of the 1830s when slavery was abolished in Jamaica and other colonies of the United Kingdom.

From Denmark Vesey's Conspiracy to Nat Turner's Revolt in the U.S. South

In the southern United States as well, the "peculiar institution" grew stronger, but, unlike in Cuba, it was due not to the importation of captives, banned since 1808, but to good sanitary conditions that allowed the number of slaves to double between 1810 and 1830. At the same time, it became practically impossible for those captives to flee or emancipate themselves, much less revolt.[14] Consequently, by 1820, nearly all the Afro-descendants in the South were enslaved, except in Maryland and Louisiana, where free African Americans represented 10 percent and 7 percent of their respective populations. Moreover, whites were the majority everywhere, except in South Carolina and Louisiana, where they represented a little less than half of the population (47 percent and 49 percent, respectively).[15] Every county had armed white militias to subdue any suspected slave unrest and pursue fugitives. Furthermore, the plantation system was very different from the one dominant in the Caribbean. Captives in every state were spread out across many plantations: only 2.5 percent of landowners had fifty slaves or more; 33.5 percent, between one and forty-nine slaves (often one or several families); and the remaining 64 percent, no slave at all. In cities, a large number of slaves were artisans, day laborers, or servants and lived in their owners' homes or independent rooms. That dispersal, often combined with the enslavement of entire families, made any collective mobilization or revolt very difficult and rapidly brought under control.[16] As a result, only two incidents had a national impact during this period: Denmark Vesey's conspiracy, in South Carolina in 1822, and Nat Turner's revolt, in Virginia in 1831.

Denmark Vesey's conspiracy was denounced by two slaves in mid-June 1822, who independently told their masters that a massive plot was being hatched for the coming days in Charleston, which would involve a very large number of slaves and free people of color killing whites and looting stores before fleeing by boat to Haiti. Beginning on 18 June, authorities made their first arrests and, following interrogations under torture, detained additional suspects, including

Vesey on 22 June. By 2 July, thirty-one blacks were behind bars, and Vesey and five slaves assumed to be accomplices had been executed by hanging. That same day, in response to criticism by a Charleston judge and member of the federal Supreme Court about the legitimacy of those executions, magistrates launched a new wave of arrests that landed eighty-two men in prison in a little more than two weeks. By the end of July, they had judged another forty-six slaves, none of whom confessed to participating in the conspiracy despite being tortured. Nonetheless, twenty-eight of them were hanged, eighteen were sold further south, and only two were acquitted. In August, new judges took over the case, but without their predecessors' zeal: of the eighteen suspects they tried, one was hanged, seven were transported, and the rest found innocent. In addition, four other suspects—all white foreigners to South Carolina: two sailors, one Scottish and the other Spanish, a German peddler, and a grocer from another state—were given prison terms. The two slave informants were emancipated.[17] Authorities also banned blacks from grieving those executed and burned down the African Methodist church to which many of them belonged. Shortly after, new laws prohibited the teaching of reading and writing to slaves, reduced their freedom to assemble, and entrusted their evangelization exclusively to authorized white missionaries.[18]

As with other similar plots, it is difficult to know whether the dozens of slaves and free blacks from Charleston and the four whites associated with Vesey's conspiracy had been concretely planning, since 1820, what could have been "the biggest slave rebellion in the history of the United States";[19] alternatively, they might have been devising or imagining various ways to escape slavery, or might have been victims of an escalating crackdown by Charleston's judges.[20] In effect, historians continue to debate the value of the main legal report about the case written after the fact by two judges and have yet to find any documentation or direct trace of Vesey's own words.[21]

Nonetheless, it remains certain that those accused were inspired by Christianity and that most of them were affiliated with the African Methodist Episcopalian Church (the AME Church) in Charleston, which was increasingly targeted by whites. Slaves and free people of color had created the church after the city's official Methodist church restricted access to its black followers in 1815. They then reached out to the African Methodist Episcopalian Church, founded in Philadelphia in 1794 by the pastor Richard Allen, in order to establish an affiliated church in Charleston. The AME Church in Charleston quickly attracted most of the county's enslaved and free African Americans, who had previously belonged to the official Methodist Church. In response, authorities arrested several black Methodists under the pretext that they had taught slaves without whites present. In July 1820, authorities banned black Methodists from holding separate religious services; furthermore, South Carolina lawmakers radically limited the possibilities of emancipation and forbade all free African Americans from entering the state, undoubtedly fearful of their collective mobilization. The number of free people of color in Charleston County had been increasing since 1800 and, in 1820, the 10,653 whites listed on that year's census had become a minority in relation to blacks, 1,475 of whom were free and 12,652 enslaved.[22] As in other cases of presumed conspiracies, the mere fact of belonging to the AME Church in 1822 could transform a free or enslaved black into a conspirator in whites' minds.

Denmark Vesey, the man who gave his name to the conspiracy, played an important role in that religious mobilization, even if his role as the supposed plot's mastermind was never proven, as most of the existing testimonies about him incriminated him after his execution. In 1822, Vesey was a fifty-five-year-old literate freedman, a regular Bible reader, and a member of the AME Church. His wife and his son were enslaved, however, as were many other Methodist followers. His life up to his execution left little trace in Charleston, where his merchant master had brought him as a slave in 1783 after acquiring him on the Danish island of St. Thomas, other than that in 1799 he had won $1,500 in the lottery, thanks to which he was able to buy his freedom for $600 and a license to work as a carpenter. Other blacks incriminated alongside him were Africans who arrived after 1800, including the enslaved artisans Gullah Jack Pritchard and Monday Gell. It is therefore possible that together those men conceived of a way to liberate slaves by drawing from the Old Testament (specifically the Book of Exodus), African cosmology, the Declaration of Independence, and the U.S. Constitution, as well as the Haitian Revolution.[23] Incidentally, those latter themes were also accessible to both white and black readers of local newspapers that would provide commentary on Haiti's recent occupation of Santo Domingo or its president Jean-Pierre Boyer's calls for black American immigration; on South Carolina congressional debates on restrictions on emancipation; or on those held in the U.S. Congress on Missouri's entrance into the Union as a slaveholding state. As a result, despite the repression suffered by its Methodist congregation in 1820, Charleston's black community had diverse reasons to imagine a better future, prompting some defendants to maintain that the late Vesey had told them: "We are made free but the White people here won't let us be so—and the only way is to raise up & fight the Whites."[24] That context was likely to generate enthusiastic statements among Charleston's blacks, and even incite some to think about how to murder whites and flee to Haiti. Even if they did not come up with a concrete plan to do so, talking about that dream of freedom already offered proof of their plotting in the eyes of local judges.[25]

News of the thirty-five executions in Charleston during the summer of 1822 spread throughout many cities in the South and put whites on high alert. In the subsequent years, incidents of captives protesting their enslavement remained isolated. Of course, some groups revolted, for example, the ninety enslaved men brought cuffed and chained by three merchants from Maryland to Kentucky in 1829 and who managed to get loose and killed two of their transporters while the third escaped to sound the alarm. But they were all subsequently captured; six were hanged for murder, and some of the others sold farther south. Slaves elsewhere seized opportunities to attack or kill masters or guards, but throughout the region whites were armed, militias ready to intervene, and rebels quickly subdued and punished.[26] However, in the East Coast states that had abolished slavery, African Americans mobilized against racial discrimination and slavery in the South. In 1827, in New York, Peter Williams Jr., a black minister from the official Episcopalian church, launched the first black newspaper in the United States, *Freedom's Journal*, with an abolitionist vision. Two years later, David Walker, one of the newspaper's occasional contributors and a follower of the AME Church, published *An Appeal to the Coloured Citizens of the World* in Boston. Drawing from the Bible and the U.S. Declaration of Independence, his pamphlet called on blacks to revolt against slavery and demand freedom and equality as well as the total and immediate abolition of slavery. He condemned the lot of black slaves in the United States as worse than that of all other enslaved peoples in the history of humanity. He compared it in particular to the conditions faced by Jews in pharaonic Egypt to underline the violence and barbarism of "the enlightened Christians of America," in contrast with the inclusiveness of Egyptians, who "were Africans or coloured people, such as we are." But Walker warned that whites would soon be punished for their sins and commanded "the coloured people of the United States" to overcome their differences and be able to recognize the leader that God would soon send them to deliver them from their misery. Walker's statements were shocking, especially in the South, where some states banned their circulation; a price was even placed on Walker's head, but he died suddenly in 1830 at the age of thirty-four. Six months later, on 1 January 1831, in Boston, the white journalist William L. Garrison launched the first issue of the newspaper *The Liberator*, which called for immediate abolition.[27]

As a result, on the night of 21 August 1831, when Nat Turner and a few dozen followers launched a deadly raid across Southampton County, in southern Virginia, and killed between fifty-five and fifty-eight whites—most of them women and children—in less than twenty-four hours, their revolt reverberated nationwide. Nonetheless, there was no indication that Turner and his accomplices had been influenced by the growth of abolitionism in the North. In Southampton, hundreds of militiamen and whites of various loyalties, backed by state and federal troops, ended the rebellion in two days, capturing or killing most of the insurgents when they surrendered. But Turner was able to elude them for more than two months and was not arrested until 30 October. Of the forty-three enslaved men tried, thirty were sentenced to death; eighteen of them, including

Turner, were hanged, but the other twelve had their sentences commuted to transportation by the governor; thirteen were found not guilty and acquitted. The white population would remain terrorized by the massacres conducted under Turner's command for a long time and suspected the rebel leader of having followers far beyond Southampton. In the bordering county of Sussex, twelve enslaved men were prosecuted for intelligence with the Southampton rebels, and ten of them executed. During the extended crackdown that followed the murders committed by rebels, twenty or thirty blacks, nearly all slaves but without any connections to Turner, were killed outside the bounds of the law in neighboring counties.[28]

Nat Turner surrendered without resistance and died proudly on 11 November 1831. However, during his imprisonment, he gave a long narrative of his motivations and how his rebellion unfolded to a journalist who immediately published it under the title *The Confessions of Nat Turner*.[29] Turner made no reference to the existent abolitionist movement, but mentioned several memorized quotations from various passages from the Bible, which he had read diligently. From the start, he presented himself as an exceptional individual since early childhood, gifted with prenatal memory and unique intelligence, destined by the Almighty to become a great prophet. With time, he had made himself a better person through prayer and fasting and developed a compelling influence over others: he even claimed to have performed miracles and baptized a white person. And most importantly, since 1825 he had witnessed a series of revelations and visions ordering him to accomplish what the Holy Spirit had preordained for him. Three years later, the Holy Spirit had commanded him to take over the burden that Christ had carried for man's sins, as "the time was approaching when the first should be last and the last should be first." But his destiny was incompatible with his status as a slave, and those who could have freed him had not done so. When Nat Turner reached the age of thirty-one, he secretly awaited signs from heaven telling him that he should start "the work of death" and "slay my enemies with their own weapons." After the solar eclipse of February 1831, he broke his silence and shared his plan with four companions over whom he wielded great authority. Those men did not betray his trust and acted loyally by targeting the families of those who had not emancipated them when they had the chance. Now, concluded Turner, he was ready to be executed, like the crucified Christ.[30]

Turner thus believed he had fulfilled his destiny, or paid back those who had not allowed him to achieve it by not freeing him. But his followers' motives remain sketchy. The rebellion was local, limited to Southampton County and its surrounding areas. But because Turner's revolt was the deadliest uprising, in terms of whites killed, in the history of the land that was now the United States, it would long incarnate white slaveowners' age-old fear of being massacred by their slaves, as demonstrates an anonymous engraving of scenes of the "horrid massacre in Virginia," which was widely circulated after 1831. For some enslaved and free African Americans, Nat Turner became the symbol of the rebellious slave, the black Spartacus announced by David Walker and awaited by many.[31]

The 1816 Barbados Revolt: "Forever with Endavourance"

Despite those revolts, slaves in the French Caribbean, Brazil, Cuba, and the southern United States were unable to weaken the institution of slavery during the years that followed the Treaty of Vienna. After 1815, however, the British Caribbean, spared the effects of the Haitian Revolution, saw the eruption of large uprisings that played a decisive role in the abolition of slavery in 1833. When the first of those insurrections broke out in Barbados in 1816, it took abolitionists in Great Britain by surprise. After the slave trade was banned by Parliament in 1807, they crusaded for France, Spain, and Brazil to eliminate it as well and encouraged the colonization of Sierra Leone by captives seized on slave ships boarded and searched by the British fleet. As for slavery in the United Kingdom's colonies, abolitionists believed that once the importation of enslaved Africans had ceased, planters would take better care of their captives, since only natural reproduction could prevent the diminishment of their labor force. Further, they thought that slavery would become more humane, "improve itself," and ultimately slowly die out on its own. In 1815, when it emerged that the number of slaves was increasing at an unusual rate on the island of Trinidad (officially a British colony since 1802), several abolitionists proposed that the House of Commons force British colonies to establish official slave registries to prevent the illegal importation of captives. Though their proposition failed, it prompted an outcry among planters, who accused them of insidiously plotting to extinguish slavery.

Particularly in Barbados, planters were at increasing odds with the London Parliament. Though they had respected the abolition of the slave trade since 1808 because they themselves were no longer importing Africans and hoped that the ban would hurt their competitors, in November 1815, during animated meetings and in the local press, they began to repeatedly criticize the proposal that masters be obliged to record their slaves on official registers as an attack on their private property, the colony's autonomy, and the very existence of slavery. Some even predicted that "all legislative interference between Master and Slave . . . encourag[ed] insubordination necessarily (if not of still more horrid evils)" among slaves who, up until then, had not shown any discontent.[32] Indeed, the last great fear of a slave rebellion in Barbados stretched back to 1692, and planters were boastful of how well they handled their captive labor force. Whites numbered approximately fifteen thousand and free people of color only three thousand, compared to a total of seventy-seven thousand slaves. Contrary to Jamaica or British Guiana at the time, 93 percent of slaves in Barbados were creoles; few were Christians, but some knew how to read and write. Moreover, apart from servants and urban workers, most captives toiled on plantations but lived in adjoining villages in which every family had a hut and plot of land on which they often produced enough to sell the surplus at nearby markets. However, those seemingly favorable conditions masked growing tensions between planters and slaves. Since the success of the Haitian Revolution, the former had been bemoaning their slaves' insolence and imprisoning the most rebellious among them in Bridgetown's "cage," a jail normally reserved for captured maroons. At the same time, despite a terrain that was nearly entirely dedicated to sugar plantations and therefore far from favorable to marronage, slave escapes multiplied.[33]

The mobilization of Barbados's planters and their virulent defense of slavery in the face of demands made by Great Britain, coincidently when the island's governor was on an official visit in London, did not go unnoticed by slaves. Some, particularly enslaved foremen and literate artisans in contact with free people of color, took planters' accusations literally and convinced themselves that emancipation had in fact been decreed in London and the governor informed, but that their masters refused to respect the decision. Some slaves undoubtedly also realized that with the end of the Napoleonic wars, the troops stationed on the small island had diminished by more than half since December 1814.[34] Subsequently, several elite slaves from the parish of St. Philipp, in the island's southwestern region, began to devise the best ways to force planters to respect the orders from London. The most active among them were overseers and servants from two neighboring plantations and belonged to a network that linked several estates in the parish all the way to Bridgetown. An enslaved man called Jackey appeared to serve as the organizer, even though the revolt would be named after the only African among the rebels, the ranger Bussa (or Bussoe). The literate domestic slave Nanny Grigg also played a major role, after she claimed to have read in a newspaper that slaves were meant to be liberated by New Year's Day but that whites opposed it. After 1 January 1816 came and went without liberation, she announced that it would take place on Easter Monday but that slaves should prepare to fight to win their freedom, as they had done in Saint Domingue. The rebellion's participants therefore organized some of the slaves on the two plantations and forged connections beyond St. Philipp. Together they created a vague plan to rebel during the Easter holiday, when the colonial elite and troops would be gathered in Bridgetown and the governor would have returned from London wielding a purported "free paper." Although some called for a strike, others wanted to "set the land on fire" like in "[Do]-Mingo" (Saint Domingue). Prematurely launched on Easter Sunday,

14 April 1816, the revolt spread rapidly, rallying several hundred slaves, possibly as many as 3,900. Unarmed or poorly armed, they scattered into various bands in an insurrection that burned down a third of the sugarcane fields in the island's western region and destroyed plantation buildings.[35]

The crackdown was swift and brutal. Militias from St. Philipp and three neighboring parishes, meaning hundreds of primarily white men, were the first to take action, followed by a West India Regiment composed of 150 "emancipated" black men and a large segment of the regular army's 1,414 European soldiers. Insurgent slaves, armed at best with machetes and sticks, stood no chance against those well-armed and trained forces. Quickly disorganized, they tried to escape rather than meet their adversaries head-on. In two days, militiamen and soldiers had more or less quashed the rebellion: they killed fifty slaves in combat (including Bussa), summarily executed seventy, and took three hundred to four hundred prisoner. As for the rebels, in total, they killed only one white civilian and two black soldiers. The suppression tactics used by security forces included burning and destroying slave huts and garden plots, followed by the indiscriminate killing of fugitives, including women and children. The governor returned from London on 24 April without an emancipation decree and extended martial law to mid-July. During a first round of trials, 111 slaves and 3 free people of color were executed in various public places throughout the island, and their bodies or heads subsequently displayed to serve as examples, continuing the macabre tradition of previous centuries. Many others were sentenced to public lashings and sale abroad, and 18 were acquitted. The trials by court martial continued for several more weeks, leading to 106 additional death penalties that the Assembly of Barbados decided to commute to transportation sentences. At the end of January 1817, those 106 slaves and others considered too dangerous by their masters to be reintegrated were deported to the mahogany forests of Belize (British Honduras). A few months later, the Assembly of Barbados passed its own law decreeing that slaves be registered, whose smooth implementation would be ensured by the planters' militia. And in January 1818, it decided to publish an official report on the revolt, which it sent to London. It was careful to place responsibility on the abolitionist William Wilberforce and two agitators from outside Barbados.[36]

Nevertheless, rebels had clearly expressed the hopes they placed in their uprising on white cotton flags covered with slogans and illustrations, which they brandished in April 1816. First of all, they repeatedly called their movement an "endavour" or "endavourance." The slogan that appeared on the top and bottom of banners, such as the one sketched at the time below, read "Happiness remains for ever with endavourance" and insisted on support from "Bretanier [Brittany]" and God in that effort. The left side bore a drawing of a tall white soldier holding a long pike with a banner reading "Royal G. R. [Georgius Rex,

Sketch of a flag taken from the insurgent slaves at Barbados, 1816.
(Courtesy of the National Archives of the United Kingdom, MFQ 1/112)

U.K. King George III] endavourance for ever," and on the right side, a large sailboat flying the British banner. At the center of this flag and others were scenes of a black royal couple, a black man coiffed and holding a stick, and various royal and military symbols. The plantation was completely absent from the flags' imagery and text, but the royal monarchy and the army were omnipresent, as was mention of the happiness associated with the movement.

By cross-checking that iconography with notes from undoubtedly violent interrogations of rebels and British military correspondence, historian David Lambert concludes that the insurgents were convinced they had the support of the British king and the Royal Army, the latter of which they expected would be arriving with reinforcements and the governor on a royal ship. They were also counting on help from the West India Regiment, which clearly explains their confusion when, on the second day of the revolt, black soldiers attacked and chased them. The motif of the black man with the white woman on some flags, also mentioned in British military correspondence, evoked a future that would break all taboos and reflected a scenario long feared by whites throughout the history of slavery: the murder by slaves of all white men and their capture of white women for their sexual desires, in a reversal of the acts of sexual violence committed by white men against enslaved women on plantations. Insurgents' flags exacerbated and played off whites' terror while claiming to be acting with the backing of the king, his army, and his navy. It was a clever way for rebels to convince illiterate slaves on plantations to join them in their "endavour."[37]

In the United Kingdom, news of the slave uprising in Barbados at first forced abolitionists to lose ground, notably Wilberforce, who agreed to withdraw his motion to establish a central slave registry. Colonial assemblies therefore created and managed their own registries, all of which were in place by 1819. However, events in Barbados coincided with the rise of protests in Great Britain by farmers and workers against industrialization and the degradation of their living conditions: strikes, riots, destruction of machines, and demonstrations by tens of thousands of people, often violently quelled and followed by liberticidal laws, multiplied. The most radical political circles gradually took an interest in those various popular uprisings at home and in the colonies, and in their causes and potential legitimacy. One of the first to establish a link between workers and slaves was an English activist newspaper that, after the bloody repression of a popular demonstration in Manchester in 1819, used the abolitionist medallion created in 1787 by Josiah Wedgwood—"Am I not a man and a brother?"—and replaced its kneeling slave with a textile worker. In the aftermath of the Barbados revolt, the slave planters' lobby insisted on the magnitude and so-called savage nature of the destruction caused by rebels, both to justify its demands for compensation for losses suffered and to revive the still terrifying images of the Haitian Revolution and demand greater autonomy for the colonies. For their part, abolitionists emphasized the differences between Saint Domingue and Barbados, notably, arguing that in the latter, few slaves were African-born and insurgents had not committed any atrocities and had only killed one white. As a result, in abolitionists' eyes, it was the planters who had reacted disproportionately and needed to be better controlled. The mass executions and subsequent displaying of the bodies of those convicted, banned from Great Britain's arsenal of punishments at the end of the eighteenth century, contributed to accusations of barbarism directed against planters, rather than their slaves. At the same time, the ban of the slave trade ten years earlier was changing opinions among politicians and activists, who were starting to think of slaves and their free or enslaved descendants as part of the British Empire, in which they should be "integrated," albeit as subalterns. As itinerant evangelism spread in Great Britain, Protestant missionaries set out to "civilize" and Christianize slaves in the West Indies.[38]

Once in the colonies, those missionaries, often from working-class backgrounds, found themselves face to face not with "African savages" but with men and women who had developed their own culture of resistance. After witnessing the violence of plantation life, as well as the physical suffering endured by slaves, many began to consider them as both "others" and "brethren in Christ." Missionaries not only converted and baptized those captives, but also trained deacons among them, who then contributed to evangelizing the colonies in turn. Some mission chapels became favored meeting places where slaves could gather away from planters and estate managers, reinterpret the Bible, and adapt lessons of salvation in the afterlife to their own spirituality or transform them into promises of immediate freedom. Like evangelized slaves in the United States, those in British colonies thrived on passages from the Old Testament about Moses liberating his people from slavery in Egypt. And like their counterparts, they also wanted the kingdom of God on earth and now, not the hell of the plantation. Worried about evangelists' interference in the private world of slave plantations, planter assemblies increased the number of laws aimed at monitoring them and restricting their actions.[39]

The Uprising of the "Brethren in Christ" in Demerara (1823)

In London, in January 1823, a group of abolitionists including Wilberforce and Thomas Clarkson established the Society for the Mitigation and Gradual Abolition of Slavery throughout the British Dominions, better known as the Anti-Slavery Society, with the goal of demanding measures to improve existing slave conditions and prepare gradual emancipation; younger militants sent the House of Commons proposals inspired by manumission laws in continental America. Although they were rejected, those proposals prompted a series of instructions about the "amelioration of slavery" in the colonies, which the royal council approved a few months later: they encouraged the evangelization of slaves by banning work and markets on Sundays; favored the Christian marriage of enslaved couples and forbid the separation of minors from their families; encouraged slaves to purchase their freedom, authorizing them to possess goods and foreseeing the establishment of savings banks; demanded that slave protectors be designated to record complaints of poor treatment and that slaves be allowed to testify in certain trials; and banned excessive punishments, all lashings of women, and the ritual whipping of laborers in the fields to increase their rate of work. However, unlike manumission laws in the northern United States and South America, those measures did not envisage the freedom, in principle, of newborns of enslaved mothers (free womb). When circulating its instructions to colonial governors, the royal council chose to make the decrees' application dependent on the willingness of colonial assemblies, but planned to test them in colonies under direct Crown rule, first in Demerara, and then in Trinidad.[40]

In general, the royal recommendations prompted anger among colonists ill disposed to reform—and, among slaves who were aware of them, at times disproportionate hopes, born from the confusion between "amelioration" and emancipation or abolition of slavery. Great Britain only implemented them in Trinidad, which it governed without the interference of a colonial assembly since its seizure from Spain in 1797 (see chapter 9). Because the crown developed slave plantations there while maintaining the Spanish Código Negro to manage slaves, planters were more willing to accept its instructions than elsewhere.[41] In the British Guiana colony of Demerara, though considered a priority due to its particularly unsanitary living conditions and the increasing exploitation to which its slaves were subjected, the governor compromised on the royal recommendations and ceded to planters' complaints. He notably limited slaves' rights to rest on Sundays and to attend religious services led by Protestant missionaries in order to favor plantation work, thus exacerbating discontent among the former. That was the backdrop against which, in August 1823, a major slave uprising erupted east of the Demerara River, which has been meticulously pieced together by historian Emília Viotti da Costa. During the night of 18 August, between 9,000 and 12,000 of the 75,000 slaves living in the colony at the time revolted—meaning one slave in seven, including children and the elderly. It was therefore a considerable movement for a territory whose inhabitants also included 2,500 whites and 2,500 free people of color.

The revolt was the result of long preparation. As soon as debates between the governor and planters began, a small group of elite slaves decided to inquire about the contents of the royal instructions. Daniel, a servant of the governor who knew how to read and write, agreed to rifle through his master's papers. The enslaved artisan Quamina, an Akan taken from the Ashanti kingdom who had recently been trained as a deacon, proceeded to glean information from his religious superior, Reverend John Smith, sent by the London Missionary Society in 1817 to evangelize slaves and living with his wife on the Le Resouvenir plantation. Quamina's son, Jack Gladstone, who was also an artisan, and Susanna, the former companion of the plantation administrator, planned to interrogate the latter. The four slaves shared and then circulated their knowledge and impressions among networks of friends and acquaintances. They came to consider the royal instructions as "new laws" that, for some, were equivalent to a decree of immediate freedom and, for others, of three free days a week—two prisms through which more and more slaves began to interpret any information or incident. According to them, they had the right to protest because planters had not respected the new royal laws. Jack Gladstone was undoubtedly the movement's instigator, but dozens of captives, whether they were creoles like him or Africans like his father, were involved in its preparation.[42] Thanks to freedom of movement and Gladstone's many family connections, as well as to gatherings held in Smith's chapel at Le Resouvenir and the system of catechesis that the missionary implemented when designating a slave teacher per plantation, the idea of protest spread across sixty estates. While many slaves were enthusiastic, others feared a movement that, in their minds, would invariably result in a cruel crackdown. Each and every one of them had reasons to revolt: the possibility of avenging an injustice, the fear of being sold and separated from one's family or, more broadly, the possibility of freedom. But slaves also feared torture and death for themselves and their loved ones.[43]

On Sunday, 17 August 1823, Jack Gladstone held a meeting during which some of his coconspirators decided to launch the protest the following day, while others, such as his father, Quamina, wanted to send a delegation to the governor. All those involved, however, were acting to obtain the "rights" supposedly granted by the king of Great Britain, and not to kill whites. On Monday evening, 18 August, slaves rose up on several plantations east of Georgetown. They forced their hesitant coworkers to join them, surrounded houses belonging to whites, and put in the stocks administrators and planters before seizing weapons and munitions they found and attacking other estates. The rebels burned down several homes and killed three whites.[44] Briefly arrested by a detachment sent from Georgetown, Quamina and his son had the good luck to be freed by a group of rebels. But they did not know that on that Monday morning, one of the plotters had reported their plans to his master, who had immediately warned the governor. Before the rebellion even began, colonists were therefore on high alert. In the evening of 18 August, the governor instituted a state of emergency and mobilized all white men able to fight. The white women in the capital were moved to safety on ships. Living on the Le Resouvenir plantation, the missionary Smith refused to join the militia; he and his wife Jane painfully monitored the events unfolding but remained at their home, confident they would not be targeted by the insurgents. On Wednesday, 20 August, Smith began to write a detailed letter to the secretary of the London Missionary Society, in which he condemned slavery and justified the captives' revolt. But he was interrupted by government forces that arrested him and his wife and imprisoned them in Georgetown. His letter and other papers, which were all confiscated, would serve as proof used to accuse him of being an external agent who had corrupted slaves with his antislavery preaching and driven them to rebel.[45]

Meanwhile, the governor was able to mobilize regular troops, the navy, and the militia, meaning over one thousand men, with weapons and munitions. The army left Georgetown on Monday night, followed by the militia shortly thereafter. On the way, both ordered the rebels to surrender and killed many of those who fled instead. At the same time, the governor was making contradictory statements, promising measures that would ameliorate slavery and the merciless punishment of rebels. By Wednesday, soldiers had already killed or injured 255 slaves. Over the following days, military units took back control of plantations, one after the other, which led to speedy trials followed by exemplary executions in front of other slaves who were then forced to decapitate the dead and place their heads on pikes. Simultaneously, in Georgetown, a court martial had been trying imprisoned slaves since 25 August. A sizable reward was offered for the capture of Jack Gladstone; his father, Quamina; and eighteen other fugitives of both sexes. Gladstone was arrested on 6 September, but Quamina preferred death to being captured alive; his body was displayed for months hanging from a chain in front of the plantation on which he had worked. Trials continued until the beginning of 1824. In total, seventy-two enslaved suspects were judged: fifty-two were sentenced to death by hanging, sixteen to lashings, and the others acquitted. In fact, of the fifty-two given the death sentence, thirty-three were executed, and the bodies or heads of a dozen of them were displayed hanging or on a stick. But the remaining nineteen were reprieved and transported as slaves, including Jack Gladstone, whom the governor preferred to ban to St. Lucia rather than risk making into a martyr. The hangings took place during public ceremonies in the capital, while the lashings (up to one thousand whiplashes over several days) were administered on plantations. In every case, the goal was to terrorize the enslaved population for a long time.[46]

However, the governor and planters also wanted to terrify missionaries and defy abolitionists in London. John Smith's court martial trial served that end. It lasted twenty-seven days and was largely covered by the local press, which also published compromising pages from the reverend's private diary. The goal of Demerara's colonial elite was to incriminate Smith for having knowingly used his evangelizing mission and Sunday sermons to incite slaves to revolt against their masters' legal authority and, therefore, against the king's peace and that of his kingdom. Knowing he was doomed from the start, Smith made his defense into an argument against slavery, which he accused of violating Christian morality, condemning the sins committed by slaveowners, plantation managers, and colonial authorities. He concluded his defense speech with the following statement: "I do, as a minister of the Gospel, in the presence of my God, most solemnly declare my innocence." But since the judges had already designed the trial as a political one, for conspiring to destroy Demerara's slavery system, they did not need tangible proof of Smith's guilt. Indeed, the absence of proof served to reinforce the theory of a secret conspiracy. On 24 November 1823, John Smith was found guilty of having made his congregation into a clandestine group intended to subvert the social order of British Guiana. He was sentenced to death by hanging—a sentence likely to receive a royal pardon, however, as he was white. The pardon was granted, but too late for John Smith, who died of exhaustion and disease in his cell in early February 1824. He was buried in great secret and the Missionary Society repatriated Jane Smith to London.[47]

The methods used by Demerara's judges to incriminate Smith nonetheless had unintended consequences in London, where the trial was widely covered and debated, especially following Smith's death. In fact, the magistrates had brought in numerous prosecution witnesses, which unusually included slaves who had been sworn in, as occurred in New York in 1741—a visible crack in the institution of slavery, which did not normally allow slaves or free blacks to testify against whites. Next the judges revealed their ambiguity toward Christianity, permitting certain biblical episodes, notably the parts of the Old Testament dedicated to Moses liberating his people from enslavement in Egypt, to be used as evidence. At the same time, the enslaved deacons or instructors ordered to report which sections of the Old or New Testament Smith had recommended to them demonstrated that not only were they good Christians, but they also knew how to read; some could write too. They were therefore human beings in their own right, and "brethren in Christ," as Smith would say.

Finally, and most importantly, the brutal repression of the Demerara rebellion moved public opinion in Great Britain, as slaves and Smith were not its only victims. In Demerara, whites had targeted missionaries and Baptist, Methodist, and even Anglican pastors in their parishes and burned down churches. Moreover, attacks against preachers and missionaries had spread to other British colonies, notably Barbados, where, in October 1823, colonists destroyed a Methodist chapel and chased away its pastor, provoking protests by several Protestant communities in Great Britain.[48] For many, John Smith was innocent and his ordeal revealed the fundamental corruption of slave societies. While the colonial lobby demanded compensation for the damage caused by enslaved rebels, strict supervision of missionaries, and an end to the "amelioration of slavery" policy, Methodists, Wesleyans, and Baptists began to condemn London's costly support of a system of slaveholding colonies that they considered illegal, anti-Christian, and politically and economically unsustainable. At the same time, politicians were using the suffering endured by Demerara's slaves to calm growing demands for social improvement and suffrage by workers and farmers in Great Britain. Even the abolitionist Clarkson stressed the relatively favorable situation of Great Britain's working class by comparison with that of slaves who could be sold, whipped, or separated from their families. However, those comparisons backfired as they primarily prompted empathy. British workers, whose conditions were deteriorating, saw more parallels than divergences in the different systems of exploitation and began to consider slaves as equal human beings. In reality, and unlike the majority of previous slave revolts, the Demerara rebellion and its cruel repression revived abolitionism, with two new developments: the participation of women and the demand for the immediate abolition of slavery. Publications and petitions multiplied. The abolition of slavery had become a demand of the British people.[49]

Simultaneously, protest movements among planters had been growing in the British Caribbean since London's attempts to impose measures to ameliorate slavery. Some colonial assemblies opposed the idea of any reform that encroached on planters' domination. In Antigua, for example, plantation owners had followed royal instructions to eliminate Sunday markets to encourage slaves' rest and evangelization, but had deliberately neglected to replace Sunday with another market day. Slaves resisted what they regarded as an attack on their limited autonomy and a violation of a traditional right—a day to be used to farm and sell any surplus from their small garden plots, livestock, or artisanal products, or for gatherings and entertainment. When markets were banned as of 18 March 1831, men and especially women gathered at the St. John's marketplace to demonstrate their refusal to comply. After declaring martial law, authorities sentenced one enslaved man to hanging and others to lashings. Acts of discontent nonetheless continued, forcing the governor to announce that the king had not abolished slavery—and planters to authorize informal markets on Saturdays.[50]

The Baptist Rebellion of 1831–1832 in Jamaica

Rumors of abolition did not disappear, and on Christmas 1831 Jamaica would be the setting for a new rebellion even larger than the preceding ones. According to historian Michael Craton, the uprising mobilized some sixty thousand slaves, which is undoubtedly an overestimate, as that figure is equivalent to one-fifth of all captives in Jamaica; but even maintaining the smaller number of twenty thousand insurgents (and as many sympathizers) proposed by sociologist Orlando Patterson, the Christmas Rebellion, also called the Baptist War of 1831–32, which shook the island's western region near Montego Bay, remains the largest in Jamaica's history.[51] As in Barbados in 1816, enslaved rebels accused planters of hiding an emancipation edict supposedly adopted by the British Parliament. As in Demerara in 1823, evangelization was also a factor in the uprising, though this time the movement's assumed instigator was not a white missionary, but an enslaved black deacon, Samuel "Daddy" Sharpe.[52]

In Jamaica, following the abolition of the slave trade, the enslaved population had dropped from 350,000 in 1808 to 310,000 in 1834, and the percentage of those born in Africa had declined from 45 percent to 25 percent. Nonetheless, abolitionists' hopes—namely, that planters would better treat their captives because they could no longer replace them—did not come true, as demonstrated by increased mortality rates and the natural decrease of the enslaved population.[53] Since 1823, the Assembly of Jamaica had resisted the majority of measures to ameliorate slavery demanded by London, but in December 1830 it granted civil rights to free blacks and mulattos, and in early 1831 it finally conceded to several reforms that benefited slaves after the British government threatened to reduce the island's autonomy.[54] Those paltry advances had been wrested from planters increasingly angry at London since the House of Commons had launched a campaign for the immediate abolition of slavery in April 1831. The

British Parliament thought it prudent to send a circular to all the colonies in June clarifying that emancipation had not been decreed and ordering slaves to remain calm. However, Jamaica's governor did not publish the letter, and anger among slaveholders continued to mount. They were convinced that Parliament was on the point of adopting a law of immediate emancipation, and their public protests multiplied. According to them, that imminent abolition would lead to the colony's ruin, the rape of white women, and the widespread massacre of whites: all the nightmares that had been haunting slaveowners since the sixteenth century were brandished once again, made more real by the Haitian Revolution. Some planters suggested taking action before catastrophe could occur, by wielding weapons and seceding from the British Empire while demanding support from slaveholders in the southern United States. Others pledged to immediately quell all vague hopes of freedom among their slaves, for example by preemptively killing enslaved men while keeping women and children. A master reportedly even told one of his slaves that "freedom was come [sic] from England, but that he would shoot every d—d black rascal before they should get it."[55]

Those kinds of statement were as common during debates at the Assembly of Jamaica as they were during gatherings and dinners of the colony's white elite, and were later repeated in the local press, providing great credibility to rumors of emancipation among slaves. The latter's hopes had already been encouraged for the past fifteen years by news of British abolitionism, which reached them indirectly and distorted through slaveowners' virulent protests. In 1815, 1816, 1823, and 1824, Jamaican authorities believed they had uncovered slave plots to murder whites and establish a black kingdom, which they suppressed by executing, transporting, or whipping the presumed conspirators. Incidentally, the evangelization and "civilization" of slaves was the impetus behind the amelioration of slavery measures demanded by London. Several English and Scottish missionary societies—notably Moravians, Presbyterians, Methodists, and Baptists—were active in Jamaica despite planters' suspicions or opposition, and their chapels offered slaves gathering places. Among those missionaries, Baptists distinguished themselves from the others because they emphasized the spiritual experience of the Holy Spirit, rather than the Scriptures and good behavior, and considered baptism a true rebirth. They were primarily based in the least developed parishes in the island's western region and their main objective was to train deacons among slaves and free people of color so they could spread Christianity to the most rural areas. Baptist missions consequently found allies among black Baptists, whose religious affiliation dated back to the end of the eighteenth century, when George Leile, an emancipated slave from Georgia, fled to Kingston to avoid being reenslaved after Great Britain's defeat in the U.S. War of Independence and established the first chapel in Jamaica. British evangelist missions also integrated Jamaican Native Baptists, who practiced a syncretic version of Baptism, extending demonstrations of divine spirituality to their ancestors and thereby creating a link to African beliefs. For Native Baptists, conversion and baptism were not only a spiritual liberation, but also a guarantee of equality for all after death, whether they were slaves, foremen, or slaveholders.[56]

By May 1831, faced with planters' unprecedented mobilization against abolitionism, slaves believed that the British Parliament or the king had indeed decreed general emancipation. Common sayings confirmed their hopes: for example, in reference to the recent extension of civil rights to free people of color, people would say, "Brown already free, black soon."[57] According to missionaries, parishes on Jamaica's northern coast were experiencing "a great outpouring of the Spirit," and slaves hurried to chapels to celebrate their imminent freedom.[58] That fervor was particularly visible among Native Baptists in St. James, a parish led by the English Baptist Thomas Burchell, who had been living in Montego Bay since 1824. In seven years, Burchell had succeeded in establishing several chapels in the neighboring parish of Hanover, which he entrusted to deacons, who were themselves often literate slaves and Native Baptists. In 1831, the latter circulated their own version of their liberation, which evoked that of Barbados's rebels fifteen years earlier: they imagined it would arrive in the form of a document decreeing general emancipation, which Burchell, who had left for Great Britain in May 1831, would bring by boat at Christmas; but, added Native Baptists, planters would do everything to oppose the decree, and slaves should therefore mobilize to obtain their emancipation. Black deacons and elite slaves slowly organized a network of activists linking the plantations in the interior region of western Jamaica, which included Hanover and St. James parishes and extended north of St. Elizabeth and northeast of Westmoreland (where the island's main revolt of 1760 had occurred). The main organizer was the aforementioned Samuel "Daddy" Sharpe, the leading deacon at Burchell's church. He was a literate domestic slave based in Montego Bay who enjoyed wide mobility, as he was allowed to circulate freely within the limits of St. James parish. A passionate and captivating preacher, close to the Native Baptists, well informed about British abolitionism, and an avid reader of the Bible, according to several statements, Sharpe had retained the following from his readings: "that the whites had no more right to hold black people in slavery than black people had to make white people their slaves."[59] He also preached that "no man can serve two masters," a phrase oft repeated by his followers which implied that slaves could not obey God and their owner at the same time.[60] The companions with whom Sharpe was preparing the arrival of emancipation were all enslaved men, overseers, or artisans, and members of Baptist, Wesleyan, or Moravian churches, and some of whom also belonged to the Native Baptists or another syncretic sect. Together, they represented a hundred plantations and, by October 1831, they were discussing strategy. Shortly before Christmas, the leaders had formed their plan, which they swore on the Bible to follow. They believed they would be freed at Christmas: if their masters then agreed to pay them wages, they would continue working as before; if not, the instructions were to sit down until they gained their freedom and only retaliate in case of attack. But since they were also expecting violent opposition by slaveowners, the organizers had prepared to defend themselves by forming a "black regiment" of 150 men led by a slave from one of the interior plantations.[61]

At the same time, Jamaican planters made it known that they were rejecting the reforms demanded by Great Britain. In November, the colony's assembly refused to debate the ban of the whipping of enslaved women demanded since 1823. Then came the announcement that although 25 December 1831 fell on a Sunday, which was already a day off, slaves would not receive an extra day in addition to the three traditionally granted for that holiday and would have to return to work at dawn on the 28. Finally, one week before Christmas, a serious incident occurred on a plantation near Montego Bay, when slaves disarmed two agents who had come to force a slave overseer to whip his own wife (already thrashed by the estate manager) and fled. Informed of the disturbance of the peace, Jamaica's governor finally published the royal circular from June denying that Parliament had voted for the immediate abolition of slavery, and then hurriedly sent additional troops to the site and ordered militias to be on alert. That announcement, added to the fact that Reverend Burchell still had not returned from England with the supposed emancipation decree, undoubtedly incited rebel leaders to gather after the Christmas service given by Burchell's replacement and agree to launch their protest movement.[62]

The uprising of slaves in western Jamaica therefore began the night of 27 December, the eve of their contested return to work. Slaves started fires on several plantations situated on hills to signal that their rebellion had begun. But by the next day, as many whites fled to the cities, the insurgents were showing their lack of cohesion: on some plantations, slaves were respecting the order to hold a nonviolent strike; elsewhere, they emptied the stores and seized anything that could be used as a weapon. The militia was the first to react. In plantations near the port of Falmouth, it rapidly contained insurgents by arresting several dozen men, women, and children. In St. James province, on the contrary, the rebels' "black regiment" was able to chase away the militia and oversee the creation of two new bands of revolting slaves. By 3 January 1832, thousands of insurgent slaves controlled the entire central region south of Montego Bay (meaning between one-sixth and one-tenth of the island's territory) as militias proved incapable of preventing the destruction and pillaging of plantations. According to one missionary, the rebels went from one plantation to the next and mobilized slaves by claiming: "We have worked enough already.... The life we live is ... the life of a dog. We wont be slaves no more; we wont lift hoe no more; we wont take flog no more. We free now, we free now; no more slaves again."[63]

However, in the meantime, the governor had proclaimed martial law, and the army, backed by maroon detachments in accordance with eighteenth-century peace treaties began to surround the rebels. Four weeks after the revolt began, troops and militias had defeated the last of the insurgents, and martial law was lifted on 7 February, though skirmishes continued for another month. In total, the slaves had partially or totally destroyed some 230 plantations and killed fourteen whites. The crackdown was incommensurate with that outcome. Several hundred slaves were killed during fighting or slaughtered outside any judicial process. In all, 626 or 627 individuals were arrested and judged, most by court martial trials held between 3 January and 7 February, and the rest by civilian courts convened after 7 February. Historian Mary Turner accounts for a total of 312 "legal" executions, and Michael Craton, 344. Both note that the majority of executions occurred under martial law and by hanging, and two-thirds of them in the most heavily impacted parishes of St. James and Hanover. In Montego Bay, where most of the trials took place, executions were done in quick succession, with three or four men hanged together in the same gallows; their bodies remained on display for several days before being thrown into a common grave to make room for other hangings. Since the goal was not only to punish but also to terrorize, it was not rare for those sentenced to death to be taken, ropes around their necks, to their plantations, where they were executed in front of their coworkers. The decapitated heads of many hanged insurgents, stuck on pikes, were displayed on public squares, along roads, and in front of plantations. Nearly all of the 626 or 627 accused men and women who were not executed were sentenced to fifty to five hundred whiplashes and/or jail; ten were transported and twenty-five acquitted.[64] During his trial, Samuel Sharpe condemned slavery as contradictory to the Bible; he was judged and executed in May 1832. According to a witness, his last words were: "I would rather die upon yonder gallows than live in slavery."[65] White missionaries—including Burchell once he returned in January 1832—were imprisoned, judged, and in the end acquitted; however, Jamaica's white residents publicly scorned and expelled them and burned down their chapels.

The Road to Freedom: Slave Revolts and Abolitionism

The three slave revolts that erupted in the British colonies between 1816 and 1831 were prompted by rumors of emancipation or of improved living conditions for slaves. All three demonstrated that at least some enslaved men and women considered their situation to be unacceptable, inhuman, unjust, and revolting. The revolts broke out at the same time that, in Great Britain, many English and Scottish people were beginning to see slavery as immoral. In effect, British abolitionism had undergone a long evolution. The fight against the slave trade, begun in the 1780s and suspended during the Saint Domingue uprising, resumed afterward, coupled with the additional argument that bossales had ignited that uprising, and triumphed at the end of 1807. Then came a wait-and-see phase that lasted until the end of the Napoleonic wars, during which abolitionists believed that the abolition of the slave trade would automatically lead to the "amelioration" of slavery. But in 1815, faced with planters' persisting cruelty and negligence, abolitionists called for concrete measures and intervention by London to evangelize slaves and improve their living conditions, prompting opposition from proslavery colonists. It was at that point, in Barbados in 1816, that rebelling slaves showed that they were not just victims, but also agents of their own destiny who wanted nothing less than immediate freedom. Abolitionists rejected the accusation that antislavery propaganda was inciting slave revolts. As explains historian Gelien Matthews, beginning in 1816, British activists could no longer consider slaves as simple beneficiaries of their actions and had to take the possibility that they would revolt into consideration. Indeed, the rebellion in Barbados pressured abolitionists and some parliamentarians to demand that the British government enact concrete amelioration measures and, following the establishment of the Anti-Slavery Society in 1823 in London, the gradual abolition of slavery without continuing to wait for colonists' voluntary cooperation. Next came the Demerara revolt of 1823, whose participants also demanded immediate freedom, and which revealed the obvious contradictions between Christianity and slavery, even as planters condemned missionaries' destabilizing activities. Abolitionists counterattacked by placing all responsibility for the revolt on inhumane masters and the institution of slavery itself. For that matter, they were able to use the facts to show that in most cases, enslaved rebels did not seek to kill all whites and destroy everything to establish a black kingdom, but that, on the contrary, they were not directly attacking their masters. Granted, slave revolts led to the destruction of property, but the few white deaths they caused were accidental. They were not demonstrations of savagery, but protests against the barbaric conditions of slavery.[66]

In contrast, deadly crackdowns and the executions of hundreds of rebel slaves by colonial forces were cruel and disproportionate, and became tangible proof that abolitionists could use to expose the inhumane nature of slavery and its proponents. The fact that some whites, particularly preachers such as John Smith in Demerara, had also been victims of acts of violence or sentenced to death by slaveowners helped them pay greater attention to the fate of rebelling slaves. On each occasion, British activists justified slave revolts, perhaps less because they showed slaves' capacity to actively participate in the fight against slavery than because the suffering inflicted on them by security forces during

To the Friends of Negro Emancipation, engraved by David Lucas after Alexander Rippingille, 1834. (Courtesy of the Victoria and Albert Museum, London)

crackdowns revealed the imminent collapse of colonial slave societies. Finally, abolitionists presented the repeated eruption of slave uprisings as proof of the need for greater intervention by London in a colonial slaveholding system that made revolt inevitable. In seeming response, in December 1831, the rebellion in Jamaica confirmed abolitionists' recent conviction that slavery should be immediately and completely abolished. Their new argument was that not only was slavery contrary to religion, morality, and humanity, but it was the very source of rebellion.[67]

While planters thought that misconceived evangelism was destabilizing slavery, a growing number of abolitionists, including men and women of all walks of life, believed that it was in fact slavery that contained the seeds of its own destruction. The British Parliament was once again assailed with thousands of antislavery petitions containing nearly 1.5 million signatures; and among working classes, demands for immediate abolition were often juxtaposed with those for social reform and the democratization of suffrage in the United Kingdom. Planters, on the other hand, attempted to highlight their essential contribution to the British Empire's economy—even though that contribution was declining as the empire spread to Asia and conquered new markets in Latin America. Finally, in 1833, Parliament approved the gradual emancipation, as of August 1834, of all 670,000 enslaved men, women, and children in its American colonies, with compensation for their owners.

It was the "Mighty Experiment." In concrete terms, masters were compensated a total of 20 million pounds, in addition to the right to labor performed by their slaves—renamed "apprentices"—for an additional six years, after which the latter would finally be free. The emancipated slaves, however, were in no way compensated for unpaid labor provided since childhood: no earnings or land, yet some hope of education for their children. Although those former slaves would embrace mission youth schools whenever available, beginning in 1835, they themselves had to face the future with nothing but what remained of their capacity to work.[68]

Unenthusiastically greeted by slaves, apprenticeship proved to be quite similar to slavery. Furthermore, some of its instruments, such as the treadmill punishment, a huge roller moved by dozens of whip-driven "apprentices," re-created all the abuses of slavery. Strikes multiplied and discontent mounted. Fearing a new large-scale revolt and increased intervention by Parliament, the majority of colonial assemblies renounced apprenticeship in 1838, thus bringing an end to slavery in British America. Of course, planters devised new forms to subordinate former slaves in the goal of linking them and their children to plantations, thus forcing them to continue their struggle for total freedom.[69] Nonetheless, from that point forward, these men, women, and children were all free.

Epilogue

When I began this diachronic project about slaves' self-liberation across the entirety of the Americas and the Caribbean, I had only one certitude, based on U.S., Latin American, Caribbean, and European historiography since the 1980s: that not only did many slaves attempt to free themselves, but some did so successfully, to the extent that they transformed their societies. Drawing from extensive studies of local, provincial, and national archives on both sides of the Atlantic, much of the published scholarship that served as major inspiration for my critical inventory focused on slaves as historical actors. That "bottom-up" perspective, which this endeavor by definition also entailed, highlighted the pioneering and ongoing role played by slaves in the long struggle against slavery across the American continent and in the Caribbean, from the beginning of the sixteenth century to the end of the revolutionary era. By mapping and organizing slaves' struggles chronologically over more than three centuries, I was able to establish a typology and compare them across time and space.

Many surprises emerged. In particular, it became clear that in the first half of the eighteenth century, another America was being quietly built even as the slave-based sugar plantation appeared to be dominant—an America of vast frontier regions and hinterlands inhabited by the descendants of fugitive slaves who had gradually blended into free populations, and also an America of cities, many of whose inhabitants were emancipated slaves and their offspring ("free people of color"). All those men and women had liberated themselves from slavery, alone or in small groups. Another discovery that emerged from my long-term comparative study was that slaves only revolted en masse on rare occasions, when several equally rare conditions were met. Far from challenging slaves' capacity to take action to shape their own destinies, that discovery reveals that, on the contrary, they had an acute understanding of their environment, waiting for cracks in the system of domination to grow before exploiting them, rather than improvising a rebellion whose outcome was inevitably cruel death.

That explains why enslaved Africans and Afro-descendants seeking to liberate themselves historically tended to choose flight, marronage, and self-purchase. However, after the Seven Years' War, rifts within the slavery system multiplied, offering slaves new opportunities for liberation. Revolt, in particular, became a possibility in the event of revolution, the weakening of planters' positions, or when an abolitionist current likely to support slaves' demands for freedom emerged. As a result, by participating in diverse but autonomous ways in movements that shook up the region from one century to another, slaves were also agents of the general history of the Americas.

My analysis ends in the year 1838, considered to be a turning point in the history of slavery in the Americas. In 1838, under pressure from enslaved populations, all the British colonies in the Americas—the Caribbean islands, including Jamaica, Antigua, Barbados, Trinidad, and many others, as well as Guyana, Belize, and Canada on the continent—did away with the gradual abolition law approved by the British Parliament in 1833 and decreed the immediate emancipation of the 670,000 enslaved men, women, and children living in their combined territories (see chapter 10). An earlier turning point came in 1804 with the Haitian Revolution, which demonstrated that the victims of slavery could defeat that oppressive system. But it also revealed the unique conditions necessary for such a victory. In addition, Haiti, a poor and fragile nation under the threat of French invasion until 1825, was in no position to actively challenge slavery elsewhere, except in neighboring Santo Domingo. In contrast, in 1838, the United Kingdom was the most powerful empire in the world and boasted an indefectible navy. The following year, the British Anti-Slavery Society became the British and Foreign Anti-Slavery Society and promoted the creation of abolitionist societies in Europe and the Americas. The Royal Navy multiplied its actions impeding the slave trade, and British consuls lobbied governments to phase slavery out. That antislavery stance by a major world power dramatically increased the prospects of freedom for the millions of men, women, and children still enslaved in the Americas.

In 1838, however, slavery remained solidly established in colonies belonging to France and the Netherlands, and in the southern United States, Puerto Rico, Cuba, and Brazil; it was still legal though more marginal in most South American republics. Indeed, it would be another fifty years before the last American nation abolished slavery—Brazil, in 1888. That half-century period attests to the predominance of slavery as a labor system and the high capital value slaves represented to their owners. It also reinforces how implausible—and suicidal—it would have been for an enslaved population to attempt to overthrow the "peculiar institution" without any external aid and any significant abolitionist movement.[1] By 1838, enslaved men and women composed the majority of the population only in the French, Dutch, and Danish colonies and in South Carolina. By law, slaves were prohibited from organizing and acquiring the most minimal means, such as money, meeting places, infrastructures, and of course weapons, to tackle the system oppressing them. Yet the abolition of slavery was almost universally the parliamentary result of violent processes such as civil war, European revolutions, or the threat of interregional conflict, in which innumerable slaves actively participated. Abolition was always declared by an executive and/or legislative power, in which slaves (and women) were as a rule excluded from representation while slaveholders held significant leverage. Faced with such an extreme power imbalance, enslaved men and women did what their predecessors had done since the sixteenth century—they adapted the liberation strategies explored in this book to new and changing contexts. Some ran away, while others endeavored to purchase their freedom or that of their loved ones by working additional hours; some enslaved men enlisted in armies in exchange for promised emancipation; and in rare cases, slaves organized major uprisings or rebelled. But as before, whenever cracks appeared in the domination system, notably during civil wars or struggles for independence, many risked—and often lost—their lives after joining and fighting for whichever camp promised or insinuated the possibility of personal freedom and general emancipation.

The impact of the 1838 British emancipation, which freed 670,000 individuals overnight, was therefore immediate in the Atlantic World. Many enslaved men and women were quick to understand its implication and in the subsequent years, thousands escaped from the United States and the French, Dutch, and Spanish islands to seek refuge and obtain freedom in the British Caribbean and Canada.[2] However, other slaveholding territories and nations did not rush to follow suit and end slavery. The first to do so were, in chronological order, the colonial powers of Sweden, Denmark, and France, fifteen years after the British Parliament voted to adopt the 1833 abolition law.[3] In France, abolitionism mirrored the British movement, beginning with the creation of the gradualist and elitist *Société Française pour l'Abolition de l'Esclavage* in 1834. In 1845, the July Monarchy adopted its own version of the British "amelioration of slavery" laws, which, as in British colonies, prompted resistance from slaveowners and effected little change in slaves' daily lives. However, many captives took advantage of certain provisions of that so-called Mackau law: the recognition of slaves' legal capacity and ownership rights, the right to self-purchase for a mutually agreed-upon price, and limits on masters' abuse, as attested to by an increase in self-manumissions and a flurry of legal complaints against abusive masters. As a result, in Guadeloupe, Martinique, and French Guiana, 36,500 slaves had obtained their manumission between 1830 and 1848, and on the eve of emancipation in 1848, between 26 and 34 percent of the Afro-descended populations were free (the remaining being enslaved). Nonetheless, planters' interests would remain unchallenged until the overthrow of the monarchy in February 1848. The Second Republic (1848–52) provided the revolutionary context necessary to bring an end to French slavery. As is widely known, deputy secretary Victor Schœlcher played a leading role in the preparation of France's act of general emancipation (with the stipulation that slaveholders be indemnified) adopted by the French provisional government on 27 April 1848 to become effective two months later. Of course, enslaved workers had no voice in the debate, but in Martinique, for example, they eagerly followed news of the revolution and its calls for emancipation thanks to information carried and shared by seamen and travelers. Martinican slaves held demonstrations in various parishes and on 20 May rallied in Saint-Pierre to demand immediate freedom. The unrest escalated, and on 23 May hundreds of slaves flooded the city, which led to limited destruction and thirty-five deaths. They forced the island's governor to declare the liberation of all Martinique's slaves on that very day, for fear of a general insurrection. Warned of the danger of revolt, the governor of Guadeloupe did the same on 27 May. Enslaved Martinicans and Guadeloupians thus succeeded in imposing immediate emancipation before France's official abolition decree reached both islands; in French Guiana, however, slaves were not emancipated until 10 August, as dictated by the law. As elsewhere, in 1848 the 244,000 French slaves (including 62,000 in Réunion) were freed but not compensated, though the short-lived Second Republic stipulated that public education be provided to their children and granted universal suffrage to all freedmen.[4]

By 1838 in the South American republics (except for Chile, where slavery was abolished in 1823), the number of slaves had dropped by half from the time of independence, and on the whole represented no more than 2 or 3 percent of the entire population. Many enslaved women worked as domestic servants in private, urban homes. Other slaves, both men and women, worked on plantations and mines, often in remote rural zones. That small enslaved population had limited possibilities to effectively and visibly fight for its freedom, especially given that abolitionism in the region was nascent or nonexistent. In fact, in the early 1840s, when the first free-womb children born after independence reached the age when they could be fully emancipated by law, several governments extended that age and reauthorized the slave trade. In general, the abolition of slavery was decreed in the context of the civil wars between liberals and conservatives (or federalists and centralists) that erupted in almost every South American republic between the late 1830s and the early 1850s. As during the wars of independence, those conflicts provided enslaved men with a chance to obtain their freedom if they were willing to enlist with one of the warring factions, with or without their masters' consent. In several cases, it was political leaders' calls to arms directed at slaves that prompted the abolition of slavery. For example, one camp would issue a decree granting freedom to those who joined its army, as well as to their families, prompting the opposing faction to respond with a broader declaration emancipating all the slaves in the republic. There was then no turning back, as enslaved populations invariably continued to fight for their liberation until abolition took effect. Hundreds of men enlisted, while plantation and mine workers took advantage of the turmoil of the civil wars to disrupt production, mutiny, and/or flee, individually or in groups, thus increasing rural unrest. In Peru in 1851, notably, hundreds of slaves from twelve estates in the Chicama Valley marched on the city of Trujillo denouncing their owners' abuses and demanding their emancipation.

Each time slavery was abolished in Hispanic South America, liberal governments were responsible: Montevideo in 1842, Colombia in 1851, Uruguay and Argentina (except in the province of Buenos Aires) in 1853, and Peru and Venezuela in 1854.[5] Particularly in Colombia, abolition mobilized the citizenry more than in the other South American republics. In 1848, in the wake of the European revolutions, a new generation of liberals there formed multiracial democratic clubs that demanded abolition as well as universal male suffrage. Following the liberals' electoral victory in 1849, Colombia's congress revitalized the provincial manumission juntas created in 1821 through increased funding and fixed emancipation prices. In May 1851, it approved a law that emancipated all enslaved Colombians as of January 1, 1852. Slaves speeded up the process by demanding that the juntas grant their manumission, to the extent that in 1851—before the law took effect—some 5,000 slaves out of a total of 16,468—had obtained their freedom, often in agreement with their masters.[6] In Argentina, by contrast, abolition did not become a popular demand and was merely limited to article 15 in the 1853 constitution, which stated "there are no slaves in the nation" and freed any remaining slaves while indemnifying their masters. Until his defeat in 1852, Argentina's dictator Juan Manuel de Rosas (1835–52) simultaneously imported African slaves, endorsed their ethnically based mutual aid societies, and courted enslaved men by enlisting them in his army, eventually emancipating and/or promoting some to officer ranks. That paternalistic policy generated support for Rosas among enslaved and free Afro-Argentinians (26 percent of Buenos Aires's population in 1836), while complicating his opponents' efforts to recruit them. In 1853 federalists unenthusiastically included the abolition of slavery in a new constitution that promoted subsidized European immigration as a means of marginalizing nonwhites. Slaves in Buenos Aires were not affected by constitutional emancipation until 1861, when the province joined the Confederation. In all likelihood, any enslaved Argentinians remaining at that point were either very old or discreetly passing for free.[7]

Unlike in the South American republics, in the United States, the 1838 British general emancipation came at a time when the issue of slavery was more contentious than ever. By 1840, slavery had profoundly divided the nation between free-soil northern states and southern states based on slave labor. With the expansion of the territory to the South and the West, the question of the legality of slavery became more critical each time a new state was formed and joined the Union. In the South, about one-third of the population (nearly 2.5

million persons in 1840) was enslaved. Southern slaves, never in a position to directly challenge the "peculiar institution," continued to try to gain freedom through flight, to the extent that the abolitionist networks that brought them to northern states and Canada were collectively dubbed the Underground Railroad. Congress's adoption of the 1850 Fugitive Slave Act, which authorized the federal government to capture suspected fugitive slaves on the sole basis of masters' claims of ownership and which criminalized officials, communities, and individuals who assisted or failed to report runaways, jeopardized the freedom of every fugitive slave and even that of free African Americans. The law also provided a chilling reminder of the realities of slavery to those living in free-soil states, notably through the terror instilled by slave catchers, which radicalized abolitionists and strengthened black communities' resistance. And despite the law, some slaves from the South were able to successfully escape to freedom alone or in small groups or families.[8]

The U.S. Civil War, which pitted Confederate slave states against free-soil and nonsecessionist slave states between 1861 and 1865, provided unprecedented occasions for African American captives to free themselves, still primarily through flight, and to contribute to the abolition of slavery. During the first year of the conflict, President Abraham Lincoln and the U.S. Congress claimed that the war was about the Union, not slavery, and refused to enlist free African American volunteers. But by the summer of 1862, tens of thousands of slaves had fled behind Union lines. In accordance with the Fugitive Slave Act, those men and women were considered property confiscated from the enemy (their Confederate owners) under the official label of "contraband" and were progressively put to work in army camps in need of manual laborers and domestic servants. Fugitives who belonged to masters in nonsecessionist slave states, however, were to be returned to their rightful owners. But in reality, among the many African American refugees arriving daily, Union military commanders were unable to distinguish between the legally free and the runaway slave or, beyond that, determine whether runaways were the property of a Confederate or a Unionist. Some in the Union government and the army became increasingly receptive to the mounting voices of African American activists, among them Frederick Douglass and Harriet Tubman, and leading abolitionists in the North, who advocated black enlistment and saw the abolition of slavery as the war's primary objective.

Whereas the endless stream of runaway slaves to Union camps was somewhat reminiscent of their predecessors' flight to the British during the U.S. War of Independence, the deciding factor that prompted President Lincoln and Congress to reverse their position on black recruitment evokes Bolívar's argument to enlist slaves in 1820: given the army's mounting losses of white soldiers, it was deemed necessary to enlist slaves, for fear that their numbers would otherwise become unmanageable. There was one major difference, however: Bolívar's racially integrated army was largely composed of men of African and Native American descent, with a minority of whites, compared to an overwhelmingly white Union army, which eventually chose to include fugitive slaves and free African Americans in separate units and under white command. In April 1862, Congress issued the Compensated Emancipation Act, which freed slaves in the district of Washington while compensating their owners. Next, in July, it decreed slaves belonging to disloyal masters "forever free of their servitude" and employable by the army in any needed capacities. On September 27, 1862, Lincoln issued a limited Emancipation Proclamation that only applied to secessionist states as of January 1, 1863. However, when the proclamation was publicly released in early 1863, enslaved men and women understood it as a general decree: they believed they were "forever free." Slaves in the South, often traveling in families, flocked behind Union lines in large numbers and, as the Union army advanced, from farther and farther south. By 1864, as many as 1 million out of a total of nearly 4 million enslaved African Americans had escaped to Union-controlled territory. In the meantime, northern free blacks were permitted to enlist in segregated Union units. A total of nearly two hundred thousand African American men, most of them fugitives from slave states, served in the Union army and navy, while some three hundred thousand men and women, overwhelmingly runaways, contributed to the war effort as manual workers, porters, nurses, domestic servants, or spies. In addition, increasingly restive slaves still in the South weakened the institution of slavery from within. Nonetheless, the bloodiest war in U.S. history would rage on until the Union victory in April 1865. In December, the Thirteenth Amendment to the U.S. Constitution cemented the abolition of slavery and declared the freedom of the almost 4 million enslaved African Americans registered in 1860. One of the few general emancipations to be decreed in the Americas without providing compensation to slaveholders, the amendment was unique in its attempt to offer comprehensive support to the formerly enslaved population—Reconstruction in the South. Intended to assist African Americans as they began to build their postslavery lives, the program was abandoned in the 1870s, leaving them alone to face former slaveowners.[9]

The year 1865, with the abolition of slavery in the United States, which had the largest enslaved population in the mid-nineteenth century, was therefore another turning point in the demise of the "peculiar institution." Yet the U.S. Civil War appears to have minimally influenced the near-simultaneous decision by the Netherlands to abolish slavery in 1863. After the 1838 British and the 1848 French general emancipations, countless slaves in the Dutch Leeward islands escaped by sea to free territories; those on St. Martin were granted de facto emancipation in 1848 to prevent their flight to the French side of the island. Between the 1830s and 1863, the Dutch government imposed "amelioration" policies on planters that were more effective than in other colonies due to their duration and to enslaved workers' successful attempts to obtain time to cultivate their own provision gardens, fish and hunt, and sell their produce to markets and plantations. As a result, in 1863, when the forty-five thousand slaves in the Dutch West Indies were freed (and their owners compensated), slavery had already lost much of its importance in Curaçao and on other islands, where slaves then accounted for one-third of the population. In Suriname, the largest Dutch colony, which had a numerous enslaved population representing 55 percent of the total number of inhabitants, abolition came with a ten-year apprentice period during which Asian indentured workers were also brought to the colony.[10]

By 1865, Spain was alone among the colonial powers to maintain slavery, in Puerto Rico and Cuba, as was Brazil among the independent nations. Since 1838, many slaves in those three territories had continued to escape, often forming entrenched palenques and quilombos in mountainous zones, interior regions, and even cities. Enslaved men and women also continued to buy freedom for themselves and their children. Brief and isolated mutinies broke out, at times successfully allowing rebels to flee and at others prompting rapid suppression. However, in Cuba in 1844, Spanish authorities implemented an extraordinary cycle of terror reminiscent of the brutal repression of alleged slave plots in the 1730s (see chapter 4). Following three violent slave uprisings in the sugar region of Matanzas, they claimed to have discovered a broad antislavery conspiracy involving plantation and urban slaves and free people of color and masterminded by British abolitionists. In what came to be known as the Year of the Lash, officials arrested over four thousand people, tortured hundreds to death while extracting confessions, used firing squads, quartering, or decapitation to execute seventy-six enslaved and free men of African descent, one white man, and one enslaved woman (many of whose heads would be publicly displayed afterward), sentenced 1,200 free and enslaved black men and women to prison, banished over 430 free people of color, and issued new slave and black codes.[11] That horrific repression decimated the island's small Afro-Cuban intellectual and professional elite and petrified slaves for the next two decades. At a time when the black and mulatto population (74 percent of them enslaved) represented 58 percent of Cuba's residents, it also convinced white planters, fearful of "another Haiti," to supplement the importation of enslaved Africans with that of Chinese indentured laborers (125,000 in 1847–74).

The institution of slavery in Cuba and Puerto Rico only began to weaken after the abolition of U.S. slavery in 1865, which ended slave imports to Cuba and destroyed any lingering hopes, particularly among Cuban slaveowning planters, of seeing slavery protected by the island's annexation to the slaveholding South. In Spain, the *Sociedad Abolicionista Española* was created on Puerto Rican initiative, and in 1868 the monarchy was overthrown, leading to six years of relative democracy in which the Cortes passed the 1870 free-womb Moret Law to be implemented in Cuba and Puerto Rico. However, in response to Puerto Rican abolitionists, in 1873, the Cortes decreed the emancipation of the 29,335 slaves registered in Puerto Rico, with indemnities to be paid to their masters and obligatory three-year work contracts with their former owners or others.[12] The Moret Law reached Cuba in the midst of its first war of independence from Spain (the Ten Years' War [1868–78]). It had little impact on the eastern provinces of Santiago de Cuba and Puerto Príncipe, where by 1870 Cuban separatists had established a provisional republican government that promised freedom to slaves. As in other wars examined in this book, in 1868 the white Cuban planters who launched the independence struggle manumitted their male slaves to enlist them in their army, but only envisioned partial or gradual emancipation with indemnification at the end of the war. As enslaved men, women, and families began to escape in large numbers to the territories held by separatist rebels, the latter proclaimed that "all inhabitants of the Republic are entirely free," while subjecting fugitive slaves to the tutelage of *patronos* and assigning most of them (and all women) to agricultural labor and some men to military service, as in Saint Domingue under Sonthonax in 1793 (see chapter 6). Again as occurred in Saint Domingue, freed slaves in eastern Cuba pressed for and obtained full freedom, backed by the increasingly powerful and numerous free black and mulatto soldiers and commanders in the proindependence army, even as the region continued to attract freedom-seeking slaves from Cuba's central sugar-producing regions. In this context, the 1870 Moret Law attempted to curb that slave exodus by offering gradual abolition while simultaneously retaining planters' loyalty to Spain. Though the law failed to convince slaves, many of whom continued to flee eastward, it secured support for Spanish rule among the immense majority of Cuban planters. The latter's attachment to slavery prevented the proindependence insurgency from spreading beyond the eastern provinces, though the war nonetheless ended in a stalemate. An 1878 peace treaty granted permanent freedom to the enslaved men who had fought, voluntarily or not, with the Spanish, as well as to all enslaved men, women, and children who had joined the rebels, in what was quite a significant victory for those fugitive slaves.

Nevertheless, Cuba maintained slavery and, with Brazil, became one of the two remaining slaveholding territories in the Western Hemisphere. Pressure for abolition increased abroad and at home, notably from Afro-Cuban veterans of the Ten Years' War, such as Gen. Antonio Maceo, and members of the renascent Afro-Cuban intelligentsia, notably Juan Gualberto Gómez, who was born a plantation slave but whose enslaved parents paid for his manumission as a child, and who, like Douglass in the United States, mobilized for abolition and racial equality through a newspaper he founded. In 1880, the Spanish Cortes approved an abolition law that declared all slaves to be *patrocinados* (apprentices) while subjecting them to an eight-year period of tutelage during which they were required to work for their masters at no charge, thus ending slavery in 1888. Once again, enslaved men and women used the law's adoption to negotiate their manumission with their owners and free themselves before 1888. As a result of both slave escapes during the Ten Years' War and manumission, in addition to the natural and free-womb demographic decline, Cuba's enslaved population fell from a total of 368,550 in 1862 to 199,094 at the end of the war in 1877, 99,566 in 1883, and 25,381 in 1886. The fact that by 1886 *patrocinados* had fallen to one-quarter of their number three years earlier demonstrates a collective will to fight for and obtain their liberation. At that date, with so few remaining *patrocinados*, most of whom were female servants, Spain decreed the definitive abolition of slavery in Cuba.[13]

Two years later, in 1888, Brazil, which alone imported 43 percent of the 10,538,000 African captives brought to the Americas through the slave trade over three centuries, finally brought a definitive end to legal slavery in the Americas. As in Cuba, the gradual demise of Brazilian slavery was accelerated by a free-womb law in 1871, with a state-supported emancipation fund. But unlike in most of the Americas, in Brazil, war seldom offered liberation opportunities to enslaved men, either during the process of independence or during the Paraguayan war (1864–70), although during the latter, 7,000 slaves (out of 90,000 soldiers) were forcibly conscripted after being granted state-compensated manumission by their owners. The proportion of slaves in Brazil's total population decreased, from about 30 percent in 1850 to 15 percent in 1872, when slaves totaled 1.5 million. Sensing an imminent end to slavery, more and more enslaved men and women purchased their freedom and used legal tactics to denounce their masters' abuses. Enslaved mothers of free-womb children were particularly active in claiming their offspring's rights and, when they managed to manumit themselves, in demanding parental rights over their children. Unrest and refusals to work hampered production in many fazendas throughout Brazil. Slaves increasingly fled to both hinterlands and cities to find refuge within free communities of predominantly African descent; at times, all the slaves from a given plantation would collectively denounce mistreatment by their owner to police in the nearest town.[14] In the 1880s, widespread slave flight, coupled with popular abolitionism, further paved the way for Brazil's general emancipation decree.

Indeed, as in the 1830s in the British Empire, abolition in Brazil mobilized tens of thousands of slaves and free citizens behind the common goal of destroying slavery. Unparalleled in any non-Anglophone region in the Americas, the Brazilian abolitionist movement that emerged in 1880 with the creation of the Brazilian Anti-Slavery Society by elite whites and middle-class Afro-Brazilians successfully organized grassroots abolitionist networks that included journalists, artists, dock and railroad workers, and ordinary men and women in street demonstrations, public performances, and active support to fugitive slaves. One of the movement's emblematic victories was the first provincial abolition of slavery, in Ceará in 1884, thanks to the popular mobilization led by Rio de Janeiro journalist José Carlos do Patrocínio, himself born to a young enslaved mother and a Catholic priest. The provinces of Goiás and Amazonas followed suit in 1885. In São Paolo, workers went on strike until the neighboring port of Santos declared itself free of slavery, after which it rapidly attracted ten thousand slave runaways; other towns also created free zones that welcomed fugitives. By that time, Brazil was becoming a patchwork of free and slave provinces and municipalities, and slaves, alone, in families, or in large groups, could count on an "Overground Railroad" that transported them to safe havens free of charge. Initially peaceful, the swelling slave exodus prompted occasional conflicts. However, slaveholders were unable to obtain official protection for their human property because of growing abolitionist sentiment. By 1887, ten of Brazil's twenty provinces had abolished slavery, and the enslaved population had dropped from 1 million in 1885 to 637,600. Rather than face the risk of civil war, in May 1888 the Parliament voted, with a large majority, to adopt the abolition of Brazil's slavery without compensation for slaveowners.[15]

⇌ Remarkably, despite a widely variable context, particularly after 1838, the liberation strategies implemented by enslaved men and women in the Americas beginning in the early sixteenth century remained quite similar until the end of slavery in 1888. During that long period, on both the American continent and the Caribbean islands, as this book has shown, many more slaves were able to liberate themselves from slavery than previously estimated. Of course, it is impossible to quantify those acts of self-liberation. There is no doubt, however, that they numbered in the hundreds of thousands, probably millions. Slaves primarily obtained their liberation through flight, though they also purchased their freedom through diverse means, or by combining those strategies. For nearly three centuries, they waged that battle alone, lacking defenders in colonial society and without any hope of bringing an end to the institution of slavery. But at the end of the eighteenth century, enslaved men, women, and children began to find allies in abolitionist and certain Protestant circles. In Saint Domingue, slaves were able to launch a protracted but ultimately successful insurrection in the wake of the 1789 French Revolution. The wars of independence and clashes between empires in the Caribbean also advantaged the emancipation of slaves, often due more to military expedience than any humanist conviction.

In 1838, however, once slavery had been definitively abolished in the United Kingdom's colonies, the system remained solidly established in most of the Americas. In order to liberate themselves, slaves on the continent and in the

Caribbean had to rely on themselves first and foremost. Even though various national narratives have long attributed the end of American slavery, between 1848 and 1888, to white individuals—Victor Schœlcher, Abraham Lincoln, and Princess Isabel of Brazil, among others—who signed decrees of permanent abolition, many slaves in those territories had won their freedom long before through self-purchase, flight, or military enlistment. And as was the case in 1838 for slaves in British colonies, those who were emancipated following those decrees had in essence purchased their freedom from their masters at the price of countless years of unpaid labor. Of course, abolitionists and their parliamentary allies aided enslaved populations by advocating for an end to the institution of slavery. But in most cases, to do so they agreed to indemnify slaveholders for the loss of their human property, while failing to compensate the newly freed for unpaid labor provided since childhood. Across the map and throughout the history of the Americas, emancipated men and women found themselves facing the future without support, equipped solely with what remained of their capacity to work and the hopes they had placed in freedom.

Notes

Introduction

1. That said, I do mention individual or collective suicides that occurred during the suppression of several slave revolts and conspiracies. Though the phenomenon was sufficiently serious to merit punishment by special laws, slave suicides have yet to be the subject of a comparative study. They have, however, been highlighted by many historians. For specific cases, see T. L. Snyder, *The Power to Die*; Bell, *We Shall Be No More*, 201–46; Pérez, *To Die in Cuba*, 25–64.
2. A. O. Thompson, *Flight to Freedom*, 127–29.
3. Blackburn, introduction, 3; Klein, *African Slavery in Latin America*, 229–30.
4. Graden, *From Slavery to Freedom in Brazil*, 199.
5. See Wheatley, *Poems on Various Subjects*; Prince, *The History of Mary Prince*; Equiano, *The Interesting Narrative of the Life of Olaudah Equiano*. Slave narratives multiplied in the United States after 1831, as shown in Gates, *The Classic Slave Narratives*. Among non-Anglophone slaves, only Juan Francisco Manzano, from Cuba, wrote his autobiography, of which only the first half has been found; it was first published in English in 1840 in a redrafted version translated by British abolitionist Richard Madden, and the original Spanish manuscript was published in Cuba in 1937 (Manzano, *Autobiografía del esclavo poeta*).
6. For a review of pre-1930 studies on slavery, see Kolchin, *American Slavery*, 273–77; Zeuske, "Historiography and Research Problems of Slavery," 90–93; Gisler, *L'esclavage aux Antilles françaises*, xii–xiv.
7. Du Bois, *Black Reconstruction in America*.
8. Aptheker, *The Negro in the Civil War*; Aptheker, *American Negro Slave Revolts*.
9. James, *The Black Jacobins*.
10. Freyre, *Casa-grande e senzala*; Ortiz, *Contrapunteo cubano del tabaco y el azúcar*; Herskovits, *The Myth of the Negro Past*.
11. Tannenbaum, *Slave and Citizen*.
12. Stampp, *The Peculiar Institution*; Elkins, *Slavery*.
13. For two seminal works, see Blassingame, *The Slave Community*; Genovese, *Roll, Jordan, Roll*.
14. See, notably, Moreno Fraginals, *El ingenio*; Fernandes, *A integração do negro na sociedade de classes*.
15. For example, Degler, *Neither Black nor White*; Cohen and Greene, *Neither Slave nor Free*; Hoetink, *Slavery and Race Relations in the Americas*.
16. For pioneer studies in this field, see Bastide, *Les Amériques noires*; Knight, *The African Dimension in Latin American Societies*.
17. E. E. Williams, *Capitalism and Slavery*; Hart, *Slaves Who Abolished Slavery*; Beckles, *Black Rebellion in Barbados*. See also Price, *Maroon Societies*.

18. Fouchard, *Les marrons de la liberté*.

19. Surinamese historian Anton de Kom pioneered such studies with *Wij slaven van Suriname* (1934), published in a German translation in Moscow in 1935. For later works, see Groot, *Van isolatie naar integratie*; Price, *The Guiana Maroons*.

20. Gaspar and Geggus, *A Turbulent Time*.

21. One of the first studies with a transnational scope was Curtin, *The Atlantic Slave Trade*. The first one to use the term "African diaspora" is V. B. Thompson, *The Making of the African Diaspora*; see also Gilroy, *The Black Atlantic*.

22. Patterson, *The Sociology of Slavery*, 260–83.

23. Genovese, *From Rebellion to Revolution*.

24. Moreno Fraginals, "Aportes culturales y deculturación."

25. For instance, Mattoso, *Ser escravo no Brasil*, 174–78, or, more recently, Barcia, *Seeds of Insurrection*.

26. Craton, *Testing the Chains*. See also M. Mullin, *Africa in America*.

27. In addition to the works by Aptheker, Hart, Beckles, and Craton cited above, see also Gaspar, *Bondmen and Rebels*; Handler, "Slave Revolts and Conspiracies."

28. J. C. Scott, *Weapons of the Weak*; J. C. Scott, *Domination and the Arts of Resistance*.

29. Costa, *Crowns of Glory*.

30. White, *Ar'n't I a Woman?*

31. Lovejoy, *Transformations in Slavery*; Thornton, *Africa and Africans in the Making of the Atlantic World*.

32. Klein and Luna, *Slavery in Brazil*, 207–8.

Chapter 1

1. This source, *Voyages: The Trans-Atlantic Slave Trade Database*, is the most complete to date and available at www.slavevoyages.org. All figures in this book are from this source unless stipulated otherwise, referred to as *Voyages* (www.slavevoyages.org/tast/assessment/estimates.faces).

2. Lovejoy, *Transformations in Slavery*, 46–67, 140–51; Morgan, "The Cultural Implications of the Atlantic Slave Trade."

3. Less studied and documented than the transatlantic (or Euro-Christian) slave trade, the trans-Saharan and eastern (or Arab-Muslim) trades probably deported over 14 million Africans through the Sahara, the Red Sea and the Indian Ocean between the seventeenth and the end of the nineteenth centuries, of whom some 3 million died along the way (Etemad, *Crimes et réparations*, 136).

4. Lovejoy, *Transformations in Slavery*; Eltis and Richardson, "West Africa and the Transatlantic Slave Trade"; Eltis, "The Volume and Structure of the Transatlantic Slave Trade." On the historiography of the trade, see J. W. Sweet, "The Subject of the Slave Trade."

5. According to *Voyages*, a total of 1,954,420 African captives perished during the Atlantic crossing.

6. Sheridan, *Doctors and Slaves*; E. R. Taylor, *If We Must Die*; Chandler, *Health and Slavery in Colonial Colombia*. On the social and spiritual impact of the slave trade on captives in Africa and during the Atlantic crossing, see V. Brown, *The Reaper's Garden*, 24–48.

7. J. C. Miller, *Way of Death*, 440–41. The estimates of slaves' death rate, from capture in Africa to adaptation in the Americas, varies from 70 percent (Postma, *The Dutch in the Atlantic Slave Trade*, 258) to much lower rates (Klein, *The Atlantic Slave Trade*, 154–58); see also Etemad, *Crimes et réparations*, 135–52.

8. D. B. Davis, *Slavery and Human Progress*, 73. The predominance of young adult men in the Atlantic slave trade stemmed from both American demand and African supply. Women,

enslaved or free, were in high demand in Africa, where they performed a large portion of agricultural labor and which had many polygamous societies. Children, who were greatly prized locally and by the Saharan and Arab slave trades, were also in high demand (Klein, *African Slavery in Latin America*, 147–48).

9. According to *Voyages*, 64.6 percent of the total of deported Africans were male, and 20.1 percent, children.

10. The islands of Aruba, Curaçao, and Bonaire, as well as three Lesser Antilles (St. Martin, St. Eustatius, and Saba) belonged to the Netherlands, those of St. Croix, St. Thomas, and St. John (Virgin Islands), to Denmark, and Saint Barthélemy, to Sweden.

11. Situated in a region neglected by the colonial powers until around 1650, the Guianas included French Guiana around Cayenne. Control of Suriname and Guiana (Essequibo, Demerara, and Berbice) was disputed by the British and the Dutch until the beginning of the nineteenth century. Suriname then officially became a Dutch colony and Guiana, a British one. For more on Dutch slave trafficking to these colonies, see Postma, *The Dutch in the Atlantic Slave Trade*, 174–95, 211–21.

12. *Voyages*.

13. Historians estimate that some 20 percent of Africans brought to Jamaica, or approximately 200,000 individuals out of 1,019,596, were reexported. When taking that surplus into account, non-Brazilian continental America absorbed 14 percent (and not 12.1 percent) of all imported Africans (Curtin, *The Atlantic Slave Trade*, 25–26).

14. *Voyages*.

15. *Voyages*. Despite the abolition of the slave trade by Denmark (1803), the United Kingdom (1807), and the United States (1808), the Danish and British Caribbean as well as Southern U.S. ports illegally imported thousands of enslaved Africans until the 1820s.

16. Bernand, *Negros esclavos y libres*, 12–20, 29–57.

17. Bennett, *Africans in Colonial Mexico*, 30–32; Bryant, "Finding Gold, Forming Slavery." See also, on the nineteenth century, Graham, *House and Street*; Fox-Genovese, *Within the Plantation Household*. Even in eighteenth-century Great Britain, possession of enslaved Africans as domestic servants indicated membership in the high nobility (Frey, *Water from the Rock*, 73).

18. Lockhart and Schwartz, *Early Latin America*, 17–29; Klein, *African Slavery in Latin America*, 16–20; Restall, "Black Conquistadors."

19. Calvo, *L'Amérique ibérique*, 28–33.

20. Lockhart and Schwartz, *Early Latin America*, 65–72, 86–121; Calvo, *L'Amérique ibérique*, 67–103.

21. *Voyages*.

22. Bowser, *The African Slave in Colonial Peru*; Klein, *African Slavery in Latin America*, 28–33; Bernand, *Negros esclavos y libres*, 99–100.

23. Klein, *African Slavery in Latin America*, 21–43; Carroll, *Blacks in Colonial Veracruz*, 21–39; Restall, *The Black Middle*; Herrera, "'Porque no sabemos firmar.'"

24. Bryant, "Finding Gold, Forming Slavery"; Acosta Saignes, *Vida de los esclavos negros en Venezuela*, 143–46, 235–36.

25. *Voyages*; Schwartz, *Sugar Plantations in the Formation of Brazilian Society*, 3–202.

26. See Emmer, *The Dutch Slave Trade*.

27. *Voyages*.

28. Klein, *African Slavery in Latin America*, 50–51; Handler and Sio, "Barbados," 218; Jordan and Walsh, *White Cargo*; *Voyages*.

29. D. Hall, "Jamaica," 194.

30. Klein, *African Slavery in Latin America*, 56–57; C. L. Miller, *The French Atlantic Triangle*, 30.

31. Debien, *Les esclaves aux Antilles françaises*, 374; V. Brown, *The Reaper's Garden*, 56, 188.

32. *Voyages*.

33. *Voyages*; Klein, *African Slavery in Latin America*, 67–88; Sharp, *Slavery on the Spanish Frontier*.

34. *Voyages*; Berlin, *Many Thousands Gone*, table 1, 369–71.

35. Berlin, *Many Thousands Gone*, 29–46, 109–41, 369; *Voyages*.

36. Berlin, *Many Thousands Gone*, 64–76, 142–76, 370; *Voyages*.

37. Berlin, *Many Thousands Gone*, 47–63, 177–94, 369; *Voyages*.

38. Winks, *The Blacks in Canada*, 1–11.

39. In 1777, Spain liberalized slave imports into Louisiana, which had a population of 20,773 enslaved and 18,737 free inhabitants in 1788, and 24,264 enslaved and 19,852 free inhabitants in 1800. See G. M. Hall, *Africans in Colonial Louisiana*, 10, 279; Vidal, "Africains et Européens au pays des Illinois," 51–68; Berlin, *Many Thousands Gone*, 370.

40. *Voyages*; Postma, *The Dutch in the Atlantic Slave Trade*, 182–95; Price, *The Guiana Maroons*, 7–9; Stipriaan, *Surinaams contrast*, 104; D. B. Davis, *Slavery and Human Progress*, 98–99.

41. *Voyages*; Curtin, *The Atlantic Slave Trade*, 216, 234.

42. Eltis, *The Rise of African Slavery*, 232.

43. Berlin, *Many Thousands Gone*, 308–9.

44. Faragher et al., *To 1877*, 297–306.

45. Faragher et al., *To 1877*, 297–306.

46. *Voyages*; Geggus, *Haitian Revolutionary Studies*, 5–8; Geggus, "Sugar and Coffee Cultivation."

47. Thomas, *Cuba*, 47–69; Helg, *Liberty and Equality*, 55–56, 85.

48. Thomas, *Cuba*, 72–84.

49. Thomas, *Cuba*, 169.

50. Paquette, *Sugar Is Made with Blood*, 131.

51. R. J. Scott, *Slave Emancipation in Cuba*, 10.

52. As a result, free people of color, who accounted for about 20 percent of Cuba's total population between 1774 and 1817, reached their lowest level in 1841, when they represented only 15 percent of the total. See U.S. War Department, *Report on the Census of Cuba*, 97–98.

53. R. J. Scott, *Slave Emancipation in Cuba*, 29.

54. Bethell and Carvalho, "Brazil from Independence to the Middle of the Nineteenth Century," 679.

55. Klein, *African Slavery in Latin America*, 129. After 1851, Brazil imported 984 additional slaves in 1852 and 320 in 1856 (*Voyages*).

56. Costa, *The Brazilian Empire*, 128–35, 144–47.

57. Klein, *African Slavery in Latin America*, 126–30.

58. Klein, "Nineteenth-Century Brazil," 314.

59. Kinsbruner, *Not of Pure Blood*, 28–31; Schmidt-Nowara, *Empire and Antislavery*, 38.

60. Klein, *African Slavery in Latin America*, 109–11; C[hevalier], "Peuplement et population de la Guadeloupe," 137.

61. Curtin, *The Atlantic Slave Trade*, 59; D. Hall, "Jamaica," 194; Holt, *The Problem of Freedom*, 118–19.

62. Andrews, *The Afro-Argentines*, 24–26, 29–41. A total of twenty-seven thousand enslaved Africans were disembarked in Rio de la Plata between 1791 and 1810, and still thirty-eight hundred between 1821 and 1840, after independence, when the slave trade was illegal (*Voyages*).

63. Mam-Lam-Fouck, *La Guyane française au temps de l'esclavage*, 118; *Voyages*.

64. Klein, *African Slavery in Latin America*, 130–36; Cohen and Greene, *Neither Slave nor Free*, appendix, table A-3, 336; Higman, *Slave Populations of the British Caribbean*, 47.

65. Morris, *Southern Slavery and the Law*, 43–49.

66. Lucena, *Les Codes noirs hispaniques*; Régent, *La France et ses esclaves*, 64–69; Wiecek, "The Statutory Law of Slavery and Race," 263–64.

67. Bowser, "Colonial Spanish America," 19–38; Klein, *African Slavery in Latin America*, 217–41.

68. Cohen and Greene, introduction.

69. Furthermore, the child of a black and a mulatto was called a "sambo" in the British colonies and a "griffe" or "câpre" in the French Antilles; the child of a white and a quadroon, a "mustee" and a "mamelouk," respectively (Vidal, "Church, Métissage, and the Language of Race in the Mississippi Colony," 139–40).

70. Helg, "La limpieza de sangre bajo las reformas borbónicas"; Klein, *African Slavery in Latin America*, 217–41.

71. See Cohen and Greene, *Neither Slave nor Free*.

Chapter 2

1. J. H. Sweet, *Recreating Africa*, 50.

2. Eltis, *The Rise of African Slavery*, 228–33; J. C. Miller, *Way of Death*, 408–10.

3. Bowser, *The African Slave in Colonial Peru*, 191–95; Lavallé, "Violence esclavagiste et marronnage à Trujillo (Pérou)"; Wood, *Black Majority*, 239–68; Berlin, *Many Thousands Gone*, 70; Bly, "'Pretends He Can Read.'"

4. In nineteenth-century Jamaica, the mortality rate was higher among whites than among blacks, due notably to yellow fever and malaria, and reached 10 percent or more each year, but was compensated by the constant arrival of English, Irish, and Scottish immigrants as well as Jews from Brazil and Suriname (V. Brown, *The Reaper's Garden*, 13, 17).

5. A. O. Thompson, *Flight to Freedom*, 40–78.

6. Price, introduction, 1–2.

7. Price, introduction, 1–2; Maestri, *L'esclavage au Brésil*, 160; Aptheker, "Maroons within the Present Limits of the United States"; V. B. Thompson, *The Making of the African Diaspora*, 273–87; Hoogbergen, *The Boni Maroon Wars in Suriname*, 10. For recent research on marronage, see Moomou and members of APFOM, *Sociétés marronnes des Amériques*.

8. Price, introduction, 2.

9. Acosta Saignes, *Vida de los esclavos negros en Venezuela*, 293–96; Patterson, *The Sociology of Slavery*, 267.

10. Palmer, *Slaves of the White God*, 122–24; Acosta Saignes, *Vida de los esclavos negros en Venezuela*, 249–59; Bowser, *The African Slave in Colonial Peru*, 187–91; Tardieu, *Cimarrones de Panamá*; Landers, *Black Society in Spanish Florida*, 10–17.

11. Acosta Saignes, *Vida de los esclavos negros en Venezuela*, 254–61.

12. Navarrete, "Los palenques," 84–85; Landers, *Black Society in Spanish Florida*, 17–18.

13. Bowser, *The African Slave in Colonial Peru*, 176–78.

14. Acosta Saignes, *Vida de los esclavos negros en Venezuela*, 251–59; Palmer, *Slaves of the White God*, 123–26.

15. Demazière, *Les cultures noires d'Amérique centrale*, 64–73; Acosta Saignes, *Vida de los esclavos negros en Venezuela*, 249–59; Beatty-Medina, "Between the Cross and the Sword"; Bowser, *The African Slave in Colonial Peru*, 187–91.

16. Guy and Sheridan, *Contested Ground*.

17. Palmer, *Slaves of the White God*, 128–31; Davidson, "Negro Slave Control and Resistance in Colonial Mexico," 92–98; Landers, "*Cimarrón* and Citizen," 121–32 (quote p. 134).

18. Vignaux, *Esclavage et rébellion*, 133–35.

19. Borrego Plá, *Palenques de negros en Cartagena de Indias*; Navarrete, *Cimarrones y palenques en el siglo XVII*, 64–114; Vignaux, *Esclavage et rébellion*, 204–74.

20. Schwartz, *Slaves, Peasants and Rebels*, 103–36; Reis, "Quilombos e revoltas escravas no Brasil," 16–20.

21. Count Dom Pedro de Almeida to the king, 20 April 1719, quoted in Conrad, *Children of God's Fire*, 396.

22. Guimarães, *Uma negação da ordem escravista*; Higgins, *"Licentious Liberty" in a Brazilian Gold-Mining Region*, 176–79.

23. Russell-Wood, *Slavery and Freedom in Colonial Brazil*, 124–26; Reis, "Quilombos e revoltas escravas no Brasil," 20–21; Cotta, "Les compagnies de mulâtres et de noirs libertos," 159–62; Higgins, *"Licentious Liberty" in a Brazilian Gold-Mining Region*, 179–90.

24. "The Code Noir"; Christian, *Black Saga*, 19, 27–28. For an analysis of Louis XIV's Code Noir, see Le Guern, "Une chose baptisée?"

25. Beckles, "From Land to Sea"; Gaspar, *Bondmen and Rebels*, 204–7; N. A. T. Hall, *Slave Society in the Danish West Indies*, 124–38. On the sugar revolution in Barbados slave plantations in the late 1640s, see Higman, "The Sugar Revolution."

26. Patterson, "Slavery and Slave Revolts."

27. Patterson, *The Sociology of Slavery*, 97.

28. Patterson, *The Sociology of Slavery*, 267–70.

29. Craton, *Testing the Chains*, 67–96; Campbell, *The Maroons of Jamaica*. For a study based on oral narratives by descendants of the Windward maroons, see Bilby, *True-Born Maroons*.

30. Sainton and Ho-Fong-Choy, "Le processus d'occupation des Petites Antilles," 249–50.

31. Debien, "Marronage in the French Caribbean," 107–9; Régent, *La France et ses esclaves*, 165.

32. Debbasch, "Le Maniel"; Geggus, *Haitian Revolutionary Studies*, 71–74.

33. La Rosa, *Runaway Slave Settlements in Cuba*, 42–62.

34. Craton, *Testing the Chains*, 115–18; Gaspar, "From 'the Sense of Their Slavery,'" 221–24.

35. Gaspar, *Bondmen and Rebels*, 194.

36. Quoted in A. O. Thompson, *Flight to Freedom*, 40.

37. Sáez, *La iglesia y el negro esclavo en Santo Domingo*, 52–55.

38. "R.C. otorgando la libertad a los esclavos que vinieran de las Antillas menores extranjeras en demanda de bautismo," 29 May 1680, in Lucena, *Regulación de la esclavitud negra en las colonias de América Española*, 194–95.

39. Quoted in Rupert, "'Seeking the Water of Baptism,'" 205.

40. Rupert, "'Seeking the Water of Baptism,'" 199, 209–11.

41. Díaz Soler, *Historia de la esclavitud negra en Puerto Rico*, 232–36; Landers, *Black Society in Spanish Florida*, 23–35. After Spain ceded Florida to Great Britain, in 1763, the freedmen of Mosé and St. Augustine and their descendants resettled in Cuba.

42. "R.C. ordenando poner en libertad los esclavos de las colonias inglesas y holandesas que huyesen...," 24 September 1750, and "R.C. extendiendo al resto de las colonias españolas la orden de liberar a los esclavos huidos de las colonias inglesas y holandesas que llegan a ellas para ser católicos," 21 October 1753, in Lucena, *Regulación de la esclavitud negra en las colonias de América Española*, 215, 217.

43. Unique in this respect is the claim list made by slaveowners in Curaçao of 604 captives who had successfully fled to Venezuela (generally Coro) between 1729 and 1775, mostly after the promulgation of the 1750 and 1753 Spanish royal orders (Aizpurúa, "En busca de la libertad," 78–81).

44. Rupert, "'Seeking the Water of Baptism,'" 200.

45. Régent, *La France et ses esclaves*, 66–67; G. M. Hall, *Africans in Colonial Louisiana*, 97–118; Berlin, *Many Thousands Gone*, 88–90.

46. Bond, "Shaping a Conspiracy," 75.

47. G. W. Mullin, *Flight and Rebellion*, 39–40, 105–21, 129; Wiecek, "The Statutory Law of Slavery and Race," 270–77.

48. Lockley, *Maroon Communities in South Carolina*, xvii–xx, 1, 6.

49. Wood, *Black Majority*, 308–20; Pearson, "'A Countryside Full of Flames.'"

50. Quoted in Helg, *Liberty and Equality*, 21. See Helg, *Liberty and Equality*, 20–39; Zuluaga R., *Guerrilla y sociedad en el Patía*, 31–66; Sharp, *Slavery on the Spanish Frontier*, 153–58; McFarlane, "*Cimarrones* and *Palenques*"; Izard, *Orejanos, cimarrones y arrochelados*; Rupert, "Inter-Colonial Networks and Revolutionary Ferment," 81–86.

51. Acosta Saignes, *Vida de los esclavos negros en Venezuela*, 249; Helg, *Liberty and Equality*, 25.

52. Guy and Sheridan, "On Frontiers"; Karasch, "Interethnic Conflict and Resistance on the Brazilian Frontier of Goaiás."

53. Helg, *Liberty and Equality*, 28–29; Boidin, "Esclaves, pardos et milices au Paraguay," 334–37. Free and enslaved Afro-descendants represented 11 percent of the population of Paraguay in the early nineteenth century, and slaves principally worked as artisans, domestics, and cowboys.

54. Price, *The Guiana Maroons*, 7–9; Goslinga, *The Dutch in the Caribbean and in the Guianas*, 359–62.

55. Stipriaan, *Surinaams contrast*, 135.

56. Price, *The Guiana Maroons*, 22–31.

57. Quoted in Goslinga, *The Dutch in the Caribbean and in the Guianas*, 374.

58. Goslinga, *The Dutch in the Caribbean and in the Guianas*, 375–415; Hoogbergen, *The Boni Maroon Wars in Suriname*, 6–13.

59. Hoogbergen, *The Boni Maroon Wars in Suriname*, 52–104; Moomou, *Le monde des marrons du Maroni en Guyane*. On the three-hundred-slave military unit, the Korps Zwarte Jagers, see Brana-Shute, "Sex and Gender in Suriname Manumissions," 189.

60. Groot, "The Maroons of Surinam," 55, 78; Price and Price, introduction, xix–xxiv; Emmer, "Who Abolished Slavery in the Dutch Caribbean?," 106.

Chapter 3

1. Lucena, "El derecho de coartación del esclavo en la América española"; Bowser, *The African Slave in Colonial Peru*, 273–74, 278–80; Russell-Wood, *Slavery and Freedom in Colonial Brazil*, 32; Paiva, "Revendications de droits coutumiers et actions en justice des esclaves dans le Minas Gerais."

2. Schwartz, "The Manumission of Slaves in Colonial Brazil"; J. H. Sweet, "Manumission in Rio de Janeiro"; Higgins, "Gender and the Manumission of Slaves in Colonial Brazil"; Libby and Graça, "Notarized and Baptismal Manumissions"; Valencia Villa, *Alma en boca y huesos en costal*, 119–53; Sharp, *Slavery on the Spanish Frontier*, 141–42. The possibility of achieving manumission in the gold mines sparked the legend of Chico Rei, an African king sold with his son as slaves in Minas Gerais at the beginning of the eighteenth century. Thanks to money made by selling gold that he found independently, Chico Rei bought his son's freedom first and then his own. Father and son then supposedly slowly purchased the freedom of every member of their tribe, who each did the same for slaves of other tribes, until they had created a kingdom in the Vila Rica district (modern-day Ouro Preto). They reportedly possessed a mine of inexhaustible riches thanks to which they established the brotherhood of St. Iphigenia and constructed the Church of the Rosary in which they held a sumptuous royal procession every 6 January (Moura, *Dicionário da escravidão negra no Brasil*, 99–100).

3. On the importance of abortion, see for example, Maestri, *L'esclavage au Brésil*, 127–39.

On enslaved men marrying free, often Indian women who would give birth to free children, see Lokken, "Marriage as Slave Emancipation in Seventeenth-Century Rural Guatemala."

4. Bowser, *The African Slave in Colonial Peru*, 281–82; Libby and Graça, "Notarized and Baptismal Manumissions," 232–33.

5. Moura, *Dicionário da escravidão negra no Brasil*, 22–24.

6. McKinley, *Fractional Freedoms*, 74–107.

7. Bowser, *The African Slave in Colonial Peru*, 280, 445.

8. See detailed cases in Bowser, *The African Slave in Colonial Peru*, 274–78, 287–97; McKinley, *Fractional Freedoms*, 176–202; Vignaux, *Esclavage et rébellion*, 137–59; Higgins, *"Licentious Liberty" in a Brazilian Gold-Mining Region*, 145–62.

9. Bowser, *The African Slave in Colonial Peru*, 125–46, 272–323.

10. Vignaux, *Esclavage et rebellion*, 179–88; Germeten, *Violent Delights, Violent Ends*, 61–68; Palmer, *Slaves of the White God*, 100–105.

11. Díaz, *The Virgin, the King, and the Royal Slaves of El Cobre*, 32–33, 39, 257.

12. Schwartz, "The Manumission of Slaves in Colonial Brazil"; J. H. Sweet, "Manumission in Rio de Janeiro"; Higgins, "Gender and the Manumission of Slaves in Colonial Brazil"; Libby and Graça, "Notarized and Baptismal Manumissions"; Valencia Villa, *Alma en boca y huesos en costal*, 127; L. L. Johnson, "Manumission in Colonial Buenos Aires," 258–79.

13. Bowser, *The African Slave in Colonial Peru*, 302–10.

14. Berlin, *Many Thousands Gone*, 36–38; Burac, *La Barbade*, 15–26.

15. Moore, "A World of Possibilities."

16. Brana-Shute, "Sex and Gender in Suriname Manumissions," 176–78; Hoetink, "Surinam and Curaçao," 67–68.

17. Handler, *The Unappropriated People*, 32; Gragg, *The Quaker Community on Barbados*, 121–41.

18. Matison, "Manumission by Purchase," 148; Christian, *Black Saga*, 27–28.

19. Handler, *The Unappropriated People*, 34–44. At the time, the annual salary of a male skilled worker was around thirty pounds.

20. Berlin, *Many Thousands Gone*, 186–87; M. Jackson, *Let This Voice Be Heard*, 14.

21. Matison, "Manumission by Purchase," 148; Christian, *Black Saga*, 27–28.

22. Beckles, *Black Rebellion in Barbados*, 67.

23. "The Code Noir."

24. Garrigus, *Before Haiti*, 40–41.

25. "The Code Noir."

26. Elisabeth, "The French Antilles," 137–43; Chauleau, *Dans les îles du vent*, 131–34; Oudin-Bastide, *Travail, capitalisme et société esclavagiste*, 227–31; Gautier, *Les sœurs de Solitude*, 141–47; Marchand-Thébault, "L'esclavage en Guyane française," 27–28; Debien, *Les esclaves aux Antilles françaises*, 380–87; Moitt, *Women and Slavery in the French Antilles*, 155; Régent, *La France et ses esclaves*, 185.

27. On increasing discriminations and harassment against free people of color in the French colonies, see Régent, *La France et ses esclaves*, 192–210.

28. Frostin, *Les révoltes blanches*, 261.

29. Frostin, *Les révoltes blanches*, 261.

30. Geggus, "Sugar and Coffee Cultivation," 79.

31. Gautier, *Les sœurs de Solitude*, 153–55.

32. Ghachem, *The Old Regime and the Haitian Revolution*, 93–104.

33. Garrigus, *Before Haiti*, 55–56, 60. In Saint Domingue in 1786 the average manumission tax was 1,274 livres by slave, when the price of an incoming bossale was between 1,800 and 2,000 livres (Régent, *La France et ses esclaves*, 53–54, 185–86).

34. G. M. Hall, *Africans in Colonial Louisiana*, 240.

35. Vidal, "Africains et Européens au pays des Illinois," 55–56.
36. G. M. Hall, *Africans in Colonial Louisiana*, 124–32, 239–42.
37. G. M. Hall, *Africans in Colonial Louisiana*, 279.
38. Hanger, "Avenues to Freedom Open to New Orleans' Black Population," 237–64.
39. See Brown and Morgan, *Arming Slaves*; Bernand and Stella, *D'esclaves à soldats*; Voelz, *Slave and Soldier*.
40. Restall, "Black Conquistadors," 171–88.
41. Restall, "Black Conquistadors," 197–98; Landers, "Transforming Bondsmen into Vassals," 122–23.
42. Mattos, "'Black Troops' and Hierarchies of Color in the Portuguese Atlantic World."
43. Higgins, *"Licentious Liberty" in a Brazilian Gold-Mining Region*, 190–95.
44. Moore, "A World of Possibilities," 41–44.
45. Garrigus, *Before Haiti*, 42–43.
46. Gaspar, *Bondmen and Rebels*, 120–24; Berlin, *Many Thousands Gone*, 66–67, 88–90, 211.
47. Ghachem, *The Old Regime and the Haitian Revolution*, 111–16.
48. E. P. Jennings, "Paths to Freedom," 274–75.
49. Smith, *Selected Philosophical Writings*, 105; Oudin-Bastide, *Travail, capitalisme et société esclavagiste*, 215.

Chapter 4

1. Briggs, *Crime and Punishment in England*, 63–70; Paton, "Punishment, Crime, and the Bodies of Slaves," 930.
2. García León, *La justicia en la Nueva España*, 55–158.
3. Quoted in V. Brown, *The Reaper's Garden*, 3, 271n3.
4. Wiecek, "The Statutory Law of Slavery and Race," 274–75; Hunt, *Inventing Human Rights*, 78.
5. See on this subject the detailed reconstitution of the discovery of an alleged slave conspiracy in Barbados in 1692, in Sharples, "Discovering Slave Conspiracies," as well as the debate on Denmark Vesey's 1822 conspiracy in Charleston, South Carolina, in "Forum: The Making of a Slave Conspiracy."
6. Paton, "Punishment, Crime, and the Bodies of Slaves," 926–27 (quotes); Kimmel, "Blacks before the Law." For Spanish legislation, see Konetzke, *Colección de documentos*; for French legislation, see "The Code Noir."
7. Paton, "Punishment, Crime, and the Bodies of Slaves," 934–36; Régent, *La France et ses esclaves*, 79–83; Oudin-Bastide, *Travail, capitalisme et société esclavagiste*, 254–60; Vignaux, *Esclavage et rébellion*, 179–88; García León, *La justicia en la Nueva España*, 161–73; Conrad, *Children of God's Fire*, 61–62, 292–97. On France and Spain, see Garnot, "Justice, infrajustice, parajustice et extra justice"; Ringrose, *Spain, Europe, and the "Spanish Miracle,"* 255–59.
8. Quoted in Irwin, *Africans Abroad*, 324–26; Palmer, *Slaves of the White God*, 133–34.
9. Palmer, *Slaves of the White God*, 16–17, 40, 135–41. Palmer qualifies the 1608 incident as an aborted rebellion but recognizes that the documents do not substantiate this hypothesis (255n53).
10. On the Iberian Peninsula, monarchies and the Catholic Church had conceived of cofradías (brotherhoods) reserved for slaves and intended to Christianize them since the fifteenth century; in America, in addition to brotherhoods, they also encouraged the establishment of cabildos de nación to facilitate the integration of slaves arriving from Africa while maintaining their ethnic divisions. Subject to control by a priest, these associations organized themselves under the protection of a saint, elected a king and a queen for Carnival, and collected contributions from their members according to their needs, such as funerals, assistance

in cases of illness or infirmity, and loans for manumissions. See Gutiérrez Azopardo, "Las cofradías de negros"; Bowser, *The African Slave in Colonial Peru*, 247–52.

11. Palmer, *Slaves of the White God*, 138–40.

12. Régent, *La France et ses esclaves*, 176–77.

13. *Voyages*; Handler, *The Unappropriated People*, 8; Higman, "The Sugar Revolution."

14. Handler, "Slave Revolts and Conspiracies," 13–19.

15. Lefebvre, *La Grande Peur de 1789*, 77–78; Sharples, "Discovering Slave Conspiracies," 833–40.

16. Handler, "Slave Revolts and Conspiracies," 22–24; Beckles, *Black Rebellion in Barbados*, 42–48.

17. Sharples, "Discovering Slave Conspiracies," 822–24.

18. Handler, "Slave Revolts and Conspiracies," 23–29; Beckles, *Black Rebellion in Barbados*, 46–51.

19. For an example of such a case, masterminded by the Cartagena elite in Colombia in 1693 in order to prevent any royal treaty with local maroons, see McFarlane, "Autoridad y poder en Cartagena."

20. Lepore, "The Tightening Vise," 78–84 (quote p. 79); Lepore, *New York Burning*, 52–53; Rosenwaike, *Population History of New York City*, 8.

21. Klein and Luna, *Slavery in Brazil*, 208–9; Régent, *La France et ses esclaves*, 176–77; Gaspar, *Bondmen and Rebels*, 210; Sharp, *Slavery on the Spanish Frontier*, 158–59.

22. Sensbach, *Rebecca's Revival*, 8–27.

23. Sensbach, *Rebecca's Revival*, 23.

24. For a general introduction on Quakers, see Barbour and Frost, *The Quakers*.

25. Theobald, "Slave Conspiracies in Colonial Virginia"; Jernegan, "Slavery and Conversion."

26. Hodges, *Root and Branch*, 89–90.

27. Carroll, *Blacks in Colonial Veracruz*, 97–99. On Yanga, see above, chapter 2.

28. G. M. Hall, *Africans in Colonial Louisiana*, 97–118; Berlin, *Many Thousands Gone*, 88–90.

29. Cooper, *The Hanging of Angélique*.

30. Gaspar, *Bondmen and Rebels*, xiii. See also Schuler, "Akan Slave Rebellions," 381–83.

31. Sharples, "Hearing Whispers, Casting Shadows."

32. Sharples, "Hearing Whispers, Casting Shadows," 39.

33. Quoted in Gaspar, *Bondmen and Rebels*, 3–5 (original spelling).

34. Gaspar, *Bondmen and Rebels*, 13, 83.

35. Gaspar, *Bondmen and Rebels*, 13–21 (quotes pp. 17, 21, original spelling).

36. Gaspar, *Bondmen and Rebels*, 21–23.

37. Sharples, "Hearing Whispers, Casting Shadows," 42–44 (quote p. 42, original spelling); Gaspar, *Bondmen and Rebels*, 23–28.

38. Gaspar, *Bondmen and Rebels*, 29–38 (quote p. 29, original spelling).

39. Quoted in Gaspar, *Bondmen and Rebels*, 29 (original spelling).

40. Abenon, *Petite histoire de la Guadeloupe*, 64–65; Lara, *La Guadeloupe dans l'histoire*, 58–59.

41. Horsmanden, *The New York Conspiracy*.

42. Horsmanden, *The New York Conspiracy*, 27; Zabin, *Dangerous Economies*, 132–40. These accusations form the bases of Peter Linebaugh's and Marcus Rediker's reinterpretation of these events as a "revolutionary conspiracy, Atlantic in scope . . . by a motley proletariat to incite an urban insurrection" (Linebaugh and Rediker, *Many-Headed Hydra*, 178–79).

43. Zabin, *Dangerous Economies*, 140–58; Doolen, "Reading and Writing Terror"; Bond, "Shaping a Conspiracy."

44. Schuler, "Akan Slave Rebellions," 373–74.

45. Klooster, "The Rising Expectations," 64.

46. Goslinga, *The Dutch in the Caribbean and in the Guianas*, 113, 546; Oostindie, "Slave Resistance," 72.

47. Long, *The History of Jamaica*, 2:447, 462.

48. Edwards, *The History, Civil and Commercial, of the British Colonies*, 2:87–88.

49. The most important studies following the interpretations of Long and Edwards are, by chronological order of publication, Schuler, "Akan Slave Rebellions," 373–75; Craton, *Testing the Chains*, 125–39; D. Hall, *In Miserable Slavery*, 92–114; Burnard, *Mastery, Tyranny, and Desire*, 170–74; V. Brown, *The Reaper's Garden*, 129–56. For an analysis considering the revolt in the context of the Ten Years' War, see Bollettino, "Slavery, War, and Britain's Atlantic Empire," 191–256. For an interactive cartographic study of the various Jamaican revolts between 1760 and 1761, see V. Brown, "Slave Revolt in Jamaica."

50. V. Brown, "Slave Revolt in Jamaica"; Craton, *Testing the Chains*, 138.

51. D. Hall, "Jamaica," 194; Bollettino, "Slavery, War, and Britain's Atlantic Empire," 19–20; V. Brown, "Slave Revolt in Jamaica."

52. On obeah (or obi), see Bilby and Handler, "Obeah."

53. V. Brown, "Slave Revolt in Jamaica"; Craton, *Testing the Chains*, 125–39; V. Brown, *The Reaper's Garden*, 148.

54. V. Brown, *The Reaper's Garden*.

55. Edwards, *The History, Civil and Commercial, of the British Colonies*, 2:64. Edwards alludes here to the slave rebellion launched in 1791 in Saint Domingue (see below, chapter 6).

56. Schuler, "Akan Slave Rebellions," 383; Maxwell, "Enslaved Merchants."

57. V. Brown, *The Reaper's Garden*, 153–55.

58. Kars, "Dodging Rebellion," 39, 44–45, 50n36.

59. Blair, "Wolfert Simon van Hoogenheim," 63–64; Goslinga, *The Dutch in the Caribbean and in the Guianas*, 465–74; Kars, "Dodging Rebellion," 45–49.

60. Goslinga, *The Dutch in the Caribbean and in the Guianas*, 476.

61. Quoted in Schuler, "Akan Slave Rebellions," 379.

62. Goslinga, *The Dutch in the Caribbean and in the Guianas*, 471–83.

63. Goslinga, *The Dutch in the Caribbean and in the Guianas*, 487–94; Blair, "Wolfert Simon van Hoogenheim," 65–66; Kars, "Dodging Rebellion," 48–50.

64. Kars, "Dodging Rebellion," 50–69.

65. Ogle, "Slaves of Justice," 286–93; Paton, "Punishment, Crime, and the Bodies of Slaves," 943–44; V. Brown, *The Reaper's Garden*, 129–32, 135–44.

66. Spierenburg, *The Spectacle of Suffering*, 66–77; Kars, "Dodging Rebellion," 191; Paton, "Punishment, Crime, and the Bodies of Slaves," 936–41.

67. Paton, "Punishment, Crime, and the Bodies of Slaves," 939–40; V. Brown, *The Reaper's Garden*, 140.

68. Many studies focus on punishments specific to slaves. See, for example, Acosta Saignes, *Vida de los esclavos negros en Venezuela*, 229–48; Paiva, "Revendications de droits coutumiers et actions en justice des esclaves dans le Minas Gerais," 117; Régent, *La France et ses esclaves*, 81; Oudin-Bastide, *Travail, capitalisme et société esclavagiste*, 155–59; Kimmel, "Blacks before the Law"; Paton, "Punishment, Crime, and the Bodies of Slaves," 946–47; Goslinga, *The Dutch in the Caribbean and in the Guianas*, 529–47.

69. V. Brown, *The Reaper's Garden*, 154–55.

Chapter 5

1. These figures are estimations, of course (see Gilbert, *Black Patriots and Loyalists,* ix–xii, 205, 309n148). The figures of eighty thousand to one hundred thousand fugitive slaves (Foote, *Black and White Manhattan,* 211) are probably overstated, and that of twenty thousand (Pybus, "Jefferson's Faulty Math"), underestimated.
2. Nash, *Race and Revolution,* 57.
3. Callahan, *The Talking Book,* xii–xiv, 2–5.
4. Wong, *Neither Fugitive nor Free,* 24–36.
5. Gilbert, *Black Patriots and Loyalists,* 7–9.
6. Quoted in Kaplan and Kaplan, *The Black Presence,* 13 (original spelling).
7. Blackburn, *The Overthrow of Colonial Slavery,* 91.
8. Frey, *Water from the Rock,* 17, 54 (original spelling).
9. See, for example, the poem "On Being Brought from Africa to America" (1770), in Wheatley, *Poems on Various Subjects,* 18.
10. Phillis Wheatley to Samson Occum (11 February 1774), *in* Wheatley, *The Collected Works,* 176–77. See also Foote, *Black and White Manhattan,* 211; Nash, *Race and Revolution,* 58.
11. Berlin, *Many Thousands Gone,* 175–76.
12. Quoted in Gilbert, *Black Patriots and Loyalists,* 6 (original spelling).
13. This chapter will refer to supporters of continuing British rule as loyalists and to supporters of independence as revolutionaries.
14. Bollettino, "Slavery, War, and Britain's Atlantic Empire," 292.
15. Berlin, *Many Thousands Gone,* 369–70.
16. Frey, *Water from the Rock,* 54–55; Piecuch, *Three Peoples,* 76–79. See notably the public hanging and cremation of the free black Thomas Jeremiah in Charleston in August 1775, for allegedly conspiring in preparation for a slave uprising, by a jury of revolutionary slaveowners in spite of the sickened opposition voiced by the city's British governor (J. W. Harris, *The Hanging of Thomas Jeremiah*).
17. Kaplan and Kaplan, *The Black Presence,* 62 (original spelling).
18. Kaplan and Kaplan, *The Black Presence,* 60–67 (quotes p. 61); Gilbert, *Black Patriots and Loyalists,* 22–23.
19. L. M. Harris, *In the Shadow of Slavery,* 54–55; Hodges, "Black Revolt in New York City," 32–33.
20. Foote, *Black and White Manhattan,* 214.
21. Foote, *Black and White Manhattan,* 215.
22. Foote, *Black and White Manhattan*; Hodges, "Black Revolt in New York City," 20–24, 28–34.
23. Nash, *Race, Class, and Politics,* 269–74. For short biographies of fugitive men and women, see Pybus, *Epic Journeys of Freedom,* 209–18.
24. Frey, *Water from the Rock,* 45; Berlin, *Many Thousands Gone,* 369–70.
25. Quoted in Frey, *Water from the Rock,* 113.
26. Gilbert, *Black Patriots and Loyalists,* 117–28; Lockley, *Maroon Communities in South Carolina,* 39–41.
27. Littlefield, "Revolutionary Citizens," 117; Berlin, *Many Thousands Gone,* 369.
28. Frey, *Water from the Rock,* 86, 108; Gilbert, *Black Patriots and Loyalists,* 71–73.
29. Between 1765 and 1776 five presumed plots by slaves seeking to kill whites were discovered in Jamaica, leading to several executions and deportations (Patterson, *The Sociology of Slavery,* 271–72). The most important one, unveiled before any concrete action, took place in the parish of Hanover during summer 1776 and ended with the execution of seventeen slaves and the transportation and flogging of many more (Craton, *Testing the Chains,* 172–79).

30. Quarles, *The Negro in the American Revolution*, 152–53.
31. Quarles, *The Negro in the American Revolution*, 143; Frey, *Water from the Rock*, 101–2, 121–24, 137–39; Gilbert, *Black Patriots and Loyalists*, 154–68.
32. Frey, *Water from the Rock*, 101–2, 106–7, 127, 167; Schama, *Rough Crossings*, 126–27.
33. Kaplan and Kaplan, *The Black Presence*, 7–10; Littlefield, "Revolutionary Citizens," 113–15.
34. Littlefield, "Revolutionary Citizens," 115–16; Frey, *Water from the Rock*, 76–79; Gilbert, *Black Patriots and Loyalists*, 98–115.
35. Piecuch, *Three Peoples*, 269–70, 325; Gilbert, *Black Patriots and Loyalists*, 160–73.
36. Garrigus, "Catalyst or Catastrophe?" These *libres de couleur* included the freeborn mulatto soldier André Rigaud and the former slave Henri Christophe, who later played a leading role in the Haitian Revolution (see chapter 6).
37. Gilbert, *Black Patriots and Loyalists*, 137–41; Frey, *Water from the Rock*, 82, 86–87, 99–120; J. K. Snyder, "Revolutionary Repercussions."
38. Frey, *Water from the Rock*, 92, 99, 122, 131; Piecuch, *Three Peoples*, 266–68; Schama, *Rough Crossings*, 107.
39. Frey, *Water from the Rock*, 144–45, 156.
40. Quoted in Frey, *Water from the Rock*, 170. For similar cases, see Frey, *Water from the Rock*, 122–24.
41. Quarles, *The Negro in the American Revolution*, 158–61.
42. Quoted in Frey, *Water from the Rock*, 172. See also Foote, *Black and White Manhattan*, 221–23.
43. Gilbert, *Black Patriots and Loyalists*, 177–80 (quotes pp. 177, 178, original spelling).
44. Gilbert, *Black Patriots and Loyalists*, 205. Piecuch estimates that nine thousand slaves left Charleston with the British before the American revolutionaries entered the city; thousands more would have left Georgia, and between five thousand and six thousand would have been evacuated from Savannah to go mainly to East Florida and Jamaica (Piecuch, *Three Peoples*, 323–26).
45. Frey, *Water from the Rock*, 101–2, 106–7, 127, 167; Lockley and Doddington, "Maroon and Slave Communities," 128–30; Diouf, *Slavery's Exiles*, 187–208.
46. Piecuch, *Three Peoples*, 320–27; Gilbert, *Black Patriots and Loyalists*, 178–90.
47. J. K. Snyder, "Revolutionary Repercussions"; Frey, *Water from the Rock*, 82, 106, 141–42, 173–83; Quarles, *The Negro in the American Revolution*, 175–76.
48. Buckley, *Slaves in Red Coats*, 6–9.
49. Quarles, *The Negro in the American Revolution*, 177; Turner, *Slaves and Missionaries*, 11.
50. Hodges, "Black Revolt in New York City," 20; Foote, *Black and White Manhattan*, 217–18; Gilbert, *Black Patriots and Loyalists*, 188–202.
51. Grant, "Black Immigrants into Nova Scotia"; Foote, *Black and White Manhattan*, 221–23; Kaplan and Kaplan, *The Black Presence*, 69; Schama, *Rough Crossings*, 169–76; Winks, *The Blacks in Canada*, 29–46.
52. In September 1781, the *Zong*, which belonged to a group of slave traders from Liverpool, left São Tomé with 440 slaves aboard, heading to Jamaica. After a navigation error prolonged the voyage, an epidemic killed 60 captives and crewmembers, and continued to spread among the survivors. Fearing he was carrying an "unsellable cargo," the captain ordered that 132 sick slaves be thrown overboard (10 others voluntarily threw themselves into the ocean) in order to be able to receive insurance compensation, and then sold the 200 survivors in Kingston. When the insurance company refused to pay the claims, the captain brought the case before a London court, in which, in 1783, the judges analyzed the case as if the slaves were merchandise. Several abolitionists, to whom the emancipated slave Olaudah Equiano had revealed the crime, tried to launch proceedings for murder. Even though their efforts were unsuccessful, the *Zong* massacre was critical to the development of British abolitionism (Walvin, *The Zong*).

53. Nash, *Race, Class, and Politics*, 274–88; Schama, *Rough Crossings*, 180–350.

54. For some sources comprising African American voices, see Foote, *Black and White Manhattan*, 293–300.

55. Moss, "The Persistence of Slavery," 301–2; Gilbert, *Black Patriots and Loyalists*, 95–115, 168–73; "Collection of pay certificates for serving in the Connecticut Line."

56. "The Migration or Importation of such Persons as any of the States now existing shall think proper to admit, shall not be prohibited by the Congress prior to the Year one thousand eight hundred and eight, but a Tax or duty may be imposed on such Importation, not exceeding ten dollars for each Person" (Constitution of the United States, article I, section 9, paragraph 1). For an analysis of the constitutional debates on slavery, see Finkelman, *Slavery and the Founders*, 3–36.

57. Constitution of the United States, article I, section 2, paragraph 3.

58. Quoted in Kaplan and Kaplan, *The Black Presence*, 29–30; Melish, *Disowning Slavery*, 64–66. For similar petitions, see Aptheker, *Documentary History of the Negro People*, 5–12.

59. See "Pennsylvania: An Act for the Gradual Abolition of Slavery." The law was amended in 1788, because it did not prevent the owner of a pregnant slave to send her to another state before the birth of her child, who then would have a slave status.

60. Menschel, "Abolition without Deliverance."

61. Menschel, "Abolition without Deliverance"; Melish, *Disowning Slavery*, 67–79. See also McManus, *Black Bondage*.

62. Nash and Soderlund, *Freedom by Degrees*, 4–9; Hodges, "Black Revolt in New York City," 39; U.S. Census Bureau, *Compendium of the Enumeration of the Inhabitants*, 368, 371.

63. Nash and Soderlund, *Freedom by Degrees*; Menschel, "Abolition without Deliverance."

64. Winks, *The Blacks in Canada*, 96–113.

65. *Voyages*; Nash, *Race and Revolution*, 14–18; U.S. Census Bureau, *Compendium of the Enumeration of the Inhabitants*, 366.

66. Callahan, *The Talking Book*, 5–6 (quote p. 5).

67. Matison, "Manumission by Purchase," 149–50, 156.

68. Nash, *Race and Revolution*, 14–18; U.S. Census Bureau, *Compendium of the Enumeration of the Inhabitants*, 371.

69. L. P. Jackson, "Manumission in Certain Virginia Cities," 281.

70. Quoted, together with other cases, in L. P. Jackson, "Manumission in Certain Virginia Cities," 282.

71. Hirschfeld, *George Washington and Slavery*, 209–23.

72. L. P. Jackson, "Manumission in Certain Virginia Cities," 285–87.

73. Sidbury, *Ploughshares into Swords*, 6–8, 210–13.

Chapter 6

1. Oudin-Bastide, *Travail, capitalisme et société esclavagiste*, 18.

2. Quoted in Dubois, *A Colony of Citizens*, 86–87. See also Geggus, "The Slaves and Free Coloreds of Martinique," 280–87. "Nous, Nègres" means "We, Negroes."

3. Quoted in Régent, *La France et ses esclaves*, 68.

4. Quoted in Bajot, *Annales maritimes et coloniales*, 555. On French legislation of slavery, see Peytraud, *L'esclavage aux Antilles françaises*.

5. See Raynal, *Histoire philosophique et politique des établissements et du commerce des Européens dans les deux Indes*; Condorcet, *Réflexions sur l'esclavage des nègres*.

6. Geggus, "The Slaves and Free Coloreds of Martinique," 284–85; Blancpain, *La condition des paysans haïtiens*, 24–25; Hurbon, "Église et esclavage au xviiie siècle à Saint-Domingue," 91–95.

7. Quoted in Geggus, "The Slaves and Free Coloreds of Martinique," 285.
8. Geggus, "The Slaves and Free Coloreds of Martinique," 283.
9. Bénot, "La chaîne des insurrections d'esclaves."
10. Bénot, *La Guyane sous la Révolution française*, 43–54; Craton, *Testing the Chains*, 224–25; Pérotin-Dumon, "Free Coloreds and Slaves," 263–64.
11. On the free mulattos Vincent Ogé and Jean-Baptiste Chavanne, see Garrigus, "Vincent Ogé *jeune*."
12. See Geggus, *Haitian Revolutionary Studies*, 5–14, 81–92; Dubois, *Avengers of the New World*, 91–131 (pp. 97 and 113 for insurgents' figures).
13. *Voyages*; Geggus, *Haitian Revolutionary Studies*, 5.
14. Geggus, "Slave and Free Colored Women in Saint Domingue," 268.
15. Geggus, *Haitian Revolutionary Studies*, 5. Several historians have stated that in Saint Domingue free people of color owned one-third of the plantations and one-quarter of the slaves without giving a historical source. As shown by Frédérique Beauvois, these proportions originate in a speech to the French national Assembly by wealthy quarteron Julien Raimond in favor of equal rights for free *gens de couleur* and were probably inflated in order to demonstrate their economic importance in the colony (Beauvois, *Between Blood and Gold*, 31).
16. *Voyages*; Geggus, "The French Slave Trade," 126, 136.
17. The proportion of African versus creole slaves at the dawn of the 1791 rebellion is difficult to establish, especially if the arrival of some seventy-three thousand new captives from Africa in 1790–91 is taken into account. Several historians have put forward that Africans made up two-thirds of Saint Domingue's slaves, thus more than half of its total population in the early 1790s, referring to Moreau de Saint-Méry, *Description topographique et politique de la partie française de l'isle de Saint-Domingue*, 1:27 (for example, Dubois, *Avengers of the New World*, 42). Geggus downgrades this estimate on the basis of a large sample of plantation inventories between 1760 and 1792 and shows that creole slaves represented 56 percent of the labor force on the longer established sugar plantations and 36 percent on the more recent coffee estates (Geggus, "Sugar and Coffee Cultivation," 78–79).
18. Dubois, *Avengers of the New World*, 105–8.
19. Thornton, "'I Am the Subject of the King of Congo,'" 207–9.
20. Hurbon, "Église et esclavage au xviiie siècle à Saint Domingue," 95–99.
21. Fick, *The Making of Haiti*, 95–110.
22. Quoted in Dubois, *Avengers of the New World*, 141; see also 122–29.
23. Barthélémy, "Les esclaves révoltés à Saint Domingue," 179–81.
24. Fick, *The Making of Haiti*, 120–25; Geggus, *Haitian Revolutionary Studies*, 99–118. These slave-soldiers were called "the Swiss," probably in reference to the Swiss guards of the king of France.
25. Fick, *The Making of Haiti*, 137–40.
26. Fick, *The Making of Haiti*, 140–45. André Rigaud was a mulatto goldsmith trained in Bordeaux and probably a veteran of the legion of volunteers sent by royalist France to aid in the siege of Savannah against the British in 1779 (Garrigus, *Before Haiti*, 245–46).
27. Fick, *The Making of Haiti*, 146–52.
28. Geggus, *Haitian Revolutionary Studies*, 137–40; Dubois, *Avengers of the New World*, 149.
29. Fick, *The Making of Haiti*, 154–56.
30. Fick, *The Making of Haiti*, 157–58.
31. On the massive exile of French colonists, who often took their slaves with them, see Meadows, "Engineering Exile."
32. Quoted in Dubois, *Avengers of the New World*, 157.
33. Geggus, *Haitian Revolutionary Studies*, 125; Fick, *The Making of Haiti*, 159–61; Barthélémy, "Les esclaves révoltés à Saint Domingue," 181–82.

34. "France Abolishes Slavery."

35. Piquet, *L'émancipation des Noirs*, 317–79.

36. Slaves freed by the general emancipation decree of 1794 were called *nouveaux libres*, to differentiate them from the former free *gens de couleur* or *libres de couleur*, who were freeborn or had been manumitted before 1794, and were now called *anciens libres* (previously free).

37. Dubois, *Avengers of the New World*, 184–87; Kafka, "Action, Reaction and Interaction"; Blancpain, *La condition des paysans haïtiens*, 54–74.

38. Blancpain, *La condition des paysans haïtiens*, 67. In 1781 Condorcet had proposed a very gradual abolition of slavery spread over seventy-seven years (Condorcet, *Réflexions sur l'esclavage des nègres*, 35–40).

39. Fick, "Emancipation in Haiti," 16–22; Kafka, "Action, Reaction and Interaction."

40. Blancpain, *La condition des paysans haïtiens*, 75–103; Dubois, *Avengers of the New World*, 196–97, 204–5, 226–28, 238–40.

41. "Toussaint Louverture's Constitution," 160.

42. Fick, "Emancipation in Haiti," 27–28.

43. Dubois, *Avengers of the New World*, 189–91, 229–30, 244.

44. "Toussaint Louverture's Constitution," 160.

45. When it came to African cultural practices, French policy was the opposite of what was implemented in Iberian colonies, where the creation of cabildos de nación (religious and cultural mutual aid societies) was encouraged in order to integrate enslaved Africans while dividing them along ethnic lines.

46. Thornton, "I Am the Subject of the King of Congo"; Dubois, *Avengers of the New World*, 198–99.

47. Dubois, *Avengers of the New World*, 251.

48. Henri Christophe was a black man born in slavery, in all likelihood in the island of Grenada, and brought to Saint Domingue, where he performed various jobs before buying his freedom. Like Rigaud, he possibly was a veteran of the French legion of volunteers that fought against the British in Savannah in 1779 (Griggs, introduction, 38–39).

49. Fick, *The Making of Haiti*, 210.

50. Dubois, *Avengers of the New World*, 256.

51. Quoted in Dubois, *Avengers of the New World*, 292. See also Fick, *The Making of Haiti*, 216–36.

52. Barthélémy, "Les esclaves révoltés à Saint Domingue," 181–82.

53. Quoted in Dubois, *Avengers of the New World*, 291–92.

54. Dubois, *Avengers of the New World*, 284–89.

55. S. E. Johnson, "'You Should Give Them Blacks to Eat,'" 67. See also Martin and Cabanis, "Choc de terreurs outremer"; Gainot, "'Sur fond de cruelle inhumanité.'"

56. This sum is the equivalent of $15,000,000 for 828,000 square miles. See Dubois, *Avengers of the New World*, 251, 254, 281–98.

57. On these estimates, see Fick, "Emancipation in Haiti," 29; Girard, *The Slaves Who Defeated Napoléon*, 343–44.

58. Barthélémy, "Les esclaves révoltés à Saint Domingue," 185.

59. Barthélémy, "Les esclaves révoltés à Saint Domingue"; Trouillot, *Silencing the Past*, 37–44, 67–69.

60. See "The Declaration of Independence."

61. Quoted in Geggus, *Haitian Revolutionary Studies*, 207; Constitution of Hayti. See Saint-Louis, "Les termes de citoyen et africain," 95; Geggus, *Haitian Revolutionary Studies*, 207–20; Girard, *The Slaves Who Defeated Napoléon*, 311–16.

62. Constitution of Hayti. See also Janvier, *Les Constitutions d'Haïti*, 30–41; Girard, *The Slaves Who Defeated Napoléon*, 317–28.

63. On these developments, see Trouillot, *Haiti, State against Nation*, 40–50.
64. Duke of Limonade to Thomas Clarkson, 20 November 1819, in Christophe, *Henry Christophe and Thomas Clarkson*, 176.
65. Trouillot, *Haiti, State against Nation*, 60–61.

Chapter 7

1. Trouillot, *Silencing the Past*, 70.
2. Geggus, "Slave Rebellion during the Age of Revolution."
3. Quoted in Pérotin-Dumon, "Free Coloreds and Slaves," 271.
4. Régent, *Esclavage, métissage, liberté*, 14–15, 247–48.
5. Régent, *Esclavage, métissage, liberté*, 250–51. See also Dubois, *A Colony of Citizens*, 23–24.
6. Régent, *Esclavage, métissage, liberté*, 238–53.
7. Régent, *Esclavage, métissage, liberté*, 266; Dubois, *A Colony of Citizens*, 140, 153–54.
8. Régent, *Esclavage, métissage, liberté*, 256–66; Dubois, *A Colony of Citizens*, 136–40.
9. Dubois, *A Colony of Citizens*, 149, 187–227.
10. Régent, *Esclavage, métissage, liberté*, 333–79.
11. Régent, *Esclavage, métissage, liberté*, 301–17; Pérotin-Dumon, "Économie corsaire et droit de neutralité."
12. Bénot, *La Guyane sous la Révolution française*, 15, 63–73, 81–91.
13. Bénot, *La Guyane sous la Révolution française*, 98–110.
14. Trani, *La Martinique napoléonienne*; Geggus, "The Slaves and Free Coloreds of Martinique," 289–90. In 1811 the authorities in Saint-Pierre discovered, thanks to one slave's information, a plot involving free and enslaved men of African descent that would have led its participants to burn down the city, seize weapons, and exterminate whites, and one of whose leaders was a free mulatto from the island who had served in the Haitian army led by the king Christophe; following judgment, sixteen suspects were hanged (Geggus, "The Slaves and Free Coloreds of Martinique," 295–97).
15. Quoted in Craton, *Testing the Chains*, 198 (original spelling).
16. Craton, *Testing the Chains*, 195–204; Gaspar, "La Guerre des Bois."
17. Dubois, *A Colony of Citizens*, 318–22, 388–99 (quotes pp. 392–93).
18. Dubois, *A Colony of Citizens*, 404–22.
19. *Voyages*.
20. Dubois, *A Colony of Citizens*, 51.
21. Bénot, *La Guyane sous la Révolution française*, 181.
22. Mam-Lam-Fouck, "La résistance au rétablissement de l'esclavage"; Marchand-Thébault, "L'esclavage en Guyane française," 71.
23. Halpern, "Les fêtes révolutionnaires"; L. C. Jennings, *French Anti-Slavery*, 3–5.
24. Goslinga, *The Dutch in the Caribbean and in Surinam*, 3–8 (quote p.3).
25. Goslinga, *The Dutch in the Caribbean and in Surinam*, 5–20 (quote p. 10).
26. Phaf-Rheinberger, "L'impossibilité d'une révolution caraïbéenne," 131–32; Oostindie, "Slave Resistance," 10–17.
27. Phelan, *The People and the King*, 110–11, 153, 193–94 (quote p. 110).
28. Stavig and Schmidt, *The Tupac Amaru and Catarista Rebellions*, 68.
29. Stavig and Schmidt, *The Tupac Amaru and Catarista Rebellions*, 127, 132. On the rebellion, see Thomson, *We Alone Will Rule*.
30. Helg, *Liberty and Equality*, 112–14.
31. Childs, *The 1812 Aponte Rebellion*, 39–40; Landers, "Spanish Sanctuary."
32. "R. instrucción sobre la educación, trato y ocupación de los esclavos" (31 May 1789), in Konetzke, *Colección de documentos*, 3:643–52.

33. Quoted in Childs, *The 1812 Aponte Rebellion*, 36–37.

34. "Consulta del Consejo de las Indias sobre el reglamento expedido en 31 de mayo de 1789 para la mejor educación, buen trato y ocupación de los negros esclavos de América" (17 March 1794), in Konetzke, *Colección de documentos*, 3:726–32.

35. Helg, *Liberty and Equality*, 91–94, 100–105.

36. By this time, the total population of Spanish Santo Domingo had reached some one hundred thousand inhabitants: 29 percent slaves, 33 percent whites and 37 percent *libres de color* (Andrews, *Afro-Latin America*, 41).

37. Quoted in Lora Hugi, "El sonido de la libertad," 113.

38. Quoted in Lora Hugi, "El sonido de la libertad," 115. Sopo is sometimes spelled Sopó.

39. Geggus, "Slave Resistance in the Spanish Caribbean," 139–47.

40. Moya Pons, "Casos de continuidad y ruptura"; Théodat, *Haïti-République dominicaine*, 127–28.

41. Baralt, *Slave Revolts in Puerto Rico*, 7.

42. Geggus, "Slave Resistance in the Spanish Caribbean," 132–39.

43. Ferrer, "La société esclavagiste cubaine," 350–56, which does not give the outcome of the trial.

44. Din, "Carondelet, the Cabildo, and Slaves."

45. *Documentos de la insurrección de José Leonardo Chirinos*; Aizpurúa Aguirre, "La insurrección de los negros de la serranía"; Gómez, "Entre résistance, piraterie et républicanisme," 95–97; Klooster, "The Rising Expectations," 65–69; Rivera, "Social Control on the Eve of a Slave Revolt." On Spain's asylum policy, see chapter 2.

46. For example, Araujo, *Shadows of the Slave Past*, 200, presents the insurrection in Coro as a slave revolt led by the maroon Chirino.

47. Helg, *Liberty and Equality*, 109–10 (quotes p. 110).

48. U.S. Census Bureau, *Census of Population and Housing*, 1790 and 1810.

49. McManus, *Black Bondage*.

50. Alderson, "Charleston's Rumored Slave Revolt."

51. Egerton, *Gabriel's Rebellion*; Sidbury, *Ploughshares into Swords*, 6–8, 40–45; Nicholls, *Whispers of Rebellion*.

52. Sidbury, *Ploughshares into Swords*, 87, 88. See also Egerton, "Slaves to the Marketplace," which stresses the impact of urbanization and monetarization of the economy on the revolt; and Callahan, *The Talking Book*, 6–7, on the Baptist dimension of the plot.

53. Sidbury, *Ploughshares into Swords*, 95–117, 139–47 (quote p. 101); Diouf, *Slavery's Exiles*, 259–65.

54. See Paquette, "'A Horde of Brigands?'"; Buman, "To Kill Whites," 66–85.

55. U.S. Census Bureau, *Census of Population and Housing*, 1810; Buman, "To Kill Whites," 52–64.

56. Buman, "To Kill Whites," 66–85; Paquette, "'A Horde of Brigands?'"

57. Reis and Gomes, "Repercussions of the Haitian Revolution," 285–87. The Tailors' Revolt referenced the French Revolution and its ideals of liberty, equality, and fraternity, denounced the Portuguese monarchy, and demanded free trade and an increase in military pay. It included whites and free pardos but no slaves (apart those turned over to the law by some elite owners to protect themselves from being accused of participating in the plot), even though it was open to the latter's demands for freedom. See Valim, "Corporação dos enteados-tensão"; Tavares, *Da sedição de 1798 à revolta de 1824 na Bahia*.

58. Cox, "Fedon's Rebellion"; Craton, *Testing the Chains*, 183–90, 207–10; Candlin, "The Role of the Enslaved in the 'Fedon Rebellion.'"

59. *Voyages*. An in-depth study of selected plantations in Jamaica and Barbados in the late

eighteenth century also shows few incidences of slave marronage in this period (Roberts, *Slavery and the Enlightenment*, 320–21).

60. V. Brown, *The Reaper's Garden*, 188.
61. Quoted in V. Brown, *The Reaper's Garden*, 131.
62. Geggus, "The Enigma of Jamaica in the 1790s."
63. On the war against maroons in Jamaica and St. Vincent, see Craton, *Testing the Chains*, 190–94, 204–7, 211–23; Craton, "The Black Caribs of St. Vincent."
64. Buckley, *Slaves in Red Coats*, 12–19, 142; Frey, *Water from the Rock*, 139; Craton, *Testing the Chains*, 169.
65. V. Brown, *The Reaper's Garden*, 228–29.
66. Buckley, *Slaves in Red Coats*, 77–80.

Chapter 8

1. Schultz, *Tropical Versailles*, 166.
2. Saunders, *A Social History of Black Slaves*, 178–79. Slavery continued to be legal in the Portuguese Empire until 1875, and then was masked under other names (*liberto* or *serviçal* contract). See Ishemo, "Forced Labour and Migration."
3. Schultz, *Tropical Versailles*, 122, 165–76; Karasch, *Slave Life in Rio de Janeiro*, 239.
4. Kraay, "'Em outra coisa não falavam os pardos.'"
5. Domínguez, *Insurrection or Loyalty*, 30.
6. *Documentos para la historia del México independiente*, 70–75 (quote p. 74).
7. *Documentos para la historia del México independiente*, 107, 131, 138 (quote p. 76).
8. For example, Van Young, *The Other Rebellion*, 39–65.
9. Carroll, *Blacks in Colonial Veracruz*, 99–111; Vincent, "The Blacks Who Freed Mexico." Morelos and Guerrero were of partial African descent.
10. Lombardi, *The Decline and Abolition of Negro Slavery in Venezuela*, 35; Domínguez, *Insurrection or Loyalty*, 30, 47–48.
11. Domínguez, *Insurrection or Loyalty*, 157–60, 174–76; Thibaud, *Républiques en armes*, 93–98; Blanchard, *Under the Flags of Freedom*, 20–21, 25–27. For similar dynamics in southern Colombia, see Echeverri, *Indian and Slave Royalists in the Age of Revolution*, 157–75.
12. Blanchard, *Under the Flags of Freedom*, 27–29; Thibaud, *Républiques en armes*, 140; Helg, "Simón Bolívar's Republic," 23. The War to the Death campaign justified the massacre of hundreds of Spaniards on Bolívar's orders in 1814.
13. Blanchard, *Under the Flags of Freedom*, 30–33.
14. Thibaud, *Républiques en armes*, 178–202.
15. Helg, "Simón Bolívar's Republic," 23–24, 27–28; Blanchard, *Under the Flags of Freedom*, 72.
16. Blanchard, *Under the Flags of Freedom*, 70–72.
17. Thibaud, *Républiques en armes*, 339; Pita Pico, *El reclutamiento de negros esclavos*, 133–44.
18. Helg, "Simón Bolívar's Republic," 24–25.
19. Blanchard, *Under the Flags of Freedom*, 76–79; Pita Pico, *El reclutamiento de negros esclavos*, 214–15.
20. Zuluaga R., *Guerrilla y sociedad en el Patía*; Echeverri, *Indian and Slave Royalists in the Age of Revolution*, 215–16.
21. Blanchard, *Under the Flags of Freedom*, 76–79; Pita Pico, *El reclutamiento de negros esclavos*, 270.
22. Helg, "Simón Bolívar's Republic," 25–26; Lombardi, *The Decline and Abolition of Negro Slavery in Venezuela*, 61–78.

23. Pita Pico, *El reclutamiento de negros esclavos*, 293; Lombardi, *The Decline and Abolition of Negro Slavery in Venezuela*, 35, 162.

24. Helg, *Liberty and Equality*, 143–57.

25. Helg, "Simón Bolívar's Republic," 26; Lombardi, *The Decline and Abolition of Negro Slavery in Venezuela*, 63–65; Blanchard, *Under the Flags of Freedom*, 172–79. See also Pita Pico, *El reclutamiento de negros esclavos*, 257–68. On the successful case of the enslaved Angela Batallas, in Guayaquil in 1823, who built on the republican rhetoric to obtain Bolívar's personal intervention and win her trial against her former owner, a wealthy patriot who was her former lover and the father of her child, and who was compelled to buy her freedom from her new master, see Townsend, "'Half My Body Free, the Other Half Enslaved.'"

26. Andrews, *The Afro-Argentines*, 44–45, 66; Borucki, "The Slave Trade to the Río de la Plata," 82–89; *Voyages*.

27. Klachko, "Le rôle de l'armée dans le processus de libération des esclaves," 280–84.

28. Lynch, *Las revoluciones hispanoamericanas*, 55–68; Andrews, *The Afro-Argentines*, 43.

29. Andrews, *The Afro-Argentines*, 27, 48–51, 54–55; Blanchard, *Under the Flags of Freedom*, 47–49.

30. Blanchard, *Under the Flags of Freedom*, 50–55; Klachko, "Le rôle de l'armée dans le processus de libération des esclaves," 284–88.

31. Blanchard, *Under the Flags of Freedom*, 59–63; Mata, "Negros y esclavos en la guerra por la independencia." In 1817, the Portuguese occupied Montevideo and promised immediate freedom to the slaves who would join their troops. At least 217 of them responded to the call and were drafted in a freedmen regiment (Bentancur, "Amos y esclavos en el viejo Montevideo," 160–61).

32. Feliú Cruz, *La abolición de la esclavitud en Chile*, 63–66; Contreras Cruces, "Artesanos mulatos y soldados beneméritos."

33. Blanchard, *Under the Flags of Freedom*, 87–92; Andrews, *The Afro-Argentines*, 116.

34. Blanchard, *Under the Flags of Freedom*, 92–112; Blanchard, *Slavery and Abolition in Early Republican Peru*, 14; Hünefeldt, *Paying the Price of Freedom*, 21–30, 87–90.

35. Klachko, "Le rôle de l'armée dans le processus de libération des esclaves," 289–300.

36. Andrews, *The Afro-Argentines*, 117–18.

37. Blackburn, *The Overthrow of Colonial Slavery*, 335.

38. Feliú Cruz, *La abolición de la esclavitud en Chile*, 91–133, 155–80 (quote p. 163–64).

39. *Voyages*; Thomas, *Cuba*, 72–84.

40. Baralt, *Slave Revolts in Puerto Rico*, 13–18.

41. Childs, *The 1812 Aponte Rebellion*, 155–71.

42. Childs, *The 1812 Aponte Rebellion*, 3–4; Palmié, *Wizards and Scientists*, 79–158.

43. Childs, *The 1812 Aponte Rebellion*, 176, 189–206.

44. Baralt, *Slave Revolts in Puerto Rico*, 21–30.

45. Baralt, *Slave Revolts in Puerto Rico*, 43–52; Díaz Soler, *Historia de la esclavitud negra en Puerto Rico*, 214–15.

46. Barcia, *Seeds of Insurrection*, 36.

Chapter 9

1. Nicholls, "Strangers Setting among Us."

2. *Voyages*.

3. Diouf, *Slavery's Exiles*, 209–29.

4. Lockley and Doddington, "Maroon and Slave Communities," 133–45.

5. Winks, *The Blacks in Canada*, 114–41; Weiss, *The Merikens*.

6. Bateman, "Africans and Indians," 33–34; Landers, *Black Society in Spanish Florida*, 220–48; Millett, *The Maroons of Prospect Bluff*; Rivers, *Rebels and Runaways*.

7. A. O. Thompson, *Flight to Freedom*, 128–29; Buman, "To Kill Whites," 45–50; Littlefield and Parins, *Encyclopedia of American Indian Removal*, 2:168–74.

8. L. M. Harris, *In the Shadow of Slavery*, 92; Berlin, *Generations of Captivity*, 168; Bordewich, *Bound for Canaan*, 11–103; Lucas, *A History of Blacks in Kentucky*, 1–2, 9, 78–79; Q. Taylor, *In Search of the Racial Frontier*, 37–39.

9. Heuman, introduction; Heuman, "Runaway Slaves in Nineteenth-Century Barbados," 106. On maritime marronage from the Danish West Indies, see N. A. T. Hall, *Slave Society in the Danish West Indies*, 124–38.

10. Ferrer, "Haiti, Free Soil, and Antislavery in the Revolutionary Atlantic," 42–43.

11. Higman, *Slave Populations of the British Caribbean*, 390–91.

12. *Voyages*.

13. Mam-Lam-Fouck, "La résistance au rétablissement de l'esclavage," 251–71; Oudin-Bastide, *Travail, capitalisme et société esclavagiste*, 298.

14. Régent, *La France et ses esclaves*, 165–66.

15. Oudin-Bastide, *Travail, capitalisme et société esclavagiste*, 300–303.

16. Hünefeldt, *Paying the Price of Freedom*, 18–19.

17. Helg, *Liberty and Equality*, 171, 186–87; Lombardi, *The Decline and Abolition of Negro Slavery in Venezuela*, 87–88.

18. La Rosa, *Runaway Slave Settlements in Cuba*, 5–12, 81–86; S. E. Johnson, "'You Should Give Them Blacks to Eat,'" 67–69. On Puerto Rico, see Nistal, *Esclavos prófugos y cimarrones*.

19. La Rosa, *Runaway Slave Settlements in Cuba*, 93–117.

20. Schwartz, "*Cantos* and *Quilombos*."

21. Karasch, *Slave Life in Rio de Janeiro*, 304–15.

22. Schwartz, *Slaves, Peasants and Rebels*, 106–7, 119. See also Moura, *Os quilombos*; Guimarães, *Uma negação da ordem escravista*.

23. Funes, "Comunidades Remanescentes dos Mocambos do Alto Trombetas," 9–10; Klein and Luna, *Slavery in Brazil*, 194–99.

24. U.S. Census Bureau, *Compendium of the Enumeration of the Inhabitants*, 368, 371. New Hampshire, with a handful of slaves recorded after 1800, did not legally abolish slavery until 1857.

25. Nash and Soderlund, *Freedom by Degrees*, 4–9; Hodges, "Black Revolt in New York City," 39; Gigantino, *The Ragged Road to Abolition*.

26. Rael, "The Long Death of Slavery," 129–33.

27. Yoshpe, "Record of Slave Manumissions," 79–80.

28. U.S. Census Bureau, *Compendium of the Enumeration of the Inhabitants*, 368, 371.

29. L. P. Jackson, "Manumission in Certain Virginia Cities."

30. Cole, "Capitalism and Freedom"; Matison, "Manumission by Purchase," 154–55; U.S. Census Bureau, *Compendium of the Enumeration of the Inhabitants*, 371.

31. Matison, "Manumission by Purchase," 150–53.

32. Klebaner, "American Manumission Laws," 443; Matison, "Manumission by Purchase."

33. U.S. Census Bureau, *Compendium of the Enumeration of the Inhabitants*, 367, 375.

34. Komisaruk, "Becoming Free, Becoming Ladino."

35. Helg, *Liberty and Equality*, 170; Andrews, *Afro-Latin America*, 64–65; Lombardi, *The Decline and Abolition of Negro Slavery in Venezuela*, 48–92. In Venezuela, the manumission juntas bought the freedom of so few slaves that in 1830 the government decreed that it would contribute to their funding in order to reach a total of twenty manumissions per year (Lombardi, *The Decline and Abolition of Negro Slavery in Venezuela*, 1).

36. Hünefeldt, *Paying the Price of Freedom*; Bentancur, "Amos y esclavos en el viejo Montevideo," 25–50.

37. Hünefeldt, *Paying the Price of Freedom*, 22, 25, 73.

38. For example, in Colombia, the number of slaves declined from 46,829 in 1825 to 38,840 ten years later (Lohse, "Reconciling Freedom with the Rights of Property," 208).

39. Handler and Sio, "Barbados," 224–30.

40. Titus, *The Amelioration and Abolition of Slavery in Trinidad*, 128–32; Spence, "Ameliorating Empire," 138–41, 174–84; Higman, *Slave Populations of the British Caribbean*, 76–77, 381.

41. Newton, "The King v. Robert James," 591–94.

42. Higman, *Slave Populations of the British Caribbean*, 381, 413–16. According to Higman, between 1808 and 1830 the yearly rate of manumission doubled to reach 2 per thousand in Demerara and Berbice, and 4 per thousand in Barbados; it remained stable in Antigua (less than 3 per thousand) and Jamaica (less than 1.5 per thousand); and it fell in Trinidad (from 6 to 4 per thousand—still comparatively high by British standards) (Higman, *Slave Populations of the British Caribbean*, 689–92). See also Handler, *The Unappropriated People*, 34–44.

43. Hoetink, "Surinam and Curaçao," 67–68. In 1817, Curaçao had a population of 2,780 whites, 4,549 free people of color, and 6,765 slaves; in 1833, it recorded 2,602 whites, 6,531 free people of color, and 5,894 slaves (Cohen and Greene, *Neither Slave nor Free*, 339).

44. *Voyages*.

45. Brana-Shute, "Sex and Gender in Suriname Manumissions," shows that in 1826, the rate of manumission was 2 per thousand for women, and 1 per thousand for men (181); Hoetink, "Surinam and Curaçao," 62.

46. Fallope, *Esclaves et citoyens*, 51, 100, 135–37.

47. Cardoso, *La Guyane française*, 393–95; Elisabeth, "The French Antilles," 143.

48. Régent, *La France et ses esclaves*, 272–82. For statistics, see Régent, *La France et ses esclaves*, 335–36, which show that with the continuation of illegal slave trade, between 1804 and 1842, the number of slaves remained stable in Guadeloupe and Martinique and increased in French Guiana after 1828.

49. Guadeloupe recorded ninety thousand slaves in the 1830s. Moitt, *Women and Slavery in the French Antilles*, 155–67; Fallope, *Esclaves et citoyens*, 80, 120–31.

50. Fallope, *Esclaves et citoyens*, 224, 278–301; Elisabeth, "The French Antilles," 146, 151–52.

51. Quoted in Childs, *The 1812 Aponte Rebellion*, 64; Bergad, García, and Barcia, *The Cuban Slave Market*, 122–28, 141.

52. Karasch, *Slave Life in Rio de Janeiro*, 335–62; Klein and Luna, *Slavery in Brazil*, 134–35.

53. Klein and Luna, *Slavery in Brazil*, 180. These are estimates as the first census of the Empire of Brazil was taken in 1872.

54. Klein and Luna, *Slavery in Brazil*, 291–92.

55. In Minas Gerais, in contrast, few new enslaved Africans were imported, and most *forros* (manumitted) continued to be urban mulatto women born in Brazil (Libby and Graça, "Notarized and Baptismal Manumissions").

56. According to Mieko Nishida, 137 manumissions were registered in Salvador de Bahia in 1808–9, 356 in 1821–22, and 396 (or a rate of 1.4 percent) in 1831–32, while the total number of slaves in the city rose from 14,696 in 1775 to 27,500 in 1835 (there are no figures available between 1775 and 1835) (Nishida, "Manumission and Ethnicity in Urban Slavery," 365, 375).

57. Nishida, "Manumission and Ethnicity in Urban Slavery"; Mattoso, *Ser escravo no Brasil*, 151.

58. See the synthesis of several studies in Klein and Luna, *Slavery in Brazil*, 254–68.

Chapter 10

1. Thésée, "La révolte des esclaves du Carbet," 560–67.
2. Thésée, "La révolte des esclaves du Carbet," 568–84. In 1816, Martinique had a population of 9,000 whites, 9,000 free people of color, and 80,000 slaves; twenty years later, the number of whites and slaves remained unchanged, but there were 30,000 free people of color who represented 19 percent of the island's total population (Elisabeth, "The French Antilles," 151). On the repression of free *gens de couleur* in Martinique and the persecution and condemnation of Cyrille Bissette, see Kennedy, "The Bissette Affair"; L. C. Jennings, "Cyrille Bissette."
3. Abénon, "Les résistances à l'oppression esclavagiste," 247–50.
4. Fallope, *Esclaves et citoyens*, 202–3 (quote p. 190).
5. Reis, *Slave Rebellion in Brazil*, 4–8, 43–44.
6. Schwartz, "*Cantos* and *Quilombos*"; Reis, *Slave Rebellion in Brazil*, 45–49.
7. Conrad, *Children of God's Fire*, 397–400; Reis, "Quilombos e revoltas escravas no Brasil," 23; Moura, *Dicionário da escravidão negra no Brasil*, 110–12.
8. Reis, *Slave Rebellion in Brazil*, 53–54.
9. Reis, *Slave Rebellion in Brazil*, 55–69.
10. Reis, *Slave Rebellion in Brazil*, 73–92. According to Reis's estimate, in 1835, the city of Salvador had 65,500 inhabitants: 42 percent were slaves, 30 percent, free people of color, and 28 percent, whites. One-third of the total population (22,000) were Africans, and among them 79 percent were slaves and 21 percent manumitted, which demonstrates the remarkable capacity of these *boçais* to (re)gain their freedom (Reis, *Slave Rebellion in Brazil*, 6).
11. Reis, *Slave Rebellion in Brazil*, 138–86 (p. 140 for statistics).
12. Reis, *Slave Rebellion in Brazil*, 189–230; Conrad, *Children of God's Fire*, 256–67.
13. Barcia, *Seeds of Insurrection*, 34–37.
14. In 1810, the U.S. South had 1 million slaves for a total population of slightly over 3 million; in 1830, 2 million slaves for 5,848,000 inhabitants (Cohen and Greene, *Neither Slave nor Free*, 339).
15. U.S. Census Bureau, *Census for 1820*, 18, 115, 123–24.
16. Faragher et al., *To 1877*, 313.
17. Egerton, *He Shall Go Out Free*, 175–202, 229–32; M. P. Johnson, "Vesey and His Co-Conspirators," 935–41.
18. Callahan, *The Talking Book*, 7–9.
19. Robertson, *Denmark Vesey*, inside cover.
20. Egerton, *He Shall Go Out Free*; M. P. Johnson, "Vesey and His Co-Conspirators," 937–40.
21. Vesey, *The Trial Record of Denmark Vesey*; Pearson, *Designs against Charleston*. For a detailed comparison of this report and two previous handwritten versions, see M. P. Johnson, "Vesey and His Co-Conspirators," 920–35. For responses to Johnson's article, see "Forum: The Making of a Slave Conspiracy," part 2, especially T. J. Davis, "Conspiracy and Credibility."
22. U.S. Census Bureau, *Census for 1820*, 115.
23. Egerton, *He Shall Go Out Free*, 101–53.
24. Quoted in M. P. Johnson, "Vesey and His Co-Conspirators," 963.
25. Egerton, *He Shall Go Out Free*, 103–20.
26. Lucas, *A History of Blacks in Kentucky*, 58, 98–99.
27. Callahan, *The Talking Book*, 130–49.
28. On the repression of the revolt, see Brophy, "The Nat Turner Trials," 1831–54.
29. Gray, *The Confessions of Nat Turner*. After an in-depth analysis of various archival

sources and contemporary newspapers, David Allmendinger concludes that the confessions presented by Gray correspond to Turner's views (Allmendinger, *Nat Turner*).

30. Gray, *The Confessions of Nat Turner*, 7–12. See also Allmendinger, *Nat Turner*, 11–24.

31. French, *The Rebellious Slave*, 7–32.

32. Quoted in Lambert, *White Creole Culture*, 114.

33. Heuman, "Runaway Slaves in Nineteenth-Century Barbados," 97–99, 105; Craton, *Testing the Chains*, 254–59; Beckles, "The Slave-Drivers' War," 105–6. On the 1692 slave revolt in Barbados, see chapter 4.

34. Geggus, "The Enigma of Jamaica in the 1790s," 294.

35. Craton, *Testing the Chains*, 258–62; Beckles, "The Slave-Drivers' War," 90–95, which gives the figure of 3,900 rebels (p. 95).

36. Craton, *Testing the Chains*, 254–66; Beckles, "The Slave-Drivers' War," 93–101.

37. Lambert, *White Creole Culture*, 127–35. See also "Sketch of a flag taken from the insurgent slaves at Barbados."

38. Matthews, *Caribbean Slave Revolts*, 58–70, 76–77; Blackburn, *The Overthrow of Colonial Slavery*, 322–26; Spierenburg, *The Spectacle of Suffering*, 92, 204; V. Brown, *The Reaper's Garden*, 201–19.

39. Turner, *Slaves and Missionaries*, 16–26, 65–70; Costa, *Crowns of Glory*, xvii–xviii.

40. Levy, "Barbados."

41. Titus, *The Amelioration and Abolition of Slavery in Trinidad*, 115–28. See also chapter 9.

42. On Akans as rebel leaders, see Schuler, "Akan Slave Rebellions."

43. Costa, *Crowns of Glory*, 167–97. For more on the Demerara revolt, see Craton, *Testing the Chains*, 267–90.

44. Costa, *Crowns of Glory*, 197–206.

45. Costa, *Crowns of Glory*, 208–16.

46. Costa, *Crowns of Glory*, 234–45; Matthews, *Caribbean Slave Revolts*, 114.

47. Costa, *Crowns of Glory*, 251–74 (quote p. 270).

48. Lambert, *White Creole Culture*, 140–42, 148–56.

49. Costa, *Crowns of Glory*, 275–92; Blackburn, *The Overthrow of Colonial Slavery*, 421–23, 434–36; Drescher, *Capitalism and Antislavery*.

50. Levy, "Barbados," 316; Gaspar, "Slavery, Amelioration, and Sunday Markets."

51. Patterson, *The Sociology of Slavery*, 273; Craton, *Testing the Chains*, 291.

52. Craton, *Testing the Chains*, 375–76 (n. 2); Geggus, "The Enigma of Jamaica in the 1790s," 294–95.

53. Higman, *Slave Populations of the British Caribbean*, 72–77, 303; V. Brown, *The Reaper's Garden*, 223. Between 1820 and 1832, average annual mortality rates of slaves in Jamaica varied between minus 2.1 per thousand and minus 4.8 per thousand (Higman, *Slave Populations of the British Caribbean*, 308).

54. Craton, *Testing the Chains*, 294.

55. Quoted in Craton, *Testing the Chains*, 295; Turner, *Slaves and Missionaries*, 150–51.

56. Turner, *Slaves and Missionaries*, 10–30, 47–59; V. Brown, *The Reaper's Garden*, 223–30. On George Leile, see chapter 5.

57. Quoted in Craton, *Testing the Chains*, 295.

58. Quoted in Turner, *Slaves and Missionaries*, 151.

59. Craton, *Testing the Chains*, 321.

60. Turner, *Slaves and Missionaries*, 154.

61. Turner, *Slaves and Missionaries*, 151–55; Craton, *Testing the Chains*, 297–301.

62. Turner, *Slaves and Missionaries*, 150, 156.

63. Quoted in Turner, *Slaves and Missionaries*, 160 (original spelling). Turner, *Slaves and Missionaries*, 156–60; Craton, *Testing the Chains*, 302–12.

64. Turner, *Slaves and Missionaries*, 160–62, 176n45; Craton, *Testing the Chains*, 314–15.
65. Quoted in Craton, *Testing the Chains*, 321; Craton, *Testing the Chains*, 291–321; Holt, *The Problem of Freedom*, 13–21; V. Brown, *The Reaper's Garden*, 232–34.
66. Matthews, *Caribbean Slave Revolts*, 180–83.
67. Matthews, *Caribbean Slave Revolts*, 4–17.
68. Holt, *The Problem of Freedom*, 92, 152.
69. Holt, *The Problem of Freedom*, 55–112; Blackburn, *The Overthrow of Colonial Slavery*, 421–57; Lambert, *White Creole Culture*, 204–6.

Epilogue

1. For comparative studies, see, for example, Engerman, *Slavery, Emancipation and Freedom*; Drescher and Emmer, *Who Abolished Slavery?*; and the helpful table 4.1 in Beauvois, *Between Blood and Gold*, 223.
2. L. C. Jennings, *French Anti-Slavery*, 123; Blackett, *Making Freedom*, 20–31.
3. On the role of slaves in the abolition of slavery in the Swedish and Danish colonies in 1847 and 1848, respectively, see Ekman, "Sweden, the Slave Trade and Slavery"; N. A. T. Hall, *Slave Society in the Danish West Indies*, 191–226.
4. L. C. Jennings, *French Anti-Slavery*, 123, 210–28, 278–84; Régent, *La France et ses esclaves*, 283–88; Régent, Gonfier, and Maillard, *Libres et sans fers*.
5. Sanders, *The Vanguard of the Atlantic World*, 30–34; Blanchard, *Slavery and Abolition in Early Republican Peru*, 113–20, 162–64, 191–207; Lombardi, *The Decline and Abolition of Negro Slavery in Venezuela*, 22–26.
6. McGraw, *The Work of Recognition*, 20–33; Lohse, "Reconciling Freedom with the Rights of Property"; Tovar, "La manumisión en Colombia."
7. Andrews, *The Afro-Argentines*, 56–58, 66–67, 96–101. Despite their large Amerindian workforce, Bolivia and Paraguay were the last former Spanish colonies on the American continent to adopt free-womb laws in 1831 and 1842, respectively, and to abolish slavery in the 1860s. Ecuador ended slavery in 1852 (Andrews, *Afro-Latin America*, 57).
8. Bordewich, *Bound for Canaan*; Blackett, *Making Freedom*.
9. D. Williams, *I Freed Myself*; Glymph, *Out of the House of Bondage*.
10. Emmer, "Who Abolished Slavery in the Dutch Caribbean?," 108–10; Oostindie, "Same Old Song?"
11. Barcia, *Seeds of Insurrection*; Paquette, *Sugar Is Made with Blood*; Reid-Vazquez, *The Year of the Lash*, 47–63.
12. R. J. Scott, *Slave Emancipation in Cuba*, 38; Schmidt-Nowara, *Empire and Antislavery*, 134–57.
13. La Rosa, *Runaway Slave Settlements in Cuba*, 93–117; R. J. Scott, *Slave Emancipation in Cuba*, 63–83, 111–72.
14. Graden, *From Slavery to Freedom in Brazil*, 53–82, 133–58; Cowling, *Conceiving Freedom*.
15. Klein, *African Slavery in Latin America*, 255–57; Graden, *From Slavery to Freedom in Brazil*, 159–96; Stein, *Vassouras*, 295.

Bibliography

Primary Sources

Aptheker, Herbert, ed. *Documentary History of the Negro People in the United States.* New York: Citadel Press, 1951.

Bajot, M., ed. *Annales maritimes et coloniales, ou recueil des Lois et Ordonnances royales [. . .]. Partie 2.* Paris: Imprimerie Royale, 1827.

Christophe, Henri, King of Haiti. *Henry Christophe and Thomas Clarkson: A Correspondence*, edited by Earl Leslie Griggs and Clifford H. Prator. Berkeley: University of California Press, 1952.

"The Code Noir, 1685." In *Slave Revolution in the Caribbean 1789–1804: A Brief History with Documents*, edited by Laurent Dubois and John D. Garrigus, 49–53. Boston: Bedford / St. Martin's, 2006.

"Collection of pay certificates for serving in the Connecticut Line in the Continental Army" (1780–82), available on http://www.scottwinslow.com/images/file/catalogs/Black_Soldiers.pdf (6 August 2017).

Condorcet, Marie Jean Antoine Nicolas Caritat de, marquis de. *Réflexions sur l'esclavage des nègres.* 1784; reprint, Paris: Flammarion, 2009.

Conrad, Robert Edgar. *Children of God's Fire: A Documentary History of Black Slavery in Brazil.* Princeton, N.J.: Princeton University Press, 1983.

Constitution of Hayti (1805). https://en.wikisource.org/wiki/Constitution_of_Hayti_(1805).

Constitution of the United States (1787). https://www.ourdocuments.gov/doc.php?flash=true&doc=9&page=transcript.

"The Declaration of Independence, 1 January 1804. Boisrond Tonnerre, *Liberté ou la mort.*" In *The Haitian Revolution: A Documentary History*, edited and translated by David Geggus, 179–80. Indianapolis: Hackett, 2014.

Documentos de la insurrección de José Leonardo Chirinos. Caracas: Fundación Historia y Comunicación, 1994.

Documentos para la historia del México independiente, 1808–1938. Mexico City: Miguel Ángel Porrúa, 2010.

Edwards, Bryan. *The History, Civil and Commercial, of the British Colonies in the West Indies.* 2 vols. 1st ed., Dublin: Luke White, 1793; 2nd ed., London: John Stockdale, 1794.

Equiano, Olaudah. *The Interesting Narrative of the Life of Olaudah Equiano, or Gustavus Vassa the African: Written by Himself.* London: Author, 1789. http://docsouth.unc.edu/neh/equiano1/menu.html.

"France Abolishes Slavery (Décret de la Convention nationale)." In *The Haitian Revolution: A Documentary History*, edited and translated by David Geggus, 112. Indianapolis: Hackett, 2014.

Gates, Henry Louis, Jr., ed. *The Classic Slave Narratives.* New York: Penguin Books, 1987.
Geggus, David, ed. and trans. *The Haitian Revolution: A Documentary History.* Indianapolis: Hackett, 2014.
Gray, Thomas R. *The Confessions of Nat Turner.* Baltimore: Lucas & Deaver, 1831. http://docsouth.unc.edu.
Horsmanden, Daniel. *The New York Conspiracy, or, A History of the Negro Plot, with the Journal of the Proceedings against the Conspirators at New York in the Years 1741–2 [. . .].*1744; reprint, New York: Southwick & Pelsue, 1810. https://books.google.ch/books?id=MSQ3AQAAMAAJ&dq=authornbsp:%22Daniel+Horsmanden%22&lr=&hl=fr&source=gbs_navlinks_s.
Irwin, Graham W., ed. *Africans Abroad: A Documentary History of the Black Diaspora in Asia, Latin America, and the Caribbean during the Age of Slavery.* New York: Columbia University Press, 1977.
Janvier, Louis Joseph. *Les Constitutions d'Haïti (1801–1885).* Vol. 1. Paris: C. Marpon et E. Flammarion, 1886.
Konetzke, Richard, ed. *Colección de documentos para la historia de la formación social de Hispanoamérica, 1493–1810.* 3 vols. Madrid: Consejo Superior de Investigaciones Científicas, 1953–62.
Long, Edward. *The History of Jamaica or, General Survey of the Antient and Modern State of the Island with Reflections on Its Situation Settlements, Inhabitants, Climate, Products, Commerce, Laws, and Government.* 3 vols. London: T. Lowndes, 1774. https://archive.org/details/historyofjamaica02long.
Lucena Salmoral, Manuel, ed. *Regulación de la esclavitud negra en las colonias de América Española (1503–1886): Documentos para su estudio.* [Alcalá de Henares, Madrid]: Universidad de Alcalá; [Murcia]: Universidad de Murcia, [2005].
———. *Les Codes noirs hispaniques.* Paris: UNESCO, 2005.
Manzano, Juan Francisco. *Autobiografía del esclavo poeta y otros escritos: Edición, introducción y notas de William Luis.* Madrid: Iberoamericana; Frankfurt am Main: Vervuert, 2007.
Moreau de Saint-Méry, Médéric-Louis-Elie. *Description topographique et politique de la partie française de l'isle de Saint-Domingue.* 3 vols. 1796; reprint, Paris: L. Guérin, 1875–76.
Pearson, Edward, ed. *Designs against Charleston: The Trial Record of the Denmark Slave Conspiracy of 1822.* Chapel Hill: University of North Carolina Press, 1999.
"Pennsylvania: An Act for the Gradual Abolition of Slavery, 1780." Avalon Project, Lillian Goldman Law Library, Yale Law School, http://avalon.law.yale.edu/18th_century/pennst01.asp.
Peytraud, Lucien. *L'esclavage aux Antilles françaises avant 1789: D'après des documents inédits des archives coloniales.* Paris: Hachette, 1897.
Prince, Mary. *The History of Mary Prince, a West Indian Slave: Related by Herself.* London: F. Westley and A. H. Davis, 1831. http://docsouth.unc.edu/neh/prince/prince.html.
Raynal, Guillaume-Thomas-François. *Histoire philosophique et politique des établissements et du commerce des Européens dans les deux Indes.* 6 vols. 1770; reprint, Amsterdam: [n.p.], 1773.
"Sketch of a flag taken from the insurgent slaves at Barbados, 1816." Originally enclosed in a dispatch dated 30 April 1816 from Admiral John Harvey. National Archives of the United Kingdom, MFQ 1/112.
Smith, Adam. *Selected Philosophical Writings.* Edited by James R. Otteson. Exeter: Imprint Academic, 2004.

Stavig, Ward, and Ella Schmidt, ed. and trans. *The Tupac Amaru and Catarista Rebellions: An Anthology of Sources*. Indianapolis: Hackett, 2008.
"Toussaint Louverture's Constitution, July 1801 (*Constitution de la colonie française de Saint Domingue*)." In *The Haitian Revolution: A Documentary History*, edited and translated by David Geggus, 160–64. Indianapolis: Hackett, 2014.
U.S. Census Bureau. *Census of Population and Housing*, 1790, 1810, 1840, 1860. www.census.gov/prod/www/decennial.html.
———. *Census for 1820*. Washington: Gale & Seaton, 1821. www.census.gov/prod/www/decennial.html.
———. *Compendium of the Enumeration of the Inhabitants and Statistics of the United States [. . .] Prepared at the Department of State*. Washington: Robert Allen, 1841. www.census.gov/prod/www/decennial.html.
U.S. War Department. *Report on the Census of Cuba, 1899*. Washington, D.C.: Government Printing Office, 1900.
Vesey, Denmark. *The Trial Record of Denmark Vesey*. Introduction by John Oliver Killens. Reprint of the 1822 ed. prepared by Lionel H. Kennedy and Thomas Parker and published as *An Official Report of the Trials of Sundry Negroes, Charged with an Attempt to Raise an Insurrection in the State of South-Carolina*. Boston: Beacon, 1970.
Voyages: The Trans-Atlantic Slave Trade Database. http://www.slavevoyages.org.
Wheatley, Phillis. *The Collected Works of Phillis Wheatley*. Edited by John C. Shields. New York: Oxford University Press, 1988.
———. *Poems on Various Subjects, Religious and Moral*. London: A. Bell, 1773. http://digital.tcl.sc.edu/cdm4/document.php?CISOROOT=/pwp&CISOPTR=138&REC=1.

Secondary Sources

Abenon, Lucien-René. *Petite histoire de la Guadeloupe*. Paris: L'Harmattan, 1993.
Abénon [sic], Lucien René. "Les résistances à l'oppression esclavagiste: Les révoltes serviles à la Martinique de 1789 à 1831." In *Rétablissement de l'esclavage dans les colonies françaises, 1802: Ruptures et continuités dans la politique coloniale française (1800–1830). Aux origines d'Haïti*, edited by Yves Bénot and Marcel Dorigny, 241–50. Paris: Maisonneuve & Larose, 2003.
Acosta Saignes, Miguel. *Vida de los esclavos negros en Venezuela*. Caracas: Hesperides Distribución-Ediciones, 1967.
Aizpurúa, Ramón. "En busca de la libertad: Los esclavos fugados de Curazao a Coro en el siglo XVIII." In *Influencias africanas en las culturas tradicionales de los países andinos: Memorias, II Encuentro para la Promoción y Difusión del Patrimonio Folclórico de los Países Andinos, Santa Ana de Coro, Noviembre 2001*, 69–102. [Caracas]: Ministerio de Educación, Cultura y Deportes, 2001.
Aizpurúa Aguirre, Ramón. "La insurrección de los negros de la serranía de Coro de 1795: Una revisión necesaria." *Boletín de la Academia Nacional de la Historia* (Caracas) 71 (July–September 1988): 705–23.
Alderson, Robert. "Charleston's Rumored Slave Revolt of 1793." In *The Impact of the Haitian Revolution in the Atlantic World*, edited by David P. Geggus, 93–111. Columbia: University of South Carolina Press, 2001.
Allmendinger, David F., Jr. *Nat Turner and the Rising in Southampton County*. Baltimore: Johns Hopkins University Press, 2014.
Andrews, George Reid. *The Afro-Argentines of Buenos Aires, 1800–1900*. Madison: University of Wisconsin Press, 1980.

———. *Afro-Latin America, 1800–2000*. New York: Oxford University Press, 2004.

Aptheker, Herbert. *American Negro Slave Revolts*. New York: Columbia University Press, 1943.

———. "Maroons within the Present Limits of the United States." In *Maroon Societies: Rebel Slave Communities in the Americas*, edited by Richard Price, 151–67. Baltimore: Johns Hopkins University Press, 1987.

———. *The Negro in the Civil War*. New York: International Publishers, 1938.

Araujo, Ana Lucia. *Shadows of the Slave Past: Memory, Heritage, and Slavery*. New York: Routledge, 2014.

Baralt, Guillermo A. *Slave Revolts in Puerto Rico: Slave Conspiracies and Unrest in Puerto Rico, 1795–1873*. Translated from Spanish by Christine R. Ayorinde. Princeton, N.J.: Markus Wiener, 2008.

Barbour, Hugh, and Jerry William Frost. *The Quakers*. New York: Greenwood, 1988.

Barcia, Manuel. *Seeds of Insurrection: Domination and Resistance on Western Cuban Plantations, 1808–1848*. Baton Rouge: Louisiana State University Press, 2008.

Barthélémy, Gérard. "Les esclaves révoltés à Saint-Domingue: Supplétifs, mercenaires et combattants." In *D'esclaves à soldats: Miliciens et soldats d'origine servile, xiiie–xxie siècles*, edited by Carmen Bernand and Alessandro Stella, 177–89. Paris: L'Harmattan, 2006.

Bastide, Roger. *Les Amériques noires, les civilisations africaines dans le nouveau monde*. Paris: Payot, 1967.

Bateman, Rebecca B. "Africans and Indians: A Comparative Study of the Black Carib and Black Seminole." In *Slavery and Beyond: The African Impact on Latin America and the Caribbean*, edited by Darién J. Davis, 29–54. Wilmington, Del.: Scholarly Resources, 1995.

Beatty-Medina, Charles. "Between the Cross and the Sword: Religious Conquest and Maroon Legitimacy in Colonial Esmeraldas." In *Africans to Spanish America: Expanding the Diaspora*, edited by Sherwin K. Bryant, Rachel S. O'Toole, and Ben Vinson III, 95–113. Urbana: University of Illinois Press, 2012.

Beauvois, Frédérique. *Between Blood and Gold: The Debates over Compensation for Slavery in the Americas*. New York: Berghahn, 2016.

Beckles, Hilary. *Black Rebellion in Barbados: The Struggle against Slavery, 1627–1838*. Bridgetown, Barbados: Antilles, 1984.

———. "From Land to Sea: Runaway Barbados Slaves and Servants, 1630–1700." In *Out of the House of Bondage: Runaways, Resistance and Marronage in Africa and the New World*, edited by Gad J. Heuman, 79–94. London: Frank Cass, 1986.

———. "The Slave-Drivers' War: Bussa and the 1816 Barbados Slave Rebellion." *Boletín de Estudios Latinoamericanos y del Caribe* 39 (December 1985): 85–110.

Bell, Richard. *We Shall Be No More: Suicide and Self-Government in the Newly United States*. Cambridge, Mass.: Harvard University Press, 2012.

Bennett, Herman L. *Africans in Colonial Mexico: Absolutism, Christianity, and Afro-Creole Consciousness, 1570–1640*. Bloomington: Indiana University Press, 2005.

Bénot, Yves. "La chaîne des insurrections d'esclaves dans les Caraïbes de 1789 à 1791." In *Les abolitions de l'esclavage: De L. F. Sonthonax à V. Schœlcher, 1793, 1794, 1848. Actes du colloque international tenu à l'université Paris-VIII les 3, 4 et 5 février 1994, organisé par l'Association pour l'étude de la colonisation européenne*, edited by Marcel Dorigny, 179–86. Paris: UNESCO; Saint-Denis: Presses Universitaires de Vincennes, 1995.

———. *La Guyane sous la Révolution française ou l'impasse de la révolution pacifique*. Kourou, French Guiana: Ibis Rouge, 1997.

Bentancur, Arturo Ariel. "Amos y esclavos en el viejo Montevideo: El combate por la libertad (1790–1820)." In *Amos y esclavos en el Río de la Plata,* edited by Arturo Ariel Bentancur and Fernando Aparicio, 15–206. Montevideo: Grupo Editorial Planeta, 2006.

Bergad, Laird W., Fe Iglesias García, and María del Carmen Barcia. *The Cuban Slave Market, 1790–1880.* Cambridge: Cambridge University Press, 1995.

Berlin, Ira. *Generations of Captivity: A History of African-American Slaves.* Cambridge, Mass.: Belknap Press of Harvard University Press, 2003.

———. *Many Thousands Gone: The First Two Centuries of Slavery in North America.* Cambridge, Mass.: Belknap Press of Harvard University Press, 1998.

Bernand, Carmen. *Negros esclavos y libres en las ciudades hispanoamericanas.* Madrid: Fundación Histórica Tavera, 2001.

Bernand, Carmen, and Alessandro Stella, eds. *D'esclaves à soldats: Miliciens et soldats d'origine servile, xiiie–xxie siècles.* Paris: L'Harmattan, 2006.

Bethell, Leslie, and José Murilo de Carvalho. "Brazil from Independence to the Middle of the Nineteenth Century." In *The Cambridge History of Latin America.* Vol. 3, *From Independence to c. 1870,* edited by Leslie Bethell, 679–746. Cambridge: Cambridge University Press, 1985.

Bilby, Kenneth M. *True-Born Maroons.* Foreword by Kevin Yelvington. Gainesville: University Press of Florida, 2005.

Bilby, Kenneth M., and Jerome S. Handler. "Obeah: Healing and Protection in West Indian Slave Life." *Journal of Caribbean History* 38 (2004): 153–83.

Blackburn, Robin. Introduction to *Paths to Freedom: Manumission in the Atlantic World,* edited by Rosemary Brana-Shute and Randy J. Sparks, 1–13. Columbia: University of South Carolina Press, 2009.

———. *The Overthrow of Colonial Slavery, 1776–1848.* London: Verso, 1988.

Blackett, R. J. M. *Making Freedom: The Underground Railroad and the Politics of Slavery.* Chapel Hill: University of North Carolina Press, 2013.

Blair, Barbara L. "Wolfert Simon van Hoogenheim in the Berbice Slave Revolt of 1763–1764." *Bijdragen tot de Taal-, Land- en Volkenkunde* 140 (1984): 56–76. www.jstor.org/stable/27863557.

Blanchard, Peter. *Slavery and Abolition in Early Republican Peru.* Wilmington, Del.: SR Books, 1992.

———. *Under the Flags of Freedom: Slave Soldiers and the Wars of Independence in Spanish South America.* Pittsburgh: University of Pittsburgh Press, 2008.

Blancpain, François. *La condition des paysans haïtiens: Du Code noir aux codes ruraux.* Paris: Karthala, 2003.

Blassingame, John W. *The Slave Community: Plantation Life in the Antebellum South.* New York: Oxford University Press, 1972.

Bly, Antonio T. "'Pretends He Can Read': Runaways and Literacy in Colonial America, 1730–1776." *Early American Studies* 6 (Fall 2008): 261–94.

Boidin, Capucine. "Esclaves, pardos et milices au Paraguay (xvii–xixe siècles)." In *D'esclaves à soldats: Miliciens et soldats d'origine servile, xiiie–xxie siècles,* edited by Carmen Bernand and Alessandro Stella, 341–64. Paris: L'Harmattan, 2006.

Bollettino, Maria Alessandra. "Slavery, War, and Britain's Atlantic Empire: Black Soldiers, Sailors, and Rebels in the Seven Years' War." PhD diss., Department of History, University of Texas at Austin, 2009. https://repositories.lib.utexas.edu/bitstream/handle/2152/ETD-UT-2009-12-543/BOLLETTINO-DISSERTATION.pdf?sequence=1&isAllowed=y.

Bond, Richard E. "Shaping a Conspiracy: Black Testimony in the 1741 New York Plot." *Early American Studies* 5 (Spring 2007): 65–94.

Bordewich, Fergus M. *Bound for Canaan: The Epic Story of the Underground Railroad, America's First Civil Rights Movement*. New York: Amistad, 2005.

Borrego Plá, María del Carmen. *Palenques de negros en Cartagena de Indias a fines del siglo diecisiete*. Sevilla: Escuela de Estudios Hispanoamericanos, 1973.

Borucki, Alex. "The Slave Trade to the Río de la Plata, 1777–1812: Trans-Imperial Networks and Atlantic Warfare." *Colonial Latin American Review* 20 (April 2011): 81–107.

Bowser, Frederick P. *The African Slave in Colonial Peru, 1524–1650*. Stanford: Stanford University Press, 1974.

———. "Colonial Spanish America." In *Neither Slave nor Free: The Freedmen of African Descent in the Slave Societies of the New World*, edited by David W. Cohen and Jack P. Greene, 19–58. Baltimore: Johns Hopkins University Press, 1972.

Brana-Shute, Rosemary. "Sex and Gender in Suriname Manumissions." In *Paths to Freedom: Manumission in the Atlantic World*, edited by Rosemary Brana-Shute and Randy J. Sparks, 175–96. Columbia: University of South Carolina Press, 2009.

Briggs, John [et al.]. *Crime and Punishment in England: An Introductory History*. London: University College London Press, 1998.

Brophy, Alfred L. "The Nat Turner Trials." *North Carolina Law Review* 91 (June 2013): 1813–80.

Brown, Christopher Leslie, and Philip D. Morgan, eds. *Arming Slaves: From Classical Times to the Modern Age*. New Haven, Conn.: Yale University Press, 2006.

Brown, Vincent. *The Reaper's Garden: Death and Power in the World of Atlantic Slavery*. Cambridge, Mass.: Harvard University Press, 2008.

———. "Slave Revolt in Jamaica, 1760–1761: A Cartographic Narrative." 2012. http://revolt.axismaps.com.

Bryant, Sherwin K. "Finding Gold, Forming Slavery: The Creation of a Classic Slave Society, Popayán, 1600–1700." *The Americas* 63 (July 2006): 81–112.

Buckley, Roger Norman. *Slaves in Red Coats: The British West India Regiments, 1795–1815*. New Haven, Conn.: Yale University Press, 1979.

Buman, Nathan A. "To Kill Whites: The 1811 Louisiana Slave Insurrection." MA thesis, Louisiana State University, 2008. http://etd.lsu.edu/docs/available/etd-07112008-110053/unrestricted/buman_thesis.pdf.

Burac, Maurice. *La Barbade: Les mutations récentes d'une île sucrière*. Bordeaux: Presses universitaires de Bordeaux, 1993.

Burnard, Trevor. *Mastery, Tyranny, and Desire: Thomas Thistlewood and His Slaves in the Anglo-Jamaican World*. Chapel Hill: University of North Carolina Press, 2004.

Callahan, Allen Dwight. *The Talking Book: African Americans and the Bible*. New Haven, Conn.: Yale University Press, 2006.

Calvo, Thomas. *L'Amérique ibérique de 1570 à 1910*. Paris: Nathan, 1994.

Campbell, Mavis. *The Maroons of Jamaica, 1655–1796*. Trenton, N.J.: African World Press, 1990.

Candlin, Kit. "The Role of the Enslaved in the 'Fedon Rebellion' of 1795." *Slavery and Abolition*. Forthcoming. https://www.tandfonline.com/doi/full/10.1080/0144039X.2018.1464623.

Cardoso, Ciro Flamarion Santana. *La Guyane française (1715–1817): Aspects économiques et sociaux. Contribution à l'étude des sociétés esclavagistes d'Amérique*. Petit-Bourg, Guadeloupe: Ibis Rouge, 1999.

Carroll, Patrick J. *Blacks in Colonial Veracruz: Race, Ethnicity, and Regional Development*. Austin: University of Texas Press, 1991.

Chandler, David L. *Health and Slavery in Colonial Colombia*. New York: Arno Press, 1981.

Chauleau, Liliane. *Dans les îles du vent, la Martinique, xviie–xixe siècle.* Paris: L'Harmattan, 1994.
C[hevalier], L[ouis]. "Peuplement et population de la Guadeloupe." *Population* 18 (January–March 1963): 137–41.
Childs, Matt D. *The 1812 Aponte Rebellion in Cuba and the Struggle against Atlantic Slavery.* Chapel Hill: University of North Carolina Press, 2006.
Christian, Charles M. *Black Saga: The African American Experience.* Boston: Houghton Mifflin, 1995.
Cohen, David W., and Jack P. Greene. Introduction to *Neither Slave nor Free: The Freedmen of African Descent in the Slave Societies of the New World,* edited by David W. Cohen and Jack P. Greene, 1–18. Baltimore: Johns Hopkins University Press, 1972.
———, eds. *Neither Slave nor Free: The Freedmen of African Descent in the Slave Societies of the New World.* Baltimore: Johns Hopkins University Press, 1972.
Cole, Shawn. "Capitalism and Freedom: Manumissions and the Slave Market in Louisiana, 1725–1820." *Journal of Economic History* 65 (December 2005): 1008–27.
Contreras Cruces, Hugo. "Artesanos mulatos y soldados beneméritos: El Batallón de Infantes de la Patria en la guerra de independencia de Chile, 1795–1820." *Historia* (Santiago) 44 (June 2011): 51–89, http://www.scielo.cl/pdf/historia/v44n1/art02.pdf.
Cooper, Afua. *The Hanging of Angélique: The Untold Story of Canadian Slavery and the Burning of Old Montreal.* Toronto: HarperCollins, 2006.
Costa, Emília Viotti da. *The Brazilian Empire: Myths and Histories.* Rev. ed. Chapel Hill: University of North Carolina Press, 2000.
———. *Crowns of Glory, Tears of Blood: The Demerara Slave Rebellion of 1823.* New York: Oxford University Press, 1994.
Cotta, Francis Albert. "Les compagnies de mulâtres et de noirs libertos: Mobilité sociale et offices militaires dans le Minas Gerais, Brésil, xviiie siècle." In *D'esclaves à soldats: Miliciens et soldats d'origine servile, xiiie–xxie siècles,* edited by Carmen Bernand and Alessandro Stella, 149–62. Paris: L'Harmattan, 2006.
Cowling, Camillia. *Conceiving Freedom: Women of Color, Gender, and the Abolition of Slavery in Havana and Rio de Janeiro.* Chapel Hill: University of North Carolina Press, 2013.
Cox, Edward L. "Fedon's Rebellion, 1795–1796: Causes and Consequences." *Journal of Negro History* 67 (Spring 1982): 7–19.
Craton, Michael. "The Black Caribs of St. Vincent: A Reevaluation." In *The Lesser Antilles in the Age of European Expansion,* edited by Robert L. Paquette and Stanley L. Engerman, 71–85. Gainesville: University Press of Florida, 1996.
———. *Testing the Chains: Resistance to Slavery in the British West Indies.* Ithaca, N.Y.: Cornell University Press, 1982.
Curtin, Philip D. *The Atlantic Slave Trade: A Census.* Madison: University of Wisconsin Press, 1969.
Davidson, David M. "Negro Slave Control and Resistance in Colonial Mexico, 1519–1650." In *Maroon Societies: Rebel Slave Communities in the Americas,* edited by Richard Price, 82–103. Baltimore: Johns Hopkins University Press, 1987.
Davis, David Brion. *Slavery and Human Progress.* New York: Oxford University Press, 1984.
Davis, Thomas J. "Conspiracy and Credibility: Look Who's Talking, about What: Law Talk and Loose Talk." In "Forum: The Making of a Slave Conspiracy," part 2, *William and Mary Quarterly* 59 (January 2002): 167–74.
Debbasch, Yvan. "Le Maniel: Further Notes." In *Maroon Societies: Rebel Slave Communities in the Americas,* edited by Richard Price, 143–48. Baltimore: Johns Hopkins University Press, 1987.

Debien, Gabriel. *Les esclaves aux Antilles françaises*. Basse-Terre, Guadeloupe: Société d'histoire de la Guadeloupe, 1974.

———. "Marronage in the French Caribbean." In *Maroon Societies: Rebel Slave Communities in the Americas*, edited by Richard Price, 107–34. Baltimore: Johns Hopkins University Press, 1987.

Degler, Carl N. *Neither Black nor White: Slavery and Race Relations in Brazil and the United States*. New York: Macmillan, 1971.

Demazière, Ève. *Les cultures noires d'Amérique centrale*. Paris: Karthala, 1994.

Díaz, María Elena. *The Virgin, the King, and the Royal Slaves of El Cobre: Negotiating Freedom in Colonial Cuba, 1670–1780*. Stanford: Stanford University Press, 2000.

Díaz Soler, Luis M. *Historia de la esclavitud negra en Puerto Rico*. 1953; reprint, [Río Piedras]: Editorial Universitaria, Universidad de Puerto Rico, 1981.

Din, Gilbert C. "Carondelet, the Cabildo, and Slaves: Louisiana in 1795." *Louisiana History: Journal of the Louisiana Historical Association* 38 (Winter 1997): 5–28.

Diouf, Sylviane A. *Slavery's Exiles: The Story of the American Maroons*. New York: New York University Press, 2014.

Domínguez, Jorge I. *Insurrection or Loyalty: The Breakdown of the Spanish American Empire*. Cambridge, Mass.: Harvard University Press, 1980.

Doolen, Andy. "Reading and Writing Terror: The New York Conspiracy Trials of 1741." *American Literary History* 16 (Fall 2004): 377–406.

Drescher, Seymour. *Capitalism and Antislavery: British Mobilization in Comparative Perspective*. New York: Oxford University Press, 1987.

Drescher, Seymour, and Pieter C. Emmer, eds. *Who Abolished Slavery? Slave Revolts and Abolitionism: A Debate with João Pedro Marques*. New York: Berghahn, 2010.

Dubois, Laurent. *Avengers of the New World: The Story of the Haitian Revolution*. Cambridge, Mass.: Belknap Press of Harvard University Press, 2004.

———. *A Colony of Citizens: Revolution and Slave Emancipation in the French Caribbean, 1787–1804*. Chapel Hill: University of North Carolina Press, 2004.

Du Bois, W. E. Burghardt. *Black Reconstruction in America: An Essay toward a History of the Part Which Black Folk Played in the Attempt to Reconstruct Democracy in America, 1860–1880*. 1935; reprint, New York: Russell & Russell, 1962.

Echeverri, Marcela. *Indian and Slave Royalists in the Age of Revolution: Reform, Revolution, and Royalism in the Northern Andes, 1780–1825*. New York: Cambridge University Press, 2016.

Egerton, Douglas R. *Gabriel's Rebellion: The Virginia Conspiracies of 1800 and 1802*. Chapel Hill: University of North Carolina Press, 1993.

———. *He Shall Go Out Free: The Lives of Denmark Vesey*. Madison, Wis.: Madison House, 1999.

———. "Slaves to the Marketplace: Economic Liberty and Black Rebelliousness in the Atlantic World." *Journal of the Early Republic* 26 (Winter 2006): 617–39.

Ekman, Ernst. "Sweden, the Slave Trade and Slavery, 1784–1847." *Revue Française d'Histoire d'Outre-Mer* 62 (1975): 221–31. 10.3406/outre.1975.1827.

Elisabeth, Léo. "The French Antilles." In *Neither Slave nor Free: The Freedmen of African Descent in the Slave Societies of the New World*, edited by David W. Cohen and Jack P. Greene, 134–71. Baltimore: Johns Hopkins University Press, 1972.

Elkins, Stanley M. *Slavery: A Problem in American Institutional and Intellectual Life*. Chicago: University of Chicago Press, 1959.

Eltis, David. *The Rise of African Slavery in the Americas*. Cambridge: Cambridge University Press, 2000.

———. "The Volume and Structure of the Transatlantic Slave Trade: A Reassessment." *William and Mary Quarterly* 58 (January 2001): 17–46.

Eltis, David, and David Richardson. "West Africa and the Transatlantic Slave Trade: New Evidence of Long-Run Trends." *Slavery and Abolition* 18, no. 1 (1997): 16–35.

Emmer, Pieter C. *The Dutch Slave Trade, 1500–1850*. Translated by Chris Emery. New York: Berghahn, 2006.

———. "Who Abolished Slavery in the Dutch Caribbean?" In *Who Abolished Slavery? Slave Revolts and Abolitionism: A Debate with João Pedro Marques*, edited by Seymour Drescher and Pieter C. Emmer, 103–11. New York: Berghahn, 2010.

Engerman, Stanley L. *Slavery, Emancipation and Freedom: Comparative Perspectives*. Baton Rouge: Louisiana State University Press, 2007.

Etemad, Bouda. *Crimes et réparations: L'Occident face à son passé colonial*. Brussels: André Versaille Editeur, 2008.

Fallope, Josette. *Esclaves et citoyens: Les Noirs à la Guadeloupe au xixe siècle dans les processus de résistance et d'intégration (1802–1910)*. Basse-Terre, Guadeloupe: Société d'histoire de la Guadeloupe, 1992.

Faragher, John Mack, Mari Jo Buhle, Daniel Czitrom, and Susan H. Armitage. *To 1877*. Vol. 1 of *Out of Many: A History of the American People*. 3rd ed. Upper Saddle River, N.J.: Prentice Hall, 1997.

Feliú Cruz, Guillermo. *La abolición de la esclavitud en Chile: Estudio histórico y social*. [Santiago de Chile]: Universidad de Chile, 1942.

Fernandes, Florestan. *A integração do negro na sociedade de classes*. São Paulo: Dominus Editôra, 1965.

Ferrer, Ada. "Haiti, Free Soil, and Antislavery in the Revolutionary Atlantic." *American Historical Review* 117 (February 2012): 40–66.

———. "La société esclavagiste cubaine et la révolution haïtienne." *Annales: Histoire, Sciences sociales* 58 (2003): 333–56.

Fick, Carolyn. "Emancipation in Haiti: From Plantation Labour to Peasant Proprietorship." *Slavery and Abolition* 21, no. 2 (2000): 11–40.

———. *The Making of Haiti: The Saint Domingue Revolution from Below*. Knoxville: University of Tennessee Press, 1990.

Finkelman, Paul. *Slavery and the Founders: Race and Liberty at the Age of Jefferson*. Armonk, N.Y.: M. E. Sharpe, 2001.

Foote, Thelma Wills. *Black and White Manhattan: The History of Racial Formation in Colonial New York City*. New York: Oxford University Press, 2004.

"Forum: The Making of a Slave Conspiracy." Part 1, *William and Mary Quarterly* 58 (October 2001): 913–76; part 2, *William and Mary Quarterly* 59 (January 2002): 135–202.

Fouchard, Jean. *Les marrons de la liberté*. Paris: Éditions de l'École, 1972.

Fox-Genovese, Elizabeth. *Within the Plantation Household: Black and White Women in the Old South*. Chapel Hill: University of North Carolina Press, 1988.

French, Scot. *The Rebellious Slave: Nat Turner in American Memory*. Boston: Houghton Mifflin, 2004.

Frey, Sylvia R. *Water from the Rock: Black Resistance in a Revolutionary Age*. Princeton, N.J.: Princeton University Press, 1991.

Freyre, Gilberto. *Casa-grande e senzala: Formação da família brasileira sob o regime de economia patriarcal*. Rio de Janeiro: Maia & Schmidt, 1933.

Frostin, Charles. *Les révoltes blanches à Saint-Domingue aux XVIIe et XVIIIe siècles (Haïti avant 1789)*. Preface by Olivier Pétré-Grenouilleau. 1975; reprint, Rennes: Presses universitaires de Rennes, 2008.

Funes, Eurípedes Antônio. "Comunidades Remanescentes dos Mocambos do Alto Trombetas." Projeto Manejo dos Territórios Quilombolas, Departamento de História, Universidade Federal do Ceará, December 2000. www.cpisp.org.br/comunidades/pdf/alto-trombetas.pdf.

Gainot, Bernard. "'Sur fond de cruelle inhumanité': Les politiques du massacre dans la révolution de Haïti." *La Révolution française*, Les massacres aux temps des révolutions, posted 8 January 2011, http://lrf.revues.org/index239.html.

García León, Susana. *La justicia en la Nueva España: Criminalidad y arbitro judicial en la Mixteca Alta (siglos XVII y XVIII)*. Madrid: Editorial Dykinson, 2012.

Garnot, Benoît. "Justice, infrajustice, parajustice et extra justice dans la France d'Ancien Régime." *Crime, Histoire and Sociétés / Crime, History and Societies* 4 (2000): 103–20.

Garrigus, John D. *Before Haiti: Race and Citizenship in French Saint-Domingue*. London: Palgrave Macmillan, 2007.

———. "Catalyst or Catastrophe? Saint-Domingue's Free Men of Color and the Battle of Savannah, 1779–1782." *Revista / Review Interamericana* 22 (1992): 109–25.

———. "Vincent Ogé *jeune* (1757–91): Social Class and Free Colored Mobilization on the Eve of the Haitian Revolution." *The Americas* 68 (July 2011): 33–62.

Gaspar, David Barry. *Bondmen and Rebels: A Study of Master-Slave Relations in Antigua, with Implications for Colonial British America*. Baltimore: Johns Hopkins University Press, 1985.

———. "From 'the Sense of Their Slavery': Slave Women and Resistance in Antigua, 1632–1763." In *More Than Chattel: Black Women and Slavery in the Americas*, edited by David Barry Gaspar and Darlene Clark Hine, 218–38. Bloomington: Indiana University Press, 1996.

———. "La Guerre des Bois: Revolution, War, and Slavery in Saint-Lucia, 1793–1838." In *A Turbulent Time: The French Revolution and the Greater Caribbean*, edited by David B. Gaspar and David P. Geggus, 102–30. Bloomington: Indiana University Press, 1997.

———. "Slavery, Amelioration, and Sunday Markets in Antigua, 1823–1831." *Slavery and Abolition* 9, no. 1 (1988): 1–28.

Gaspar, David B., and David P. Geggus, eds. *A Turbulent Time: The French Revolution and the Greater Caribbean*. Bloomington: Indiana University Press, 1997.

Gautier, Arlette. *Les sœurs de Solitude: La condition féminine dans l'esclavage aux Antilles du XVIIe au XIXe siècle*. 1985; reprint, Rennes: Presses universitaires de Rennes, 2010.

Geggus, David. "The Enigma of Jamaica in the 1790s: New Light on the Causes of Slave Rebellions. *William and Mary Quarterly* 44 (April 1987): 274–99.

———. "The French Slave Trade: An Overview." *William and Mary Quarterly* 58 (January 2001): 119–38.

———. *Haitian Revolutionary Studies*. Bloomington: Indiana University Press, 2002.

———. "Slave and Free Colored Women in Saint Domingue." In *More Than Chattel: Black Women and Slavery in the Americas*, edited by David Barry Gaspar and Darlene Clark Hine, 259–78. Bloomington: Indiana University Press, 1996.

———. "Slave Rebellion during the Age of Revolution." In *Curaçao in the Age of Revolutions, 1795–1800*, edited by Wim Klooster and Gert Oostindie, 21–56. Leiden: KITLV Press, 2011.

———. "Slave Resistance in the Spanish Caribbean in the Mid-1790s." In *A Turbulent Time: The French Revolution and the Greater Caribbean*, edited by David B. Gaspar and David P. Geggus, 131–55. Bloomington: Indiana University Press, 1997.

———. "The Slaves and Free Coloreds of Martinique during the Age of the French and Haitian Revolutions: Three Moments of Resistance." In *The Lesser Antilles in the Age of European Expansion*, edited by Robert L. Paquette and Stanley L. Engerman, 280–301. Gainesville: University Press of Florida, 1996.

———. "Sugar and Coffee Cultivation in Saint Domingue and the Shaping of the Slave Labor Force." In *Cultivation and Culture: Labor and the Shaping of Slave Life in the Americas*, edited by Ira Berlin and Philip D. Morgan, 73–98. Charlottesville: University Press of Virginia, 1993.

Genovese, Eugene D. *From Rebellion to Revolution: Afro-American Slave Revolts in the Making of the Modern World*. Baton Rouge: Louisiana State University Press, 1979.

———. *Roll, Jordan, Roll: The World the Slaves Made*. New York: Pantheon, 1974.

Germeten, Nicole von. *Violent Delights, Violent Ends: Sex, Race, and Honor in Colonial Cartagena de Indias*. Albuquerque: University of New Mexico Press, 2013.

Ghachem, Malick Walid. *The Old Regime and the Haitian Revolution*. New York: Cambridge University Press, 2012.

Gigantino, James J., II. *The Ragged Road to Abolition: Slavery and Freedom in New Jersey, 1775–1865*. Philadelphia: University of Pennsylvania Press, 2014.

Gilbert, Alan. *Black Patriots and Loyalists: Fighting for Emancipation in the War for Independence*. Chicago: University of Chicago Press, 2012.

Gilroy, Paul. *The Black Atlantic: Modernity and Double Consciousness*. London: Verso, 1993.

Girard, Philippe R. *The Slaves Who Defeated Napoléon: Toussaint Louverture and the Haitian War of Independence, 1801–1804*. Tuscaloosa: University of Alabama Press, 2011.

Gisler, Antoine. *L'esclavage aux Antilles françaises: Xviie–xixe siècle, contribution au problème de l'esclavage*. Fribourg: Éditions universitaires, 1965.

Glymph, Thavolia. *Out of the House of Bondage: The Transformation of the Plantation Household*. New York: Cambridge University Press, 2008.

Gómez, Alejandro E. "Entre résistance, piraterie et républicanisme: Mouvements insurrectionnels d'inspiration révolutionnaire franco-antillaise dans la côte de Caracas, 1794–1800." *Travaux et Recherches de l'UMLV* 11 (January 2006): 91–120.

Goslinga, Cornelis Ch. *The Dutch in the Caribbean and in the Guianas, 1680–1791*, edited by Maria J. L. van Yperen. Assen, Netherlands, and Dover, N.H.: Van Gorcum, 1985.

———. *The Dutch in the Caribbean and in Surinam, 1791/5–1942*. Assen, Netherlands: Van Gorcum, 1990.

Graden, Dale Torston. *From Slavery to Freedom in Brazil: Bahia, 1835–1900*. Albuquerque: University of New Mexico Press, 2006.

Gragg, Larry Dale. *The Quaker Community on Barbados: Challenging the Culture of the Planter Class*. Columbia: University of Missouri Press, 2009.

Graham, Sandra Lauderdale. *House and Street: The Domestic World of Servants and Masters in Nineteenth-Century Rio de Janeiro*. Cambridge: Cambridge University Press, 1988.

Grant, John N. "Black Immigrants into Nova Scotia, 1776–1815." *Journal of Negro History* 58 (July 1973): 253–70.

Griggs, Earl Leslie. Introduction to Henri Christophe, King of Haiti, *Henry Christophe and Thomas Clarkson: A Correspondence*, edited by Earl Leslie Griggs and Clifford H. Prator, 3–80. Berkeley: University of California Press, 1952.

Groot, Silvia W. de. "The Maroons of Surinam: Agents of Their Own Emancipation." In *Abolition and Its Aftermath: The Historical Context, 1790–1916*, edited by David Richardson, 55–77. London: Frank Cass, 1985.

———. *Van isolatie naar integratie: De Surinaamse Marrons en hun afstammelingen; officiele documenten betreffende de Djoeka's (1845–1863)*. s-Gravenhaage: M. Nijhoff, 1963.

Guimarães, Carlos Magno. *Uma negação da ordem escravista: Quilombos em Minas Gerais no século XVIII*. São Paulo: Icone Editora, 1988.

Gutiérrez Azopardo, Ildefonso. "Las cofradías de negros en la América Hispana: Siglos XVI–XVIII." N.d. http://www.africafundacion.org/IMG/pdf/Frater.pdf.

Guy, Donna J., and Thomas E. Sheridan. "On Frontiers." In *Contested Ground: Comparative*

Frontiers on the Northern and Southern Edges of the Spanish Empire, edited by Donna J. Guy and Thomas E. Sheridan, 3–15. Tucson: University of Arizona Press, 1998.

——, eds. *Contested Ground: Comparative Frontiers on the Northern and Southern Edges of the Spanish Empire*. Tucson: University of Arizona Press, 1998.

Hall, Douglas. "Jamaica." In *Neither Slave nor Free: The Freedmen of African Descent in the Slave Societies of the New World*, edited by David W. Cohen and Jack P. Greene, 193–213. Baltimore: Johns Hopkins University Press, 1972.

——. *In Miserable Slavery: Thomas Thistlewood in Jamaica, 1750–86*. London: Macmillan, 1989.

Hall, Gwendolyn Midlo. *Africans in Colonial Louisiana: The Development of Afro-Creole Culture in the Eighteenth-Century*. Baton Rouge: Louisiana State University Press, 1992.

Hall, Neville A. T. *Slave Society in the Danish West Indies: St. Thomas, St. John, and St. Croix*. Edited by B. W. Higman. Baltimore: Johns Hopkins University Press, 1992.

Halpern, Jean-Claude. "Les fêtes révolutionnaires et l'abolition de l'esclavage en l'an II." In *Les abolitions de l'esclavage: De L. F. Sonthonax à V. Schœlcher, 1793, 1794, 1848. Actes du colloque international tenu à l'université Paris-VIII les 3, 4 et 5 février 1994, organisé par l'Association pour l'étude de la colonisation européenne*, edited by Marcel Dorigny, 187–98. Paris: UNESCO; Saint-Denis: Presses Universitaires de Vincennes, 1995.

Handler, Jerome S. "Slave Revolts and Conspiracies in Seventeenth-Century Barbados." *New West Indian Guide* 56 (1982): 5–43.

——. *The Unappropriated People: Freedmen in the Slave Society of Barbados*. Baltimore: Johns Hopkins University Press, 1974.

Handler, Jerome S., and Arnold A. Sio. "Barbados." In *Neither Slave nor Free: The Freedmen of African Descent in the Slave Societies of the New World*, edited by David W. Cohen and Jack P. Greene, 214–57. Baltimore: Johns Hopkins University Press, 1972.

Hanger, Kimberly S. "Avenues to Freedom Open to New Orleans' Black Population, 1769–1779." *Louisiana History: The Journal of the Louisiana Historical Association* 31 (Summer 1990): 237–64.

Harris, J. William. *The Hanging of Thomas Jeremiah: A Free Black Man's Encounter with Liberty*. New Haven, Conn.: Yale University Press, 2010.

Harris, Leslie M. *In the Shadow of Slavery: African Americans in New York City, 1626–1863*. Chicago: University of Chicago Press, 2003.

Hart, Richard. *Slaves Who Abolished Slavery*. 2 vols. Kingston, Jamaica: Institute of Social and Economic Research, University of the West Indies, 1980–85.

Helg, Aline. *Liberty and Equality in Caribbean Colombia, 1770–1835*. Chapel Hill: University of North Carolina Press, 2004.

——. "La limpieza de sangre bajo las reformas borbónicas y su impacto en el Caribe neogranadino." *Boletín de Historia y Antigüedades* (Academia Colombiana de Historia) 100, no. 858 (January–June 2014): 143–80.

——. "Simón Bolívar's Republic: A Bulwark against the 'Tyranny' of the Majority." *Revista de Sociologia e Política* 20 (June 2012): 123–47, www.scielo.br/pdf/rsocp/v20n42/04.pdf.

Herrera, Robinson A. "'Porque no sabemos firmar': Black Slaves in Early Guatemala." *The Americas* 57 (October 2000): 247–67.

Herskovits, Melville J. *The Myth of the Negro Past*. New York: Harper, 1941.

Heuman, Gad. Introduction to *Out of the House of Bondage: Runaways, Resistance and Marronage in Africa and the New World*, edited by Gad Heuman, 1–8. London: Frank Cass, 1986.

——. "Runaway Slaves in Nineteenth-Century Barbados." In *Out of the House of Bondage: Runaways, Resistance and Marronage in Africa and the New World*, edited by Gad Heuman, 95–121. London: Frank Cass, 1986.

Higgins, Kathleen J. "Gender and the Manumission of Slaves in Colonial Brazil: The Prospects for Freedom in Sabará, Minas Gerais, 1710–1809." *Slavery and Abolition* 18, no. 2 (1997): 1–29.

———. *"Licentious Liberty" in a Brazilian Gold-Mining Region: Slavery, Gender, and Social Control in Eighteenth-Century Sabará, Minas Gerais*. University Park: Penn State University Press, 1999.

Higman, Barry William. *Slave Populations of the British Caribbean, 1807–1834*. Baltimore: Johns Hopkins University Press, 1984.

———. "The Sugar Revolution." *Economic History Review* 55 (May 2000): 213–36.

Hirschfeld, Fritz. *George Washington and Slavery: A Documentary Portrayal*. Columbia: University of Missouri Press, 1997.

Hodges, Graham Russell. "Black Revolt in New York City and the Neutral Zone, 1775–1783." In *New York in the Age of the Constitution, 1775–1800*, edited by Paul A. Gilje and William Pencak, 20–47. Rutherford, N.J.: Fairleigh Dickinson University Press, 1992.

———. *Root and Branch: African Americans in New York and East Jersey, 1613–1863*. Chapel Hill: University of North Carolina Press, 1999.

Hoetink, H[arry]. *Slavery and Race Relations in the Americas: Comparative Notes on Their Nature and Nexus*. New York: Harper & Row, 1973.

———. "Surinam and Curaçao." In *Neither Slave nor Free: The Freedmen of African Descent in the Slave Societies of the New World*, edited by David W. Cohen and Jack P. Greene, 59–83. Baltimore: Johns Hopkins University Press, 1972.

Holt, Thomas C. *The Problem of Freedom: Race, Labor, and Politics in Jamaica and Britain, 1832–1938*. Baltimore: Johns Hopkins University Press, 1992.

Hoogbergen, Wim S. M., *The Boni Maroon Wars in Suriname*. Leyden: E. J. Brill, 1990.

Hünefeldt, Christine. *Paying the Price of Freedom: Family and Labor among Lima's Slaves, 1800–1854*. Berkeley: University of California Press, 1994.

Hunt, Lynn. *Inventing Human Rights: A History*. New York: W. W. Norton, 2007.

Hurbon, Laënnec. "Église et esclavage au xviiie siècle à Saint-Domingue." In *Les abolitions de l'esclavage: De L. F. Sonthonax à V. Schœlcher, 1793, 1794, 1848. Actes du colloque international tenu à l'université Paris-VIII les 3, 4 et 5 février 1994, organisé par l'Association pour l'étude de la colonisation européenne*, edited by Marcel Dorigny, 87–100. Paris: UNESCO; Saint-Denis: Presses Universitaires de Vincennes, 1995.

Ishemo, Shubi L. "Forced Labour and Migration in Portugal's African Colonies." In *The Cambridge Survey of World Migration*, edited by Robin Cohen, 162–65. Cambridge: Cambridge University Press, 1995.

Izard, Miquel. *Orejanos, cimarrones y arrochelados*. Barcelona: Sendai Ediciones, 1988.

Jackson, Luther P. "Manumission in Certain Virginia Cities." *Journal of Negro History* 15 (July 1930): 278–314.

Jackson, Maurice. *Let This Voice Be Heard: Anthony Benezet, Father of Atlantic Abolitionism*. Philadelphia: University of Pennsylvania Press, 2009.

James, C. L. R. *The Black Jacobins: Toussaint Louverture and the San Domingo Revolution*. London: Secker and Warburg, 1938.

Jennings, Evelyn P. "Paths to Freedom: Imperial Defense and Manumission in Havana, 1762–1800." In *Paths to Freedom: Manumission in the Atlantic World*, edited by Rosemary Brana-Shute and Randy J. Sparks, 121–41. Columbia: University of South Carolina Press, 2009.

Jennings, Lawrence C. "Cyrille Bissette, Radical Black French Abolitionist." *French History* 9 (March 1995): 48–66.

———. *French Anti-Slavery: The Movement for the Abolition of Slavery in France, 1802–1848*. Cambridge: Cambridge University Press, 2000.

Jernegan, Marcus W. "Slavery and Conversion in the American Colonies." *American Historical Review* 21 (April 1916): 504–27.

Johnson, Lyman L. "Manumission in Colonial Buenos Aires, 1776–1810." *Hispanic American Historical Review* 59 (May 1979): 258–79.

Johnson, Michael P. "Vesey and His Co-Conspirators." *William and Mary Quarterly* 58 (October 2001): 915–76.

Johnson, Sarah E. "'You Should Give Them Blacks to Eat': Waging Inter-American Wars of Torture and Terror." *American Quarterly* 61 (March 2009): 65–92.

Jordan, Don, and Michael Walsh. *White Cargo: The Forgotten History of Britain's White Slaves in America*. New York: New York University Press, 2008.

Kafka, Judith. "Action, Reaction and Interaction: Slave Women in Resistance in the South of Saint Domingue, 1793–94." *Slavery and Abolition* 18, no. 2 (1997): 48–72.

Kaplan, Sidney, and Emma Nogrady Kaplan. *The Black Presence in the Era of the American Revolution, 1770–1800*. Greenwich, Conn.: New York Graphic Society, 1973.

Karasch, Mary. "Interethnic Conflict and Resistance on the Brazilian Frontier of Goaiás, 1750–1890." In *Contested Ground: Comparative Frontiers on the Northern and Southern Edges of the Spanish Empire*, edited by Donna J. Guy and Thomas E. Sheridan, 115–34. Tucson: University of Arizona Press, 1998.

Karasch, Mary C. *Slave Life in Rio de Janeiro, 1808–1850*. Princeton, N.J.: Princeton University Press, 1987.

Kars, Marjoleine. "Dodging Rebellion: Politics and Gender in the Berbice Slave Uprising of 1763." *American Historical Review* 121 (February 2016): 39–69.

Kennedy, Melvin D. "The Bissette Affair and the French Colonial Question." *Journal of Negro History* (January 1960): 1–10.

Kimmel, Ross M. "Blacks before the Law in Colonial Maryland." MA thesis, 1974. Maryland State Archive, Special Collection, http://msa.maryland.gov/msa/speccol/sc5300/sc5348/html/title.html.

Kinsbruner, Jay. *Not of Pure Blood: The Free People of Color and Racial Prejudice in Nineteenth-Century Puerto Rico*. Durham, N.C.: Duke University Press, 1996.

Klachko Rotman, Maïté. "Le rôle de l'armée dans le processus de libération des esclaves au Río de la Plata: Le cas des '*libertos*' de Buenos Aires (1806–1821)." In *D'esclaves à soldats: Miliciens et soldats d'origine servile, xiiie–xxie siècles*, edited by Carmen Bernand and Alessandro Stella, 279–300. Paris: L'Harmattan, 2006.

Klebaner, Benjamin Joseph. "American Manumission Laws and the Responsibility for Supporting Slaves." *Virginia Magazine of History and Biography* 63 (October 1955): 443–53.

Klein, Herbert S. *African Slavery in Latin America and the Caribbean*. New York: Oxford University Press, 1986.

———. *The Atlantic Slave Trade*. Cambridge: Cambridge University Press, 1999.

———. "Nineteenth-Century Brazil." In *Neither Slave nor Free: The Freedmen of African Descent in the Slave Societies of the New World*, edited by David W. Cohen and Jack P. Greene, 309–34. Baltimore: Johns Hopkins University Press, 1972.

Klein, Herbert S., and Francisco Vidal Luna. *Slavery in Brazil*. Cambridge: Cambridge University Press, 2010.

Klooster, Wim. "The Rising Expectations of Free and Enslaved Blacks in the Greater Caribbean." In *Curaçao in the Age of Revolutions, 1795–1800*, edited by Wim Klooster and Gert Oostindie, 57–74. Leiden: KITLV Press, 2011.

Knight, Franklin W. *The African Dimension in Latin American Societies*. New York: Macmillan, 1974.

Kolchin, Peter. *American Slavery, 1619–1877*. New York: Hill and Wang, 1993.
Kom, Anton de. *Wij slaven van Suriname—Wir Sklaven von Surinam*. Moscow: Verlagsgenossenschaft Ausländischer Arbeiter in der UdSSR, 1935.
Komisaruk, Catherine. "Becoming Free, Becoming Ladino: Slave Emancipation and *Mestizaje* in Colonial Guatemala." In *Blacks and Blackness in Central America: Between Race and Place*, edited by Lowell Gudmundson and Justin Wolfe, 150–74. Durham, N.C.: Duke University Press, 2010.
Kraay, Hendrik. "'Em outra coisa não falavam os pardos, cabras, e crioulos': O 'recrutamento' de escravos na guerra da Independência na Bahia." *Revista Brasileira de História* 22, no. 43 (2002): 109–26.
Lambert, David. *White Creole Culture, Politics, and Identity during the Age of Abolition*. Cambridge: Cambridge University Press, 2005.
Landers, Jane. *Black Society in Spanish Florida*. Urbana: University of Illinois Press, 1999.
———. "*Cimarrón* and Citizen: African Ethnicity, Corporate Identity, and the Evolution of Free Black Towns in the Spanish Circum-Caribbean." In *Slaves, Subjects, and Subversives: Blacks in Colonial Latin America*, edited by Jane G. Landers and Barry M. Robinson, 111–45. Albuquerque: University of New Mexico Press, 2006.
———. "Spanish Sanctuary: Fugitives in Florida, 1687–1790." *Florida Historical Quarterly* 62 (January 1984): 296–313.
———. "Transforming Bondsmen into Vassals: Arming Slaves in Colonial Spanish America." In *Arming Slaves: From Classical Times to the Modern Age*, edited by Christopher Leslie Brown and Philip D. Morgan, 120–45. New Haven, Conn.: Yale University Press, 2006.
Lara, Oruno. *La Guadeloupe dans l'histoire: La Guadeloupe physique, économique, agricole, commerciale, financière, politique et sociale de 1492 à 1900*. 1921; reprint, Paris: L'Harmattan, 1999.
La Rosa Corzo, Gabino. *Runaway Slave Settlements in Cuba: Resistance and Repression*. Translated from Spanish by Mary Todd. Chapel Hill: University of North Carolina Press, 2003.
Lavallé, Bernard. "Violence esclavagiste et marronnage à Trujillo (Pérou) au xviie siècle." In *La Violence en Espagne et en Amérique (xve–xixe siècles): Actes du colloque international "Les raisons des plus forts,"* edited by Jean-Paul Duviols and Annie Molinié-Bertrand, 271–90. Paris: Presses de l'université Paris-Sorbonne, 1997.
Lefebvre, Georges. *La Grande Peur de 1789, suivi de Les Foules révolutionnaires*. 1932; reprint, Paris: Armand Colin, 1988.
Le Guern, Erwann. "Une chose baptisée? Le statut juridique de l'esclave des colonies françaises sous l'Ancien Régime." Mémoire pour le DEA d'histoire du droit, Université Rennes-I, 2002–3, http://partages.univ-rennes1.fr/files/partages/Recherche/Recherche%20Droit/Laboratoires/CHD/Theses/LeGuern.pdf.
Lepore, Jill. *New York Burning: Liberty, Slavery, and Conspiracy in Eighteenth-Century Manhattan*. New York: Knopf-Vintage Books, 2005.
———. "The Tightening Vise: Slavery and Freedom in British New York." In *Slavery in New York*, edited by Leslie Harris and Ira Berlin, 57–89. New York: New Press, 2005.
Levy, Claude. "Barbados: The Last Years of Slavery, 1823–1833." *Journal of Negro History* 44 (October 1959): 308–45.
Libby, Douglas Cole, and Alfonso de Alencastro Graça Filho. "Notarized and Baptismal Manumissions in the Parish of São José do Rio das Mortes, Minas Gerais (c. 1750–1850)." *The Americas* 66 (October 2009): 211–40.
Linebaugh, Peter, and Marcus Rediker. *Many-Headed Hydra: Sailors, Slaves, Commoners, and the Hidden History of the Revolutionary Atlantic*. Boston: Beacon, 2000.

Littlefield, Daniel C. "Revolutionary Citizens: 1776–1804." In *To Make Our World Anew*, vol. 1: *A History of African Americans to 1880*, edited by Robin D. G. Kelley and Earl Lewis, 103–68. Oxford: Oxford University Press, 2005.

Littlefield, Daniel F., Jr., and James W. Parins, eds. *Encyclopedia of American Indian Removal*. 2 vols. Santa Barbara, Calif.: Greenwood, 2011.

Lockhart, James, and Stuart B. Schwartz. *Early Latin America: A History of Colonial Spanish America and Brazil*. Cambridge: Cambridge University Press, 1983.

Lockley, Tim, and David Doddington. "Maroon and Slave Communities in South Carolina before 1865." *South Carolina Historical Magazine* 113 (April 2012): 125–45.

Lockley, Timothy James, ed. *Maroon Communities in South Carolina: A Documentary Record*. Columbia: University of South Carolina Press, 2009.

Lohse, Russell. "Reconciling Freedom with the Rights of Property: Slave Emancipation in Colombia, 1821–1852, with Special Reference to La Plata." *Journal of Negro History* 86 (Summer 2001): 203–27.

Lokken, Paul. "Marriage as Slave Emancipation in Seventeenth-Century Rural Guatemala." *The Americas* 58, no. 2 (October 2001): 175–200.

Lombardi, John V. *The Decline and Abolition of Negro Slavery in Venezuela, 1820–1854*. Westport, Conn.: Greenwood, 1971.

Lora Hugi, Quisqueya. "El sonido de la libertad: 30 años de agitaciones y conspiraciones en Santo Domingo (1791–1821)." *Clío, Órgano de la Academia Dominicana de la Historia* 80 (July–December 2011): 109–40.

Lovejoy, Paul E. *Transformations in Slavery: A History of Slavery in Africa*. Cambridge: Cambridge University Press, 1983.

Lucas, Marion Brunson. *A History of Blacks in Kentucky: From Slavery to Segregation, 1760–1891*. Frankfort: University Press of Kentucky, 2003.

Lucena Salmoral, Manuel. "El derecho de coartación del esclavo en la América española." *Revista de Indias* 59, no. 216 (1999): 357–74.

Lynch, John. *Las revoluciones hispanoamericanas, 1808–1826*. 1976; reprint, Barcelona: Editorial Ariel, 1989.

Maestri Filho, Mário José. *L'esclavage au Brésil*. Paris: Karthala, 1991.

Mam-Lam-Fouck, Serge. *La Guyane française au temps de l'esclavage, de l'or et de la francisation (1802–1946)*. Petit-Bourg, Guadeloupe: Ibis Rouge, 1999.

———. "La résistance au rétablissement de l'esclavage en Guyane française: Traces et regards (1802–1822)." In *Rétablissement de l'esclavage dans les colonies françaises, 1802: Ruptures et continuités dans la politique coloniale française (1800–1830): Aux origines d'Haïti: Actes du colloque international tenu à l'université Paris-VIII les 20, 21 et 22 juin 2002*, edited by Yves Bénot and Marcel Dorigny, 251–71. Paris: Maisonneuve & Larose, 2003.

Marchand-Thébault, M.-L. "L'esclavage en Guyane française sous l'Ancien Régime." *Revue française d'histoire d'outre-mer* 47 (first quarter 1960): 5–75.

Martin, Michel Louis, and André G. Cabanis. "Choc de terreurs outremer: Haïtiens et Français à Saint-Domingue, 1802–1804." In *Justice et politique: La Terreur dans la Révolution française*, edited by Germain Sicard, *Études d'histoire du droit et des idées politiques* 1 (1997): 327–44.

Mata, Sara E. "Negros y esclavos en la guerra por la independencia, Salta 1810–1821." In *"Negros de la patria": Los afrodescendientes en las luchas por la independencia en el antiguo Virreinato del Río de la Plata*, edited by Silvia C. Mallo, Ignacio Tellesca, and Alex Borucki, 131–48. Buenos Aires: Editorial SB, 2010.

Matison, Sumner Eliot. "Manumission by Purchase." *Journal of Negro History* 33 (April 1948): 146–67.

Matthews, Gelien. *Caribbean Slave Revolts and the British Abolitionist Movement*. Baton Rouge: Louisiana State University Press, 2006.

Mattos, Hebe. "'Black Troops' and Hierarchies of Color in the Portuguese Atlantic World: The Case of Henrique Dias and His Black Regiment." *Luso-Brazilian Review* 45, no. 1 (2008): 6–29.

Mattoso, Kátia M. de Queirós. *Ser escravo no Brasil*. São Paulo: Brasiliense, 1982.

Maxwell, Clarence. "Enslaved Merchants, Enslaved Merchant-Mariners, and the Bermuda Conspiracy of 1761." *Early American Studies* 7 (Spring 2009): 140–78.

McFarlane, Anthony. "Autoridad y poder en Cartagena: La herencia de los Austrias." In *Cartagena de Indias en el siglo XVIII*, edited by Haroldo Calvo Stevenson and Adolfo Meisel Roca, 221–59. Bogotá: Banco de la República, 2005.

———. "*Cimarrones* and *Palenques*: Runaways and Resistance in Colonial Colombia." *Slavery and Abolition* 6, no. 3 (1985): 131–51.

McGraw, Jason. *The Work of Recognition: Caribbean Colombia and the Postemancipation Struggle for Citizenship*. Chapel Hill: University of North Carolina Press, 2014.

McKinley, Michelle A. *Fractional Freedoms: Slavery, Intimacy, and Legal Mobilization in Colonial Lima, 1600–1700*. New York: Cambridge University Press, 2016.

McManus, Edgar J. *Black Bondage in the North*. Syracuse: Syracuse University Press, 1973.

Meadows, R. Darrell. "Engineering Exile: Social Networks and the French Atlantic Community, 1789–1809." *French Historical Studies* 23 (Winter 2000): 67–102.

Melish, Joanne Pope. *Disowning Slavery: Gradual Emancipation and "Race" in New England, 1780–1860*. Ithaca, N.Y.: Cornell University Press, 1998.

Menschel, David. "Abolition without Deliverance: The Law of Connecticut Slavery 1784–1848." *Yale Law Journal Online* 111 (September 2001): 183–222. https://www.yalelawjournal.org/pdf/452_udpoi658.pdf.

Miller, Christopher L. *The French Atlantic Triangle: Literature and Culture of the Slave Trade*. Durham, N.C.: Duke University Press, 2008.

Miller, Joseph C. *Way of Death: Merchant Capitalism and the Angolan Slave Trade, 1730–1830*. London: J. Currey, 1988.

Millett, Nathaniel. *The Maroons of Prospect Bluff and Their Quest for Freedom in the Atlantic World*. Gainesville: University Press of Florida, 2013.

Moitt, Bernard. *Women and Slavery in the French Antilles, 1635–1848*. Bloomington: Indiana University Press, 2001.

Moomou, Jean. *Le monde des marrons du Maroni en Guyane (1772–1860): La naissance d'un peuple: Les Boni*. Matoury, French Guiana: Ibis Rouge, 2004.

Moomou, Jean, and members of APFOM, eds. *Sociétés marronnes des Amériques: Mémoires, patrimoines, identités et histoire. Du XVIIe au XXe siècles: Actes du colloque, Saint-Laurent-du-Maroni, Guyane française (18–23 novembre 2013)*. Matoury, French Guiana: Ibis Rouge éditions, 2015.

Moore, Christopher. "A World of Possibilities: Slavery and Freedom in Dutch New Amsterdam." In *Slavery in New York*, edited by Leslie Harris and Ira Berlin, 29–56. New York: New Press, 2005.

Moreno Fraginals, Manuel. "Aportes culturales y deculturación." In *África en América Latina*, edited by Manuel Moreno Fraginals, 13–33. Mexico: Siglo Veintiuno Editores, 1977.

———. *El ingenio: El complejo económico social cubano del azúcar*. 3 vols. Havana: Editorial de Ciencias Sociales, 1978.

Morgan, Philip D. "The Cultural Implications of the Atlantic Slave Trade: African Regional Origins, American Destinations, and New World Developments." *Slavery and Abolition* 18, no. 1 (1997): 122–45.

Morris, Thomas D. *Southern Slavery and the Law, 1619–1860*. Chapel Hill: University of North Carolina Press, 1999.

Moss, Simeon F. "The Persistence of Slavery and Involuntary Servitude in a Free State (1685–1866)." *Journal of Negro History* 35 (July 1950): 289–314.

Moura, Clóvis. *Dicionário da escravidão negra no Brasil*. São Paulo: Editora da Universidade de São Paulo, 2004.

———. *Os quilombos e a rebelião negra*. São Paulo: Brasiliense, 1981.

Moya Pons, Frank. "Casos de continuidad y ruptura: La revolución haitiana en Santo Domingo (1789–1809)." In *La crisis estructural de las sociedades implantadas*. Vol. 5 of *Historia General de América Latina*, edited by Germán Carrera Damas and John V. Lombardi, 137–61. Madrid: Trotta; Paris: UNESCO, 1999.

Mullin, Gerald W. *Flight and Rebellion: Slave Resistance in Eighteenth-Century Virginia*. New York: Oxford University Press, 1972.

Mullin, Michael. *Africa in America: Slave Acculturation and Resistance in the American South and the British Caribbean, 1736–1831*. Urbana: University of Illinois Press, 1992.

Nash, Gary B. *Race, Class, and Politics: Essays on American Colonial and Revolutionary Society*. Urbana: University of Illinois Press, 1986.

———. *Race and Revolution*. Madison, Wis.: Madison House, 1990.

Nash, Gary B., and Jean R. Soderlund. *Freedom by Degrees: Emancipation in Pennsylvania and Its Aftermath*. New York: Oxford University Press, 1991.

Navarrete, María Cristina. *Cimarrones y palenques en el siglo XVII*. Cali: Editorial Facultad de Humanidades, 2003.

———. "Los palenques, reductos libertarios en la sociedad colonial, siglos XVI y XVII." *Memoria y Sociedad* (Bogotá) 7, no. 14 (April 2003): 77–96.

Newton, Melanie J. "The King v. Robert James, a Slave, for Rape: Inequality, Gender, and British Slave Amelioration, 1823–1834." *Comparative Studies in Society and History* 47 (July 2005): 583–610.

Nicholls, Michael L. "Strangers Setting among Us: The Sources and Challenge of the Urban Free Black Population of Early Virginia." *Virginia Magazine of History and Biography* 108, no. 2 (2000): 155–79.

———. *Whispers of Rebellion: Narrating Gabriel's Conspiracy*. Charlottesville: University of Virginia Press, 2012.

Nishida, Mieko. "Manumission and Ethnicity in Urban Slavery: Salvador, Brazil, 1808–1888." *Hispanic American Historical Review* 73 (August 1993): 361–91.

Nistal Moret, Benjamín, ed. *Esclavos prófugos y cimarrones: Puerto Rico, 1770–1870*. Río Piedras: Editorial de la Universidad de Puerto Rico, 1984.

Ogle, Gene E. "Slaves of Justice: Saint Domingue's Executioners and the Production of Shame." *Historical Reflections / Réflexions historiques* 29 (Summer 2003): 275–93.

Oostindie, Gert. "Same Old Song? Perspectives on Slavery and Slaves in Suriname and Curaçao." In *Fifty Years Later: Antislavery, Capitalism and Modernity in the Dutch Orbit*, edited by Gert Oostindie, 143–78. Leiden: KITLV Press, 1995.

———. "Slave Resistance, Colour Lines, and the Impact of the French and Haitian Revolutions in Curaçao." In *Curaçao in the Age of Revolutions, 1795–1800*, edited by Wim Klooster and Gert Oostindie, 1–22. Leiden: KITLV Press, 2011.

Ortiz, Fernando. *Contrapunteo cubano del tabaco y el azúcar (advertencia de sus contrastes agrarios, económicos, históricos y sociales, su etnografía y su transculturación)*. Havana: J. Montero, 1940.

Oudin-Bastide, Caroline. *Travail, capitalisme et société esclavagiste: Guadeloupe, Martinique (xviie–xixe siècle)*. Paris: La Découverte, 2005.

Paiva, Eduardo França. "Revendications de droits coutumiers et actions en justice des esclaves dans le Minas Gerais du xviiie siècle." In *Brésil: Quatre siècles d'esclavage: Nouvelles questions, nouvelles recherches*, edited by Jean Hébrard, 115–31. Paris: Karthala, 2012.

Palmer, Colin A. *Slaves of the White God: Blacks in Mexico, 1570–1650*. Cambridge, Mass.: Harvard University Press, 1976.

Palmié, Stephan. *Wizards and Scientists: Explorations in Afro-Cuban Modernity and Tradition*. Durham, N.C.: Duke University Press, 2002.

Paquette, Robert L. "'A Horde of Brigands?': The Great Louisiana Slave Revolt of 1811 Reconsidered." *Historical Reflections / Réflexions historiques* 35 (Spring 2009): 72–96.

———. *Sugar Is Made with Blood: The Conspiracy of La Escalera and the Conflict between Empires over Slavery in Cuba*. Middletown, Conn.: Wesleyan University Press, 1988.

Paton, Diana. "Punishment, Crime, and the Bodies of Slaves in Eighteenth-Century Jamaica." *Journal of Social History* 34 (Summer 2001): 923–54.

Patterson, Orlando. "Slavery and Slave Revolts: A Sociohistorical Analysis of the First Maroon War, 1665–1740." In *Maroon Societies: Rebel Slave Communities in the Americas*, edited by Richard Price, 246–92. Baltimore: Johns Hopkins University Press, 1987.

———. *The Sociology of Slavery: An Analysis of the Origins, Development and Structure of Negro Slave Society in Jamaica*. 1967; reprint, Rutherford, N.J.: Fairleigh Dickinson University Press, 1975.

Pearson, Edward A. "'A Countryside Full of Flames': A Reconsideration of the Stono Rebellion and Slave Rebelliousness in the Early Eighteenth-Century South Carolina Lowcountry." *Slavery and Abolition* 17, no. 2 (1996): 22–50.

Pérez, Louis A., Jr. *To Die in Cuba: Suicide and Society*. Chapel Hill: University of North Carolina Press, 2005.

Pérotin-Dumon, Anne. "Économie corsaire et droit de neutralité: Les ports de la Guadeloupe pendant les guerres révolutionnaires." In *L'Espace caraïbe: Théâtre et enjeu des luttes impériales, xvie–xixe siècles*, edited by Paul Butel and Bernard Lavallé, 239–75. Bordeaux: Maison des Pays Ibériques, 1996.

———. "Free Coloreds and Slaves in Revolutionary Guadeloupe: Politics and Political Consciousness." In *The Lesser Antilles in the Age of European Expansion*, edited by Robert L. Paquette and Stanley L. Engerman, 259–79. Gainesville: University Press of Florida, 1996.

Phaf-Rheinberger, Ineke. "L'impossibilité d'une révolution caraïbéenne: Curaçao et Venezuela, 1795–1817." In *Haïti 1804: Lumières et ténèbres. Impact et résonance d'une révolution*, edited by Léon-François Hoffmann, Frauke Gewecke, and Ulrich Fleischmann, 125–41. Madrid: Iberoamericana; Frankfurt am Main: Vervuert, 2008.

Phelan, John Leddy. *The People and the King: The Comunero Revolution in Colombia, 1781*. Madison: University of Wisconsin Press, 1978.

Piecuch, Jim. *Three Peoples, One King: Loyalists, Indians, and Slaves in the Revolutionary South, 1775–1782*. Columbia: University of South Carolina Press, 2008.

Piquet, Jean-Daniel. *L'émancipation des Noirs dans la Révolution française (1789–1795)*. Paris: Karthala, 2002.

Pita Pico, Roger. *El reclutamiento de negros esclavos durante la independencia de Colombia 1810–1825*. Bogotá: Academia Colombiana de Historia, 2012.

Postma, Johannes M. *The Dutch in the Atlantic Slave Trade, 1600–1815*. Cambridge: Cambridge University Press, 1990.

Price, Richard. *The Guiana Maroons: A Historical and Bibliographical Introduction*. Baltimore: Johns Hopkins University Press, 1976.

———. "Introduction: Maroons and Their Communities." In *Maroon Societies: Rebel Slave Communities in the Americas*, edited by Richard Price, 1–30. Baltimore: Johns Hopkins University Press, 1987.

———, ed. *Maroon Societies: Rebel Slave Communities in the Americas*. Baltimore: Johns Hopkins University Press, 1987.

Price, Richard, and Sally Price. Introduction to *Stedman's Surinam: Life in an Eighteenth-Century Slave Society*, edited by Richard Price and Sally Price, xi–lxxv. Baltimore: Johns Hopkins University Press, 1992.

Pybus, Cassandra. *Epic Journeys of Freedom: Runaway Slaves of the American Revolution and Their Global Quest for Liberty*. Boston: Beacon, 2006.

———. "Jefferson's Faulty Math: The Question of Slave Defections in the American Revolution." *William and Mary Quarterly* 62 (April 2005): 3–64.

Quarles, Benjamin. *The Negro in the American Revolution*. 1961; reprint, Chapel Hill: University of North Carolina Press, 2012.

Rael, Patrick. "The Long Death of Slavery." In *Slavery in New York*, edited by Leslie Harris and Ira Berlin, 111–46. New York: New Press, 2005.

Régent, Frédéric. *Esclavage, métissage, liberté: La Révolution française en Guadeloupe, 1789–1802*. Paris: Grasset, 2004.

———. *La France et ses esclaves: De la colonisation aux abolitions (1620–1848)*. Paris: Grasset, 2007.

Régent, Frédéric, Gilda Gonfier, and Bruno Maillard. *Libres et sans fers: Paroles d'esclaves français. Guadeloupe, Île Bourbon (Réunion), Martinique*. Paris: Fayard, 2015.

Reid-Vazquez, Michele. *The Year of the Lash: Free People of Color in Cuba and the Nineteenth-Century Atlantic World*. Athens: University of Georgia Press, 2011.

Reis, João José. "Quilombos e revoltas escravas no Brasil." *Revista da Universidade de São Paulo* 14 (December 1995–February 1996): 14–39, www.usp.br/revistausp/28/02-jreis.pdf.

———. *Slave Rebellion in Brazil: The Muslim Uprising of 1835 in Bahia*. Translated by Arthur Brakel. Baltimore: Johns Hopkins University Press, 1993.

Reis, João José, and Flávio dos Santos Gomes. "Repercussions of the Haitian Revolution in Brazil, 1791–1850." In *The World of the Haitian Revolution*, edited by David Patrick Geggus and Norman Fiering, 284–313. Bloomington: Indiana University Press, 2009.

Restall, Matthew. "Black Conquistadors: Armed Africans in Colonial Spanish America." *The Americas* 57 (October 2000): 171–205.

———. *The Black Middle: Africans, Mayas, and Spaniards in Colonial Yucatan*. Stanford: Stanford University Press, 2009.

Ringrose, David R. *Spain, Europe, and the "Spanish Miracle," 1700–1900*. Cambridge: Cambridge University Press, 1996.

Rivera, Enrique Salvador. "Social Control on the Eve of a Slave Revolt: The Case of Coro, 1795." MA thesis, University of Maryland, College Park, 2013. http://drum.lib.umd.edu/bitstream/handle/1903/14152/Rivera_umd_0117N_14289.pdf?sequence=1&isAllowed=y.

Rivers, Larry Eugene. *Rebels and Runaways: Slave Resistance in Nineteenth-Century Florida*. Urbana: University of Illinois Press, 2012.

Roberts, Justin. *Slavery and the Enlightenment in the British Atlantic, 1750–1807*. New York: Cambridge University Press, 2013.

Robertson, David M. *Denmark Vesey: The Buried History of America's Largest Slave Rebellion and the Man Who Led It*. New York: Alfred A. Knopf, 1999.

Rosenwaike, Ira. *Population History of New York City*. Syracuse: Syracuse University Press, 1972.

Rupert, Linda M. "Inter-Colonial Networks and Revolutionary Ferment, Curaçao and

Tierra Firme." In *Curaçao in the Age of Revolutions, 1795–1800*, edited by Wim Klooster and Gert Oostindie, 75–96. Leiden: KITLV Press, 2011.

——. "'Seeking the Water of Baptism': Fugitive Slaves and Imperial Jurisdiction in the Early Modern Caribbean." In *Legal Pluralism and Empires, 1500–1850*, edited by Lauren Benton and Richard J. Ross, 199–231. New York: New York University Press, 2013.

Russell-Wood, A. J. R. *Slavery and Freedom in Colonial Brazil*. 1982; reprint, Oxford: Oneworld, 2002.

Sáez, José Luis. *La iglesia y el negro esclavo en Santo Domingo: Una historia de tres siglos*. Santo Domingo, Dominican Republic: Patronato de la Ciudad Colonial de Santo Domingo, 1994.

Saint-Louis, Vertus. "Les termes de citoyen et africain pendant la révolution de Saint-Domingue." In *L'Insurrection des esclaves de Saint-Domingue (22–23 août 1791): Actes de la table ronde internationale de Port-au-Prince (8 au 10 décembre 1997)*, edited by Laënnec Hurbon, 75–95. Paris: Karthala, 2000.

Sainton, Jean-Pierre, and Lydie Ho-Fong-Choy Choucoutou. "Le processus d'occupation des Petites Antilles (du milieu du XVIe au début du XVIIe)." In *Histoire et civilisation de la Caraïbe (Guadeloupe, Martinique, Petites Antilles)*, vol. 1: *Le temps des genèses, des origines à 1685*, edited by Jean-Pierre Sainton, Raymond Butin, Richard Château-Degat, Lydie Ho-Fong-Choy Choucoutou, and Georges B. Mauvois, 187–380. Paris: Maisonneuve & Larose, 2004.

Sanders, James E. *The Vanguard of the Atlantic World: Creating Modernity, Nation, and Democracy in Nineteenth-Century Latin America*. Durham, N.C.: Duke University Press, 2014.

Saunders, A. C. de C. M. *A Social History of Black Slaves and Freedmen in Portugal, 1441–1555*. Cambridge: Cambridge University Press, 1982.

Schama, Simon. *Rough Crossings: Britain, the Slaves and the American Revolution*. London: BBC Books, 2005.

Schmidt-Nowara, Christopher. *Empire and Antislavery: Spain, Cuba, and Puerto Rico, 1833–1874*. Pittsburgh: University of Pittsburgh Press, 1999.

Schuler, Monica. "Akan Slave Rebellions in the British Caribbean." 1970; reprinted in *Caribbean Women: An Anthology of Non-Fiction Writing, 1890–1980*, edited by Veronica Marie Gregs, 366–92. Notre Dame, Ind.: University of Notre Dame Press, 2005.

Schultz, Kirsten. *Tropical Versailles: Empire, Monarchy, and the Portuguese Royal Court in Rio de Janeiro, 1808–1821*. New York: Routledge, 2001.

Schwartz, Stuart B. "*Cantos* and *Quilombos*: A Hausa Rebellion in Bahia, 1814." In *Slaves, Subjects, and Subversives: Blacks in Colonial Latin America*, edited by Jane G. Landers and Barry M. Robinson, 247–72. Albuquerque: University of New Mexico Press, 2006.

——. "The Manumission of Slaves in Colonial Brazil: Bahia, 1684–1745." *Hispanic American Historical Review* 54 (November 1974): 603–65.

——. *Slaves, Peasants, and Rebels: Reconsidering Brazilian Slavery*. Urbana: University of Illinois Press, 1996.

——. *Sugar Plantations in the Formation of Brazilian Society: Bahia, 1550–1835*. Cambridge: Cambridge University Press, 1985.

Scott, James C. *Domination and the Arts of Resistance: Hidden Transcripts*. New Haven, Conn.: Yale University Press, 1990.

——. *Weapons of the Weak: Everyday Forms of Peasant Resistance*. New Haven, Conn.: Yale University Press, 1985.

Scott, Rebecca J. *Slave Emancipation in Cuba: The Transition to Free Labor, 1860–1899*. Princeton, N.J.: Princeton University Press, 1985.

Sensbach, Jon F. *Rebecca's Revival: Creating Black Christianity in the Atlantic World.* Cambridge, Mass.: Harvard University Press, 2005.

Sharp, William F. *Slavery on the Spanish Frontier: The Colombian Chocó, 1680–1810.* Norman: University of Oklahoma Press, 1976.

Sharples, Jason T. "Discovering Slave Conspiracies: New Fears of Rebellion and Old Paradigms of Plotting in Seventeenth-Century Barbados." *American Historical Review* 120 (June 2015): 811–43.

———. "Hearing Whispers, Casting Shadows: Jailhouse Conversation and the Production of Knowledge during the Antigua Slave Conspiracy Investigation of 1736." In *Buried Lives: Incarcerated in Early America*, edited by Michele Lise Tarter and Richard Bell, 35–59. Athens: University of Georgia Press, 2012.

Sheridan, Richard B. *Doctors and Slaves: A Medical and Demographic History of Slavery in the British West Indies, 1680–1834.* Cambridge: Cambridge University Press, 1985.

Sidbury, James. *Ploughshares into Swords: Race, Rebellion, and Identity in Gabriel's Virginia.* Cambridge: Cambridge University Press, 1997.

Snyder, Jennifer K. "Revolutionary Repercussions: Loyalist Slaves in St. Augustine and Beyond." In *The Loyal Atlantic: Remaking the British Atlantic in the Revolutionary Era*, edited by Jerry Bannister and Liam Riordan, 165–84. Toronto: University of Toronto Press, 2012.

Snyder, Terri L. *The Power to Die: Slavery and Suicide in British North America.* Chicago: University of Chicago Press, 2015.

Spence, Caroline Quarrier. "Ameliorating Empire: Slavery and Protection in the British Colonies, 1783–1865." PhD diss., Harvard University, Faculty of Arts and Sciences, 2014. http://dash.harvard.edu/bitstream/handle/1/13070043/Spence_gsas.harvard.inactive_0084L_11797.pdf.

Spierenburg, Pieter. *The Spectacle of Suffering: Executions and the Evolution of Repression. From a Preindustrial Metropolis to the European Experience.* Cambridge: Cambridge University Press, 1984.

Stampp, Kenneth M. *The Peculiar Institution: Slavery in the Ante-Bellum South.* New York: Knopf, 1956.

Stein, Stanley J. *Vassouras: A Brazilian Coffee County, 1850–1900: The Roles of Planter and Slave in a Plantation Society.* Princeton, N.J.: Princeton University Press, 1985.

Stipriaan, Alex van. *Surinaams contrast: Roofbouw en overleven in een Caraïbische plantagekolonie, 1750–1863.* Leiden: KITLV Uitgeverij, 1993.

Sweet, James H. "Manumission in Rio de Janeiro, 1749–1754: An African Perspective." *Slavery and Abolition* 24, no. 1 (2003): 54–70.

———. *Recreating Africa: Culture, Kinship, and Religion in the African-Portuguese World, 1441–1770.* Chapel Hill: University of North Carolina Press, 2003.

Sweet, John Wood. "The Subject of the Slave Trade: Recent Currents in the Histories of the Atlantic, Great Britain, and West Africa." *Early American Studies* 7 (Spring 2009): 1–45.

Tannenbaum, Frank. *Slave and Citizen: The Negro in the Americas.* New York: Vintage Books, 1946.

Tardieu, Jean-Pierre. *Cimarrones de Panamá: La forja de una identidad afroamericana en el siglo XVI.* Madrid: Iberoamericana; Frankfurt am Main: Vervuert, 2009.

Tavares, Luís Henrique Dias. *Da sedição de 1798 à revolta de 1824 na Bahia: Estudos sobre a sedição de 12 de agosto de 1798.* Salvador: EDUFBA; São Paulo: UNESP, 2003.

Taylor, Eric Robert. *If We Must Die: Shipboard Insurrections in the Era of the Atlantic Slave Trade.* Baton Rouge: Louisiana State University Press, 2006.

Taylor, Quintard. *In Search of the Racial Frontier: African Americans in the American West, 1528–1990.* New York: W. W. Norton, 1998.

Theobald, Mary Miley. "Slave Conspiracies in Colonial Virginia." *Colonial Williamsburg Journal* 28 (Winter 2006): 26–31, www.history.org/Foundation/journal/Winter05-06/conspiracy.cfm.

Théodat, Jean-Marie. *Haïti-République dominicaine: Une île pour deux, 1804–1916.* Paris: Karthala, 2003.

Thésée, Françoise. "La révolte des esclaves du Carbet à la Martinique (octobre–novembre 1822)." *Revue Française d'Histoire d'Outre-Mer* 80 (fourth quarter 1993): 551–84.

Thibaud, Clément. *Républiques en armes: Les armées de Bolívar dans les guerres d'indépendance du Venezuela et de la Colombie.* Rennes: Presses Universitaires de Rennes, 2006.

Thomas, Hugh. *Cuba, or, The Pursuit of Freedom.* 2nd rev. ed. New York: Da Capo, 1998.

Thompson, Alvin O. *Flight to Freedom: African Runaways and Maroons in the Americas.* Kingston, Jamaica: University of the West Indies Press, 2006.

Thompson, Vincent Bakpetu. *The Making of the African Diaspora in the Americas: 1441–1900.* White Plains, N.Y.: Longman, 1986.

Thomson, Sinclair. *We Alone Will Rule: Native Andean Politics in the Age of Insurgency.* Madison: University of Wisconsin Press, 2002.

Thornton, John K. *Africa and Africans in the Making of the Atlantic World, 1400–1680.* Cambridge: Cambridge University Press, 1992.

———. "'I Am the Subject of the King of Congo': African Political Ideology and the Haitian Revolution." *Journal of World History* 4 (Fall 1993): 181–214.

Titus, Noel. *The Amelioration and Abolition of Slavery in Trinidad, 1812–1834: Experiments and Protests in a New Slave Colony.* Bloomington: AuthorHouse, 2009.

Tovar, Jorge A. "La manumisión en Colombia, 1821–1851: Un análisis cuantitativo." Documentos CEDE 004387, Universidad de los Andes-Centro de Estudios sobre Desarrollo Económico, November 2007, https://core.ac.uk/download/files/153/6325261.pdf.

Townsend, Camilla. "'Half My Body Free, the Other Half Enslaved': The Politics of the Slaves of Guayaquil at the End of the Colonial Era." *Colonial Latin American Review* 7 (1998): 105–28.

Trani, Lionel. *La Martinique napoléonienne, 1802–1809: Entre ségrégation, esclavage et intégration.* Preface by Bernard Gainot. Paris: Éditions SPM, 2014.

Trouillot, Michel-Rolph. *Haiti, State against Nation: The Origins and Legacy of Duvalierism.* New York: Monthly Review Press, 1990.

———. *Silencing the Past: Power and the Production of History.* Boston: Beacon, 1995.

Turner, Mary. *Slaves and Missionaries: The Disintegration of Jamaican Slave Society, 1787–1834.* Urbana: University of Illinois Press, 1982.

Valencia Villa, Carlos Eduardo. *Alma en boca y huesos en costal: Una aproximación a los contrastes socio-económicos de la esclavitud, Santafé, Mariquita y Mompox, 1610–1660.* Bogotá: Instituto Colombiano de Antropología e Historia, 2003.

Valim, Patrícia. "Corporação dos enteados-tensão, contestação e negociação política na Conjuração Baiana de 1798." PhD diss., Universidade de São Paulo, 2012. http://www.teses.usp.br/teses/disponiveis/8/8137/tde-02042013-115539/pt-br.php.

Van Young, Eric. *The Other Rebellion: Popular Violence, Ideology, and the Mexican Struggle for Independence, 1810–1821.* Stanford: Stanford University Press, 2001.

Vidal, Cécile. "Africains et Européens au pays des Illinois durant la période française (1699–1765)." *French Colonial History* 3 (2003): 51–68.

———. "Church, Métissage, and the Language of Race in the Mississippi Colony during the French Period." In *Louisiana: Crossroads of the Atlantic World,* edited by Cécile Vidal, 125–46. Philadelphia: University of Pennsylvania Press, 2013.

Vignaux, Hélène. *Esclavage et rébellion: La construction sociale des Noirs et des mulâtres (Nouvelle-Grenade, xviie siècle)*. Montpellier: Presses Universitaires de la Méditerranée, 2007.

Vincent, Ted. "The Blacks Who Freed Mexico." *Journal of Negro History* 9 (Summer 1994): 257–76.

Voelz, Peter Michael. *Slave and Soldier: The Military Impact of Blacks in the Colonial Americas*. New York: Garland, 1993.

Walvin, James. *The Zong: A Massacre, the Law and the End of Slavery*. New Haven, Conn.: Yale University Press, 2011.

Weiss, John M. *The Merikens: Free Black American Settlers in Trinidad, 1815–16*. London: McNish & Weiss, 2002.

White, Deborah Gray. *Ar'n't I a Woman? Female Slaves in the Plantation South*. New York: W. W. Norton, 1985.

Wiecek, William M. "The Statutory Law of Slavery and Race in the Thirteen Mainland Colonies of British America." *William and Mary Quarterly*, 3rd ser., 34 (April 1977): 258–80.

Williams, David. *I Freed Myself: African American Self-Emancipation in the Civil War Era*. New York: Cambridge University Press, 2014.

Williams, Eric E. *Capitalism and Slavery*. Chapel Hill: University of North Carolina Press, 1944.

Winks, Robin W. *The Blacks in Canada: A History*. New Haven, Conn.: Yale University Press, 1972.

Wong, Edlie L. *Neither Fugitive nor Free: Atlantic Slavery, Freedom Suits, and the Legal Culture of Travel*. New York: New York University Press, 2009.

Wood, Peter H. *Black Majority: Negroes in Colonial South Carolina, from 1670 through the Stono Rebellion*. New York: W. W. Norton, 1975.

Yoshpe, Harry B. "Record of Slave Manumissions in New York during the Colonial and Early National Periods." *Journal of Negro History* 26 (January 1941): 78–107.

Zabin, Serena. *Dangerous Economies: Status and Commerce in Imperial New York*. Philadelphia: University of Pennsylvania Press, 2009.

Zeuske, Michael. "Historiography and Research Problems of Slavery and the Slave Trade in a Global-Historical Perspective." *International Review of Social History* 57 (April 2012): 87–111.

Zuluaga R., Francisco U. *Guerrilla y sociedad en el Patía: Una relación entre clientelismo político y la insurgencia social*. Cali: Universidad del Valle, Facultad de Humanidades, 1993.

Index

Page numbers in *italics* refer to illustrations.

Abenon, Lucien-René, 98, 247
Abner, Andrew (in Connecticut), 131
abolition of slavery, 3, 7, 13–14, 275–76; in Brazil, 283–84; in Caribbean colonies, 5, 10, 13, 152–53, 160, 237, 281–83; France and, 140, 152, 165–66, 174–75, 198, 276–77; Great Britain and (*see* abolition of slavery and Great Britain); liberals and, 277–78; in Mexico and Guatemala, 199–201, 232; Netherlands and, 176, 280–81; Portugal and, 197, 305n2; in Hispanic South America, 169, 197, 214, 232–33, 275, 277–78; Spain and, 178, 281–83; in United States, 29, 133–35, 136, 229–31, 254, 279–80, 307n24. *See also* revolt and abolitionism; *under specific colonies, countries, and states*
abolition of slavery and Great Britain: "amelioration" recommendations and, 261–62; movement of, 9–10, 194, 245, 256, 260, 265, 271–73, 275, 299n52; Parliament and, 5, 34, 136, 266–67, 273
abolition of slave trade, 19–20, 28, 29, 33, 195, 201, 218, 256, 289n15
abortion, 66
Accarra (in Berbice), 105, 107
Act for the Gradual Abolition of Slavery, 134, 300n59
Africa, as source of slave trade, 17, 20, 27; colonization of, 130, 256; origin of slaves in, 17. *See also* Akans; Angolas; Bambaras; Kongos; Hausas; Igbos; Mandingas; Minas; Yorubas
African diaspora studies, 10, 288n21
African Methodist Episcopalian (AME) Church, 252–53

Afro-descendants, free: discrimination of, 37–38. *See also* free people of color; *under specific colonies, countries, and states*
afterlife, slave beliefs in, 108
agriculture militarization, 154–56, 158, 160, 162, 168, 170, 181
Akans, 17, 54, 88, 92, 96, 101–6, 191, 262
Alabama, 137, 224, 231
Alaou (in Saint Domingue), 157
Alfonso XIII (king of Spain), 36
Allen, Richard, 252
All Saints Bay, Brazil, 248
Amazonian region, Brazil, 228, 284
"amelioration of slavery," 226, 235, 261–63, 265, 267, 271–73, 276, 280–81
American Dilemma: The Negro Problem and Modern Democracy, An (Myrdal), 8
American Revolution. *See* War of Independence (U.S.)
Amerindians: blood purity and, 38; conquest against, 77–79, 82; enslaved, 21–22, 23, 27, 45, 58, 76, 86, 123, 135; labor tribute of, 22, 45, 69, 177, 234; marronage and, 44, 47, 48, 49, 51, 52, 54, 58, 60, 106; Natchez, 58; population, 21–23, 60, 184, 201; revolt by, 82, 177–78; selling of slaves by, 129; Seminoles, 223–24; trade with, 28
Amherstburg, Canada, 224
Ana María (in Boca Nigua), 181
anciens libres, 159, 160–61, 162, 168, 302n36
Andean region, 177–78, 212
Angélique (in Montreal), 95
Angolas, 17, 48, 51, 59, 78
Antigua: emancipation in, 72, 236, 275, 308n42; marronage in, 56, 226; revolt

and conspiracy in, 95–98, 104, 109; slave population of, 95; slave treatment in, 266
Antioquia province, Colombia, 26, 46, 177
Anti-Slavery Society, 261, 271, 275, 283–84
Antonio (in Boca Nigua), 181
Antonio, Domingo (in Argentina), 213
Aponte, José Antonio, 216
Aponte's conspiracy, 216
Appea (in Barbados), 225
Appeal to the Coloured Citizens of the World, An (Walker), 254
apprentices: slaves as, 195, 273, 281, 282–83
Aptheker, Herbert, 7
Arbuthnot, Robert, 96
Argentina, 38, 208–10, 214, 278. See also Río de la Plata
Armand (in Saint Domingue), 149, 151
Armistead, James (in Virginia), 131, *132*
Army of the Andes, 209–10, 306n31
asylum policy of Spain, 56–58, 59, 60–61, 178, 185, 292n43
Atanásio, King (in Brazil), 228
Atta (in Berbice), 106, 107
Attucks, Crispus, 123
Aztec Empire, 21, 22

Bahamas, the, 92, 128, 237
Bahia, Brazil, 51, 192, 198, 227–28, 247–50. See also Salvador de Bahia, Brazil
Baker, Briston (in New Haven), 131
Bambaras, 17, 95
Baoruco Mountains, Santo Domingo, 151
baptism of slaves: by Catholic Church, 35, 93, 94, 108, 115, 239; emancipation and, 57, 66–67, 74, 75, 93–94, 115, 239; religious development and, 128, 267–68. See also evangelization of slaves
Baptist General Committee of Virginia, 137
Baptist Rebellion in Jamaica, 266–70
Baptists, 115, 136, 137, 265, 267; black, 128–29, 188, 267–68. See also Native Baptists
Barbados: emancipation in, 72, 235, 236, 237, 308n42; marronage in, 53–54, 226, 257; protest in, 73; reexportation of slaves from, 26; revolt and conspiracy in, 88–90, 245, 256–67, *259*, 271; slave imports and population of, 24, 88, 89, 256–57; sugar plantation model and, 24–25
Bardales, Juan (in Central America), 78
Barlovento, Venezuela, 201, 202
Barthélémy, Gérard, 161
Basse-Terre, Guadeloupe, 55, 98, 172, 226
Batavian Republic, 175
Battle of Vertières, 160
Bayamo, Cuba, 216
Bayamón, Puerto Rico, 217
Bear Creek, 127
Beauvois, Frédérique, 301n15
Beckles, Hilary, 10
Belize, 258, 275
Bell, Graham, 138
Ben (in Barbados), 89–90
Bénech, Gilles (in Saint Domingue), 158
Benkos (in Colombia), 49
Bennett, Herman, 21
Bénot, Yves, 170
Berbice, 34; population of, 104–5; revolt in, 101, 104–7, 308n42
Berlin, Ira, 26
Bermuda, 104, 223
Bett, Mum (in Massachusetts), 133
Biassou, Georges (in Saint Domingue), 144, 147, 149, 151, 152, 156, 157
Bill of Rights of 1689, 85
Bioho, Domingo (in Colombia), 49
Birch, Samuel, 129
Birchtown, Canada, 129
Bissette, Cyrille, 246
Black Brigade, 120, 129
black companies in Continental Army, 123
black companies in Royal Army, 120, 122, 128, 129, 194–95
Black Dragoons, 122, 128
Black Jacobins, The (James), 7
Black Reconstruction in America (Du Bois), 7
blood purity, 37–38, 39
Boas, Franz, 7
boçais, 21, 24, 51, 241, 242–43, 309n10; emancipation and, 241–42
Boca Nigua, Santo Domingo, 180–81
Bohio, Juana (in Lima), 66
Bois-Caïman ceremony, 144
Bolívar, Simón, 202–7, 212, 279–80, 305n12, 306n25

Bolivia, 34, 232–33, 311n7
bombas, 217
Bonaparte, Napoleon, 33, 140–41, 157–59, 163, 171–72, 197
bossales, 21, 30, 34, 56, 76, 239, 247, 271, 294n33; in Saint Domingue revolt, 140, 145–46, 156, 159
Boston, 104, 114, 118
Boston King (in Charleston), 126, 130
Boukman (in Saint Domingue), 144, 146
Bourbon reforms, 176–79
Boves, José Tomás, 202, 203, 204
Boyer, Jean-Pierre, 163, 181, 217, 253
bozales, 21; Cuba and, 31, 216; emancipation and, 77–78, 240; marronage and, 45–46, 47; Peru and, 23; revolt and conspiracy and, 87, 182; Río de la Plata and, 199, 208
Bran, Antón (in Lima), 67
Brazil: abolition of slavery in, 275, 283–84; emancipation in, 36, 65–67, 78–79, 241–43, 293n2, 308n55; Haitian Revolution impact in, 192; historiography of, 6, 8, 9; independence of, 198; marronage in, 48, 50–51, 52, 60, 79, 227–29; Portuguese monarchy in, 197–98, 218; revolt in, 247–50; slave imports and population of, 18, 20, 22, 23, 25–26, 28, 32–33, 227, 241–42, 283; slavery in, 8, 23–24, 32–33; war of independence of, 198, 249. *See also specific cities and regions in*
Bridgens, Richard, 235
Brigand War, 170–71
Britain. *See* Great Britain
British and Foreign Anti-Slavery Society, 275
British Guiana, 34–35, 289n11; emancipation in, 308n42; revolt in, 245, 261–65, 271. *See also* Demerara
British West Indies: emancipation in, 71–72, 235, 237; Haitian Revolution impact in, 192–95; historiography of, 9–10, 11; planters in, 256–57, 265; slave imports and population of, 18, 19, 24–25, 289n13, 289n15. *See also* Great Britain; *specific colonies of*
brotherhoods, black, 87–88, 263n3, 295–96n10
Brown, Vincent, 108
Bucks of Massachusetts, 123

Buenos Aires, Argentina, 34, 208, 209–10, 213, 278
Burchell, Thomas, 268, 269, 270
Burton, Mary, 99–100
Bush Negroes, 62
Bussa (in Barbados), 257, 258

cabildos de nación, 216, 295–96n10, 302n45
Cachoeira region, Brazil, 249
Cádiz Cortes debates, 215, 216
Canadian provinces, 135–36, 223, 224, 275, 276
Cangé (in Saint Domingue), 158, 161
Cap, Jean-Baptiste (in Saint Domingue), 146
capitães do mato, 52, 79
capital, slaves as, 20–21, 68, 73–74, 275, 289n17
Caracas, Venezuela, 57, 101, 179, 201, 202–3
Carbet, Martinique, 245–46
Carleton, Guy, 127
Carpata, Bastiaan (in Curaçao), 175–76
Cartagena de Indias, Colombia, 22, 49–50, 79, 186, 296n19
Casa-grande & senzala (Freyre), 8, 9
castas, 38, 60, 70, 199
Catholic Church: concubinage and, 37, 73; marriage of enslaved couples and, 67, 233; Saint Domingue revolt and, 156; slavery and, 8, 35, 68, 108, 142, 178–79, 295–96n10; Spain's asylum policy and, 48, 56–57, 58, 98, 178. *See also* baptism of slaves
Cauca province, Colombia, 204–5
Cayenne, French Guiana, 169–70, 174
Ceará, Brazil, 284
Charles IV (king of Spain), 178
Charles X (king of France), 163
Charleston, S.C., 27, 29; African Methodist Episcopalian (AME) Church in, 252–53; emancipation in, 231; marronage and, 222; revolt in, 59–60, 119, 187, 251–53; War of Independence and, 127, 299n44
Charnock, George (in New York), 230
Charnock, Thomas, 230
Chichima, Francisco, 47
Chico Rei (in Brazil), 293n2
children, emancipation of: by baptism, 66–67, 71, 72, 238, 239; Code Noir and,

73–74, 75–76; self-purchase and, 66–67, 71, 293n2; in United States, 229. *See also* free womb
Chile, 210–11, 214, 232, 277–78
Chilpancingo, Mexico, 199, 200
Chinese laborers, 32, 281
Chirino, José Leonardo (in Coro), 185
Chocó, Colombia, 26, 65, 92
Christianity: enslavement incompatibility with, 93–94, 114–15, 117–18, 139, 264, 271; slave conversion to, 35, 71, 114–15, 260–61. *See also* baptism of slaves; Catholic Church; Protestants; *specific denominations of*
Christophe, Henri, 157–58, 159, 161, 162–63, 216, 299n36, 302n48. *See also* Henri I
cimarrones, 44, 46–47, 60, 226–27
civil wars: emancipation and, 199, 276; in Hispanic South America, 202, 209, 277–78; in United States, 7, 279–80
Clarkson, Thomas, 261, 265
Clinton, Henry, 121, 129
coartación/coartação, 36–37, 65, 67, 69, 72, 231, 240–41
Cockpit Country, Jamaica, 54–55, 195
cocoa, 26, 32, 48, 105, 201, 228
Code Noir, 38, 53, 58, 73–74, 85; restoration of, 171, 173, 238
Código Negro, 178–80, 201, 213, 231, 262
Coercive Acts, British, 118
coffee: Berbice and, 104; Brazil and, 32, 241; Cuba and, 31; Haiti and, 162; Saint Domingue and, 30, 145, 147, 153, 155; Suriname and, 28, 61; trade of, 25, 30, 32
Coffij (in Berbice), 105–6
Cofradía de Nuestra Señora, 87
Cointet, François-Maurice, 169–70
Cole, Patty, 138
Colombia: abolition of slavery in, 278; emancipation in, 204–5, 232–33; Haitian Revolution impact in, 186; marronage in, 46–47, 49–50, 60; revolt and conspiracy in, 92, 177, 186; slave population in, 207, 278; slavery in, 23, 26; slave trade and, 22, 26; war of independence in, 204–7. *See also specific cities and regions in*
Compensated Emancipation Act, 280
concubinage, 37, 67, 72, 73, 74, 75, 238
Condorcanqui, José Gabriel, 177–78

Condorcet, Marie Jean Antoine Nicolas Caritat de, 141–42, 302n38
confession and justice, 6, 83–84, 87, 97, 182, 183, 196, 255, 281
Confessions of Nat Turner, The (Gray), 255, 309–10n29
Congo, Antonio (in Puerto Rico), 217
Congo, Louis (in Louisiana), 76
Congo, Mariano (in Cuba), 183
Congress of Angostura, 205
Connecticut, 118, 123, 134–35
Consolidated Slave Act of 1826, 236
conspiracy, 6, 11, 82–83, 84, 88, 100; Haitian Revolution and, 164–65; historiography of, 11, 84–85, 295n5. *See also* revolt and conspiracy; rumors; *specific conspiracies; under specific colonies and countries*
Constitutional Convention of 1787, 29, 131
constitutions: of Argentina, 278; of Brazil, 32, 241; of Chile, 214; of Colombia, 206; of France, 152–53; of Haiti, 161–62, 225; of Hispanic South America, 232; Louverture's, 155, 156; of Mexico, 200; of Spain, 203; of United States, 131–34, 232, 280, 300n56; of Venezuela, 201, 206
Continental Army, 118, 122–24, 126, 130–31
Continental Congress, 118, 123–24
Coro, Venezuela, 60; revolt in, 184–86, 195–96Corps of Loyal Rangers, 192
Cortes, the, 203, 282–83
Costa, Emilia Viotti da, 262
cotton, 29–30, 32, 33, 155, 187
coup of 18 Brumaire, 171
Court (in Antigua), 96–97
Craton, Michael, 11, 266, 270
Criollo, Domingo (in Colombia), 50
Cuba: abolition of slavery in, 281–83; emancipation in, 68–69, 80–81, 240–41; Haitian Revolution impact in, 178–79, 182–83; marronage in, 56, 226–27; revolt and conspiracy in, 215–16, 217–18, 250–51, 281; royal slaves in, 68–69; slave imports and population of, 20, 28, 30–31, 178, 215, 226, 283; slavery in, 30–32; slave trade and, 250. *See also specific cities and regions in*
Cubah (in Jamaica), 103
Cúcuta, Colombia, 206, 207, 208
Cudjoe (in Jamaica), 54–55

Cuffee (in Barbados), 88
Cul-de-Sac plain, Saint Domingue, 149, 151, 152
cultivators, 153–56, 158, 160, 162, 168–69, 171–73
cultural practices, African-derived, 2, 102, 103, 104, 144, 156, 302n45
Curaçao: abolition of slavery in, 281; Haitian Revolution impact in, 165, 195, 196; marronage in, 185, 292n43; population of, 175, 237, 281, 308n43; revolt in, 101, 175–76, 185, 195–96; self-purchase emancipation in, 71, 237
curés des nègres, 142, 146
Curiepe, Venezuela, 57
Cuzco, Peru, 177–78
Cyrille Bissette affair, 246

Daniel (in Demerara), 262
Danish West Indies, 289n10; abolition of slavery and, 7, 276, 311n3; abolition of the slave trade in, 19, 289n15; slavery in, 18, 56, 92, 275, 307n9
David (black preacher, Charleston), 117
Debret, Jean-Baptiste, *243*
Declaration of Independence of Haiti, 161
Declaration of Independence, U.S., 131, 133
Declaration of the Rights of Man and the Citizen, 143, 146
Delaware, 29, 118, 137, 231
Delgrès, Louis, 172, 174
Demerara, 34–35, 289n11; emancipation in, 308n42; revolt in, 245, 261–65, 271; slave imports and population in, 34, 262
Denmark, 7, 276, 289n10
Denmark Vesey conspiracy, 137, 251–52, 253
Dérance, Lamour (in Saint Domingue), 158, 161
descendants of fugitive slaves, 47–48, 61, 63, 76, 274
Deslondes, Charles (in Louisiana), 191
Dessalines, Jean-Jacques, 154, 156–58, 159, 160, 161–62
Dias, Henrique, 78–79
Díaz, María Elena, 68–69
Dieudonné (in Saint Domingue), 157
Dominica, 53, 92, 143
Douglass, Frederick, 279
Drake, Francis, 47, 78

Du Bois, W. E. B., 7
Dunmore, John Murray, 119–20, 123
Dutch, the. *See* Netherlands, the
Dutch West Indies, 18, 37, 39, 289n10; abolition of slavery in, 280–81; emancipation in, 71, 72, 237; marronage in, 57, 58, 280; slave revolt in, 92, 101, 175–76. *See also* Berbice; Suriname
Dutch West India Company, 71, 101

Ecuador, 22, 23, 48, 60, 214, 311n7
Edwards, Bryan, 101–2, 103, 104, 193
Egyptian slavery analogy, 115, 117, 119, 189, 254, 261, 265
Eighth Infantry Battalion, 210, 213
El Castigo, Colombia, 206
El Cobre, Cuba, 68–69
Elkins, Stanley, 8–9
El Portillo, Cuba, 56
emancipation, 3, 4, 81, 244; baptism of slaves and, 57, 66–67, 93–94, 115, 239; change from restriction to endorsement of, 234–40, 308n42; of children (*see* children, emancipation of); civil wars and, 199, 276; Código Negro and, 179; concubinage and, 37, 67, 72, 73, 74, 75, 238; differences in slave system access to, 36–37; of families, 233–34; French restrictions on, 238–39; French Revolution and, 140, 148; gradual (*see* gradual emancipation); Great Britain and, 3, 118–22, 239, 275, 276; in Hispanic South America, 232–34; military service for (*see* military service for emancipation); in mining, 66, 293n2; for protecting whites, 72, 96, 188, 217, 252; record of, 6; self-purchase (*see* self-purchase emancipation); in slaveowners' wills, 36, 67–68, 70, 71–72, 74, 138, 233, 239; taxes on, 72, 74, 76, 80, 235, 237–38, 294n33; through Spain's asylum policy, 57–58; women and, 66, 242–43, *243*. *See also* abolition of slavery; emancipation in U.S. War of Independence; free womb; rumors of emancipation and abolition of slavery; *under specific colonies and countries*
emancipation in U.S. War of Independence: after British defeat, 125–30; British promises of, 118–22, 139; claims by African

Americans, 114–18; Continental Army and, 123–25; in postwar North, 130–36; in postwar South, 133–39
Emancipation Proclamation of Abraham Lincoln, 280
Emanuel (in Antigua), 96–97
encomienda, 22, 23, 78
equality, 115, 133–34, 143–44, 152–53, 192
Equiano, Olaudah, 299n52
Estanislao (in Cuba), 182–83
Estrada, Francisco (in Argentina), 213
Ethiopian Regiment, 119
evacuation, post–U.S. War of Independence, 125–27, 129–30
evangelization of slaves: British encouragement of, 93, 261; emancipation and, 72, 115, 116, 236; as a factor in revolt and protest, 252, 261, 266, 267–68, 271, 273; Great Awakening and, 114–15; France and, 142, 146; Spain and, 178

Fabulé, Francisque (in Saint Domingue), 55
Fallope, Josette, 240, 247
Fédon, Julien, 192–93
"Feelings of the Chilpancingo Nation," 200
Ferdinand VI (king of Spain), 58
Ferdinand VII (king of Spain), 198, 199, 203, 216
fictional purchase of slaves, 231, 236
flag of Barbadian insurgents, 258–60, *259*
Flick, Carolyn, 150
flight. *See* marronage
Florida: Britain's ceding to Spain of, 29, 128; flight and marronage in, 57, 59, 124–25, 223–24, 299n44; population in, 128, 231. *See also specific cities in*
Fort Nassau, Berbice, 105
Fort St. Andries, Berbice, 105, 106
Fox, George, 72
France: abolition of slavery and, 7, 74, 140–41, 153, 160, 174–75, 198, 276–77; Haiti and, 162–63; restoration of slavery by, 33, 159, 171–75, 238; revolution in, 140–41, 144, 152; Saint Domingue and, 30; slave trade and, 24, 28, 145; war with Great Britain and, 165–66. *See also specific colonies of*
freedmen/freedwomen, 38, 72, 148, 153–57, 208, 277. *See also libertos/libertas*; *nouveaux libres*

freedom, lottery, 209; as a natural right, 81, 113, 116–18, 138, 147, 172, 196; slaves' strategies to gain, 1–5
Freedom's Journal, 254
Freeman, Elizabeth (in Massachusetts), 133
free people of color, 1, 18; abduction and enslavement of, 138; discrimination of, 38–39, 74–75; fictitious purchase of slaves by, 231; maroons as, 45; revolt and conspiracy and, 143, 144, 146, 148, 167, 192, 248, 281. *See also libres de color*; *libres de couleur*; free people of color population
free people of color population: before 1775, 1, 23, 25; 1775 to 1799, 30, 175, 242, 290n52; 1800 to 1820, 31, 190, 235, 237, 253, 256–57, 290n52, 308n43, 309n2; 1823 to 1872, 33–34, 236, 237, 242, 263, 290n52, 308n43, 309n10; impact of growth of, 37, 70, 75
free womb: in Hispanic South America, 206–7, 209, 211, 233–34, 277, 283, 311n7; in Mexico, 215; Moret Law and, 282, 283; in United States, 134–35, 229
French, the. *See* France
French Antilles: abolition of slavery in, 168, 276–77; British invasion of, 165–66, 168; emancipation in, 73, 76, 79, 239–40, 276; historiography of, 10; impact of French revolution in, 143, 168; marronage in, 55–56, 225–26; revolt and conspiracy in, 98, 143, 167, 172–73, 246–47; slave imports and population of, 18, 19, 20, 28, 74, 166, 225. *See also specific colonies of*
French Guiana, 289n11; abolition of slavery in, 169; emancipation and, 240, 276, 277; Haitian Revolution impact in, 170, 174; marronage in, 247; slave imports and population of, 18, 34, 169, 308n48
French Revolution, 13, 140–41, 144, 148, 152
Frey, Sylvia, 121
Freyre, Gilberto, 8, 9
Frossard, Simon (in French Guiana), 174
Fuertes, Francisco (in Cuba), 182–83
Fugitive Slave Act of 1793, 222, 224
Fugitive Slave Act of 1850, 279
fugitive slaves: laws on, 47, 52, 53, 55, 208, 222, 224, 279; slave hunters and, 79; in Spanish American wars of independence, 200, 202, 211, 214, 282; in U.S. Civil War, 279–80; in U.S. War of Independence,

121–22, 126, 127–28, 129, 130, 298n1; in War of 1812, 223. *See also* marronage

Gabriel's conspiracy, 188–90
Galán, José Antonio, 177
Ganga Zumba (in Brazil), 51
Garrido, Juan (in Mexico), 77–78
Garrison, William L., 254
Gaspar, David, 95
Gautier, Arlette, 75
Geggus, David, 165, 193–94
Gell, Monday (in Charleston), 253
gender: slave imports and, 18; slave labor and, 21, 66, 153; struggle against slavery and, 11. *See also* women
Genovese, Eugene, 10
gens de couleur libres. See free people of color; *libres de couleur*
George (in South Carolina), 119
George II (king of Great Britain), 119
George III (king of Great Britain), 118, 119
Georgetown, Demerara, 263–64
Georgia: emancipation and, 137; marronage in, 57, 222, 223; revolt and conspiracy in, 116; slave imports and population of, 27, 137, 231; slave trade and, 29; War of Independence and, 118, 120, 121, 124, 127, 128, 299n44
Gilbert, Alan, 127
Girard, Philipp, 160
Gladstone, Jack (in Demerara), 262–63, 264
Goiás, Brazil, 284
Gómez, Juan Gualberto, 282
González, José Caridad (in Coro), 185
Gracia Real de Santa Teresa de Mosé, Fla., 57–58
gradual emancipation: Brazil and, 283; Britain and, 34, 261, 271, 273; Chile and, 211; coartación/coartação, 36–37, 65, 67, 69, 72, 231, 240–41; Cuba and, 282; French colonies and, 141–42, 276, 302n38; Hispanic South America and, 206, 218, 221, 244, 311n7; Portugal and, 197; United States and, 133, 134–35, 136, 139, 229, 230, 244, 300n59. *See also* free womb
Grande-Terre, Guadeloupe, 98
grand marronage, 43–44, 61–62
Gray, Thomas R., 255, 310–11n29
Great Awakening, the, 114–15

Great Britain: Argentina and, 208; Cuba and, 30; emancipation and, 3, 118–22, 239, 275, 276; French Antilles and, 165–66, 168, 170; marronage and, 54–55, 194; planter discontent with, 256–57, 260, 265–67, 269, 273; slave trade and, 24, 25, 34, 193; war between France and, 165–66. *See also* abolition of slavery and Great Britain
Great Dismal Swamp, 59, 222
Great Negro Plot of 1741, 99–100, 296n42
Grenada, 128, 192–93
griffes, 37, 76, 291n69
Grigg, Nanny (in Barbados), 257
Guadeloupe: emancipation in, 167, 239–40, 276, 277; Haitian Revolution impact in, 165–69, 171–74, 195; marronage in, 55, 226; population in, 75, 166, 174, 308nn48–49; revolt and conspiracy in, 98, 143, 247; slavery in, 33; sugar plantation model and, 24, 25. *See also specific cities and regions in*
Guatemala, 78, 232
Guerrero, Vicente, 200, 305n9
guerrilla warfare, 62, 122, 146, 156, 170, 174, 206
Guianas, the, 18, 28, 143, 225, 239, 289n11. *See also* Berbice; British Guiana; Demerara; French Guiana; Suriname
Güines, Cuba, 182–83
Gwin (in New York), 99–100

Haiti, 140, 160–63
Haitian Revolution, 140, 164, 275; historiography of, 10. *See also* Haitian Revolution impact; Saint Domingue revolt
Haitian Revolution impact, 164–65, 195–96; Bourbon reforms and, 176–79; in Brazil, 192; in British West Indies, 192–95; Curaçao revolt and, 175–76; in other French colonies, 165–71; *nouveaux libres and* restoration of slavery, 171–75; in Spanish America, 179–87; in United States, 187–90
Hammon (in Barbados), 89
Hanger, Kimberly, 77
Hanover parish, Jamaica, 268–70, 298n29
Hart, Richard, 10
Hausas, 192, 228, 247–48, 250
Henri I (king of Haiti), 162–63. *See also* Christophe, Henri

Henson, Josiah (in Kentucky), 224
Herskovits, Melville J., 8
Heuman, Gad, 225
Hidalgo y Castillo, Miguel de, 199–200
Higman, Barry, 237, 308n42
Hispaniola, 46, 57, 64, 180–81. *See also* Saint Domingue; Santo Domingo
historiography of slavery, 5–11; sources for, 6–7
Hughson, John, 99–100
Hugues, Victor, 168, 170–71, 174, 192, 225
Hünefeldt, Christine, 233
Hurbon, Laënnec, 146
Hyacinthe (in Saint Domingue), 149

immigration: to Argentina, 278; to Canadian provinces, 135–36; to Cuba, 31, 215; to Jamaica, 291; to Saint Domingue, 147; to United States, 135
importation of slaves. *See* slave imports and population
Inca Empire, 21, 22
indentured workers, 22, 24, 26, 32, 71, 88, 134, 281
Independence. *See* Declaration of Independence; War of Independence (U.S.); wars of independence
Indians. *See* Amerindians
Infantes de la Patria, 211
infanticide, 66
Irish Catholics, 24, 26, 53, 71, 88, 89, 99, 100
Islam. *See* Muslims

Jackey (in Barbados), 257
Jacuí, Brazil, 52
Jamaica: Baptists in, 128–29; emancipation in, 235, 236, 237, 308n42; Haitian Revolution impact in, 193; marronage in, 54–55; mortality in, 291n4; reexportation of slaves from, 26; revolt and conspiracy in, 100–104, 107, 109, 245, 266–70, 273, 298n29; slave codes of, 85; slave imports and population of, 18, 25, 33–34, 54, 266, 289n13; sugar plantation model and, 25. *See also specific cities and regions in*
Jamaica (in Jamaica), 102–3
James, C. L. R., 7
Jean-Dominique (in Martinique), 141, 142
Jean-François (in Saint Domingue), 144, 147, 149, 151, 152, 156, 157

Jean-Louis (in Martinique), 246
Jeannot (in Saint Domingue), 144
Jefferson, Thomas, 121
Jemmy (in South Carolina), 59–60
Jewish planters, 28, 61
João VI (king of Portugal), 197–98
juntas, 199, 207, 211, 233, 278, 307n35

Kars, Marjoleine, 107
Kellers camp, Saint Domingue, 226
Kentucky, 224
Kermené (in St. Lucia), 170
Kina, Jean (in Saint Domingue), 150
Kongos, 17, 56, 60, 61, 146, 156, 157, 181, 182, 185
Kook (in Louisiana), 191

Labatut, Pierre, 249
Lacrosse, Jean-Baptiste Raymond de, 171, 173
ladinos, 21, 47, 77
Lafayette, Marquis de, 126, *132*
Lambert, David, 259
Lara, Oruno, 98
Las Casas, Bartolomé de, 22
laws: anti-emancipation, 238; conspiracy, 84; differences in slavery system, 35; free womb, 134, 282, 283; emancipation, 71, 72, 73–75, 76, 232–33, 235–36, 237, 238–39; marronage and, 47, 48, 53, 59, 208, 222, 224, 226–27; slave treatment, 85, 91, 141, 178–79. *See also* slave codes
Le Cap, Saint Domingue, 55, 144–45, *151*, 151–52, 156, 157, 160
Le Clerc, Francis, 78
Leclerc, Victor-Emmanuel, 157–59, 161
Leeward Maroons, 54–55, 56
Leile, George, 128–29, 267
Le Maniel, Saint Domingue, 56
Le Resouvenir plantation, Demerara, 262–63
Lettre aux bailliages (Condorcet), 141–42
liberals and abolitionism, 277–78
liberation strategies, 3–5, 12, 13
Liberator, The, 254
libertos/libertas, 68, 209–10, 211, 212, 213–14, 241, 305n2
libres de color: in Argentina, 208; in Colombia, 206; in Cuba, 37, 178, 182, 215–16, 251, 281; discrimination of, 38;

marronage and, 49, 61, 69, 70; revolt and conspiracy and, 87, 176; taxes on, 38, 70, 199; in Venezuela, 184, 185, 201, 202, 204. *See also* free people of color

libres de couleur: in French Antilles, 74–75, 166, 174, 240; in Louisiana, 183; in Saint Domingue, 75, 76, 145, 148–49, 150, 151, 152, 160, 301n15, 302n36, 304n36; in U.S. War of Independence, 124, 299n36. *See also* free people of color population

libres de fait, 226, 239–40

libres de savane, 74–75, 226, 239–40, 243–44

Lima, Peru, 23, 48, 66, 67, 211–12, 233

limpieza de sangre. *See* blood purity

Lincoln, Abraham, 279–80

Linebaugh, Peter, 296n42

Lisboa, Antônio Francisco (pseud. Aleijadinho), 67

London Missionary Society, 262, 263, 264

Long, Edward, 101

Louis XIV (king of France), 27, 53, 74, 89, 141

Louisiana: control of, 28, 77, 163, 184; emancipation in, 76–77, 231; marronage in, 58, 76, 224; population of, 28, 190, 251; revolt and conspiracy in, 95, 180, 183–84, 190–91, 195; slave displacement to, 224; U.S. purchase of, 159, 163, 302n56

Louis-Philippe (king of France), 240

Louverture, Toussaint, 152, 154–58, 160–62, 181

Lovejoy, Paul, 11

loyalists of U.S. War of Independence, 118, 121, 123, 124–25, 126–28, 136

Lucas, David, 272

Macaya (in Saint Domingue), 157, 158

Maceo, Antonio, 282

Madden, Richard, 287n5

Malê rebellion, 249–50. *See also* Hausas

Malpic, José de Jesús (in Colombia), 206

mancha de la esclavitud. *See* stain of slavery

Mandingas, 17, 56, 61

manumission. *See* emancipation

Manzano, Juan Francisco, 287n5

Maracaibo, Venezuela, 186

Marcos Xiorro conspiracy, 217

Marc (in Martinique), 141, 142

Mario (in Puerto Rico), 217

maroon, 44; societies, 9, 11, 39, 43, 44, 45, 53, 54, 149. *See also* marronage

marronage, 1, 3, 4, 10, 43–44, 45–46, 63, 221, 243–44; abolition of slavery and, 279–80, 282–83, 283–83; Amerindians and, 48, 51, 60; grand, 43–44, 61–62; historiography of, 6, 9–11; laws on, 47, 48, 53, 59, 222, 224, 226–27; maritime, 53–54, 57, 60, 128, 171, 224, 225, 226, 280, 307n9; palenques and, 46, 48–50, 56, 60, 186, 206, 227, 281; peace treaties and, 48, 54–55, 56, 62, 102, 194; petit, 43, 44; quilombos and, 44, 49–53, 60, 192, 227–29, 248, 249, 281; record of, 6; repression of, 49–50, 52–53, 59, 98, 62, 226–27; revolt and conspiracy and, 44–47, 82–83, 189, 248; sanctuary policy of Spain and, 56–58, 59, 60–61, 292n43; in sugar-producing Caribbean, 53–56; transimperial, 56–58; in U.S. War of Independence, 119–21, 124, 127; in wars of independence, 200, 202, 203, 207, 211, 282. *See also under specific colonies and countries*

Martial (in Saint Domingue), 149, 151

Martinique: emancipation in, 239, 240, 276, 277; Haitian Revolution impact in, 166, 170, 171, 303n14; marronage in, 55, 226; population of, 75, 141, 240, 308n48, 309n2; protest in, 141–43; revolt in, 245–47; slave trade and, 33; sugar plantation model and, 24, 25. *See also specific cities in*

Maryland: emancipation and, 136, 137, 139, 230; marronage in, 244; population in, 118, 137, 251; slave trade in, 26, 137; War of Independence and, 124

Massachusetts, 26, 114, 116, 118, 123, 133

Matthews, Gelien, 271

Matuna, Colombia, 49

Mendoza, Antonio de, 86

Mendoza, Argentina, 210

Ménénius, Hector (in French Guiana), 170

Mercier, Louis (in Curaçao), 175, 176

"Meriken" Company Villages, Trinidad, 223

Methodists, 1, 115, 136, 252–53, 265, 267

Mexico: abolition of slavery and, 199–201, 232; emancipation in, 232; marronage in, 48, 50, 200, 224; revolt and conspiracy in, 86–87, 94, 295n9; slave imports and population of, 22, 23, 86–87, 176, 199; war of independence in, 199–200. *See also specific cities in*

Index   345

Mexico City, 86–87, 295n9
Michigan, 136
Middleton, George, 123
Miguel, Negro (in Venezuela), 46
militarized agriculture, 154–56, 158, 160, 162, 168, 170, 181
military service for emancipation, 3, 4–5, 64, 77–81; French Revolution and, 140, 146; Haitian Revolution impact and, 194–95; Hispanic South American civil wars and, 278; Saint Domingue revolt and, 148, 152, 154, 301n24; U.S. Civil War and, 280; U.S. War of Independence and, 118–25; War of 1812 and, 223; wars of independence and, 198, 203, 204, 206–7, 208–10, 282
Minas Gerais, Brazil: emancipation in, 66, 67, 79, 293n2; marronage in, 51–52, 60, 228; slave imports and population of, 25–26, 308n55
mining, 23, 25–26, 46, 47, 48, 51–52, 60, 66, 68–69, 92, 177, 206, 228, 293n2
missionaries, 56, 142, 146, 260–61, 265, 267–68
Mississippi, 28, 137, 224, 231
Mississippi River, 58, 183, 190–91
Missouri, 253
mita, 22, 69, 70
mixed-blood people, 37–39, 66, 291n69. *See also* castas, griffes; mulattos; pardos; quadroons and quinteroons; zambos
mocambos, 44, 50, 51, 52, 227, 228
Montego Bay, Jamaica, 266, 269–70
Montes de María, Colombia, 49, 50
Monteverde, Juan Domingo de, 202
Montevideo, Uruguay, 213, 278, 306n31
Montreal, New France, 27, 95, 135
Morales, Francisco Tomás, 202, 203
Morelos, José María, 199–200
Moreno Fraginals, Manuel, 10–11
Moret Law, 282, 283
Morillo, Pablo, 203, 204–5
mortality: of slaves, 17–18, 25, 108, 266, 288n5, 288n7, 310n53; of whites, 44, 291n4
mulattos: discrimination and, 37–39, 78; emancipation and, 65, 66, 73, 74–76; revolt and, 159, 161, 172, 174
Munro, Pamela (in Trinidad), 236
Muslims, 37, 247–48, 249–50

Mutiny Act of 1807, 195
Myrdal, Gunnar, 8

Ñanga (in Mexico), 48–49
Nanny Town, Jamaica, 54
Nash, Gary, 114
Natchez Indians, 58
Native Americans. *See* Amerindians
Native Baptists, 267–68. *See also* Baptists
Nat Turner's revolt, 251, 254–55
Nazaré das Farinhas, Brazil, 248
nègres marins, 168–69
Nepomuceno, Juan (in Venezuela), 203
Netherlands, the: abolition of slavery and, 7, 176, 237, 280–81; abolition of slave trade, 19; attacks on maroon communities by, 50; Jews and, 28; military service for emancipation and, 79; revolt and conspiracy and, 106; slave trade and, 18, 23, 24, 25, 26, 27, 237; sugar plantation model and, 24. *See also specific colonies of*
New Amsterdam, 79. *See also* New York
New Brunswick, 127, 136
New France, 27, 28, 135, 290n39
New Hampshire, 118, 133–34, 307n24
New Jersey: abolitionism in, 229; emancipation in, 134; revolt and conspiracy in, 93–94; slave population of, 27, 119, 135, 187, 229, 230; War of Independence and, 120, 129
New Netherland, 71
New Orleans, 28, 77, 190–91
New York: abolitionism and, 229; emancipation in, 134, 136, 230; marronage in, 58–59; revolt and conspiracy in, 90–91, 99–100, 109, 254, 296n42; slave population of, 27, 120, 135, 229, 230; War of Independence and, 120, 121, 129, 131
New York Mercury, 120
Nishida, Mieko, 241–42, 308n56
North American British colonies: emancipation in, 71–72; marronage in, 53, 57, 58–62; revolts and conspiracies in, 93–94, 98–100; slave codes in, 83, 84; slave imports and population of, 18, 19, 26–27, 118–19. *See also* Great Britain; United States; War of Independence (U.S.); *specific colonies*
North Carolina, 27, 59, 118, 119, 137, 222

nouveaux libres: in French Guiana, 169–70; in Guadeloupe, 168–70; in Saint Domingue/Haiti, 153–57, 160–61, 304n36; restoration of slavery and, 171–75
Nova Scotia, 127, 129–30, 136, 223

obeah, 102, 103, 104
Ocumare, Venezuela, 202
Oldendorp, C. G. A., 56
Old Testament, 253, 261, 265
Oriente province, Cuba, 226–27
Ortiz, Fernando, 8
Oudin-Bastide, Caroline, 81

Padilla, Domingo (in Colombia), 50
Páez, José Antonio, 204
Palenque de San Basilio, Colombia, 49, 50
palenques, 46, 48–50, 56, 60, 186, 206, 227, 281
Palmares, Brazil, 50–51
Panama, 22, 47–48, 50
Paraguay, 61, 232–33, 283, 293n53, 311n7
pardos, 37, 201–2, 204
Parliament, British: abolition of slave trade and slavery by, 5, 34, 136, 195, 234, 266–67, 273; colonial representation in, 115–16; planters and, 256. *See also* Great Britain
partus sequitur ventrem, 35, 70, 73, 134
Pasto, Colombia, 206
Patía Valley, Colombia, 206
Paton, Diana, 85
patrocinados, 282–83
Patrocínio, José Carlos do, 284
Patterson, Orlando, 10, 266
pearl fishing, 23, 45
Peculiar Institution, The (Stampp), 8
Pélage, Magloire, 172, 173
Pennsylvania, 26, 59, 72, 134, 230, 300n59
Pernambuco, Brazil, 24, 50, 51, 78–79, 228
Peru: abolition of slavery in, 233, 278; emancipation in, 232–34; marronage in, 48, 211, 226; revolt in, 47, 177–78, 278; slave imports and population of, 22–23, 212, 214; military service for emancipation in, 211–13; war of independence in, 211–12. *See also specific cities in*
Peters, Thomas (in New York), 120, 130
Petersburg, Va., 138, 231
Pétion, Alexandre, 157, 159, 161, 162, 204

petit marronage, 43, 44
petition, antislavery, 71, 113, 116, 133, 198, 249, 265, 273, 300n58
Pharaoh (in Richmond), 187–88, 189–90
Philadelphia, 72, 119, 252
Philémon, Father, 146
Piar, Manual, 204
Pierrot (in Saint Domingue), 152
Piñero, Ramón (in Venezuela), 203
piracy, 46–47, 48, 78
Plaine du Nord, Saint Domingue, 5, 140, 144–47, 193
planters, 25–28; discontent with Código Negro, 179; discontent with Great Britain of, 236, 256–57, 260, 265–67, 269, 273; impact of Haitian Revolution on, 165–66, 169–71, 179–80; influence in British Parliament of, 115, 256; Saint Domingue revolt and, 150, 151, 154, 155; slave registration and, 74, 256, 258, 260; slave trade and, 31–32, 34, 221, 239, 247; U.S. South and, 224, 231; U.S. War of Independence and, 123, 124–25; wars of independence and, 200, 201, 205, 215, 282
Platons, Saint Domingue, 149–51, 152
Plummer, James, 138
Poems on Various Subjects, Religious and Moral (Wheatley), 116–17
Pointe-à-Pitre, Guadeloupe, 172
Pointe Coupée, La., 183–84, 196
Pointis, Baron de, 79
Polverel, Étienne, 150, 151, 152, 153
Pompée (in French Guiana), 225
Ponce region, Puerto Rico, 33, 217
population, natural growth of: in Brazil, 32; in Cuba and, 31, 69; of free people of color, 236, 242; in United States, 26–27, 29, 187, 251. *See also* free people of color population; slave imports and population; white population
Port-Salut, Saint Domingue, 147
Portugal: abolitionism and, 197, 305n2; marronage and, 51–52; slave asylum of, 197; slave population in, 21; slave trade and, 22, 24, 28–29
Price, Richard, 45
Prieur, Petit-Noël (in Saint Domingue), 158, 161
Prince (in New York), 99–100
Pritchard, Jack (in Charleston), 253

privateering, 125, 127–28, 168–69
Prospect Bluff, Fla., 223
Prosser, Gabriel (in Richmond), 188–89, 190
Protector of Slaves Office (Bridgens), 235
Protestants, 8, 35–36, 89, 94, 115, 117, 128, 142, 236, 260, 262. *See also specific denominations*
publications, antislavery, by slaves and/or free people of color, 7, 113, 116–17, 246, 254, 265, 287n5
pueblos de indios, 22, 23, 49, 69
Puerto Príncipe, Cuba, 182, 216, 282
Puerto Rico: abolition of slavery in, 281–82; marronage in, 57; revolt and conspiracy in, 182, 215, 217; slave population and imports in, 18, 215; slavery in, 33, 38, 240punishment for revolt and conspiracy, 5, 6, 11, 12, 83–86, 88–100, 107–9, 142–43, 171–72, 175–76, 185, 188, 191–92, 216, 217, 246–250, 252, 254–55, 258, 260, 263–64, 270, 281. *See also specific revolts and conspiracies*
purchasing freedom. *See* self-purchase emancipation

quadroons and quinteroons, 37, 70, 149
Quakers, 1, 72, 93, 115, 136
Quamana (in Louisiana), 191
Quamina (in Demerara), 262–63, 264
Quebec, 135
quilombos, 44, 49–53, 60, 192, 227–29, 248, 249, 281

race relations scholarship, 8
racial discrimination, 18, 37–39, 67, 74–75, 76, 129, 152, 173, 208, 238, 309n2; mobilization against, 182, 192, 193, 206, 246, 254, 282
Raimond, Julien, 301n15
Ramos, María (in Lima), 66
rancheadores, 226–27
rape, 35, 73, 74, 259–60
Recôncavo, Brazil, 227, 248–50
Reconstruction in U.S. South, 7, 280
Rediker, Marcus, 296n42
Régent, Frédéric, 167
Règlement de culture, 154–55
Reis, João, 249, 309n10
religious mobilization of African Americans, 252–53

Remedios, Colombia, 46–47
resistance, historiography of, 10–11
Restall, Matthew, 77
restoration of slavery by France, 171–75, 238
revolt and abolitionism, 245–73; in Caribbean, 246–47; in U.S. South, 251–56
revolt and conspiracy, 3, 5, 11–13, 82–83, 107, 274; 1700 and before, 86–90, 295n9; 1700 to 1730, 90–94; 1730 to 1741, 95–100; 1741 to 1763, 100–107; 1792 to 1811, 164–96; 1816 to 1832, 245–69; British instigation of, 118–19; colonial justice and, 83–86; historiography of, 6, 11–12; marronage and, 44–47, 82–83, 189, 248; punishment for, 5, 6, 83–86, 107–9, 246–50, 263–64, 281; reasons for fear of, 82–83, 91–93, 196, 217, 255–56, 259–60; record of, 6; in Spanish Caribbean, 215–18; spectacle of execution and, 12, 107–9, 246, 270. *See also* conspiracy; revolt and abolitionism; Saint Domingue revolt; *under specific cities, colonies, and countries*; *under specific revolts and conspiracies*
Rhode Island, 27, 123, 131, 134–35
Richepance, Antoine, 172, 173, 174, 247
Richmond, Va., 187–90, 196, 230–31
Rigaud, André, 149, 154, 156, 157, 158, 299n36, 301n26
Rio de Janeiro, Brazil, 32, 51, 197–98, 228, 241, 243
Río de la Plata, 208–14, 232–33; slave imports and population of, 34 199, 208, 290n62. *See also* Argentina
Rochambeau, Donatien Marie Joseph de, 126, 159, 160
rochelas, 60
Rondeau, José, 213
Rosas, Juan Manuel de, 278
Rosete, Francisco, 202, 203
Royal Army, 121, 122, 125–26, 194–95
Royal Navy, 23, 122, 123, 126, 129–30, 195, 275
royal slaves: British, 194–95; Spanish, 68–69
rumors, 94
—of emancipation and abolition of slavery: in Brazil, 249; in British colonies, 93–94, 100, 121, 267, 268, 270; in Curaçao, 175; in French Antilles, 141–42, 143, 166, 247; in Spanish America, 94, 101, 180, 181–82, 215, 249; in United States, 190

—of slave conspiracies, 89, 90, 107, 119, 187, 190, 193, 249
Rupert, Linda, 58

Saint-André, Sabathier (in St. Lucia), 170
Saint Domingue: economy of, 30; emancipation in, 75–76, 79, 80, 145, 152–53, 294n33; impact of French Revolution in, 143; *libres de couleur* in, 75–76, 145, 301n15; marronage in, 55–56; slave imports and population of, 18, 25, 30, 145, 301n15, 301n17; sugar plantation model and, 251. *See also* Saint Domingue revolt; *specific cities and regions in*
Saint Domingue revolt, 5, 13, 31, 139, 140, 143–44, 163, 221; bossales and, 140, 145–46, 156, 159, 301n17; freedmen's resistance to labor codes and, 153–56; French abolition of slavery and, 150–53; and independence war, 156–60; *libres de couleur* and, 143, 147, 148, 149, 152, 159, 160, 301n11; marronage in, 149–50, 152, 154, 155–60, 161, 162; in Plaine du Nord, 140, 144–47; in Southern Saint Domingue, 147–50. *See also* Haitian Revolution impact
Sainte-Anne, Guadeloupe, 167, 173
Saint Patrick's Plot. *See* Great Negro Plot of 1741
Saint-Pierre, Martinique, 141–43, 246–47, 277, 303n14
Salem, Peter (in Massachusetts), 123
Sally (in Virginia), 138
Salvador de Bahia, Brazil, 26, 60, 192, 227–28, 242, 247–50, 308n56, 309n10
Sambo (in Barbados), 89
Samson (in Barbados), 89
sanctuary policy of Spain, 56–58, 59, 60–61, 178, 185, 292n43
San Felipe, Venezuela, 46
San Lorenzo de los Minas, Santo Domingo, 49
San Lorenzo de los Negros, Mexico, 49
San Martín, José de, 210, 211–12
San Miguel Arcángel, Colombia, 49, 50
Sans-Souci, Jean-Baptiste (in Saint Domingue), 144, 158, 161
Santa Marta, Colombia, 50
Santiago, Chile, 211
Santiago de Cuba, 78, 282

Santo Domingo (future Dominican Republic), 30, 37, 55, 57, 180–81, 275, 304n36
São Paolo, Brazil, 32, 241, 284
Savannah, Ga., 122, 127, 299n44
scenario of slave conspiracy, 87, 90, 92, 183, 246, 259–60; and Haitian Revolution, 140
Schœlcher, Victor, 276–77
Scott, James, 11
secret societies of Africans, 146, 156
self-purchase emancipation, 4, 36–37, 64, 81, 244, 276, 293n2; in Brazil, 65–70, 198, 241–43, 283; in British and Dutch America, 70–73, 235–38; in Cuba, 240–41, 282; in French America, 75–76, 77, 238–40, 277; in Hispanic South America, 232, 233–34, 235–36, 277–78; historiography of, 11, 69; military service and, 79; in Spanish America, 65–70, 179; in United States, 137, 138, 230–31; in wars of independence, 203, 212–14. *See also military service for emancipation*
Seminoles, 223–24
Seventh Infantry Battalion, 209
Seven Years' War, 13, 24, 80–81, 101–2, 192
Sharp, Granville, 117–18, 130
Sharpe, Samuel "Daddy" (in Jamaica), 266, 268–69, 270
Sharples, Jason, 95
Sheppard, Tom (in Richmond), 187–88, 189–90
Sierra Leone, 130, 256
Siete Partidas, 36, 68, 85, 178
Simon (in Jamaica), 104
Slave and Citizen (Tannenbaum), 8–9
slave codes: Code Noir (*see* Code Noir); Código Negro (*see* Código Negro); differences in, 35–36; of Dutch and British colonies, 71, 85, 237. *See also* laws
slave hunters, 6, 52, 79, 226–27, 279. *See also capitães do mato; rancheadores*
slave imports and population, 17, 18–20, *19–20*, 288n5, 288nn7–9, 289n13, 289n15; 1501 to 1650, 22–24; 1650 to 1775, 24–28, 290n39; 1775 to 1870, 28–35. *See also* population, natural growth of; *under specific colonies and countries*
slave narratives, 7, 287n5
slaveowners: property rights of, 2, 35, 68, 73, 81, 83, 115, 215, 178, 232, 256, 279;

Index   349

and wills as source of emancipation, 36, 67–68, 70, 71–72, 74, 138, 233, 239.
Slavery: A Problem in American Institutional and Intellectual Life (Elkins), 8–9
Slavery Abolition Act of Great Britain, 136
slavery, 1–5, 8–9, 18, 20–21, 25–27, 35–39, 288–89n8, 289n17
slaves as social actors, historiography of, 5–9
slaves as capital, 20, 21, 68, 90, 234, 275; as human property, 2, 35, 73, 102, 108, 125, 178, 229, 236, 239, 284, 285
slaves' strategies to gain freedom, 1–5. *See also under specific strategies*
slave trade, 1, 17–18; 1501 to 1650, 21–24; 1650 to 1775, 24–28; 1775 to 1870, 30–35; abolition of, 19–20, 28, 195, 256, 271, 289n15; Africa as source of, 17, 20, 27; during and after wars of independence, 136–37, 221; *nègres marins* and, 168–69; post–Seven Years' War growth of, 109, 115; Saharan and Arab, 17, 288n3; sugar plantation model and, 24, 27; within United States, 29–30, 125, 128, 224. *See also* slave imports and population; *under specific colonies and countries*
Smith, Adam, 81
Smith, Jane, 262, 264
Smith, John, 262–65, 271
Sociedad Abolicionista Española, 281–82
Société des Amis des Noirs, 141, 153
Société Française pour l'Abolition de l'Esclavage, 276
Society for the Mitigation and Gradual Abolition of Slavery, 261, 271, 275, 283
Soler, María Demetria Escalada de (in Argentina), 210
Solitude (in Guadeloupe), 172
Somerset, James, 115–16
Sonthonax, Léger Félicité, 150, 151, 152, 153
Sopo, Francisco (in Boca Nigua), 181
Southampton, Va., 254–55
South Carolina: emancipation in, 72, 137, 231; marronage in, 53, 59–60, 222; slave imports and population of, 27, 118, 137, 231, 251, 253; revolt in, 251–53; Saint Domingue refugees in, 187; sea escape and, 224; War of Independence in, 121, 122, 124. *See also specific cities and regions in*

Spain: abolition of slavery and, 178, 281–83; asylum policy of, 56–58, 59, 60–61, 178, 185, 292n43; Haitian Revolution impact in, 176–80; Saint Domingue revolt and, 152; slave population in, 21–22; slavery and, 178, 198–99. *See also specific colonies of*
spectacle of execution, 107–9, 246, 270
stain of slavery, 38, 39, 70, 74, 76
Stampp, Kenneth, 8
St. Augustine, Fla., 57–58, 59–60, 125
St. Bartholomew parish, S.C., 119
St. David parish, Jamaica, 100–101
St. James parish, Jamaica, 268–70
St. John Island, 92–93, 94, 107, 289n10
St. John's, Antigua, 95–98, 266
St. Kitts, 55
St. Lucia, 53, 143, 166, 170–71, 195, 196
St. Martin, 280, 289n10
Stono Rebellion, 59–60, 98
St. Philipp, Barbados, 257–58
sugar plantations, 21, 23, 24–28, 30–33, 53, 61, 88
suicide as a liberation strategy, 3, 10, 11, 36, 287n1; during repression, 18, 51, 88, 92, 102, 104, 106, 173, 183, 217, 248
Surarregui, José Amborsio (in Venezuela), 204, 207–8
Suriname, 10, 289n11; abolition of slavery in, 281; emancipation in, 71, 72, 237–38; marronage in, 44, 61–62; slave imports and population of, 34, 238, 281, 308n45; sugar plantation model and, 28
Susanna (in Demerara), 262
Sweden, 276
Sylla (in Saint Domingue), 158, 161

Tabacal, Colombia, 50
Tacky (in Jamaica), 101–3, 109
Tacky's Rebellion, 101–4, 109
Tadó, Colombia, 92
Tailors' Revolt, 192, 304n57
Tannenbaum, Frank, 8–9
taxes: emancipation, 72, 74, 76, 80, 167, 235, 237–39, 294n33; on free people of color, 38, 70, 199; on slave importation, 29, 133, 300n56
Tennessee, 224, 231
Ten Years' War, 282

terror: against slaves, 5, 84, 107–8, 140, 158–59, 168, 173, 193, 260, 264, 270, 279, 281; spread by slaves, 92, 121–22, 140, 144–45, 159, 254. *See also* punishment for revolt and conspiracy; spectacle of execution

Texas, 29, 200–201

Thirteenth Amendment of U.S. Constitution, 280

Thornton, John, 11, 157

tobacco, 21, 24, 26, 27, 28, 29, 30, 187, 228

Tobago, 53, 171

Tomboy (in Antigua), 96–97

Toral, Sebastián (in Mexico), 78

torture, 5, 6, 12, 83–85, 108–9. *See also* punishment for revolt and conspiracy; *specific revolts and conspiracies*

To the Friends of Negro Emancipation (Lucas), 272

trade, slave. *See* slave trade

transculturation, 8

treatment of slaves: contestation of, 68–69, 73, 116; criticism of, 108–9; death from, 18, 25; differences in slave systems and, 35–36; laws on, 85, 91, 141, 178–79, 233; Portuguese monarchy in Brazil and, 197–98

Treaty of Amiens, 171

Treaty of Bale, 180

Treaty of Paris, 126–27, 135

tributary labor, 22, 69, 70

Trinidad: amelioration of slavery and, 261–62; emancipation in, 235–36, 275, 308n42; population of, 235, 236, 256; freedmen displacement to, 223; Spanish asylum policy and, 57

Trois-Rivières, Guadeloupe, 166

Trombetas River, Brazil, 228

Trouillot, Michel-Rolph, 164

Trujillo, Peru, 278

Tubman, Harriet, 279

Tula (in Curaçao), 175–76

Tupac Amaru II. *See* Condorcanqui, José Gabriel

Turner, Mary, 270

Turner, Nat (in Virginia), 254–56, 310–11n29

Underground Railroad, 279

Union Army, 279–80

United States: abolition of slavery and, 133–35, 229–30, 279–80, 307n24; Civil War in, 279–80; constitutions of, 131–34, 232, 280, 300n56; emancipation in, 137, 138, 230–31; Haitian Revolution impact in, 187–90; marronage in, 114, 222–24, 279; slave imports and population of, 28, 29, 114, 187, 251, 278–79, 298n1, 309n14; slavery in territory expansions of, 29–30, 221, 224; slavery of North versus South in, 131–33, 229–32, 278–79, 307n24; slave trade and, 29, 131–33, 134. *See also specific states;* War of Independence (U.S.)

Uruguay, 234, 278

Valdivia, Juan de, 78

Valiente, Juan (in Chile), 78

van Hoogenheim, Wolfert Simon, 105–6

Vaudoux (voodoo), 156

Venezuela: abolition of slavery in, 278; emancipation in, 232–33, 307n35; marronage in, 201, 203; population of, 184, 201, 207; revolt and conspiracy in, 101, 184–86; slavery in, 23, 26, 34; war of independence in, 201–4. *See also specific cities in*

Ventura (in Argentina), 209

Veracruz, Mexico, 22, 23, 47–49, 107, 199

Vermont, 133, 136, 229

Vesey, Denmark (in Charleston), 137, 252, 253

Vilcabamba, Peru, 47

Virginia: emancipation in, 72, 115, 131, 136, 137, 138–39, 230, 231; Haitian Revolution impact in, 187–90, 196; marronage in, 53, 59, 125, 244; revolt and conspiracy in, 93–94, 187–90, 254–56; Saint Domingue refugees in, 187; slave imports and population of, 26, 118, 137; War of Independence and, 120, 124, 125, 131. *See also specific cities in*

Virginia Gazette, 59

Voyages: The Trans-Atlantic Slave Trade Database, 17, 18–19, *19–20*, 288n1, 288n5, 289n9

Walker, David, 254, 256

Walker, Quock (in Massachusetts), 133

Wardall, Thomas, 72

Index 351

War of 1812, 222–23
War of Independence (U.S.), 114, 118, 139; fate of slaves post, 125–30, 136–39, 299n44; slaves in liberated territories during, 122–25. *See also* emancipation in U.S. War of Independence
War of Jenkins' Ear, 98
wars of independence: in Argentina, 208–10; in Brazil, 198, 249; in Chile, 211; in Colombia, 204–8; in Cuba, 282; in Mexico, 199–201; in Peru, 211–12; and slavery, 205, 210, 212–14; in United States (*see* War of Independence [U.S.]); in Venezuela, 201–4, 206–8
Washington, George, 118, 122–23, 126–27, 138
Wedgwood, Josiah, 260
Wesleyans, 265, 268
West India Regiment, 194–95, 258, 259
Westmoreland parish, Jamaica, 102, 103–4
Wheatley, Phyllis, 116–17
whip bans, 149, 153, 155, 269
White, Deborah, 11
white population: 1775 and before, 24; 1775 to 1799, 30, 31, 33–34, 141, 145, 169, 175, 303n36; 1800 to 1820, 190, 251, 253, 308n43, 309n2; 1823 to 1835, 262, 309n10
Wilberforce, William, 258, 260, 261
Williams, Eric, 9–10
Williams, Peter (in New Jersey), 131

Williams, Peter, Jr. (minister), 254
wills, emancipation in. *See* emancipation: in slaveowners' wills
Wilmington, N.C., 119
Windward Maroons, 54
Women slaves: agriculture work of, 153–54, 155, 160, 168, 210; in Berbice revolt, 107; concubinage and, 37, 67, 72, 73, 74, 75, 238; emancipation and, 66, 218, 233, 237–38, 242–43, *243*, *308n45*; maroon abductions of, 46, 48, 53, 55; rape of, 35, 73, 74; roles of, 21, 23; in U.S. War of Independence, 116–17, 121; wages of, 153–54; in wars of independence, 210, 212, 213. *See also* free womb
working-class comparison to slavery, British, 265, 273

Xiorro, Marcos (in Puerto Rico), 217

Yanga, Mexico, 48–49
Year of the Lash, 281
Yorktown, Va., 125–26, 131
Yorubas, 17, 156, 157, 248, 250, 251

zambos, 37, 47–48, 65, 70, 177
Zaragoza, Colombia, 46–47
Zong, 130, 299n52
Zumbi dos Palmares (in Brazil), 51